D1276106

Political Leadership in Industrialized Societies

STUDIES IN COMPARATIVE ANALYSIS

70527

LEWIS J. EDINGER, EDITOR

Department of Public Law and Government
Columbia University

John Wiley & Sons, Inc.   NEW YORK   LONDON   SYDNEY

OLD WESTBURY LIBRARY

JC 571
.E 2t
Copy 1

Copyright © 1967 *by John Wiley & Sons, Inc.* All Rights Reserved. This book or any part thereof must not be reproduced
in any form without the written permission of the publisher.

Library of Congress Catalog Card Number: 67-23324
Printed in the United States of America

The Contributors

Samuel H. Barnes is Associate Professor of Political Science at the University of Michigan and has also taught at the Universities of Florence and Rome. He is the author of *Party Democracy: Politics of an Italian Socialist Federation* and has contributed numerous articles to various symposia and professional journals.

Lewis J. Edinger is Professor of Government and Politics at Columbia University. He has written extensively on political leadership and comparative politics and is the author of *West German Armament, German Exile Politics*, and *Kurt Schumacher: A Study in Personality and Political Behavior* and co-author of *Germany Rejoins the Powers, Foreign Policy in World Politics*, and *France, Germany, and the Western Alliance*.

Erwin Hargrove is Associate Professor of Political Science at Brown University. He is the author of *Leadership in American Government* and various articles on related subjects. He is presently engaged in a comparative analysis of the political implications of social change in industrialized societies.

Stanley Hoffman is Professor of Government at Harvard University. His publications include *Le mouvément Poujade, Contemporary Theory in International Relations, In Search of France* (co-author), *The State of War*, and many articles on French and international politics. At present he is completing a book on American foreign policy.

Harold D. Lasswell is Edward J. Phelps Professor of Law and Political Science at Yale University. He is particularly concerned with the study of psychological and cultural factors affecting authority and control, and his publications in this area include *Psychopathology and Politics, World Politics and Personal Insecurity, Power and Personality*, and *Power Sharing in a Psychiatric Hospital* (co-author).

Alfred G. Meyer is Professor of Political Science at the University of Michigan. He is the author of *Leninism, Stalinism, Communism*, and *The Soviet Political System*, co-author of *The Incompatible Allies*, and a frequent contributor to professional journals. His current studies focus on the comparative analysis of political authority, particularly in Communist systems.

Alexander Mitscherlich is Director of the Psychosomatic Clinic at the University of Heidelberg as well as Director of the Sigmund Freud Institute for Psychoanalytic Training and Research in Frankfort, Germany. His numerous publications include *Doctors of Infamy, Auf dem Weg zur vaterlosen Gesellschaft,* and *Die Unwirklichkeit unserer Städte.*

Glendon Schubert is William Rand Kenan Professor of Political Science at the University of North Carolina (Chapel Hill). Among his publications are *The Judicial Mind, Judicial Policy-Making, The Public Interest, Constitutional Politics,* and *The Presidency in the Courts.* His latest book is *Dispassionate Justice.*

Joseph A. Schlesinger is Professor of Political Science at Michigan State University. He has long been a student of political leadership and career patterns and is the author of *How They Became Governors, Ambition and Politics,* and numerous articles and essays in other books and professional journals.

Lester Seligman is Professor of Political Science at the University of Oregon. Presently at work on a comparative study of political parties, he has written widely on political leaders, their recruitment, and their mobility in the United States and other countries. His most recent book is *Leadership in a New Nation* and his *Political Recruitment* will soon be published.

E. Victor Wolfenstein is Assistant Professor of Political Science at the University of California (Los Angeles). He has just published *The Revolutionary Personality: Lenin, Trotsky, Ghandi,* and is now working on a study of Winston Churchill as well as a book on personality and politics.

Contents

1. Editor's Introduction

LEWIS J. EDINGER

"E Pluribus Unum"

The bibliography of American social science literature has in recent years been vastly expanded by the proliferation of symposia that range from "*Festschrifts*" which lay no claim to a common focus to collections of conference papers and readings that do. Some of the latter kind have provoked irate reviewers to label them "nonbooks," allegedly held together by little more than a binding and the labored efforts of their editors to find a common denominator where none exists. As one such critic wrote not long ago, you can no more make a dry martini by pouring vermouth into a cocktail shaker and shouting "gin!" than produce a book by juxtaposing a number of disjointed essays preceded by an introduction that seeks to make a scholarly virtue of an editorial necessity.

A few remarks about an editor's role is perhaps a good way to launch into a discussion of leadership. Assembling a collection of previously published pieces for inclusion in a reader provides an editor with a particularly high degree of control over the contributors. Those who "belong" are allowed to come along for the journey into print—or rather reprint—and those who do not "fit" are autocratically excluded by editorial fiat. A collection of original essays requested by the editor, on the other hand, allows him a minimal degree of control, subject to the voluntary agreement of his contributors to help him achieve his objectives. They may choose to gallop off in separate directions wherever their fancy takes them, leaving him in the position of the proverbial Frenchman who ran after a crowd, explaining, "I am their leader and must therefore follow them!" If an editor is fortunate, however, he may achieve that ideal mixture between the extremes of anarchic laissez faire and totalitarian absolutism which rests on the consensual editorial principle that if coauthors do not hang together, they may in the end hang separately over the fires of their critics.

Thanks are due to John H. Kautsky, Donald Searing, and Victor LeVine for comments on an earlier version of this essay and to Washington University (St. Louis) for clerical and financial support in its preparation.

The reader will have to judge for himself how close this particular symposium has come to the ideal. It originated in a series of panels organized by the editor for the 1966 Annual Meeting of the American Political Science Association. The essays by Barnes, Hoffmann, Mitscherlich, Schlesinger, Schubert, Seligman, and Wolfenstein are revised versions of papers presented at that time; those by Hargrove, Lasswell, and Meyer were written subsequently by panel members who agreed to the editor's request to help expand the scope of the symposium. He sought largely to confine his role to that of a bargaining and negotiating agent, attempting to promote what he conceived to be the common group objectives, but in the last analysis depending upon the cooperation of the authors and their particular perception of these objectives.

As conceived by the editor, the symposium was to serve two major functions. One was to make available in a single book a series of comparative studies which might suggest similarities and differences between political leaders and forms of leadership in modern industrialized societies and identify factors resulting in converging, diverging, or parallel patterns. Thus one of the basic questions posed by such comparative analyses is whether societies that share certain socioeconomic characteristics because they are industrialized also produce similar structures of leadership recruitment and analogous leadership roles and functions. Or, alternatively, are there fundamental differences, rooted in quite dissimilar institutional arrangements and authority norms, which distinguish political leadership patterns in various industrialized societies and perhaps link their "political cultures" more closely to those of less industrialized or even nonindustrialized societies?

Questions such as these seem particularly relevant in view of a plethora of recent studies which more or less sharply differentiate between the politics of so-called "developing" or "underdeveloped" areas on the one hand and those of "developed" areas on the other. In some instances, developed areas are collectively associated with "modern" forms of political leadership that are perceived as the inevitable product of industrialization; in others the patterns of political leadership in industrialized societies are believed to be so different that they preclude cross-societal generalizations.

The essays in this book suggest that comparisons between the politics of industrialized societies may be particularly meaningful and useful, both for contrasting them with each other and for comparing them with those of economically less advanced societies. They also detach such comparative analysis from prevalent geocultural and ideological categorizations which distinguish, for example, between Western and non-Western societies and between Free World democracies and Communist autocracies.

The book's second major function was to present a variety of theoretical and methodological approaches to the comparative analysis of political leadership. In this respect, the symposium was not intended to bring together a group of experts on the politics of a particular area or country who shared a common analytical framework, but rather meant to include very different and even conflicting views about the ways and means of comparative leadership analysis. Unavoidably, the essays do not constitute a representative sample of the vast and growing literature about political leadership in general and in industrialized societies in particular. To supplement them, the annotated bibliography at the end of the book has been designed to direct the interested reader to other investigations employing a large variety of different theories and methods. It also serves to illustrate more specifically many of the points considered in only a very summary fashion in the following general observations.

The Comparative Analysis of Political Leadership

The study of political leadership is as old as the study of politics for the one is inseparable from the other. Since time immemorial men have asked, debated, and sought to establish who governs or should govern, what are or ought to be the bases of political authority in a community, and why and how some individuals obtain and exercise exceptional influence over the making of public rules and policies when others do not. And, implicitly or explicitly, such questions have also embodied comparative generalizations. When we evaluate the fitness of candidates for public offices, judge the performance of governmental decision-makers, or compare our political leaders with those who aspire to displace them or rule other peoples we compare and we generalize. When we say here is an effective leader, a wise statesman, a just ruler, or, on the other hand, call a leader a tyrant, an opportunist, or a fraud, we make comparisons between what we see in a leader and what we expect of one.

Professional observers and practitioners of political leadership, from the time of Plato and Aristotle to our own, have made it their special business to formulate such comparative generalizations. Some of these have been ostensibly descriptive, as in the case of historical chronicles and studies of "power elites" in American cities. Others again have been explicitly prescriptive and have sought to establish principles of "proper" political leadership on the basis of generalized assumptions about the nature of man, society, and authority. One need not have read *The Federalist* or the works of Tocqueville and Lenin to be familiar with comparative generalizations of the latter type; they can be found on the editorial pages of the daily papers, in the textbooks of civic courses, and even in the fictional works of novelists, poets, and playwrights.

In recent decades the scope and focus of comparative leadership analysis has been profoundly affected by a number of developments. Older theories and methods seem no longer adequate to explain similar types of leadership in very different cultures and societies and dissimilar patterns in what appear to be kindred ones. The rise and fall of an unprecedented form of autocracy—"totalitarian" dictatorships—in industrialized as well as nonindustrialized societies (that is, China) have posed the question whether Fascist and Communist dictatorships are cut off the same cloth along similar patterns, or only superficially similar manifestations of entirely different phenomena. Is authoritarianism only a characteristic of developing societies and was the Nazi dictatorship in "modern" Germany therefore an aberration, or does industrialization, in fact, promote autocratic and oligarchic leadership in contemporary mass societies? Can Hitler's and Stalin's rules be explained as the manifestations of pathological individual or mass behavior patterns or were they reflections of more basic and permanent socioeconomic and cultural factors in German and Russian society?

New theories, new modes of analysis, and new research opportunities have been no less important than substantive political events for the development of comparative leadership analysis, particularly among social scientists in the United States. New methods and facilities for collecting quantifiable data have provided scholars with an unprecedented amount of information about leadership patterns in past as well as contemporary societies. The "computer revolution" has made it a great deal easier than formerly to analyze and compare aggregate data and to test theoretical propositions about the behavior of leaders and followers in various political systems. Interdisciplinary collaboration has promoted the search for new analytic models and concepts which can facilitate exact and logically consistent explanations and predictions.

All of these developments have extended the research frontiers of leadership analysis, but they have also created new problems and disputes, and accentuated older ones, complicating the common search of social scientists for valid comparative generalizations. Essentially, these issues focus on the questions of what can be compared, for what purpose, and in what manner.

The Subject of Comparison

At the beginning of all comparison stands the definition of concepts. One cannot investigate and analyze leadership patterns without first stating what one is talking about in terms that are noncontradictory and inclusive as well as exclusive. Conceptual definitions identify factors considered relevant for analysis and form the basis of all comparative generalizations.

The search for clear, precise, and generally applicable analytical terms has been a major concern of contemporary efforts to study political leadership in various societies, but it has also been an important obstacle to progress in this direction. As social scientists have learned to probe beneath the manifest aspects of leadership and have become correspondingly more sensitive to the relevance of numerous and complex latent factors, they have found it more difficult to agree on what leadership is and does. It is a great deal easier to distinguish between voters and candidates in electoral studies, or between superiors and inferiors in formal political organizations, than to establish clear, operational boundaries that discriminate between leaders and followers in all situations. Whereas in the former case the difference is clearly one of kind, in the latter it is more likely to be one of degree. Followers may lead and leaders follow and individuals who may be leaders in one situation may be followers in another.

Generally, leadership is variously defined in the contemporary social science literature as influence, authority, power, and control over others. (See Table 1.1.) But how such concepts are to be defined and applied for comparative purposes remain a matter of considerable disagreement. Apparently identical or similar concepts—such as elite, authoritarianism, and leadership roles—may be defined in terms of very different operational criteria. On the other hand, various authors may define seemingly very different conceptualizations of power, influence, authority, and control—in quite similar operational terms. Or yet again, significantly different concepts *and* operational criteria may be employed to study similar subjects, such as decision and policy making.[1]

Some scholars identify political leadership with formal positions, offices, tasks, and functions along more or less traditional lines. Others emphasize performance: what leaders do and how they do it. Leadership is seen as the ability to guide and structure the collective behavior patterns of a given group in a desired direction, so that the decisions of the leader are implemented by group action. The leader is followed because he is loved, admired, respected, or feared, because he can coerce, persuade, or manipulate group members, because he can offer psychic as well as material rewards and punishments, or because compliance with his wishes is sanctioned by habit, traditional or legal-rational behavior norms. Still other

[1] In a somewhat different connection, these points are emphasized by Robert T. Golembiewski's "Small Groups and Large Organizations" in James C. March, *Handbook of Organizations*, Chicago, Ill., Rand McNally, 1965, p. 90.

Table 1.1. Selected Concepts and Organizational Criteria
For the Study of Political Leadership
(Derived from Leadership Literature)

Concept	Definition	Operational Criteria	Illustrative Data
Leadership authority	A relationship of inequality sanctioned by the legitimacy of leaders to make and enforce policy.	The nature and extent of legitimating group norms.	Elite and/or mass consensus on rights and duties of formal positions, on means and ends of leadership behavior.
Leadership control	The actual or perceived ability to provide or withhold benefits and apply sanctions.	Extent of leaders' ability to extract conforming group behavior.	Comparing means of control (for example, coercion, manipulation) with compliance on the part of group members.
Leadership autonomy	The extent to which leaders are independent of environmental factors.	Leaders' ability to be their own referent.	Intra- and extra-systemic variables interacting with leadership views and actions.
Leadership skills	The nature, possession, and application of methods designed to gain compliance.	Predisposition and capabilities of leaders and receptivity of group members to leadership cues.	Comparing goal orientations of leaders with success or failure to achieve group behavior conforming with goals.
Statescraft	A measure of the successful or unsuccessful exercise of legitimate authority in sovereign entities and sub-components thereof.	Determination of the efficacy of such authority in achieving stipulated goals.	Extent of achievement of stipulated objective or subjective communal goals (for example, political stability, defense of the national interest).

Table 1.1. (*Continued*)

Concept	Definition	Operational Criteria	Illustrative Data
Policy-making	The process of choosing among alternative goals, decision-makers, and courses of action.	a. The ingredients which enter into the process.	a. Extent of available information, perceived goals and capabilities, emotions, time pressure.
		b. The interaction process between relevant agents.	b. Rules and interpersonal relations in legislative, judicial, and administrative bodies.
		c. The relationship between policy inputs and outputs.	c. Comparing demands articulated by voters, interest associations, foreign governments with behavioral response of policy-makers.
Leadership roles	Three definitions involving inequality between actual or aspiring group leaders and actual or potential followers:		
	a. The position of leaders.	a. Offices occupied or sought, rights and duties associated with position.	a. The American presidency and its veto power over legislation.

Table 1.1. (*Continued*)

Concept	Definition	Operational Criteria	Illustrative Data
	b. The behavioral "style" of leaders.	b. Nature of interaction with other relevant actors.	b. The extent to which behavioral congruence is attained through coercion, manipulation, persuasion, etc.
	c. Orientations toward the incumbents of leadership positions.	c. Determination of reciprocal expectations associated with position.	c. Perception of representative or delegated functions, degree of conformity with group norms in the view of followers.
The personality of a leader	Individual, as distinguished from collective characteristics which influence attitudinal and behavioral patterns.	Determination of personality syndromes, their source, degree of adaptability and general impact on leader and/or follower.	Instinctive needs requiring satisfaction, learned repression, expression, and want patterns, degree of internalization of cultural norms, etc.
Leadership recruitment	The process of leadership selection.	a. The variables which promote or hinder the acquisition of leadership	a. Social background, ambition, skills, charisma, respect, material values, connections.
		b. The general process through which leaders are chosen and displaced.	b. Electoral processes, career patterns, revolutions, etc.

definitions are couched primarily in psychological rather than sociological terms. Here leadership is conceived as an attitudinal phenomenon in the mind of an actor who ascribes it to others, to himself, or both and responds accordingly to stimuli from his social environment. In short, varying definitions of leadership prevail and give rise to corresponding differences over what is the subject of comparison.

Another matter of dispute is the question at what level of comparison generalizations about leaders and leadership may be considered valid and meaningful. The avalanche of new data has greatly added to the store of information, and it has also brought into sharper focus the unique aspects of relevant individual and group behavior in particular situations and moments of time. The higher and broader the level of generalization, the greater, too, is (1) the distance from such empirical data and (2) the diversity of discrete variables encompassed.

For many area specialists, historians, and biographers engaged in micro-analytic investigations of specific men and events, the new data substantiate their belief that generalized comparisons across time and space can all too easily distort empirical reality and obscure significant differences between individual leaders, cultures, and societies. On the other hand, social scientists pursuing macro-analytic studies have not hesitated to employ the new data aggregatively, and at a correspondingly higher level of abstraction, in order to establish and test empirical propositions about classes of leaders and patterns of leadership. In the one case, the scope of comparison is relatively narrowly defined in order to give it greater depth, in the other the search for universally valid generalizations gives greater emphasis to breadth at the expense of unique factors. Thus a specialist on Soviet politics may insist that a singular combination of historical, socioeconomic, and cultural variables gives Russian Communist leadership a *sui generis* quality which sharply distinguishes it from all other types, or, at least, from leadership in non-Communist systems. However, a student of political decision-making or elite recruitment and behavior patterns may view the same phenomenon as but a variation of ubiquitous leadership functions in all political systems.

The Purpose of Comparison

The purpose of comparative leadership analysis, intimately related to matters of conceptualization and scope, constitutes another problem area. What should be the ultimate object of such studies is disputed among scholars. Some insist that as social scientists they are above all committed to seek knowledge and in their search for more precise and universally valid propositions have become increasingly wary of "value-laden" definitions and generalizations. What may be "common-sense" in one society may be considered "nonsense" in another, they point out, and moral truths which are thought to be eternal at one point in time may in the long run prove to be only fleeting values.

At least in their professional capacity, these social scientists are inclined to take a correspondingly relativist view of "democratic" and "authoritarian" forms of leadership. In their view, whether one or the other may be considered more "effective" for the attainment of the objectives of a particular leader or group or for the "systemic" needs of a political organization or community, depends on the nature of the problem one chooses to investigate. Whereas this choice may be dictated by a scholar's personal values, his search for the objective explanations and predictions must be unencumbered by subjective assumptions and normative value judgment if his data are to be collected and analyzed "scientifically." Accordingly, what constitutes a "great leader," for example, is considered a matter of definition in terms of the problem under investigation. To some he may be a man who gets things done, such as furthering economic development or winning elections or wars; to others he may be a leader who maintains the "stability" of a political system in time of stress or who introduces major innovations into political processes.

This relativist approach has been severely criticized by other scholars, especially on two grounds. In the first place, the premise on which it rests is said to be false. Social scientists allegedly cannot exclude their personal preferences from their investigation of political leadership. Culturally imbedded values, it is said, may exclude, for example, the use of certain techniques, such as the employment of dangerous drugs in small group leadership experiments. More important, the nature of the problems investigated by social scientists encourages personal involvement, in this view, since they are usually participant observers. Claims to the contrary serve only to delude the investigator and to conceal his inevitable bias toward one type of leadership or another.

In the second place, it is argued that students of political leadership have an obligation to employ their findings for public policy ends. Even assuming that they can and should strive for a maximum degree of objectivity in research and analysis, their ultimate purpose must be to study "important" political and moral problems. For instance, comparative leadership studies ought to suggest ways to prevent war and oppression, promote democracy and honest government, and indicate what sort of men and leadership structures can most effectively advance the welfare of a particular society, community, or political organization. If they fail to do this, the claim for "scientific objectivity" allegedly represents but an evasion of the scholar's responsibilities toward his fellow men.

The Method of Comparison

Finally, there is considerable disagreement over the most effective way to study and compare political leaders for whatever purpose. What kind of data are needed and how should they be interpreted? To what extent should one focus on the leaders and to what extent on the context in which they operate, particularly their followers? How much attention should be paid to such leadership characteristics as social background, career patterns, and personality make-up, and how much to such environmental factors as prevailing socioeconomic conditions, cultural patterns, and political structures? The answers provided by students of political leadership depend today, as in the past, on their explicit or implicit analytical framework or theoretical models.

Such analytic schemes are legion and not infrequently mutually exclusive in approach. Some are empirically oriented and strive for comparative generalizations based on observed phenomena. Others again deliberately ignore "the real world" and seek to explain leadership patterns on the strength of mathematical abstractions. Some favor an inductive approach which proceeds from the particular to the general, other deduce specific patterns from general propositions. Some embrace deterministic theories, some probabilistic explanations based on statistical inferences. Certain scholars consider psychological and cultural factors particularly important, whereas others ignore these entirely in favor of social or economic variables. One approach may be holistic and insist on the relevance of a host of complex factors, another may be monistic and associate leadership patterns with a major causal variable or set of variables, such as urbanization or social stratification. By and large, however, one can distinguish among these different approaches in terms of the (1) focus, (2) relative weight attached to the autonomy of a leader, and (3) space and time dimension for comparative analysis.

As indicated in Table 1.2, the *focus* of comparative studies may be the identity of leading actors in various political systems or subsystems. Who they are is thought to indicate the patterns of leadership recruitment and/or—at least by inference—dominant political values and interpersonal relations in the groups they lead in fact if not in form. For example, data on social background, career patterns, and the like may thus be employed as indices of similar or different types of leadership selection processes and performance styles in various political parties and governmental structures.

Another, and frequently complementary, approach to the questions of

Table 1.2.   Approaches to the Study of Political Leadership

I. Focus on the leading actors
   A. Elite analysis—leaders studied as collectivities
      1. Elite identification (recruitment, composition, and circulation of leading participants in political processes)
         a. By position
         b. By reputation
      2. Elite attitudes
      3. Elite behavior patterns
   B. The study of individual leaders
      1. Standard political biographies
      2. Psychobiographies
II. Focus on interaction between leaders and context
   A. Leaders as subjects (for example, the event-making man)
   B. Leaders as objects of social forces, group norms, organizational structures, etc.
   C. Leaders as actors in interpersonal relationships (leader-leader, leader-followers, etc.)
      1. Systems analysis
      2. Influence analysis
      3. Issue analysis
      4. Analysis of social movements and small groups
      5. Situational analysis (for example, "crisis" leadership)

---

why some individuals become leaders when others fail and why the leaders of structurally similar groups behave often very differently, is to examine the attitudes of leaders as well as followers. Here the emphasis tends to be placed upon subjective sociopsychological and sociocultural factors which predispose some men to lead and others to follow them and some leaders to choose one course of action and some another. For example, an investigator may conclude that congruent mass and elite orientations toward political authority and leadership roles promote effective and stable leadership patterns, whereas discordant attitudes may shatter group cohesion and paralyze or even destroy its leader or leaders. Or he may trace differential patterns of leadership behavior to individual personality characteristics, or to learning experiences that vary in time and space.

Rather than ask who leads and why, the comparative analysis may focus on leadership processes in different or similar situations. The investigator may seek his answer by constructing an abstract system or decision-making model which posits that given conditions will produce one or more behavioral outcomes in light of the options which are logically open to a leader. This is the approach favored by game theorists, who view leadership in terms of alternative choices made by actors assumed to act entirely rationally in pursuing their interests. A related but more empirical method rests upon the theory that leadership is the product of logical exchange relationships among leaders and between leaders and followers. For example, a legislator is thought to buy or trade votes in exchange for services rendered or promised to other leaders or his interest group clients.

More psychologically oriented scholars are prone to view leadership processes in terms of individual or group dynamics and relate them to subjective factors. For example, they may ask what kind of cues provided by a leader will elicit the desired responses from group members he wants to follow him. Are they psychologically predisposed to react positively to an authoritarian or a democratic style of leadership? Are they members of an ideological movement based upon a strong sense of emotional identification between leaders and followers? Do they look for a leader who will magically deliver them from conditions which they consider beyond their own control or do they expect the leader to conform to their demands?

Other approaches again may focus on sociological factors, such as organizational structures and norms that promote or limit strong leadership in political parties and public bureaucracies. Leadership performance may be compared in terms of focal issues of policy-making in local or national governmental bodies, in terms of patterns of influence, or both. The analytical framework may stipulate that knowledge provides political power and that those who are best informed about who is who and who does what in public affairs also exercise the greatest amount of political influence.

Last, the methodological focus may be directed toward the consequences of different types of leadership and styles of leadership performance. Scholars interested in the preservation of political stability under varying conditions of stress and strain may investigate the requisites for strong governmental authority. Leadership patterns most likely to promote certain group goals may be the concern of others. One study may examine comparatively the most efficient forms of political control for economic development, another may examine under what circumstances authoritarian or democratic styles of leadership are most effective in mobilizing mass support behind party or governmental officials. Comparisons between presidents and prime ministers, or between one legislature and another, may lead to generalizations about effective and ineffective public leadership, strong and weak political leaders, innovating and stabilizing authority patterns.

The question of a *leader's autonomy* from the context in which he operates has always been a matter of controversy. One school of thought has held that leadership, particularly "heroic" or "event-making" leadership, is the function of individual qualities, and should be examined in these terms. De Gaulle's assertion that "History in its great moments tolerates in position of authority only those men capable of directing their own course," [2] has been echoed by scholars who hold that a Hitler or Stalin, a Churchill or Roosevelt, should not be studied as the mere embodiment of social forces. They may be situationally relevant, but they are not situationally determined, in this view, and their actions shape the environment rather than being molded by it.

Such an approach is emphatically rejected by most contemporary American social and political scientists. In their view, all leadership is more or less a function of the environment. According to a leading political scientist, a leader is but "a bus driver whose passengers will leave him unless he takes them in the direction in which they wish to go. They leave him only minor discretion as to the road to be followed." [3] Who leads, how, and why are thus believed to be more or less situationally determined. But proponents of this view by no means agree which environmental factors are particularly relevant in circumscribing the autonomy of various leaders in different settings. Neo-Marxists may single out economic variables, proponents of a "national character" approach are likely to focus on cultural patterns, students of large-scale organizations on formal rules and institutional norms, and scholars who concentrate on small group dynamics are prone to stress the limitations which the psychological predispositions of the members of large as well as small groups are believed to impose upon their leaders.

The *space and time dimensions* employed also tend to be significantly influenced by, as well as to influence, various theories and methods of comparative leadership analysis. Cross-sectional comparison *in time*, within or between particular societies, cultures, and political systems, frequently treat historical factors as irrelevant or even misleading for an understanding of contemporaneous leadership patterns. Thus many students of community power structures, for example, tend to see little or no need to delve into the past in their search for generalizations about the ongoing present. On the other hand, scholars who seek to compare the development of leadership patterns *over time* are correspondingly more likely to emphasize historical analogies or differences. For instance, they may discern in the "charismatic" leadership of a George Washington, a

---

[2] Charles de Gaulle, *Memoirs*, Vol. III, New York, Simon and Schuster, 1960, p. 75.
[3] Herbert Simon, *Administrative Behavior*, New York, Macmillan, 1947, p. 134.

Napoleon, or a Lenin styles of performance considered typical for all "modernizing" societies. Or, on the contrary, allegedly unique factors, identified with particular and unparalled historical developments or personages, may be singled out to explain patterns of political leadership said to vary significantly in space as well as time.

Political Leadership in Industrialized Societies

In planning this volume, its editor proceeded from certain theoretical assumptions which, as will be seen, were neither fully shared by all the contributors nor always sustained by their analyses. They are, nonetheless, presented in this introductory essay for two reasons. In the first place, these controlling assumptions will indicate the general editorial criteria that led to the inclusions of some countries and the exclusion, or only peripheral consideration, of others. In the second place, taken together, the following essays suggest that by and large these assumptions may serve as a common focus for the comparative analysis of political leadership in time as well as over time.

Assumption 1. A society may be defined as a collection of individuals sharing a process of patterned interaction and multiple interdependent functions and tasks.

Assumption 2. Leadership is a position within a society which is defined by the ability of the incumbent to guide and structure the collective behavior patterns of some or all of its members. It is at all times relational, interpersonal, and is based upon inequality of influence between the leader as the influencing agent and the followers as the objects of his efforts to cue their behavior so that it will conform with his personal objectives.

Assumption 3. Politics revolves around competition for control over the distribution of public benefits and obligations in a society organized in the form of a large-scale, geographically distinct and formally defined group called a political community.

Assumption 4. Political leadership involves the direct or indirect exercise of influence over the distribution of public benefits and obligations in a political community.

Assumption 5. The study of political leadership focuses (1) on the relationship between those who exercise such influence and those who are subject to it, as well as (2) on the competition between individuals for access to positions which provide influence.

Assumption 6. The selection and behavior of political leaders are products of the interaction between the characteristics of the key actors and the characteristics of the contextual milieu in which they operate. Under the former, one might include such innate factors as the physiological and psychological traits of actual or aspiring leaders—for instance, their sex, age, and capacity for rational decisions and sustained activity— as well as such social characteristics as education, religion, and political affiliations, positions, and value commitments. Qualities of the contextual milieu, on the other hand, may encompass a much wider range of interdependent variables extending beyond the confines of the political community. Parameters for leadership activities may, for example, be drawn by limitations on policy choices imposed by factors external to a community, such as the authority of a superior political agency or linkages to other communities. But, generally speaking, internal factors inherent in the milieu are likely to be of greater importance. These may include prevailing cultural norms and institutional structures and, more particularly, formal and informal orientations and relationships governing political intercourse between leaders and nonleaders.

Assumption 7. The environmental conditions for political leadership in industrialized societies are distinguished from those which prevail in other societies by certain common characteristics. The adjective "industrialized"—like "developed" or "modern"—describes, of course, a relative, rather than absolute stage of socioeconomic development. Moreover, social scientists differ and often are not very explicit about the specific criteria which identify industrialized societies. Some employ economic criteria, others add sociological indicators. Some are content to speak in broad terms about societies considered industrialized, others seek to go farther by speaking of fully industrialized or even postindustrialized societies.

For the purposes of this book, societies were considered industrialized on the basis of the following general socioeconomic criteria: [4]

1. A self-sustaining flow of capital accumulation for expanding the production of goods and services through the application of technology using impersonal sources of energy. (See Lasswell, Chapter 11 of this book.)
2. A high rate of mass consumption of the goods and services of the Gross National Product (GNP).

[4] Many of these are listed in Bruce M. Russett, Hayward R. Alker, Karl W. Deutsch, and Harold Lasswell, *World Handbook of Political and Social Indicators*, New Haven, Conn., Yale University Press, 1964; and Arthur Banks and Robert T. Textor, *A Cross-Political Survey*, Cambridge, Mass., MIT Press, 1963. See also Samuel P. Huntington, "Political Development and Political Decay," *World Politics*, XVII, 3 (April, 1965), 386 ff, and the references cited there, and Lucian W. Pye, *Aspects of Political Development*, Boston, Mass., Little Brown, 1966, p. 45 ff.

3. A *per capita* GNP at least twice as high as the world average.
4. The sources of the GNP are primarily nonagricultural.
5. The nonagricultural labor force exceeds the agricultural.
6. At least one-third of the population is urbanized (that is, lives in cities with populations of 20,000 or more).
7. At least two-thirds of the adult population is literate, and extensive, centralized mass media of communications facilitate a common focus of attention and expectations toward societal leaders.
8. The vast majority of the population participates in extensive, complex, and multifunctional transactions involving a high rate of exchange of goods and services within the society.
9. An integrated network of specialized leadership positions facilitates the mass mobilization of skills and energies and the coordination of functionally differentiated economic, social, and political structures.

In terms of the world population as a whole at the time of analysis, all of the societies called "modern" or "industrialized" by the contributors to this volume were relatively highly advanced by these criteria. They were either already "mass-consumption" societies—like the United States, Canada, Britain, France, Germany, and Australia—or rapidly approaching that state—like Japan, the Soviet Union, Czechoslovakia, Poland, and Hungary. By comparison, such European countries as Greece, Portugal, and Albania—not to mention the "developing" societies of Asia, Africa, and Latin America—are still nonindustrialized today.

Thus, as here defined, the term industrialized societies cuts across the distinction between "Western" and "non-Western" societies and between "democratic" and "authoritarian" political systems. It includes some European countries and excludes others and it accommodates certain Communist states but not some others.

The "typical" *political characteristics* of industrialized societies—and corresponding political leadership patterns—are again subjects of considerable disagreement among social scientists. It seems to be generally accepted that industrialization serves to extend mass involvement in political activities. But whether such intensified mass mobilization leads to greater or diminished popular participation in the selection of political leaders and public policies is another question. A second issue is whether industrialization produces converging, parallel, or diverging political patters in different societies. Both questions are either explicitly or implicitly considered by a number of the contributors to this book.

In the view of some social scientists, industrialization inevitably produces greater political and social democracy in all societies. In the opinion of others, it has the very opposite effect and leads to greater controls from above and increased curbs on individual freedom and democratic processes. Similarly, on the second question, some social scientists believe that industrialization gives rise to uniformities in organization, skills, education, and mobility and corresponding common outlooks and values among the members of different societies. Ideologies generated during earlier periods of class conflict are said to be giving way to a common industrial "culture" based on the acceptance of an "open" pluralist society, a mixed economy, and the need for social planning. According to this "convergence" theory, distinct national value systems and political cultures will increasingly decline in importance before "rationalizing" institutions and technocratic elites. Thus "modern" Communist and non-Communist systems, for example, will more and more come to resemble one another.[5]

The critics of this approach suggest that national value systems have great vitality and that the patterns of political leadership, organization, and values in industrialized societies will take correspondingly more or less different, if not divergent forms. Thus both American and Soviet scholars emphatically deny that industrialism is producing similar or analogous political systems in "modern" Communist and non-Communist societies and do not look upon the United States and Russia as mere variants of advanced industrial cultures.[6]

In the last analysis, both of these issues pose theoretical propositions demanding a great deal of further empirical research to prove them true or false. For that matter, it may be that none of them are entirely correct. At the present time, as Lasswell observes in this book, the diversity of the available data seems to preclude scholarly agreement on an empirical model that encompasses the characteristic political features of leadership in all industrialized society.

Studies in Comparative Analysis

All of the following essays focus on political leadership in industrialized societies, but they vary considerably in scope, theory, and method of comparative analysis. In scope they range from broad, macroanalytic studies of leadership patterns in several societies to microanalytic investi-

[5] See, for example, Clark Kerr et al., *Industrialism and Industrial Man*, Cambridge, Mass., Harvard University Press, 1960; and Pitirim Sorokin, "Mutual Convergence of the United States and the U.S.S.R.," *International Journal of Comparative Sociology*, I (September, 1960), 143–176.

[6] See Robert C. Tucker, "On the Comparative Study of Communism," *World Politics*, XIX (January, 1967), 250–252 and references cited there.

gations limited to a single society and/or a few specific leaders. As to theory and method, some of the contributors deduce comparative generalizations from more or less hypothetical models, others employ an inductive approach to advance empirical propositions based on their analysis of aggregate data, and some attempt to use an inductive-deductive analytical framework.

Second, all of the authors look upon their contributions as exploratory in nature and tentative in conclusions, as suggestive rather than definitive. Each brings to his analysis a particular set of theoretical assumptions that are not always shared by the others and, for the most part, the comparative generalizations offered are explicitly limited in terms of the particular context or actors examined, the model employed, and the available data. Thus each author says, in effect: This is the way it looks to me, from my point of view, in this particular instance, on the basis of what I can observe at this time.

Mitscherlich's psychiatric interpretations of the impact of advanced industrialization on patterns of political authority focuses on psychological factors assumed to have universal application. Manifest value commitments to one type of political order or another seem to him only to obscure converging trends in all modern mass consumption societies. Employing a Freudian psychoanalytic model and analogies based on clinical observations, the German psychiatrist maintains that in these societies the specialization and routinization of socioeconomic functions, on the one hand, and an unprecedented degree of general mass affluence on the other, have been accompanied by a distinct change in the psychological foundations of political authority. The passing of traditional authority patterns has, in his opinion, led to a "depaternalization" of political leadership, without, however, producing thus far new forms of emotionally satisfying and acceptable role relationships. In place of the symbolic father figure who formerly expressed a relatively stable, hierarchic type of paternal authority, Mitscherlich sees the instrumental leadership of competing specialists in political management who owe allegiance only to themselves.

At the present time, this type of "fraternal" leadership is said to rest for the most part on unstable peer group relationships because it encourages "sibling rivalries" among men who recognize no superiors in the psychological sense. Below this leadership stratum Mitscherlich perceives the broad masses who demand material satisfaction but lack a psychologically satisfying relationship with those who exercise political authority over them. Manifestly apathetic and unwilling to participate in politics, they are seen as latently disposed to be aggressive and likely to become destructive if new acceptable authority patterns do not emerge. All this suggests to Mitscherlich the possibility of a new form of political stratification in all industrialized societies that bifurcates their members into a small minority of cooperating or competing political managers at the top and a more or less manipulated mass at the bottom.

Barnes, in the following chapter, examines the impact of industrialization on political orientations toward leadership in terms more familiar to social scientists. Whereas Mitscherlich deduced comparative generalizations from his psychoanalytic model, the American political scientist relies largely on survey research data for his inductive analysis; and whereas the psychiatrist saw the impact of industrialization in terms of concomitant curbs on mass participation in politics, Barnes considers the limitations which efforts to mobilize mass support for their goals may impose upon political leaders, including those committed to the realization of "democratic" objectives in industrialized societies.

On the strength of his interviews with members of the Italian Socialist Party, as well as other studies of the politics of industrialized societies, Barnes concludes that effective mass mobilization calls above all for styles of political leadership congruent with the sense of political competence of those who are to be led. According to Barnes, when the led feel incompetent to influence the choice of leaders and policies, a sense of popular participation is not a requisite for the political mobilization of mass support by the leaders. Even though the ostensible goal of a political movement may be egalitarian mass participation, he suggests that such democratic ends may be more effectively achieved by nondemocratic means as long as the masses to be mobilized lack a sense of participatory competence. In other words, leadership for democracy need, in fact, not be leadership through democracy, a theme which recurs in other chapters of this book.

Meyer's discussion of political authority patterns in Communist regimes again employs essentially a deductive approach—in part by choice, in part of necessity in view of the paucity of adequate empirical data. It uses a developmental model for a comparative analysis of various Communist systems and the efforts of their leaders to establish their authority in the wake of a revolutionary transformation of a political system. According to Meyer, the origin and ideological basis of such regimes complicate this task. It is only in "mature" Communist regimes, those that have developed social and economic systems similar to those of other industrialized societies, that the tensions between the revolutionary challenge to authority and the need for stable authority has been overcome. Thus although the nature of political authority in comparatively developed Communist countries may incorporate cultural and instittuional features which still distinguish it from that in other industrialized societies, their "modernization," claims Meyer, has produced analogous, if not similar authority patterns. He therefore concludes that comparisons between leadership in "developed" and "underdeveloped" Communist systems and between political authority patterns in industrialized Communist and non-Communist societies, on the one hand, and less industrialized societies, on the other, may illuminate heretofore neglected aspects of comparative politics.

The contributions by Hoffmann, Wolfenstein, Hargrove, Schubert, and Schlesinger shift the focus of comparative analysis from more general aspects of political leadership in industrialized societies to a consideration of particular leaders and elite groups. The first two authors consider exceptional leaders in exceptional situations, the other three are primarily concerned with more routinized and institutionalized forms of leadership recruitment and behavior.

Hoffmann's analysis of three French crisis leaders—Pétain, Mendes-France, and de Gaulle—is a comparison over time between leadership styles under various regimes, but within a single society. It differs from other essays in this book not merely in this deliberate restriction of the scope of the investigation to one country, but in the theoretical assumptions underlying it.

First of all, Hoffmann distinguishes sharply between what he identifies as the "psychological" and "political" approach to the study of political leadership and maintains that it is necessary to choose between one or the other analytic framework if a clear theoretical focus is to be achieved. His own preference is to disregard the personality characteristics and deeper motivations of a leader in order to concentrate on the efficacy of his performance as key actor in the political system.

Second, Hoffmann questions the utility and validity of cross-national comparisons which assume that common elements in the political leadership patterns of industrialized societies clearly distinguish these from those in other societies. Like a number of other critics of "developmental" approaches to comparative politics, he challenges the assertion that socio-economic and political structures and norms in industrialized societies develop necessarily interdependently and along similar, if not converging lines. Primarily on the strength of his analysis of French society, Hoffmann holds that political authority relationships tend to be largely autonomous and to reflect particular historical and cultural factors that are, at best, only marginally related to socioeconomic "modernization." Therefore he concludes that the political implications of industrialization are too varied and tenuous to permit meaningful and theoretically sound cross-cultural generalizations about the similarity of political leadership and authority patterns in industrialized societies.

In sharp contrast, Wolfenstein's analysis of crisis leadership in Britain and Germany stresses the psychodynamic aspects of Churchill's and Hitler's behavior patterns and places correspondingly less emphasis on institutional, socioeconomic, and politico-cultural environmental factors. Wolfenstein deduces from his psychoanalytic model that the personality characteristics of these men suggest that crisis leaders in general tend to be individuals who successfully express their inner needs through a style of performance which is congruent with the role expectations and emotional predispositions of the masses they mobilize behind them. Thus, whereas the psychogeneric origins of the crisis leaders' "abnormal" behavior patterns may vary considerably from case to case, their deviancy from established political leadership styles in time of crisis not only becomes acceptable but is considered highly functional by their followers. By extending his comparative analysis beyond industrial societies to include the crisis leadership of Lenin and Ghandi, Wolfenstein suggests that regardless of socioeconomic and cultural differences in the societal context, the role of the crisis leader tends to be effectively played by men who are attracted to it by strong inner compulsions.

The relevance of cultural and institutional patterns for cross-national comparisons of leadership recruitment and style of performance in industrialized societies—and the related question of converging patterns—are central to the empirical investigations presented by Hargrove, Schubert, and Schlesinger. Each of them focuses for the purposes of comparison on functionally more or less similar key government positions in several political systems, and each includes in his analysis two or more societies which are not only industrialized, but ostensibly distinguished by common roots in an "Anglo-Saxon" political culture.

Hargrove, like Schubert in the following and Lasswell in the concluding chapter, endeavors to accommodate psychological as well as non-psychological factors in the analysis of political leadership. His comparative analysis of the role of the chief executive in the United States, Canada, and Great Britain takes account of the political "resources" available to government leaders in these three "Anglo-Saxon" industrialized societies and seeks to explain significant differences in their styles of performance, both in terms of variations in the cultural and institutional environment and in terms of variations in individual personality characteristics.

Hargrove's observations lead him to agree with Hoffmann that, in general, significant variations in the efficacy of governmental leaders are primarily a function of the degree of their congruence with distinctive cultural role perceptions defined by the authority norms of different "political formulas." Thus even analogous institutional and cultural patterns in three societies at roughly the same level of advanced industrialization do not appear to Hargrove to yield identical or converging orientations toward the role of the chief executive. Within the confines of a distinct political culture, however, the personality characteristics of a particular president or prime minister may give rise to significant variations in leadership style. He therefore finds room in his scheme of analysis for psychodynamic studies of crisis as well as noncrisis leaders.

Schubert's essay offers two major contributions to this volume. First, his investigation of the political leadership functions of four sets of judicial elites provides a further test of the convergence hypothesis by extending the comparative analysis beyond "Anglo-Saxon" and industrialized societies. Second, his report on judicial policy-making in the United States, Australia, Japan, and the Philippines suggests the use of a quantitative approach to multivariate analysis which would endeavor to be more precise and integrated than the intuitive juxtaposition of political institutions, cultures, and leaders.

Employing a decision-making model, Schubert examines the relationship between institutional, socioeconomic, sociocultural and psychocultural "input" variables, on the one hand, and variations in the "outputs" of the four judicial systems, on the other. Correlational tests of the rank order of association between these input and output variables indicate that the most and the least industrialized societies in his sample—the United States and the Philippines—are most similar in the style and extent of political leadership by the members of the supreme judicature. These findings suggest to Schubert that such affinity is the result primarily of half a century of direct American influence upon the development of Philippine political (including, of course, judicial) institutions and norms. Other factors that were examined but found to be less significant include degrees of industrial development, and sharing of Anglo-Saxon legocultural traditions.

Schlesinger's comparative study of the function of political parties in the recruitment of public leaders introduces yet another mode of analysis. As he indicates at the outset of the chapter, his examination of the career patterns of legislators and cabinet members in the United States, Canada, Britain, Australia, and France rests upon theoretical assumptions radically different from those of other contributors. The model used factors out all the independent variables which other authors consider relevant for the study of such dependent variables as leadership selection and performance. Schlesinger assumes simply that all party leaders who seek and hold elective public offices are motivated by a constant and universal factor, ambition, and will rationally choose the most logical strategy for furthering their political careers in a particular institutional setting. Therefore career data are thought to reflect the structure of political opportunities available in different societies, and their analysis, according to Schlesinger, will permit cross-national comparisons between the career perspectives of politicians and the recruitment functions of party organizations.

His investigations over time of the careers of legislators and cabinet officers in five countries leads Schlesinger to the conclusion that distinctly different party structures are primarily conditioned by the aggregate ambitions of their leaders for public office. On the other hand, similar governmental structures appear to accommodate a wide variety of opportunities for the advancement of such political careers; different ideological goals seem to have little or no influence on the organization of political parties serving as recruitment structures for public leaders.

Seligman's contribution demonstrates how a theoretical focus for comparative analysis similar to that of Schlesinger's empirical investigation may be expanded to develop generalizations based upon a broader and more abstract mode of analysis. Seligman also conceives political leadership in industrialized societies in terms of complex organizational tasks and roles and the recruitment of political leaders in terms of the interaction between party organizations and the larger sociopolitical and sociocultural environment. Like Schlesinger he (1) views political parties as mediating structures between individual ambition for and the attainment of public office and (2) assumes that the internal dynamics of party organizations are decisively influenced by, as well as influence themselves, the opportunities and risks which different political systems provide for office-seeking party leaders. Party organizations, according to Seligman, tend to control the selection of political leaders in societies with single as well as multiparty systems; and who is recruited and how varies in accordance with the interaction between such organizations and the environment in which they function. Therefore, he asserts, the patterns of leadership recruitment may indicate why large-scale party organizations operating in very diverse environments appear to give rise to similar roles and behavior patterns, even though in form they seem to vary widely.

The essay by Lasswell concludes the symposium literally as well as figuratively. Broadly conceived in substance as well as theory, it brings together much of what has preceded in a cross-national survey built around a problem-oriented approach to political leadership in industrialized societies. That is, Lasswell looks at this phenomenon in terms of the end product, the values which are to be realized, and he considers leadership recruitment and performance as processes designed to achieve given values in a given setting. His "configurative" approach holds that in any society political leadership patterns result from the interaction between the political culture of the community and the "political personalities" of leading actors.

Lasswell's emphasis on generalized sociocultural value patterns, on the one hand, and individual psychocultural patterns, on the other, accommodates most—though by no means all—approaches employed by the studies in this as well as other works on political leadership. He allows that the cultural diversity and developmental dynamics of advanced industrialized societies give rise to extremely complex and varying forms of political leadership. But he believes that there are sufficient common features to allow him to develop a probabilistic "developmental construct" for identifying the requisites of stable political leadership in modern mass-consumption societies. This is the theoretical model that he recommends as an analytical framework for descriptive and explanatory research studies, as well as for prescriptive, policy-oriented formulations based upon the extrapolation of their findings into the future.

Unity in Diversity

The variety in scope, theory, method, and data presented here and in other studies of political leadership may cause one to wonder whether a comprehensive approach can ever be achieved. The answer, as a social psychologist recently suggested, depends largely upon one's aspirations.[7] The editor of this symposium shares his belief that the task of integration may be difficult but not impossible, provided one's approach is broad enough to encompass research by all the social sciences on many societies and political systems. Comparisons between multiple political leadership patterns may reveal important similarities and differences in time and space that will permit a tighter theoretical integration of seemingly quite heterogeneous phenomena.

There can be unity in diversity, many roads may lead to Rome, but they are all designed to get us there. Although the point of departure may vary, side roads merge into major avenues of approach to a common objective. And if we take the trouble to observe the efforts of our fellow travelers, we may learn to profit from their achievements as well as their errors. As in other fields of scholarly endeavor, the road to progress in political leadership analysis is not so much paved with good intention as with the products of collaborative and mutually reinforcing efforts to find the answers to questions of common concern. If this book will help to stimulate discussion and to further comparative studies, it will have achieved the editor's principal objectives.

[7] Dorwin Cartwright, "Influence, Leadership, and Control," in March *op cit.*, p 40f.

2. Changing Patterns of Political Authority: A Psychiatric Interpretation

ALEXANDER MITSCHERLICH

The Author's Frame of Reference

The following reflections present one possible way of interpreting the phenomenon of "political authority"—that of a psychoanalyst. In the nature of things he gains most of his insight into human behavior from treating his patients, apart, of course, from his own personal experience of life. For a psychoanalyst his patients are samples in whom he can examine features of behavior peculiar to his contemporaries. From them he learns what makes his contemporaries suffer, the problems they solve satisfactorily and those they solve inadequately, where they feel comparatively sure and where they feel helpless. It must, however, be conceded that these samples seen by the analyst (even when he is in research work and financially independent, as I am) are not entirely random.

The patients who seek treatment are suffering and want to be cured. But it need not therefore be thought that what is revealed in them is purely pathological.[1] In a way they represent a select group of people with a higher sensitivity to so-called normal stress. We have learned to realize that it is an error to make distinctions between illness with organic causes and illness with nonorganic, emotional causes—organic disturbances too can be decisively motivated by emotional factors. Today we also know that the majority of patients are not to be regarded only as a group characterized to begin with by having more problems of adjustment, as, for instance, in the case of the "ambivalents" in Robert Presthus's classification of types.[2] One cannot rate them as a negative selection and

[1] Our study of the neuroses to which, after all, we owe the most valuable pointers to an understanding of normal conditions . . . ." S. Freud, *Standard Edition of the Collected Works*, Vol. XXI, p. 135.

[2] R. Presthus, *The Organizational Society*, New York, Vintage Books, 1962.

leave it at that. The distinction between individual illness and the social structure has proved just as arbitrary as that between the organic and the psychogenic. For if one knows how to read the patients' symptoms, one finds that they reflect the characteristic frustrations or pressures that are widespread in their society. It is possible that they reacted more violently than other individuals, but it may also be that they were forced to live under unusually strong but nevertheless typical pressure and that their reaction to this was pathological. At any rate, experience has taught us that many who have fallen ill under emotional stress were more sensitive in their reaction to characteristic frustrations than the great majority. This is a subjective problem for them, but for our purpose these patients give us the opportunity to observe contingencies to a degree of subtlety that cannot be achieved by experimental investigation of behavior.

Moreover, so-called normality conceals a number of psychopathological reactions which are, however, sanctioned by the tendency of the times. Many of these traits of behavior which the psychoanalyst has the opportunity to observe when treating his patients have no direct pathogenic significance. They are subsidiary findings, but sometimes it is quite easy to trace their origin, easier than it would be within the framework of a mere economic or moral approach. In our group of patients we found far fewer cases that could be described as extreme constitutional variants (to use the classic terminology, psychopaths, for instance), and therefore casuistic curiosities, than cases which presented frequently recurring conflicts motivated by the conditions of life in society as a whole. We must not forget that every society has its dark pathogenetic side, and adaptation is often synonymous with coercion to adopt pathological, that is, alienating patterns of behavior. But why do people create societies whose self-made institutions invariably make them ill? This question is perhaps inadequate, but it points to the unrest shaping the rises and falls of human history.

These remarks are intended to make it clear that the following reflections are based on clinical observation; they have been arrived at as a result of case study and not experimentally. They cannot, therefore, be allowed any statistical conclusiveness; in all probability much is not simply verifiable by empirical methods but only by the same process, namely, the psychoanalytical method. Nevertheless we are, it seems to me, justified in taking a critical interest in such behavior even if it cannot be immediately dissected by differential psychological methods.

The desire to be cured moves patients to make observations which one usually does not because at first they undermine one's self-esteem. But the therapy is only successful when more of the patient's motivation becomes apparent to him than he has so far been able to discover about himself. Through this therapeutic process, far more diverse and hidden behavior becomes visible than can become accessible to experimental research with its necessarily circumscribed approach. Observation in the course of treatment, however, brings to light a great many specific stereotypic attitudes and value judgments characteristic of various age brackets, political and religious groups, or occupations. For this reason these psychiatric investigations provide information of value to the political observer too.

My manner of presentation is bound to be sketchy in many places. At times it may fly off at a tangent. I have made no attempt to streamline my presentation because I considered it important not to allow the manner of communication to cover up completely the many-layered complexity of psychical processes and then arouse the impression that we are speaking of comparatively simple nexuses.

The theoretical framework of reference within which I make my remarks is taken from psychoanalytical social psychology, particularly from Freud's classic studies "Group Psychology and the Analysis of the Ego" and "Civilization and its Discontent."

Historical Patterns of Authority

The definition of political authority from which I proceed aims at the reality of power; authority rests with him who is in a position to make decisions and then get others to act in accordance with them. Such an authority imposes a hierarchy of social behavior. This is an etiological interpretation of the concept, but it will suffice for the purposes of this study.

It must first be determined whether political authority finds independent expression within the social compass and to what extent it makes use of the mode of expression of other authorities. Take, for instance, certain representatives of authority which we observe today. There we obviously must realize that not every contemporary phenomenon is truly expressive of our time: many of ther are anarchronistic, and some of them are intentionally so. A glance at Charles de Gaulle provoking and returning with outstretched arms the acclamation of the crowd apprises us of his intention to celebrate a political authority bordering on the religious. In line with Max Weber's ideas, he sees himself as a political priest, as the *charismatic leader of the nation.*

For the psychologist it is interesting to observe how such authoritative appeal can come about. The priest-politician stands by his grandiose fantasies in public and projects them into the cosmic: He *knows* that God is with him. This is the oldest justification of political authority. It is frankly and openly expressed in all forms of the Divine Right of Kings, such as Augustus' claim that his rule was founded on a "higher legitimation," [3] on the "consensus universorum."

This pretension to charismatic distinction on the part of political authorities, however, requires a society prepared to submit to such leadership. The charismatic leader's megalofantasy, then, is in accordance with a megalofantasy in which collective desires converge. The fantasy may be an infantile indulgence and the expression of an unintellectual sense of life, but it may also be formed as a reaction to a marked lack of self-assurance and to feelings of guilt. In the French this need for self-assertion may be rooted in the defeat of 1940. The guilt feelings may have grown from the war in Algeria following the disaster of Dien Bien Phu. The atrocities of the Algerian war (reminding many Frenchmen of their own experiences under Hitler) are in shocking contrast to the humanitarian aims of the French revolution. Whether it was for these feelings that General de Gaulle was reelected is, of course, mere speculation. At any rate, in the course of history there seem to have been constantly recurring situations in which security has been sought—probably mainly regressively—from charismatic political authorities.

Secondly, there is a *bourgeois version of political authority* based on a theory of strength resulting from conformity with the ruling class. An example of this was to be found in the Federal Republic of Germany. When Ludwig Erhard was Chancellor, he also liked to bring himself to the public's attention in the guise of a performer of miracles. He wanted to be seen as the incarnation of affluence regained. When he appeared on television to make a political speech, then almost without fail some potted plants were in the background or family photos were on a shelf—elements which simply could not be more characteristic of the middle-class style of living. Be it unintentional, or be it thanks to ingenious stage-management, the speaker was obviously addressing his audience in *their* living-rooms from his living-room with the authority of a paterfamilias. In this case, then, political authority borrows power to impress from the stereotype of middle-class paternalism.

Really "modern" political authority has arisen along with *bureaucracy*. It took on its first recognizable form in the Russian "apparatchik." In post-revolutionary Russia bureaucracy acquired a new function: it did not organize the sphere of power of traditional political force (as, for instance, Prussian bureaucracy served the feudal power of Prussia); it was itself

[3] Eleonore Sterling, *Der unvollkommene Staat*, Frankfurt, Europäische Verlagsanstalt, 1965, p. 284.

part of a new ideology. The sheer survival of the ideological concept (for example, of Bolshevism in Russia) depended on the functioning of this newly established bureaucracy and of the authoritarian supervisory organs which, however, emerged from its own ranks. This development was the stepping stone for bureaucracy and gave the figures in key political positions in the administration of the country the decisive increase in power which they managed to extend in spite of all setbacks. The leading ideologists are at the same time the leading bureaucrats. Often there is no clear distinction between politics and administration.

Meantime it has become a commonplace that bureaucracy acquires new positions of power where industrial civilization spreads. "The organisation increasingly determines the working conditions of the individual"[4]—and thus the conditions of life in general: "Sleep faster, comrade!"

The pictures of politicians appearing daily in the mass media help to delineate the characteristic traits of this contemporary political authority. The type which crops up most frequently is no longer the much-decorated monarch or the autocrat in his ostentatiously unpretentious uniform whom the revolution has carried to the top, but men without any striking characteristic, wearing inconspicuous civilian suits. This inconspicuousness, or rather this smart conformity in dress and bearings, represents the outwardly imperceptible power of a *reciprocally equalizing specialism* which, however, remains under control in the political, bureaucratic institutions. But this control acts as if it in turn were subject to democratic supervisory organs, whereas in practice it makes its position more and more impregnable so that the root $\kappa\rho\alpha\tau\epsilon\iota\sigma$, or rule, in the words bureaucracy and technocracy acquires a more intensive significance far removed from the trace of irony connected with it decades ago.

In spite of the undeniable fact that a new caste society is being born here, a contrary tendency can also be observed. The mass of technicians in our society recognize themselves in these political technicians. There are signs of a new kind of "depaternalized" *fraternal society* for which history provides no models of political authority. Wherever they meet, most strikingly at congresses (and that seems to be one of their major important functions), the specialists form a fraternal society in which they vie for authority among their peers. It is difficult to inspire enthusiasm in them for the old ideological or national antagonisms. Some specialists, such as physicists, biologists, and sociologists, who operate with energy in dangerous quantities or with far-reaching technological processes (the artificial mutation of genes or the influencing of the mass media for instance), look around for universal humanitarian principles, which are precisely what the

[4] R. Presthus, *ibid.*, p. 32.

traditional powers do not offer. Political rebels such as Klaus Fuchs who try to subordinate the power acquired through research to an "ideal" political authority they are forever seeking are rarer than "professors" who, with the power of their knowledge behind them, call the political authorities to order. The tendency to regard positivistic specialism as the true basis of political authority is undoubtedly winning out in the mass societies. In practice, committees of the legislature and the executive cooperate extremely closely in such societies. But whether it is always in the best way for the public is dubious.

The detached objectivity of specialists' decisions is itself often a myth. The positions of authority held by the conservative powers (which include Western socialism) are being undermined, it is true, by the intensified division of labor and the rapid increase in the specialists' knowledge. This also makes it impossible to go on establishing positions of authority on paternal lines. But many of the so-called objective decisions are only pseudo-objective. In reality, when the specialist's emotions become involved and conflict arises he is caught up in the mechanism of unconscious "rationalization." That is to say that under the cloak of rational motivation the way is to be paved for instinctive urges. Think of the privileges of status that accompany authority. The specialist does not see his power as so distinct from his own person that he does not try to bolster it up even with specious arguments. For anyone not completely familiar with the matter this rationalizing argumentation is difficult to recognize.

But there is yet another widespread form of authority to consider, which is at once traditional and modern, namely, *military authority*. Regions in which the transition from traditional political authorities and ruling cliques to industrial conditions of power is taking place do not have an established corps of specialists or a functioning bureaucracy; on the other hand, the masses to be governed by the new bureaucracy lack the typical routine attitude of obedience and consciousness of obedience displayed by those who have grown up in a technical civilization. Instead, in many places manifestations of feudal power inseparably accompanied by corruption and frequently linked with an underdeveloped economy survive into the phase of new national independence.

We observe that in the developing countries the forms of authority withdrawn from circulation are not being replaced, as had been hoped, by enlightened representatives of political authority schooled in the standards of the red brick universities; instead, as the increasing number of military juntas shows, an apparently timeless form of authority, that is, one which can be revived at any time, is elbowing its way to power; it embodies power in its direct physical form. The army represents the only supralocal authority. In these societies executive power falls to the lot of the strongest in accordance with the laws governing the struggle for leadership in the herd; in this way he becomes the politically effective authority. But how do the "strong men" of those countries orient themselves? Are the struggles for authority we observe on the world-wide political scene only regressions or are they repetitions of the old forays between chiefs fought with the new technological weapons? This form of authority of the "strongest" is different from the instances we depicted before (in France and Germany) and also different from military authority exercised under normal governmental control.

There is no doubt, however, that we are witnessing very heavy *regressions to forms of authority based on brutal force.* The Nazi dictatorship under Hitler was its prototype. The psychologist observes in individuals as well as in groups of every size that abrupt breaches in the traditional forms of living—like the economic crises of the thirties, that unexpected concomitant of industrialization [5]—mobilize high degrees of anxiety. More or less unconscious destructive phantasies with the accompanying vague but oppressing feelings of guilt, persecutory and retaliatory fears unite to weaken the resistance against processes of social decay. In extreme cases of deterioration, about the only political institution that then remains is the law of the jungle.

The usurper, whom contemporary history has taught in so many instances how unstable his power is, tries to set up a defense against fear by means of concentrated military power. For their parts, his subjects expect protection from the usurper as from an omnipotent father and in return are prepared to concede to him the degree of cruelty as a tool of government that approximately corresponds to their own repressed destructive fantasies. Thus the authority of the role is safeguarded only by the power available for demonstration at the moment. Since there is no stable identification with the incumbents of power, authorities may be overthrown and vanish into nothing in the constantly recurring crises. It is the "irregular power of force" [6] that is being exercised. The effect of the fear of insecurity is that a vicious circle between the averted realization of powerlessness and the soaring fantasies of allpowerfulness uppermost in the conscious develop in all the members of such an unstable group. The legal insecurity resulting from despotism fans the flames of destruction fantasies which in turn provoke fears of retaliation and guilt. Thus in the end everyday behavior is determined by unrealistic fantasies (by primary-process thinking) rather than by adherence to reality.

[5] This is one of the surface motivations of Hitlerism; I have tried to describe other chains of motivations in a paper: *Die Unfähigkeit zu trauern,* Munich, 1967.

[6] Robin M. Williams, Jr., *American Society,* New York, 1951.

Moreover, *homosexual impulses* (taking unconscious effect) undoubtedly play an important part in the military demonstrations of authority; regarded from the aspect of anxiety they are also to be seen at work in the markedly paranoiac elements in all instances of terrorism. It is not, however, possible to go into further detail on the subject of these vicissitudes of the libido.

Such authoritative patterns of behavior, however, can only come into existence or survive where self-critical knowledge, or rather critical self-knowledge, has remained circumscribed and where the demand of self-criticism has not yet penetrated. This, of course, applies to all "retarded," backward areas and not just to the geographically distant, so-called developing countries.

It must be added that not only knowledge of a subject or field but also knowledge of oneself—that is *psychological knowledge*—has become a power that confers authority. This power can be abused like any other. The original trend can be reversed and, instead of leading to critical self-examination, knowledge of self can be used for "rationalization," that is, for the fallacious establishment of reasons for one's own emotions and instincts, in other words, for self-deception.

An Emergent Pattern of Authority: The Specialist

Here we want to propose a thesis, namely, that the truly *modern form of authority is that of the specialist*. The explosive increase of our knowledge has made the specialist irreplaceable. It is a fact that knowledge became one of the ideals of our civilization, which had the concomitant effect of intensifying the increase of knowledge. Here the interest of our times is focused. Molecular chains have replaced the *summae theologiae* of Thomas Aquinas as proof of knowledge.

However, one persisting obstacle has reared up with renewed vehemence. The emotional resistance against the application of psychological knowledge for the better understanding of ourselves has not lost much of its force. Self-knowledge has developed very much more slowly than other fields of knowledge. Russia is interesting in this respect: there a downright split in the ideal of knowledge has come about. Specialized knowledge in all imaginable fields is highly respected and esteemed, whereas psychological knowledge must not break with the established ideological premises.

One hesitates simply to add the true modern form of authority, that of the specialist—in particular the specialist in the game of politics—to the end of the series of figures embodying power familiar to us from history.

That may have been possible with the bureaucrat in a feudal state who identified himself with the reigning monarch. The apparatchik, the manager type, is something quite new. As a person he can only identify himself with himself, for his frame of orientation is a body of potentially analyzable and augmentable knowledge instead of the orders of some potentate of unquestionable authority, protected by the taboo of being exempt from criticism.

Above the *polit-specialist* of our times there are no father-figures of the kind against whom the age of Enlightenment stood up. The functionary is, as his name says, a function of an institution; the institutions themselves are made up by functionaries in action. There is no "meta"—no metapolitics of a kind one can believe in—outside. Historically seen this is perhaps the essential point in the change political authority has undergone. In our own life time we observe something like an oscillation between progressive developments—namely the developments enforced by the factual realities of our technological civilization—and regressive moods. Phenomena like Napoleon, Hitler, and Stalin show how difficult men find it to live without fathers. They cannot relinquish the protecting father of their childhood, they cling to a superfather who will regulate all their activities and also determine the "meta." Nevertheless, man has also had the strength to start the analytical exploration of nature and history to destroy old fantasies about the world, however frustrating this disenchantment was. Now neither the political specialist nor anybody else can be satisfied with the guidance of great fathers; all that is left are rather abstract ideologies—for instance, the (infallible) "party," "christianity," "the western world." He is part of the administrated society. No feelings of awe or tragic hate are cherished toward him. Instead he is one of a host of *"eminences grises,"* of "hidden persuaders" who exercise power that is considerable, yet at the same time only confers limited authority. Whoever is directed by analytically gained knowledge as the basis of authority cannot exercise power in the sense of times before the age of Enlightenment. The rational veto, a right acquired with great efforts, is the newly accrued possession of our time.

In a psychological view of political authority we should perhaps distinguish *two kinds of motives for acquiring knowledge.* For the sake of brevity I speak of them as if they were alternatives; but as alternatives they are only the exteme poles of possible reactions. The specialist uses knowledge according to his own mental economy, namely, his instinctual needs and the claims of his critical ego. There is the type of (political) specialist who acquires knowledge for the sake of deepening his understanding. He may enjoy it on an ego-commensurate and sublimated level;

the acquisition of knowledge is libidinized, so to speak. Although learning with him was not primarily connected with a purpose, he may use it in relative freedom for a quick and flexible handling of problems. At the other end of the scale we perceive a politician who acquires knowledge for the sake of gaining and exercising power. His satisfaction is immediately connected with the instinctual sphere. What is libidinized and cherished is the power.

This is an old antithesis. The shrewd pragmatist warns the young politician against infection by the "pallor of thought," and as long as politics consisted of only territorial strife, he might have been right. In this sense national policy has always been territorial policy and is so up to these days. Political decisions which have universal consequences require Hamlet's ponderings.

I have called the reader's attention to these contrasting possibilities of using power because in my view we are faced with an independent variable persistently influencing political life. The two hypothetically presented types of politicians are men who for very different reasons feel attracted by their job. They are the products not of politics but of far-reaching chains of conditions. Inborn talents and social influences make one individual more prone to id-gratifications—satisfaction of instinctual drives—and another to the satisfactions of ego-functions.

According to my personal conviction—which I do not wish to conceal— only the *team* can cope with the complexities of the modern entanglements of power. In a team the differing attitudes toward power will come to a certain balance. The manipulation of power is not such a fatal threat for a democratic state as long as the political managers are not ideologically unified. The use of the concept "democracy" for a state is legitimate only where a functioning system of more than one political party exists. It is interesting to observe that the one-party, so-called "people's democracies" have always had severe struggles between factions of the one party. In those political systems thinking in alternatives is, so to speak, a sin—which nevertheless happens.

On the whole one can say that the political specialist is no type in himself. His way of handling authority is that of a specialist among others. His behavioral pattern is—as we shall illustrate later—that of a conformist and a member of a social elite in one. Unlike the charismatic or military leader he is not intent on revealing striking characteristics. These political specialists try to look harmless and nonmartial because to be the opposite would earn them the hostility of their rivals, compared with whom they do not enjoy such a vastly superior starting position as did hereditary monarchs, for instance.

On the Psychological Management of the New Masses

As the functions of the state grow tremendously and the machinery of administration expands, political power is being increasingly transferred to the hands of the specialist. He must be established as a *confidence-inspiring image,* since it is now practically impossible for the individual to acquire personal information. Here the same methods of advertising strategy are used as those that direct other needs. With the help of psychological knowledge (for instance, how to suggest trustworthiness) the image of a political authority is established. Not infrequently this image differs from reality just as much as the peace and quiet of a bathing-beach on a billboard advertisement differs from the reality of the mass invasion which has long since taken place there. This is an apt illustration of information colored to serve a purpose, and here we observe the abuse of the specialist's ideal of information as the basis of knowledge. Factual communications, in technology, for example, must be foolproof or else they are not taken for serious information. In the political sphere, however, the tacticians have recourse to the propagation of wishful imagery, mingling truth and fantasy. Political slogans are devised to appeal not to the critical mind but to emotional urges. This may have short-lived success: the political decisions of the masses very often appear uninfluenced by rational and factual considerations.

But the psychological manipulation of the voters has its pitfalls for the political managers themselves. The trends of public opinion which are studied by specialists and allegedly translated into action by the political leaders are, in fact, at least partly, the result of purposeful information fed to the voters through the mass media. This kind of circular process is an almost insurmountable obstacle impeding the specialist's task of finding the "truth." The art of the politician must then consist of keeping his head and avoiding self-deception [7] in spite of the seemingly unavoidable manoeuvres of the trade. There ought to be a problem of conscience connected with the fact that inherent in the striving for power is the coercing necessity of being successful if any of the projects and promises are to become reality. Should the politician tell the voters that the consequences of his electoral slogan of "economical administration" means less money for educational purposes? An ephemeral success might entail lasting dam-

[7] Self-deception as a major weakness of totalitarian governments has been frequently cited by various authors, for example, Karl W. Deutsch, *The Nerves of Government,* New York, Free Press, 1963.

age, and the egotistical interpretation of the coercion to be successful may well lead to rationalizations in order to justify an unreasonable action. One of these rationalizations is that of the smaller evil. Here lies a specific danger of democracy.

The "image" of a politician is *per se* a regression to an older form of authority as critical thinking is replaced by idealization. For the sake of power, psychological insights are used to bring about that regression. Only differentiating psychological knowledge could protect the voter against purposeful attempts to influence and deceive; and where should he have acquired such knowledge? It is likewise impossible for most of us to check the information the political managers serve us; are we to be informed or to be influenced for a purpose? The news consumer is induced either to trust uncritically or to mistrust all and everything. The feeling of being fooled by purposive deceptions is one of the elements behind the growing apathy toward political news.

Thus the chances for correct information are unequal. Moreover, the political pragmatist has the lead over the specialists at work in the social field, for he has made the manipulation of party or bureaucracy into his particular skill. He is in a position to *manipulate power*. His specialist training, it is true, allows him to view the world only from the specialist perspective. Traditional obligations, that is, identifications which would commit him to fundamental humanitarian duty, are not features of this realist attitude, but his wealth of experience in the technique of acquiring political power makes him a much sought-after partner. He is a positivist, tending to overestimate what is offered as the easiest solution to a problem. He takes into account that knowledge and political conditions may change and enforce an early revision of the decrees. But this will not disavow him; it is always the losers who are disavowed. If he is left in the lurch it is for his obtuseness, not because of his unshakable political convictions. Political management, that is, administrational routine, is paralleled by the dissolution of identity. It is, as we have seen, no longer the contents of one or the other political program but an easy adjustability and efficient saving of face that determine the modern politician's "image."

Apparently neither the politician himself nor so-called public opinion is any longer conceiving his appointment as a national responsibility conferred upon him; he is simply managing a section of the public business and his own responsibility is limited. This explains the phenomenon of the *lobbyist* whose purpose is to procure for the expert access to political committees which, for their part, lack expert specialized knowledge. Here the processes of communication are a matter of almost equal give and take; the tactical dodge can only bring about minor increases or decreases in authority. For some experts, such as nuclear physicists, it can become an acute problem of conscience to find ways and means of acquiring influence over the political machinery.

Recent history has shown that bitter struggles between the specialists can take place above all when problems of self-understanding are inextricably bound with problems inherent in a particular branch of learning. A determining factor in this is the personality structure and the difference between personality structures. Problems of concrete fact tend to be of secondary importance and acquire their coloring from the tactical moves. For instance, a great deal depends on what sort of personality a nuclear physicist or an opinion leader working through the mass media is. If he is someone who accepts the prevailing pattern of authority within his group or class comparatively uncritically, then we know that we can expect that he will, in general, react conservatively, that, for instance, he will be hostile toward the trade unions and in all probability will approve of war as an instrument of policy.[8] Attitudes are not isolated psychological processes; they influence one another and form so-called clusters.

These remarks may serve to indicate the borderline between the genuine rationalization of knowledge and the pseudo-rationalization that seeks to justify emotional positions. ". . . In bureaucratic organizations too (there are) conflicts both about the goal to be set and about the best way of achieving it, and, not least, conflicts between the personal desires and the obligations of their members." [9] But this fact is kept out of the image of the political authority that is to be "plugged." Ambivalent feelings must not be aroused; the strategy of public relations must shift what is negative onto the shoulders of any rivals there may be. It is, then, nonsense to suggest that the specialist in modern specialized institutions is *per se* a more objective administrater of the state's instruments of power than any earlier politician. It is true that his activities may be better screened from observation from without. The ideals on the conscious level derived from the measuring sciences are unconsciously molded by the identifications that the politicians in their personal life happened to have. This explains the proposal made by James Conant that advisory committees should be composed of experts with a variety of political views. For this can take on the greatest importance if, for instance, the aggressive-authoritarian character-structure of a highly respected nuclear physicist happens to be paired with a foreign minister or Secretary of State with the same type of personality. It might tip the scale for peace or war. The way in which

[8] R. Stegner, "Attitudes Towards Authority," *Social Pathology*, 40, 210.
[9] Renate Mayntz, Epilogue to Presthus, in German Edition. Frankfurt/Main, S. Fischer, 1965.

people in key positions experience their world—in paranoiac or decidedly ethnocentric fashion, for example—is of scarcely less decisive importance than at the court of an absolute monarch such as Louis XIV.

Fraternal Rivalry in Leadership

These remarks by no means describe the most important characteristics of the (political) expert. Thus we must admit that a certain quite contrary assertion hits the mark as far as some aspects of highly industrial and highly bureaucratic states are concerned; namely, the claim that specialization goes along with a limiting of the power to make decisions. Specialists, as we have already indicated, identify themselves with models but also jealously constrict each other's scope for action. This is the phenomenon of *fraternal rivalry*. Under the old preindustrial conditions of life brothers were only in agreement as long as they had a common father above them who subdued them. There has evidently been no change in this law of behavior from the Diadochian struggles to the succession of rivalries among army officers disputing among themselves the office of president in South American or African states. And yet it must be asked whether in a society which to begin with no longer has motives for maintaining the idea of a superior paternal authority—because no father or charismatic leader can know so much more, can be so much more potent then a well-coordinated group of specialists—the development of a new modus vivendi, a new pattern of authority, is not required. Responsibility is spread among a group and the citizens also have high hopes of such group leaderships. In this connection it will be interesting to learn the motivation for the disappearance of the personality cult in Russia. We will also recall the extraordinary readiness of an enlightened President like John F. Kennedy to cooperate with advisers and how well it was received by the public. The authority of political leaders prepared to secure the advice of specialists and thus share their power with them is obviously in accordance with the scientific ideal of our times. Here we observe an affirmative *communis opinio*.

This development may perhaps be described in terms of object-relations, as this concept is used in psychoanalysis. The quality of the attitude toward political power is either a narcissistic one or one oriented upon reality. The two cannot, it is true, be cleanly separated, but a tendency may be recognizable. Therefore the observer of the political scene may ask by what motivations an individual politician or a group striving for political power is guided: is it their own grandiose fantasies they are trying to impose on the masses or is it a more mature wish for power in order to change reality according to a fuller understanding of the existing forces in their society?

If power for its own sake ranks first, we are faced with people guided by a narcissistic personality structure compelling them to subordinate intellectual satisfaction to the—often insatiable—desire for recognition. Their development is not unknown to the psychologist: at some point in their early lives a fixation of libido to the self has taken place. Objects from the outside world offering themselves at later developmental stages may then be perceived and even assessed but play no decisive part for the person's self-esteem. The structure of the society then decides upon which kind of personality is preferred in the common opinion: the narcissistic one or the one capable of understanding for and acceptance of objects outside the self. There is little doubt that our civilization offers more satisfaction to the narcissistic than to the altruistic personality. This is, of course, a generalizing judgment which should be specialized. As an illustration it is enough to cite the role of posters, for instance, the ever-present pictures of leaders in authoritarian countries.

Maybe one of the tasks for the development of consciousness consists in disengaging the fraternal team from the fruitless narcissistic fixations and introducing a liberating element, namely, the truly humane ideal of enlightenment which would allow the individual to use knowledge for empathy rather than for a narcisstic exploitation of the object. This would be a revolution in the sense of George Thomson's remark (quoted previously). Knowledge as an instrument of power can be a secondary aim only. Knowledge as an ideal, liberated of narcissistic needs, could mitigate the fraternal rivalry of the specialists. And since such an ideal would strengthen the functioning of the critical ego, the tendencies to aggressive-defensive grandiose feelings might in turn decrease.

To the more remote observer it may seem that the extremely high esteem in which advisers are held indicates a change in the delicate structure of political authority. The self-confidence of the team-oriented political leader is evidently little prone to pathological change: with his election to the presidency, for instance, he is not cut off in his inner self-assessment from his capacities of critical judgment. In his exertion of power he remains conscious of reality and must not give in to instinctual drives urging him to use his increased chance for narcissistic satisfaction. In other words: His rise in the power hierarchy does not weaken his reality-control—for instance, that he is dependent on the team—and does not promote the uncontrolled fusion of instinctual wishes with an archaic omnipotent ego-ideal.

This attempt at the description of a structural change is, of course, an idealized characterization of a team-leader; in reality, the omnipotent ego-ideal on one side and envy on the side of the experts will never be fully overcome. Again we must look at signs of a general tendency: an apparently slight shift of the ideal from the narcissistic satisfaction to object-conscious responsibility may very perceptibly change the decisions. One of the consequences of specialist learning is the correcting effect it has on the ego-ideal which will be nearer to consciousness and self-criticism. In the midst of his advisers, the politician will better resist allowing himself to be manoeuvred into the precast attitudes expected of him by those around him and thus into self-idealization. This resistance certainly requires considerable critical strength on the part of the ego.

At this point it may be added that this account concentrates on the dangerous tendencies in present developments—for they are obtrusive—rather than on the successful attempts at solving the problem of authority. The politician is not, of course, only concerned with satisfying his desire for power. He undoubtedly pursues ideals, however eccentric they may be at times. He will scarcely become a politician if shouldering responsibility for others is not part of his character. After all, assuming responsibility usually means supporting and protecting dependents or trying to realize ideas that seem important to the present and future welfare of the group. *This identification with parental functions* is an important driving force in the politician. At times, it is true, these altruistic ideals become forgotten in the necessity to hold one's own in the struggle for power.[10]

The shift from authority models constructed in accordance with a graduated hierarchy of fathers to a multiplicity of individual specialist spheres on a par with one another cannot be undone. The older types of authority are associated with a comparatively closely knit, static, and highly traditional world-picture, whereas specialist authority is coupled with the rapid development of knowledge, with the still progressing dynamic force of inventions that outstrip one another.

To sum up: *The quality of political authority is now measured by its ability to integrate specialist, detailed knowledge with specialist striving for power.* It is typical that in the old institutions of learning, such as academies and universities, the rudiments of rule by a *primus inter pares* could already be discerned. The continuation of this pattern among the most gifted of the specialists is being furthered, for their critical awareness of the complexity of the situation is growing. At the same time, how-

[10] It seems that we have neglected to consider the role of women. Their part in the structuralization of authority is indeed not very distinct, although the reference to parental functions like protecting dependents would include the maternal attitude. In Germany women have little institutionalized political authority, but they constitute the majority of voters and their decision determines the political line.

ever, learning how to exercise power collectively is obstructed because the concentration of the instruments of power leads to impressive conglomerations which are struggled for "fiercely," that is to say, without much moral restraint. There is tacit acceptance by all participants of this background feuding which lacks all humanity and in which hardly any holds—or indeed no holds at all—are barred. Not a few people believe that here, where the struggle is in secret-service style, they can hear the heart of politics beating. Careful sociological and psychological research into the extent and the limits within which the settling of political differences uninhibited by any law is sanctioned would be highly rewarding.

It is a recognizable fact that in many respects other abilities are now coupled with the function of constructive leadership than once stood alone. A political leader who wants to contribute to the solution of the decisive problems of our times will find no precedents for how to proceed. There is still no accepted pattern for the role of "fraternal authority" comparable to the many there were for paternal authority. The tragic death of President Kennedy was such a political catastrophe because he was the first representative of a modern statesman surrounding himself with a team of advisers. Little as he intended to become a charismatic leader, the impression he produced was convincing; he understood the new obligations resting with a modern politician, and presently public opinion changed and became receptive for the new ideal. (Incidentally, it is interesting to see that the Kennedy family and certain people of his coterie try to transform Kennedy posthumously into a charismatic leader.)

There were already indications of the change in the structure of political authority after World War I when Robert Michels spoke of "the iron law of the oligarchical process;" [11] he had the German political parties in mind. This tendency toward the *rule of the few* has made itself felt in many places as the successor of monarchical authority and of the personality cult. There are many indications that in the future, oligarchies will be the working form adopted by the political specialist going about his business in relative concealment. Perhaps the unobtrusive way he does his political job is the specialist's self-protection against *jealousy*.

It requires no particular gift of prophecy to foresee that the dominant emotional problem for these bodies will be the problem of *jealousy*, of *sibling rivalry*, just as in a hierarchical society it was that of the relation to paternal authority. A strong father-figure is not envied, for the son identifies with him. The ambivalent feelings are either repressed or find their expression in a coup d'état. In the case of a successful "patricide" a new authority figure immediately takes over. The specialists, on the con-

[11] R. Michels, *Political Parties*, Glencoe, Ill., Free Press, 1949.

trary, experience themselves as a select caste; they strive for prestige among themselves; public approbation has little appeal for them; they are satisfied to exercise their impenetrable power. The implicit resignation to certain narcissistic satisfactions (indispensable to the authoritarian personality, who has to demonstrate his power) is a specific adaptational achievement of the new caste of team-workers.

On Overpopulation and Destructive Aggressiveness

It is only when one picks out a few of the greatest political problems of our times that it becomes clear that so far neither a traditional authority nor one of the more modern political authorities has been up to coping with them, for the dimensions of these conflicts and developments surpass the range of our optical integrative faculty. We are often quite literally unable to "visualize" these processes now in operation and their effects.

Two such conspicuous problems are *overpopulation* and the tremendous *increase in destructive aggressiveness* which can be observed almost all over the world. Wherever industrial civilization, with its rigid rhythm of work,[12] with its highly developed division of labor, and with the concentration of capital and producer goods in large-scale organizations, makes its appearance, this aggressive irritability, which is easily aroused, is unconfined by social conventions and seeks an immediate outlet, makes itself felt with comparative rapidity. It is behavior that has appeared on the scene in a great variety of places in a great variety of societies, and we are bound to receive the impression that it is increasing more and more.

Means of combating *overpopulation* have been found that make it seem possible to check it. There is even hope that in the not too distant future the consciousness of the human race will reach a point from which birth control can be felt to be the moral obligation of each individual. This insight has of course to overcome some old, established resistances of large groups to whom the new behavioral patterns come as a shock. Inventions like the modern ovulation inhibitors are indeed upsetting the dictates of traditional morality, and without the threat of punishment.

[12] Fewer work-hours and rationalization entail the suppression of irregular but tolerated short breaks amounting to 30 and even 40 minutes. This means the elimination of self-regulation, of the individual's adjustment to the rigid working rhythm. The shorter but constantly strained concentration is felt like being hurried . . . The heterogeneous rhythm of the machine is more and more overlaying the individual rhythm." L. Kroeber-Keneth, "Gesund und Krank zugleich," *Frankfurter Allgemeine Zeitung*, Oct. 16, 1965.

Therapy for the *destructive tendencies,* elemental outbursts of which can ruin any political order, seems remote; the danger of such outbursts is, however, great. We have nothing like sufficient information about what frustrations are the origin of these violent outbursts. The industrialized civilization which we are continually expanding makes little allowance for many of the fundamental biological needs of our nature and, indeed, often contradicts them brutally. One need only recall the *rigid rhythm of work* mentioned previously which is set for people with the most varying types of temperament or remember that it is quite unphysiological to restrict people for technological reasons to a *fractional participation in the manufacture of a product* or in an administrative process. The need to produce a "complete" achievement, a "creation," is based on age-old tradition and it may even be conditioned by instinct mechanisms of the kind we observe in nesting.

Thus in jobs in mass-producing factories and in modern office work a large measure of constructive imagination and productive potential on the part of the individual is alienated and frustrated. The unpleasure engendered here has motivated the great stream of *surrogate satisfactions* on the market. Stimulation of an addictive nature, hallucinatory drugs, etc., have to siphon off the permanent unpleasure and the pent-up feelings of aggression which develop at work. The outbreaks of destructive activity, however, show that this is by no means sufficiently successful because the methods of surrogate satisfaction frequently have a stimulative effect and only lead to exhaustion without relaxation. In this connection I call attention to the desire for extensive holiday trips, supposedly for health reasons, which are, however, actually a permanent repetition of the same round of stimuli and irritants in other surroundings.

Our civilization, then, does not escape unshorn the objective conditions that it creates. A look at the pains bestowed by the so-called "amusements"—which have long been economically exploited with all the psychological tricks—makes it clear that in this respect the contemporary consciousness lags behind the conditions under which it has developed. The individual has too little idea of the extent to which he is deformed by the manipulated exploitation of his *instincts and desires* as he once was by the exploitation of his *labor.* We can observe this phenomenon in the pursuit of high status symbols—and the symbol of political authority is one. It frequently shortens life through cardiac failure, but the need of many for aggressive satisfaction and self-assertion is stronger and allows them to ignore the danger signals; the same applies to the many forms of addiction resulting from narcissistic-libidinous instinctual hunger. All such withdrawals from reality have in common that they are caused by frustrations; and indeed the citizens of the industrial nations are subjected to many frustrations. The fate of many of them might be called "traceless work." [13] The work they do for their subsistence cannot be demonstrated and its meaning is not recognized by the people who have meaning for the workers. But the recognition of these people is the root of self-esteem, and whenever self-esteem cannot be founded on recognizable achievements, a pathological development is imminent. The very necessity to perform fragmented, alienated work is pathogenic. All this engenders unstable character structures. The political leaders have to take that into account—but they themselves may have had to suffer that impact either directly or by way of identification.

Early Infantile Social Experiences: Frustrations and Overindulgence

The attempts at explanation (at least by sociologists) that have so far appeared seem to me to neglect the idea that it may be primary, *early infantile social experiences* that lead to the unbridled outbreaks of excess aggressive instinct that burst in on society. Experience gained from giving psychoanalytical treatment suggests that it is highly probable that changes in the family structure and thus in the form of family life promote this strange increase in aggression; this point seems to deserve further investigation. It should also be noted that such outbreaks occur in persons who may otherwise be quite apathetic. It is entirely objective factors in our society that have a slackening effect on the object-relations of the primary group. In particular, the fulfillment of every wish which our affluent economy and social security have ready for us has weakened or ousted entirely the pattern of behavior that had been valid, in which each man knew his role.

We must bear in mind the fact that man can only adjust himself to any conceivable society by *suppressing instincts*. Not until he gains control—never more than relative—of his instincts, a control which makes the procrastination and possibly even renunciation of a desire necessary, does he become a tolerable member of society. Sociologists have pointed out often enough that so far societies have taken care of this in a mainly repressive—at times brutally repressive—manner. At any rate the immediate predecessor of the affluent society, namely, bourgeois capitalism, was marked by such repressive features. Here a change has taken place, for it is no longer economic shortage that justifies the frustration of desires. Now that the manifold fulfillment of desires is achievable, a certain psychological mechanism has been ignored, which has so far been at least

[13] A. Mitscherlich, *Auf dem Weg zur vaterlosen Gesellschaft*, München, 1963.

as important as learning to control instincts in the process of making the individual a social being. Commandments always came from persons who could be directly experienced by the senses. They invited an emotional relation: anger, for instance, or disappointment when satisfaction was denied. On the other hand the satisfaction of instincts also proceeded from the same people; in this way an ambivalent emotional relation came about. In the course of these experiences the child learned to make sacrifices for a person: to do something to please a person; and that means that at a second stage the unpleasure-provoking process of renunciation can after all be cathected with libido. Renunciation is then felt to be approved as a socially valuable behavior. The self-assertion experienced by the child seems to have an inhibiting influence on aggression. Overindulgence and pampering may keep the child quiet for a time, but they do not help to transform his aggressiveness, since they fail to fortify his ego. The ego, however, and the ego's special function, the superego, are the agencies exercising a dependable control over aggression.

The matter may be reduced to the following pattern: the intensity of reciprocal emotional relations, such as those between mother and child, declines when unpleasure becomes avoidable. Superficially the assumption would appear more probable that frustrations disturb the object-relation and are more likely to lead to an inner withdrawal of interest from the object. But surprisingly enough this is precisely what happens when the satisfaction of desires becomes too much a matter of course. If, however, in the child's immediate experience the unpleasure caused by renunciation can be overcome with regard to the person who requires the renunciation, then the result is not alienation after all but intensification of emotional relations, for the mother sees the renunciations as evidence of love.[14] The acknowledgement and approval of the *achievement* renunciation represents compensate, at least in part, for the frustration. There evolves that ambivalent object-relation which is a mixture of experiences of pleasure and unpleasure, and which forms the basis of all emotional social relations. This *ambivalence* marks any mature relation to authority. As long as ambivalence is not so pathologically intensified as to make the individual vacillate between idealization and debasement, the ambivalence of the emotional relation promotes the ability to form judgments consonant with reality. It seems to me that the democratic order furthers this critical attitude toward authority just as on the other hand it needs this dauntlessness in dealings with authority so that it can function properly.

[14] This emotional process clears the way for further identification. "Thus social feeling is based upon the reversal of what was first a hostile feeling into a positively-toned tie in the nature of an identification." S. Freud, *Standard Edition*, Vol. XVIII, p. 121.

In everyday life, of course, such emotional relations, here reduced to schematically simplified terms, are overlaid by other behavior which is the result of more complicated instinctual vicissitudes. For instance, the pleasure of being able to forbid a child things may be for the otherwise so often powerless adults a welcome aggressive satisfaction in itself, which then overshadows the objective necessity of the prohibition. Such "sadistic" repression does, in fact, intensify the ambivalent emotional relation with paralyzing effect. For our purposes, however, the important thing was to demonstrate the elementary genesis of ambivalent relations and to emphasize that this fusion of contrasting feelings is a fundamental prerequisite for the process of socialization. This might also be put as follows: If social learning is to be promoted, it must be made possible to experience renunciation as something meaningful. Renunciation must intensify the love of both partners in the relation for one another, to the parent for the child, and vice versa. The emotional potential as it has been formed in childhood will, in comparable situations in later life, interact afresh with the then significant authorities. Therefore both authority and obedience permeate a society in all its social relations, in countless decisions and actions.

In our affluent society, renunciation, for example, of oral gratifications, is often unnecessary. Necessity no longer compels. Oral satisfaction is taken as a matter of course, as something automatically granted in this world. Now it can be observed that satisfaction arouses satiation but by no means gratitude toward the object (the parents, for instance).[15] The parents, on the other hand, are frustrated in their expectation of loving attention from their children by the *absence of gratitude* for their efforts. Gratitude as a spontaneous emotion cannot develop unless what is given to the child is meaningful for his self-esteem. The child must be able not only to consume the gift but use it for his development. This again is felt by the parents as a "repayment."

Of course, lack of interest on the part of the parents for the children's exhausting claims on their attention may often lead to compensatory oral or other overindulgence. Behavior analysis may show that much of the passive-apathetic demanding attitude displayed by the citizen of the welfare state is conditioned by this spiritless spoiling in childhood, by the feeling of having been fobbed off with indulgences.

One might also adduce indulgence in connection with the expression of aggressive behavior. Permissive education was doomed to failure; the point of it was to inhibit childish behavior as little as possible, to tolerate

[15] Here I should like to mention briefly that primary forms of renunciation such as weaning from the breast or bottle, or toilet training remain unavoidable, oedipal desires cannot be gratified either. These basic renunciations form the "storm-center" which stimulates adjustment to social conditions.

many "misdemeanors," without setting the child any limits. This freedom evidently has not made the children that went through this treatment happy; partly because in the end they had to make the fundamental instinctual renunciations (including those of an oedipal nature) anyway, and partly because they were unable to go through the experience of receiving love from the persons important to them in their object-relations in return for renunciation.

Let us pursue further the theory that the definite social behavior of an adult is directly related to infantile experience. The feasibility of producing a superabundance of consumer goods and of distributing them extensively in our society deprives of their justification a number of moral rules which were originally made necessary by states of permanent emergency. The management of the little there was, the task of economizing, was entrusted to foresighted authority. Now foresightedness is required to prevent overproduction. This revolution in the life of the affluent society robs many of the moral precepts we take for granted of their cogency and condemns them to decay. One can appeal only to the dietetic of esthetic angle or to ascetic-philosophical arguments if one wants to resist the *oral indulgences* which today nearly everyone can afford daily and which were reserved for high days and holidays half a century ago. The lack of risk now involved in sexual relations is a parallel case.

But what is the result as regards the behavior of the adult if in childhood no strong ambivalent emotional relations have been set up with the whole force of unsatiated instinctual urges behind them? What new potentialities in emotional relations present themselves, in our civilization now freed from so much lasting distress? We must accustom ourselves to making as unprejudiced an examination as possible of the conditions of our environment (that we take so much for granted but which are nevertheless the product of our highly complex civilization) for their unplanned side-effects in the emotional sphere. The idea that we are confronted by permanent progress without a dark side would, in truth, be a delusion.

The changes in the roles and patterns of political authority as we see them here thus are released by the incisive alterations in the social sphere. The contributions provided by specialism allow one to view authority as an unclosed process capable of development. Another important factor is the increase in population in numbers as well as in density in the districts of industrial production and administration. A humane form of handling large masses of people packed together in densely populated quarters is still to be found. We do not know, for instance, the measurements of the minimum living-space that must be granted to the individual living in the immense urban agglomerations if he is to retain a sense of personal responsibility and individual value. The administrational acts, unavoidable as they may well be, to which the individual is subject give him a stifling feeling of being reduced to a mass particle; his basal, all-invading experience is then not one of his significance but utter insignificance as an individual. He must evoke very archaic omnipotential fantasies as a surrogate which, however, cannot really satisfy.

The effect on the individual's relations to political authority is a double one. On the one hand the representatives of authority are fantasied to be much more powerful than they are; they are ascribed the faculty of solving all kinds of conflicts. On the other hand political authority vanishes beyond the emotional horizon of the masses. They feel helplessly exposed to the processes of communal as well as world policy and do not invest any emotional energy in it. Any pleasure or unpleasure tensions they experience are spent in apolitical social contacts. This kind of *public passivity weakens political authority* as an instrument for deciding upon matters of society as a whole, a "disease" of the modern democracies which is not immediately discernable. One of the consequences is that the political climate is determined by administrative decrees, and their language is authoritarian rather than democratic. The specialists employed in official administrative jobs do not enjoy the same high esteem as the engineers or natural scientists—and they would rarely deserve it.

Political Apathy in the West—Authority Worship in the East

We shall now add to our reflections just a few brief remarks on the infantilism of concerted authority worship, on feelings of guilt, and on the increasing tensions between the suppression of instincts and the development of consciousness. In this connection Freud [16] has afforded us deep insight into psychosocial processes. Nevertheless, we admit that in forming a judgment it is extremely difficult to distinguish decisive from irrelevant influences.

From a geographical point of view, various stages of emotional development in various regions may serve as object-lessons in how authority is treated. *In the West* we may observe advancing technology and rational planning in almost every field including political power—with all the disadvantages of increasingly uncontrollable manipulation. This much at least seems quite plain: the experiencing of authority is no longer so closely connected with this form of power. On the contrary, there are some most enlightened views on the reach of politicians' intelligence. Moreover, large sections of the population abstain from having anything

[16] Cf. S. Freud, *Group Psychology and the Analysis of the Ego, Standard Edition of the Collected Works*, Vol. XVIII.

to do with political questions. Whether it is one of the citizen's privileges not to take an interest in politics or whether the reason for the fact that political appeals fall on deaf ears is to be sought in the social processes themselves remains an open question.

In countries with autoritarian governments, on the contrary, the factual elimination of the citizens' influence on the political fate is screened from consciousness by creating artificial affective ecstasies. *In Russia* the once extreme personality cult is being combated. This looks like a development: a development toward an oligarchy in the shape of the party. Some critical statements have been made, and it seems that criticizing the idealized leaders is no longer a death warrant. The role of the political specialist is well-adjusted to the requirements of technological development, perhaps more so than in the rest of the world. The "apparatchik," it is true, has been the target of derision inside and outside Russia. What caused the grinding of the state machinery was, however, not so much the narrowmindedness of bureaucracy, but the fact that no well-defined roles, useful experiences, or conscientious responsibilities were available for the construction of a state whose survival was dependent upon quick technological development. Both the governing and the governed groups were likewise unprepared to fulfill the tremendous tasks. Maybe in the course of the next decades the extraordinary costs of the Russian Revolution will be repayed.

In China this personality cult is in full flower. A nation of 700 million people unites in repeated mass demonstrations—at present under the banner of the "cultural revolution" (dictated from above)—around the person of their leader Mao Tse-tung. The fact that in this "cultural revolution" specialism and the independence of the technicians are being attacked is bound to arouse our interest. From a tactical point of view this can only mean that the masses are to be kept unorganized, without the support afforded by individual groups, that is, without a starting point for criticism in the worship of the party and their practically sacrosanct leader. But present-day judgments on the development in China cannot be more than attempts made to gain some insight (wishful thinking would only lead to misinterpretations, as did the biased judgments at the time of the Russian Revolution).

That the new "cultural revolution" is a textbook case of manipulated worship can be seen in the way in which all the naturally ambivalent feelings are channelled away from the hero figure. Only the feelings of religious worship for the infallibility he has realized within the framework of the party are for Mao the leader—as they once were for Stalin or Hitler or the absolute monarchs. The energy issuing from rebellious thoughts and attempts at critical judgment is branded as heresy and projected. It is not oneself but "sinister criminal elements" who "resist the party, its chairman and his teachings." The similarity to the kind of leader-worship practiced in past and present fascist nations is a deceptive one. In these countries the answer to the hardships of industrialization was a regressive reaction—like the "blood and soil" mythology in Nazi Germany. In Russia and nowadays in China the brutal methods of herding the masses, of keeping the individual down on the level of the collective, and the leader-worship are concomitants accompanying industrialization, and not its reverberations. Although the final phenomena look similar—total collective control under the vigilant eye of big brother—their political function may differ. China was forced from the outside to take the way of industrialization and thus restore her injured self-esteem. But it was not on the basis of Puritan capitalism and philosophical enlightenment that China developed leader-worship and her own atomic bomb. The functions of the Mao-cult are perhaps something like a local matter; on the other hand the universal interrelation of world politics no longer allows a conception like the Monroe doctrine. Even a homemade ideology meant for internal use only is bound by the sheer existence of the world-wide communicative media to offer its kind of solution as a panacea for every social illness. The drop of the influence is by nо means from West to East only. This is another viewpoint we have to take into account when we try to evaluate the changes occurring in our ideas on political authority.

One is tempted to regard these varying kinds and conditions of authority as phases in the historical development of large individual collectives and to assign them to the development of their general consciousness and in particular of their consciousness of their own situation in the various phases. One point must, of course, be borne in mind: political unification as a national and ideological unit is only achieved by having recourse to intensive identification with a leader. To the psychologist it seems just as plausible to reason that the general need brings out the required leader as to take the view, so common in popular belief, that at such moments men make history. As Freud puts it, the leader represents the ego-ideal of the masses. Above all, when traditions are broken and historical developments surge forward into an uncertain future, the regressive urges of the crowd mount. Safe escort into the unknown is sought. Traditionally calmer times merely conceal the fact that finding an independent way through the processes of education, as has so far been usual in societies, is only being partially encouraged; as Freud remarked in the year 1909, "You cannot exaggerate the intensity of people's inner lack of resolution and craving for authority." [17] In China too, the technique of the party

[17] S. Freud, *Standard Edition*, Vol. XI, p. 146.

machinery is evidently being fully used to generate and direct regressive inclinations in order to make Mao the undisputed ego-ideal of the masses. The quasi-paradoxical situation has arisen in that no freedom of critical thinking is possible without stable identifications which the individual must have acquired. This freedom, however, perished under the oppression of too much dirigism exerted by a strong authority. The Chinese leaders, for instance, made use of the decay of the traditional government; on the psychological level this means a loss of the support provided by identifications. The emerging regressive needs are used to bring about a "transformation of man," a "gigantic experiment in our century," as an observer of the Far East has called it.[18]

It is indeed a dangerous fact that the great majority of people, including educated people, are easily induced to merge the ego and the ego-ideal, that is, to fuse themselves with a leader with the greatest enthusiasm, whenever they find themselves in conflicts which at first seem to overtax their wits. "In many individuals the separation between the ego and the ego-ideal is not very far advanced; the two still coincide readily; the ego has often preserved its earlier narcissistic self-complacency." [19] As long as this identification—which in moments of extreme stimulation can, however, be not just identification but the experience of total fusion—can be maintained, it is possible to persecute and combat without mercy the enemies of the ego-ideal *without feelings of guilt*, indeed with the subjectively clearest of conscience. The masses are capable of the greatest cruelties if the ego-ideal personified in a "Führer" and if the individuals forming the mass are unified in the identification with him. Feelings of guilt return with the breakdown of these conditions—as was the case in Germany. Then part of the people return to older ideals and identifications, another part is calling for new images from outside. One must not underestimate the persistence of old images in the neighborhood of omnipotent fantasies. This is clearly shown in the rigid dogmatism of religion. Adherence to their old myths of deity and the beyond requires a considerable ego-split.

People seem not unwilling to seize upon this permission granted by such an ego-ideal to indulge in aggressive misdeeds. It is felt to be a powerful inducement to join such mass movements and their authorities. In contrast to idealizing views of man, this thirst for aggressive unburdening becomes more intelligible when we recall another remark of Freud's: "Our civilization consists in more and more of our instincts succumbing to repression." [20] Venting aggressions on an unworthy fiend with impunity

[18] Lily Abegg, "Jeder Chinese ein Robinson Crusoe," *Frankfurter Allgemeine Zeitung*, August 15, 1966.

[19] S. Freud, *Standard Edition*, Vol. XVIII, p. 129.

[20] See E. Jones, *Sigmund Freud—Life and Work*, Vol. III, p. 362.

can be compared to leaving the sphere of civilization for a paradise free from the burdens of repression. Of course, the individual must not be aware that he is just discharging instinctual drives; he must believe in some exalted aim he is serving.

In this process ideologies only play the part of a release mechanism, a cue. In China aggression is directed at the "Soviet revisionists and imperialists." All the feelings of hate, which the methods of continual persuasion to induce decent behavior there are bound to arouse, are projected at them. In Indonesia recently it was the communists themselves that had to endure all the brutalities of a witch-hunt and a crusade. The emotional processes which are aroused and kept alive within the jurisdiction of these popular idols are as alike as two peas in a pod. From the first the individual is not trained to develop independent reactions or to form independent judgments of reality but to yield unquestioning childish obedience, a phenomenon with which our history through the long centuries down to the great religious revolutions has made us familiar. They are the "sons of man" who should think themselves fortunate to have found such a good father.

To put it in psychological terms, political authority is not a power which one discovers as one develops in the social field and toward which one slowly acquires an attitude—ambivalent, critical, convinced, etc., as the case may be; all social conditions are such that this leader appears to the individual to be an incarnation of his own omnipotent fantasies. Between the two there is the same intimate relation as that between the believer and his God. He does not respect him as one respects a person with whom one exchanges experiences, from whom one learns, but as the group ideal of a "leader" he is part of each individual's experience, each is identified with him. This powerful leader has "taken the place of the ego ideal." [21] The ego obeys as if hypnotized.

The Return of the Moralist: Authority and Education

Here we have to add a contrasting theoretical conclusion. The individual in the highly specialized industrial civilizations in which the very thing has happened that Mao's party is trying to prevent, namely, the formation of "castes" of specialists who might doubt the primateship of the party and its omniscience—this individual who has grown up among pluralistic ideas may again be in danger. The threat is *constraint towards self-alienation* from other causes than in the mass states of Asia. In spite of a comparatively long period of freedom from such uniformative coer-

[21] S. Freud, *Standard Edition*, Vol. XVIII, p. 113.

cion in matters of belief as can now be seen practiced in China, the political judgment of the majority of citizens of the Western societies is still comparatively hazy.[22] Little success has been achieved in trying to extend their interest to political events in a wider context. Perhaps future politics will differ from what we understand by this concept by the same margin as the future cities differ from the polis of classical antiquity. The crassest expression of this is the apathy displayed by the population at elections. The reasons for this may vary from one country to another. One factor, however, is comparable in all the variants of Western democracy and that is the weakening of the early object-relations by processes which, as we have indicated, have affected society as a whole. This leads to a comparatively high degree of inurement to feelings of guilt. But it is not until the individual has learned from the reaction of the others to perceive clearly that he has acted without consideration for them, and not until feelings of guilt have gradually taught him to be more considerate, that "civilization" can develop.

Before guilt can be felt the child must have developed meaningful object-relations. Just the reversed development is happening under authoritarian governments, where the individual is not allowed to show ambivalent object-relations and where dependence from the externalized ego-ideal, the "Führer," is being intensified to a maximum. It was one of Freud's greatest insights when he proposed ". . . to represent the sense of guilt as the most important problem in the development of civilization and to show that the price we pay for our advance in civilization is a loss of happiness through the heightening of the sense of guilt."[23] The "happiness" which Freud is referring to is the infant's paradise; it is therefore an infantile hope to return to it. But this may make it even more enticing.

At first it will be thought that this stress on guilty feelings is a Puritan legacy in Freud's theory. However, this insight does seem to be pertinent to a more general set of circumstances. A feeling of guilt reflects our own behavior in the eyes of the others at whom our action was directed. With the maturation of ego-functions, guilt feelings are connected with conflicts of opinion. Real and illusionary guilt begin to be differentiated. Our ego learns to experience conflicts of opinion without overdue guilt and to overcome the infantile, outlived feelings of shame and guilt. The feeling of guilt contains the basis of the discovery that I and you, the ego and the object, are separate beings. At the beginning of our lives we cannot manage without identification with the great parental authority in order to

---

[22] Cf. J. Habermas et al., *Student und Politik*, Neuwied, Luchterhand, 1961.
[23] S. Freud, *Standard Edition*, Vol. XXI, p. 134.

learn to control our instinctual inclinations. We identify ourselves with and introject that powerful object with whom we feel one. That should not have to be the end of the matter. Only if, as in China's political leadership (here taken merely as an example), no negative feelings towards authority are allowed to be felt and only if we are compelled to make vigorous use of repression, namely, repression of all ambivalence in our feelings towards authority, do we remain in that fairyland in which there are heroes, sinister criminals, imperialists—but no human beings.

Normally the child's development proceeds to another level. After he has discovered that he does not become all-powerful by means of fusion and identification, he has to order his emotional ties anew. Now love and hate are concentrated on the same object and finally we begin to choose between the objects we value. Political authority, which in a democracy is composed of many separate entities, with many opinions and organized in parties, calls for object-*choice*. Certainly the choice will be partly determined by the identifications we have made before in the course of our lives. But these prototypes should exert no iron constraint. Democratic society does not require that we should persist in the identification with political authority that compels obedience. Perhaps democratic society has been so relatively unsuccessful in influencing the masses, in helping them to tolerate deviant opinions and ambivalent feelings, even toward a highly respected authority—an attitude which should be an outstanding feature of democratic life—because of its inconsequence. In matters of religious authority it clings to the handed-down tradition of unconditioned obedience. We do not refer to the individual and his attitude in religious matters, but insofar as religious convictions are used as instruments for a Christian power policy (or in the Communist countries their specific eschatology) we do not hesitate to state that here a specimen of unenlightened collective behavior lives on.

Of demagogues like Hitler or Mussolini it is true that under their influence a stage of differentiation in the cultural process already reached was lost again and the process became retrograde; one may say that ". . . object-choice has regressed to identification." [24] I cannot presume to reach a verdict on the situation in China in its historical and genetic context, to decide whether the hero-worship of Mao is a fixation on or a regression to infantile father ideals; but perhaps this at least suggests a suitable angle of approach to the question. The forced reeducation makes use, that much we can say, of the means of forced regression. This is very clearly shown in Lifton's [25] book. However, when a country unifies and

[24] S. Freud, *Standard Edition*, Vol. XVIII, p. 107.
[25] Robert J. Lifton, *Thought Reform and the Psychology of Totalism*, New York, Norton, 1961.

becomes legalized to the extent that it is no longer necessary to bribe the custom officials at the frontiers of the provinces and one is not set upon by bands of highwaymen on the roads, this is, of course, regarded by the inhabitants as a great, liberating step forward, and he who made it possible is celebrated as one of the greats of history. The more objective observer sees the price to be paid at the same time, namely, the artificial and at bottom mendacious enthusiasm for the demagogue who has not only brought about unification but also specifically new types of bondage. Only at the cost of as complete as possible a denial of all constraints or their reversal into the opposite can the new master be raised to become the ideal ego. Furthermore, such exalted fanaticism is not innocuous for neighboring countries, for such exuberance can easily bring them into the firing line of projection.

If one contrasts this homogenization of the masses by means of an iron grip, namely, identification with the leader, which forces them all to regard themselves as his children and to encourage and supervise each other in this role, and if one contrasts the intensity of their hostile feelings which are directed outwards with the widespread political apathy of the masses in the West, one cannot altogether rejoice in a feeling that the danger of such social terror has been banished. For in the West, too, it is not only occasional acts of regression, such as the mass identification with Hitler, which have precipitated the most grievous catastrophes. The *process of alienation* that lies in the development of societies on an advanced level of technology and specialism sets in in earliest childhood— just as *indoctrination* does in authoritarian societies where technology has as yet made little advance. We have already pointed to the decay of early object-relations which is caused by a host of conditions. There is the absence of the father, the tracelessness of his work, the increasing trend of the mother's absence from the home, her job being as unreal for the child's imagination as the father's is. Early interaction, training in a recognizable role (say, the father's business as a farmer or a cabinet-maker) is replaced by oral spoiling, which is but an insufficient substitute for a genuine object-relation. In the affluent society no less than in any other society the child is exposed to early "conditioning" experiences influencing the economy of his instincts and his ensuing behavior in the social context. The differences in comparison with religious or ideological indoctrination seem almost negligible, and, of course, the needs of the species remain unaltered.

The crucial question is whether a society allows its members to proceed from the more primitive interactional patterns such as identification to the maturer relation of *object-choice*. This concept means that the individual is capable of perceiving the real person in front of him and of interacting with him or her as with an equal partner. (This kind of equality is not to be confounded with conformism.) We tried to show that inherent in our society is the danger of symbiotic dependence. The individual has not learned to distinguish between self and non-self and remains fixated to a providing object. This infantile fixation is promoted by a welfare state which acts as a nourishing and spoiling provider but at the same time depreciates its citizens and reduces the individuals to mere numbers. If the wellsprings of the state at which the citizens are nourishing themselves do not flow as required, then aggressive irritation arises and seeks aimlessly for outlets; it is this mood that renders people susceptible to seduction by a demagogue.

In 1909 in the discussion following a lecture by Alfred Adler on the Psychology of Marxism, Freud [26] named the two main tendencies of cultural development as he saw them—and he adhered to this view; in his eyes they were: ". . . the gradual widening of human consciousness and the constant increase in repression." He thus pointed to the two contradicting stress factors of our times. A complex society with explosively increasing populations concentrated in densely populated industrial areas has to demand an extraordinary amount of instinctual renunciations; in reward the individual is gorged with consumer goods.

If one looks at developments in the theaters of contemporary history as a neutral observer, then it may indeed be that on the individual who is used to the particular civilization in question the very events pilloried by the other side as dangerous impress themselves as progress. And yet we believe that we can point to a decisive difference that lies in the line taken by the evolution of consciousness. It can be inferred from the relation to authority. "If everyone," wrote David Riesman, "is the prisoner of the character structure of his childhood, the formation of which lies beyond the range of his control, it can easily be inferred that all his later motives, inclinations, and judgments are not really his own." [27] This argument seems to hold water, but it overlooks one fact. There is the dynamic interrelation of infantile and mature positions, of early conditioning childhood experiences and the character structure of the adult person. In every civilization we can think of, the young member has a long way to go before he has found his self. Maturation of the critical faculties is a slow process that requires all the help of adults. The alienation caused by the conditions of work and life in a modern society must be counteracted in the firm encouragement of the critical ego-functions offered to the young members during their educational period. They must be given the feeling

---

[26] E. Jones, *Sigmund Freud—Life and Work*, Vol. III, London, 1957, p. 360.
[27] D. Riesman, *Freud und die Psychoanalyse*, Frankfurt, 1963, p. 54.

also that the complex conditions of current society may be actively met and, if necessary, reformed, instead of surrendering to them in passive adaptation. By acting according to this insight we would be a step ahead of those authoritarian states where the problem is concealed and no doubt is allowed to be entertained that what is really alienation and the subjection of the individual constitute this orthodoxy.

But can we be sure that the political authority exercised by the specialists will be equal to that educational task? In my view this is not a specialist's job but a problem to be solved by politicians motivated by a genuine desire for knowledge. Man must be enabled to define himself as one who is responsible not only for his own but also for the welfare of his beloved objects. As in past times the political leaders are expected to set the example so that the members of their group can identify with them.

No one in our society, which has gone through the development of Enlightenment, will be naive enough to postulate that a single person can be the best model for all of us. Our stimulus to preserve for ourselves the possibility of choice so that life is worth living may not consist of much more than this knowledge. But it would be careless optimism to believe that our own cultural development does not promote processes which may lead to the suppression of what has brought us true progress. Freud called this anti-force, counter to the libido which binds men together, the *death-drive,* and was attacked for it by the biologists among his readers. Perhaps the explorers of human society will understand him better.

3. Leadership Style and Political Competence

SAMUEL H. BARNES

Woven into the fabric of much of Western political thought is an ambiguous dual concern: there is a tradition of respect for the individual, regardless of his rank and wealth, and there is also a recurring warning against the potential danger of the masses in politics. These concerns have been reflected in numerous schools of thought and have received diverse formulations since Aristotle equated the rule of the masses with tyranny, and it is perilous to seek common themes in competing and conflicting theories; but at the risk of unjustifiable oversimplification and with apologies for the inevitable distortions resulting from lumping together sheep and goats, hawks and doves, it seems to me that this fear of the masses in politics reflects primarily a concern with the effects of the low political competence of mass publics and their susceptibility to deviant styles of leadership.

Individual policy preferences concerning the role of mass publics in politics do not and cannot derive from scientific premises. They stem from personal choices based on normative preferences. However, a dispassionate analysis can at least point up the practical ramifications of certain value positions and also indicate the feasibility, if not the desirability, of the attainment of certain values. It is in this spirit, then, that the following analysis is conceived, and not with the intention of suggesting either the possibility or the impossibility of mass participatory democracy. It is an analysis of relationships, not a prescription for policy.

It is my thesis in this chapter that effective political mobilization requires a congruence between leadership style and political competence. In the analysis that follows I will (1) briefly examine the problem as viewed theoretically in the work of some contemporary thinkers, (2) review some of the empirical literature on the subject, (3) present new evidence from a study of an Italian Socialist Federation, and (4) discuss some implications of my general proposition and other findings relative to political competence and leadership style.

By leadership style I mean the nature of the relationship between leaders and followers—whether the relationship is democratic, authoritarian, manipulatory, or another type. Leadership style has been operationalized in diverse ways, as will be made evident.

Political competence consists of political skills plus the sense of efficacy necessary for effective political action. This differs from the definition of Gabriel Almond and Sidney Verba in *The Civic Culture,* which, it seems to me, would render most people in nondemocratic systems and many in democratic systems incompetent because of the characteristics of the systems, not those of the individual: ". . . It is only when officials act because they fear the consequences of not acting that a group may be considered to be politically influential and a participant in the decision. If the individual can exert such influence, we shall consider him to be *politically competent;* or if he *believes* he can exert such influence, he will be *subjectively competent.*" [1] This formulation was excellent for their purpose— the study of democracies—but the concept of political competence is potentially of great use in analyzing all political systems, and it should not be confined by a restrictive meaning.

Political competence is a concept that avoids both the extremes of vagueness of terms such as political sophistication and the technical connotations of terms like political efficacy, knowledge, education, or ideological sensitivity. Political competence is an individual attribute involving technical abilities such as some knowledge and interpersonal and organizational skills as well as a psychological orientation that makes political action possible. Sense of efficacy, knowledge, education, ideological sensitivity, and so on, all are closely correlated with political competence without, however, being identical with it. It is a mixture of all of them; and since political competence cannot presently be measured directly, these variables will be examined as indices of it.

My use of the term democracy also merits a brief introductory comment. Democracy is a term with many usages, many of them indefensible from a historical, logical, or linguistic point of view.[2] My intent here is not to define democracy but rather to show some of the implications of certain conceptions of it. These will be strictly defined later in the chapter. When I use the term democracy in the more general sense I am referring to formulations that involve participation by followers in decision making or choice between alternatives. For this reason I find it

[1] Italics in the original. Princeton, N.J., Princeton University Press, 1963, pp. 180–181.

[2] On this point see Giovanni Sartori, *Democratic Theory,* New York, Praeger, 1965 (second American edition). The original Italian edition was *Democrazia e definizioni,* Bologna, Il Mulino, 1957.

necessary to qualify some formulations of democracy as democratic-manipulatory if goals and decisions are made solely by leaders and the task of leadership is viewed as one of inducing acceptance of the goals or decisions by manipulation of the followers.

A final introductory comment on my approach is needed. I take the point of view that leadership is a *relationship* between leaders and followers. The study of leaders is not the study of leadership: It may tell us a great deal about decision making but little about leadership unless the followers and the relationship between them and leaders are studied simultaneously. Research on leadership by political scientists has concentrated heavily on leaders. I am seeking to remedy this deficiency by concentrating on the relationship.

The Fear of Mass Publics in Politics

A fear of the political impact of mass publics has been expressed by thinkers as different as Lenin, Ortega y Gasset, and Lipset. Frequently these diverse thinkers share no important assumptions, and treating them together, even for our limited purpose, involves dangers of misrepresentation and distortion. But the fear of mass publics in politics is widely shared; it has not been limited to any particular tradition or school of thought, and any attempt to equate it with antidemocratic thought would be unjustified.

Lenin wrote eloquently of the need for a professional revolutionary elite to overcome the inadequacies of the proletariat. He developed the communist party as the organizational tool par excellence for mobilizing people of low political competence. Another Marxian analyst, Nikolai Bukharin, although admitting the general incompetence of the masses, argued that it would disappear: "This incompetence is by no means an attribute of every social system; it likewise is a product of the economic and technical conditions, expressing themselves in the general cultural being and in the educational conditions." [3] Bukharin's statement contains an important insight concerning the relationship between political competence and general cultural conditions, and we will return to this subject later.

From another philosophical tradition, aristocratic theorists of mass society have stressed the decline of standards and the tyranny of mediocrities resulting from the political power of the masses.[4] De Tocqueville

[3] From *Historical Materialism*, quoted in *Union Democracy*, S.M. Lipset, Martin Trow, and James Coleman, New York, Free Press, 1956, p. 454.

[4] For an introduction to these and other criticisms of democracy, especially in the twentieth century, see David Spitz, *Patterns of Anti-Democratic Thought*, New York,

and Burckhardt in the nineteenth century and Ortega y Gasset, Le Bon, and Arendt in the twentieth—to sample the diversity of viewpoints— have restated the aristocratic critique. Their points of view tend to be historical-analytical rather than social scientific; although their analyses are empirical as well as normative, their value preferences make them suspect to many democratically oriented social scientists.

Equally suspect but perhaps taken more seriously by contemporary social scientists are the works of the twentieth-century elitists—the school referred to by James Burnham as the "Machiavellians," including Burnham himself.[5] The values of Michels, Mosca, Pareto, and Burnham, their interpreter, may be suspect, but they are more serious opponents because they inaugurated and furthered some important concerns of contemporary social science—the study of oligarchy in complex organizations and a theoretical concern for elite-mass relationships.[6]

S.M. Lipset and William Kornhauser are two contemporary writers who merit closer examination, for they have analyzed the question of the relationship between political competence and political leadership from the perspective of American liberal democratic social scientists; neither their motives nor their methodologies are suspect in the same sense that a social scientist might reject out of hand the conclusions of some of the thinkers previously mentioned.[7] For that and other reasons their views merit closer attention.

On first examination, Kornhauser's *Politics of Mass Society* does not relate directly to leadership and political competence.[8] It develops the

---

Free Press, 1965 (revised edition). For a review of the tradition of the "mindless masses" see Daniel Bell, "Notes on Authoritarian and Democratic Leadership," in *Studies in Leadership*, ed. by Alvin W. Gouldner, New York, Russell and Russell, 1965 (first edition, 1950), pp. 395–408.

[5] For a beginning see James Burnham, *The Machiavellians*, New York, John Day, 1943.

[6] The publication of Robert Michels' *Political Parties* (the first English edition was 1915; the available English edition is New York, Dover, 1959) alone has resulted in a huge scholarly outpouring that shows no sign of abating. Most books on organizational theory, political parties, and political theory will provide an introduction to the literature dealing with the "iron law of oligarchy."

[7] That is not to suggest that they are above criticism. On their normative implications see Jack L. Walker, "A Critique of the Elitist Theory of Democracy," *American Political Science Review*, 60 (June, 1966), 285–96; the reply by Robert A. Dahl, "Further Reflections on 'the Elitist Theory of Democracy,'" *ibid.*, 296–306; and Walker's rejoinder, *ibid.*, 391–92. See also S.M. Miller and F. Reisman, "Working class Authoritarianism: a Critique of Lipset," *British Journal of Sociology*, 12 (September, 1961), 263–76.

[8] New York, Free Press, 1959.

theory of mass society, the properties of which "are relations which engender both readily accessible elites and readily available nonelites." [9] Since they are not insulated from one another by intermediate groups, masses are available for mobilization by elites and elites are vulnerable to mass appeals; along with a decay of values and standards there is a decay in the autonomy of elites.

This formulation is important for our general discussion because it implicitly recognizes a distinction between participation and mobilization.[10] Political mobilization is the general process whereby individuals are incorporated into networks that involve them either directly or indirectly in public affairs. Mobilization can be achieved by means of industrial activity, propaganda through the mass media, clientelistic relationships, voluntary or coerced participation in political organizations, a combination of these, or still other forms. In the modern polity high levels of mobilization seem necessary for the achievement of national goals, regardless of what these goals are.

Participation is but one form of mobilization. The empirical distinction between participation and mobilization is important, but the differing normative implications of the two are even more basic. For the theory of mass society suggests that if democratic participation is not achieved in modern society, then other forms of potentially successful mobilization are available. An ever increasing proportion of the population involved in the national polity seems to be an important dimension of modernization. It has been one of the sad discoveries of our century that mass publics can be effectively mobilized (and perhaps even satisfactorily mobilized from their point of view) in ways that are not compatible with the democratic system as it is viewed by most American social scientists.

Inability or unwillingness to differentiate between participation and mobilization has led to certain inconsistencies in our outlooks, inconsistencies more apparent in our ad hoc evaluations of particular political systems than in our theoretical concerns. There is, on the one hand, a

---

[9] *Ibid.*, 115.

[10] Little has been written specifically on political mobilization, though much is available under other headings such as analyses of totalitarianism and, more generally, propaganda. Several works of Karl Deutsch reflect an interest in mobilization, but his concern is more with social than strictly political mobilization: "Social Mobilization and Political Development," *American Political Science Review*, **55** (September, 1961), 493–514; and *Nationalism and Social Communication*, Cambridge, Mass., MIT Press, 1953. The literature on participation is extensive. For a beginning see Lester W. Milbrath, *Political Participation*, Chicago, Ill., Rand McNally, 1965, and Robert E. Lane, *Political Life*, New York, Free Press, 1959.

tendency on the part of some to view positively any system of mobilization that is effective, that is, that does not show outward signs of internal disaffection. On the other hand, some political systems are criticized because of a lack of meaningful democratic participation. We need to distinguish between effective political mobilization and democratic participation. The greatest need of many contemporary polities is to find ways of mobilizing the population for the achievement of national goals. We should perhaps devote more effort to devising methods of political mobilization compatible with future democratization than to trying to export "instant democracy," which is often irrelevant. It is the merit of Kornhauser's work that he examined some of the negative possibilities associated with the entry of the masses on the political stage.

Lipset's work represents a more systematic attempt to come to grips with democratic participation. It is at once more empirical and implicitly normative than that of Kornhauser. His field study of a socialist party in Western Canada,[11] his study (with Coleman and Trow) of democracy in an American trade union,[12] and his *Political Man*,[13] especially the chapter on "Working-class Authoritarianism," reflect the attempt of an enlightened if not disillusioned liberal to separate the desirable and the feasible in democracy. The earlier empirical study of the Canadian socialist party in a single province reached generally optimistic conclusions; the study of trade union democracy, which concentrated on a union that was internally democratic, reached pessimistic conclusions concerning the democratic potential of most unions. The reasons for this conclusion are numerous and complex, and the interested student should study the work carefully.

The common thread uniting the various obstacles to democracy in unions is the unequal levels of political competence of leaders and rank and file in most unions. Thus most workers are poorly educated and lacking in sense of efficacy. Leaders have a virtual monopoly of skills. Only in a union such as the International Typographical Union, in which members are well-educated and well-paid and also deeply involved in the union, and where distinctions between leaders and rank and file can be kept to a minimum, is it possible to have a two party system and rotation in office. *Union Democracy* operationalizes Michels' concern with oligarchy and demonstrates how difficult it is for members of working class organizations to control their leaders effectively.

In "Working-class Authoritarianism" Lipset presents a depressing body of evidence for the authoritarian tendencies of the working class in many

[11] *Agrarian Socialism*, Berkeley, Calif., University of California Press, 1950.
[12] *Union Democracy.*
[13] Garden City, N. Y., Doubleday, 1960.

countries.[14] One does not have to conclude that the working class has special authoritarian propensities to be convinced that under many circumstances it may not be a bulwark against authoritarianism. Lipset cites low education, low participation in political or voluntary organizations, little reading, isolated occupations, economic insecurity, and authoritarian family patterns as some of the most important elements contributing to authoritarian predispositions within the lower class.[15] It would be difficult to list six characteristics that are more descriptive of the condition of the mass of mankind.

Although Lipset is talking about lower-class individuals in Western society, there are few reasons to believe that these characteristics are rarer outside of Western society: It is difficult to underestimate the political competence of mass publics anywhere. Lipset cities many factors that may serve to channel working-class political energies in a democratic direction. What the working class seems to lack is the ability to see the larger picture or take the long view. The working class is not so much antidemocratic as it is uncommitted; and being uncommitted, it is available for mobilization, democratically or otherwise.[16] In Lipset's words, "The proposition that the lack of a rich, complex frame of reference is the vital variable which connects low status and a predisposition toward extremism does not necessarily suggest that the lower strata will be authoritarian; it implies that, other things being equal, they will choose the least complex alternative." [17]

For the American social scientist, democratic forms of mobilization have a particular legitimacy not shared with other forms. For Lipset as for

[14] *Ibid.* Lewis Lipsitz reaches similar conclusions on the basis of a small sample of workers: "Work Life and Political Attitudes: A Study of Manual Workers," *American Political Science Review*, **58** (December, 1964), 951–62. These conclusions are somewhat qualified in another article by Lipsitz using survey data. He found that 1. ". . . A reanalysis of survey data indicates that education is the major factor contributing to the relatively greater authoritarianism of the working class. With education controlled, the working class may be no more authoritarian than the middle class," and 2. ". . . That different indices of "authoritarianism" may measure quite different dimensions of people's attitudes and that, especially within a working class sample, no simple assumption of correspondence can be made." "Working-class Authoritarianism: a Re-evaluation," *American Sociological Review, 30* (February, 1965), 103–9.

[15] *Political Man,* 100–01.

[16] It may be that much of the seeming authoritarianism of the working class is response-set or mere acquiescence. See Bernard M. Bass, "Authoritarianism or Acquiescence," *Journal of Abnormal and Social Psychology,* **51** (November, 1955), 616–23. In an experiment in which he could control for acquiescence three-fourths of the F scale (from *The Authoritarian Personality*) was associated with acquiescence and only one-fourth with authoritarianism.

[17] *Political Man,* p. 116.

Kornhauser the nondemocratic potential of the masses is something to be deplored and overcome; it is not used as an argument for the impossibility of democracy. In fact, the normative assumptions of American social scientists have probably contributed to our general reluctance to draw disquieting conclusions from much of the evidence. Before presenting some new evidence I will review and evaluate some empirical research concerning the relationship between leadership style and political competence.

Leadership Style and Political Competence: A Review of the Evidence

There is a vast literature on the subject of leadership. The empirical evidence eludes simple interpretation and, especially for the political scientist, it has severe limitations as a source of firm generalizations. Much of it is contradictory and requires care and caution in application to politics. In fact, few studies deal directly with political leadership in an empirical setting and fewer still in an experimental setting. Experimental work on leadership is heavily concentrated in the area of industry, presumably because financial support is more easily available for research with an immediate practical payoff, and among students, presumably because they provide an inexpensive captive audience. Much experimental work is doubly handicapped: the research population is not only inappropriate for the political scientist's interests, but it is also difficult to evaluate the relevance of controlled experiments to the lively confusion of most real-life political situations. It is possible in an experimental situation to control other variables while manipulating those being investigated. This is seldom possible in other types of research, including that presented below, though statistical controls exist that allow assessment of the independent contribution of particular variables. The experimental situation permits a precise evaluation of relationships among the variables, and for that reason special attention will be devoted to several experiments concerning leadership style and competence; unfortunately the studies examined do not deal specifically with political competence.

By reviewing the literature on leadership it is possible to conclude that considerable progress has been made, at least in a negative sense. In recent years the "trait" approach has largely been abandoned. There seem to be few general traits or personal qualities common to leaders; or, to indulge in proper scholarly qualification, leadership "traits" may exist but they have not yet been isolated. Nor has the "great man" theory of leadership involves a *relationship* between leaders and led. Leadership is not tiated thing, and the nature of leaders varies according to the nature of the activity and—a point to which we will return—the characteristics of those being led. The fact that leadership is seemingly functionally specific suggests caution in applying the findings of nonpolitical leadership studies to politics, but too much caution leads to inactivity when there is a need for new departures, not inhibitions. Consequently, much of the following discussion rests on assumptions concerning the comparability of political and nonpolitical leadership that may not be well founded or that will require subsequent modification.

One of the best grounded propositions in the literature is that leadership involves a *relationship* between leaders and led. Leadership is not something possessed by the leaders but rather a relationship in which the followers and their characteristics are as important as the leaders and their characteristics. On this point there is general agreement.[18] This simple finding has immense implications for politics and is the basic evidence for the hypothesis concerning the need for congruence between leadership style and level of political competence. It seems to vitiate the significance of much of the literature on leaders that is concerned with their characteristics, social background, and attitudes. These factors are important in understanding decision making, but they have limited relevance for the study of leadership. One can also speculate that elite theorists such as Pareto, Mosca, and Michels might have reached differing conclusions had they considered the impact of mass education and high average level of political competence on the dominance of elites.[19] A well-grounded study of political leadership must deal with this relationship.

It is surprising how little attention has been paid in experiments to differences in the levels of competence of followers and the nature of the tasks performed by the group. The most important single proposition in the field is the "participation hypothesis," which has been stated by Herbert Simon as follows: [20]

"Significant changes in human behavior can be brought about rapidly only if the persons who are expected to change participate in deciding what the change shall be and how it shall be made."

The most suggestive single experiment on leadership style and group

[18] See Sidney Verba, *Small Groups and Political Behavior*, Princeton, N.J., Princeton University Press, 1961, pp. 117 ff; Robert T. Golembiewski, "Small Groups and Large Organizations," in *Handbook of Organizations*, ed. by James G. March, Chicago, Ill., Rand McNally, 1965, pp. 87–141; Luigi Petrullo and Bernard M. Bass, eds., *Leadership and Interpersonal Behavior*, New York, Holt, Rinehart and Winston, 1961, xviii.

[19] John D. May makes a related point with respect to Michels, "Democracy, Organizations, Michels," *American Political Science Review*, **59** (June, 1965), 417–429.

[20] "Recent Advances in Organization Theory," *Research Frontiers in Politics and Government*, Washington, D.C., Brookings Institution, 1955, 28–29.

performance was the now famous series of experiments by Kurt Lewin.[21] Lewin had groups of children perform cooperative tasks, directed by adults who were trained to utilize three different styles of leadership. In the "laissez faire" groups the leader permitted the children to do as they pleased; he exercised a minimum of leadership. In the "authoritarian" groups the leader provided strong direction, even in the details to be carried out by each individual. In the "democratic" group the leader encouraged and aided the members to work together, formulating policies through discussion and mutual accommodation.

The "democratic" style resulted in higher morale and better quality work. The "authoritarian" style led to equally high productivity, but morale was low and the work of the group ceased when the leader was absent. Furthermore, the authoritarian group manifested signs of high aggressiveness when the leader left the room.

Lewin's study contains several types of methodological problems and concealed normative concerns.[22] The time of the study (the late 1930s) and the public debate over the relative efficacy of democracy and authoritarianism undoubtedly made a certain outcome desirable. The use of children is questionable. Perhaps most open to criticism from our point of view is the nature of the "democratic" style: since the goals of the group were established by the leader and he carefully and consciously sought to lead the group in a predetermined direction, it can be argued that this style is in reality a "manipulatory" rather than "democratic" style. The "laissez faire" style might be more in keeping with classical notions of democracy. However, the experiment is excellent evidence for the point I am making: the children (presumably of low competence) when left to themselves were unable to accomplish a great deal, whereas with "authoritarian" and "democratic" (manipulatory) styles of leadership the predetermined goals were achieved. The seeming superiority of the democratic-manipulatory style over the authoritarian may suggest why armies and state bureaucracies ("authoritarian") are generally not as effective as mass parties such as the Communist ("manipulatory") in effecting compliance with the goals of modernization and, more generally, in mobilizing groups of low political competence.

Some studies have tended to confirm the participation hypothesis.

[21] This experiment is described and discussed in numerous texts and readers. For the original reports see Lewin and Ronald Lippitt, "An Experimental Approach to the Study of Autocracy and Democracy," *Sociometry*, 1 (January–April, 1938), 292–300; and Lippitt, "An Experimental Study of Authoritarian and Democratic Group Atmospheres," *University of Iowa Studies*, 16 (1940), 43–198.

[22] It should be noted that Lewin himself did not make the leap from small groups to the political system, as have some of his interpreters.

Others report conflicting and inconclusive findings.[23] However, there is increasing evidence that its applicability may be severely limited. An experiment by Shaw [24] demonstrated that authoritarian leadership resulted in better group performance and lower group morale than non-authoritarian. Vroom [25] studied the relationship between job performance and leadership style among people who scored differently on tests concerning need for independence and authoritarianism. He concluded that "attitudes toward the job of low authoritarian persons and of persons with high independence needs are favorably affected by opportunities to participate in making decisions in their jobs. On the other hand, the attitudes of highly authoritarian individuals and of individuals with low independence needs are relatively unaffected by this experience." [26] In other words, participation is not nearly as important for authoritarians.

Other studies demonstrate the importance of skill levels. Verba concluded that permissive leadership "if it is to be effective, must relate the level of skill of the group members to the group task." [27] An important experiment by A.D. Calvin, F.K. Hoffman, and E.L. Hardin concluded that groups of bright students benefitted from permissive leadership, whereas dull groups produced more with authoritarian leadership.[28] Verba concluded, "If productivity is to increase through group participation in decision-making, the group must possess enough skill to produce high-quality decisions." [29]

Verba also notes the importance of the expectations of members and the cultural norms concerning leadership.[30] And he and Almond emphasize the importance of the norm of participation in *The Civic Culture*.[31] Golembiewski likewise emphasizes the importance of atmosphere and norms.[32] He presents evidence that the participation hypothesis has severe limitations in other cultures. This point has not been adequately researched, to my knowledge, but work by R.S. Weiss [33] and J.R.P. French,

[23] See Golembiewski, *op. cit.*, 115.

[24] M. E. Shaw, "A Comparison of Two Types of Leadership in Various Communication Nets," *Journal of Abnormal and Social Psychology*, 50 (January, 1955), 127–34.

[25] Victor H. Vroom, "Some Personality Determinants of the Effects of Participation," *Journal of Abnormal and Social Psychology*, 59 (November, 1959), 322–27.

[26] *Ibid.*, 324.

[27] *Op. cit.*, 235.

[28] "The Effect of Intelligence and Social Atmosphere on Group Problem Solving Behavior," *Journal of Social Psychology*, 45 (February, 1957), 61–74.

[29] *Op. cit.*, 235.

[30] *Ibid.*, 178.

[31] *Ibid.*, 178.

[32] *Op. cit.*, 93.

[33] "A Structure-function Approach to Organizations," *Journal of Social Issues*, 12, No. 2 (1956), 61–67.

Jr., J. Israel, and D. As [34] suggests that it has a limited applicability in other cultures. Almond and Verba note that "In Germany and Italy participation does not appear to lead to more frequent positive evaluation of the system as a whole." [35]

Several elements combine to reduce the saliency of democratic norms for many people. Lipset writes:

"Acceptance of the norms of democracy requires a high level of sophistication and ego security. The less sophisticated and stable an individual, the more likely he is to favor a simplified view of politics, to fail to understand the rationale underlying tolerance of those with whom he disagrees, and to find difficulty in grasping or tolerating a gradualist image of political change." [36]

In compiling a list of the basic variables affecting organizational capacity, Arthur L. Stinchcombe,[37] in an analysis of the relationship between organizations and society, simultaneously enumerates many of the factors associated with individual competence: (1) general literacy and specialized advanced schooling; (2) urbanization; (3) money economy; (4) political revolution; and (5) the density of social life, especially the existence of a rich organizational life. He concludes: "Perhaps the most fundamental difference between men for the social scientists' purposes is the difference between functionally literate men and illiterates." [38] It is difficult for men without an adequate mix of these qualities to manage an effective organization, and it is highly unlikely that they will habitually be concerned that it be managed democratically.

An American student of trade unions suggests that members desire strong oligarchic leadership: "There is good reason to think that strong (that is, oligarchic) leadership in unions is what many members want—for pragmatic reasons, at least—and that there is relatively little "psychological" motivation on the part of most members militating in the direction of democratic unionism. Democracy in unions is not a deeply felt personal value for many members." [39] Lipset and his colleagues reach similar conclusions.[40]

This point has not been widely researched within political parties or

[34] "An Experiment on Participation in a Norwegian Factory," *Human Relations,* 13 (February, 1960), 3–19.

[35] *The Civic Culture,* 250.

[36] *Political Man,* 108.

[37] "Social Structure and Organizations," in *Handbook of Organizations,* ed. by James March, Chicago, Ill., Rand McNally, 1965, p. 150.

[38] *Ibid.*

[39] Arnold S. Tannenbaum, "Unions," in James March, ed., *op. cit.,* 750.

[40] *Union Democracy,* 440–469.

other more specifically political organizations. In the next section I will present some data from a study of an Italian Socialist Federation that will suggest that the same dynamics probably apply to many political organizations.

Conception of Democracy and Political Competence

In the previous section data were reported from several studies relating the effectiveness of various styles of leadership to levels of political competence. This section indicates the results of a study of the relationship between several measures of political competence and conceptions of democracy among a sample of members of an Italian Socialist Federation. It will demonstrate that people of low political competence within this Federation held conceptions of democracy that did not involve their direct participation or choice in decision making.[41] Forced to choose one of three conceptions of democracy, a large majority of the members of low political competence selected a statement that incorporated the view that democracy was an end product, rather than a process.

Thus even within a party that aspires to internal democracy, a majority of members are not concerned with democratic processes. The party leaders consequently must live with the tension resulting from the joint concern with internal democracy, which most of them share with many of the members, and the need for effective direction of those who are concerned primarily with the end product. This suggests that one of the reasons for the attraction of people of low political competence to nondemocratic styles of leadership is simply their lack of concern with democratic processes. A further implication is that a democratic style of leadership may not be the most effective style for mobilizing people of low political competence. Finally, these findings clarify several aspects of the oligarchical tendencies of working-class organizations. I will present some evidence in support of these points and then return to them.

The 301 respondents were from a one-of-three systematic sample of the membership lists of the Italian Socialist Party (PSI) in the commune of Arezzo, a city, commune, and province in Central Italy. Only 272 of the respondents answered the question concerning their conception of democracy. Most of those who did not respond were low on the indices of politi-

---

[41] In Almond and Verba's terms, they are subjects, not citizens: ". . . If the ordinary man is interested in political matters, he is more likely to be interested in the output than in the input process. He is concerned about who wins the election, not about how it is carried on; he cares about who is benefitted by legislation, not about how legislation is passed." *The Civic Culture*, 161.

cal competence used in the analysis, so their inclusion would merely have strengthened the relationships demonstrated herein. Further details of sampling procedures and measurements employed have been described elsewhere.[42]

The three statements were printed on separate cards, which were shuffled between interviews. The respondent could study and rearrange them at will. The statements were designed to reflect the *Classic* conception of democracy as participation, the *Neoliberal* notion of democracy as choice between alternative sets of leaders and policies, and the *Marxian* view of democracy as the dominance of the interests of the neediest and most numerous class:

> Classic—A political party is democratic when the members are able to participate and influence the policies of the party.
>
> Neoliberal—A political party is democratic when the members have the possibility of choosing among various leaders and political policies that are proposed.
>
> Marxian—A political party is democratic when it represents the true interests of the most numerous and needy class of the population.

The forced choice method was used because pretests had demonstrated that it was extremely difficult for the rank and file to articulate their opinions and attitudes on open-ended questions. But the forced choice between set alternatives also involved some difficulties. The statements themselves, for example, are neither completely unambiguous nor necessarily mutually incompatible. It could be argued that they apply to different dimensions of the notion of democracy. Furthermore, there is no way of knowing how they were interpreted by the respondents: people bring different frames of reference to the act of choosing and consequently employ differing criteria. Yet the fact remains that the respondents did choose, and it seems that they did not choose randomly.

The responses are extremely illuminating in examining the relationship between leadership style and political competence. They demonstrate that many respondents view democracy as a goal rather than a process, but that those who are highly competent politically are deeply concerned with democratic processes. The highly competent usually also rate high on measures of participation, which suggests that participation and political competence, and not ideology, encourage respect for opposition and other components of conventional notions of democracy.

[42] Samuel H. Barnes, "Participation, Education, and Political Competence: Evidence from a Sample of Italian Socialists," *American Political Review*, **60** (June, 1966), 348–53; and Barnes, *Party Democracy: Politics in an Italian Socialist Federation*, New Haven, Conn., Yale University Press (forthcoming).

Of the 272 members who responded to this question, 169 (62 per cent) chose the Marxian conception. When this group is broken down by level of participation, important differences emerge, as Table 3.1 indicates.[43]

Table 3.1.   Conception of Democracy and Level of
Party Participation

	Nominal Member	Marginal Member	Participant Member	Militant Member
Classic	12%	12%	24%	36%
Neoliberal	18	17	16	16
Marxian	70	71	60	48
	100%	100%	100%	100%
N =	33	93	74	69

The drop in the percentage selecting the Marxian conception is particularly remarkable between the first two categories, neither of which is active in party life, and the two higher categories. It is equally important that the increase in those preferring the non-Marxian categories is due solely to the increase in those choosing the Classic conception. The proportion choosing the Neoliberal is remarkably constant, suggesting a certain randomness in selection of this category.

Similar findings emerge from an examination of the relationship between total associational memberships and conception of democracy.[44] Less than half the PSI members who belong to two or more associations preferred the Marxian conception, whereas 71 per cent of those who belonged to no association but the party preferred that conception (see Table 3.2).

[43] A measure of participation was obtained for each member based on information about his attendance at meetings and activities for the party. Members were divided into four categories, which correspond closely with conventional notions of participation. The *militant* member (25 per cent of the total) is the most active, followed by the *participant* (27 per cent). The *marginal* member (34 per cent) had little to do with the party, and the *nominal* member (14 per cent) had done nothing more than take a card.

[44] Associational memberships include only formal organizations, such as trade unions, cultural and recreational clubs, etc. Church membership is not included; most members were nominally Catholic but this meant little to any of them in associational terms.

Table 3.2.   Total Memberships and Conception
of Democracy

	Party Only	Party + One Other	Party + Two Others
Classic	13%	20%	33%
Neoliberal	16	14	21
Marxian	71	66	46
	100%	100%	100%
$N =$	104	92	60

Since the PSI is a Marxian party, perhaps it is not surprising that almost half of the militants chose what we consider the Marxian conception. It should not be assumed that those members are unconcerned with internal democracy; for example, they could have chosen the Marxian conception for ideological reasons. There is some evidence that they did not, for the more ideologically sensitive members tended more often to select non-Marxian conceptions (see Table 3.3).[45] It is unfortunate that our small number of respondents does not allow further breakdowns.

There is confirmation from another source that ideology is not the

Table 3.3.   Conception of Democracy and Ideological Sensitivity
(with some categories combined)

	Ideologues and Near Ideologues	Group Benefits	Personalities
Classic	32%	19%	20%
Neoliberal	23	20	12
Marxian	45	61	68
	100%	100%	100%
$N =$	41	103	89

[45] The measure of ideological sensitivity is adapted from Angus Campbell, Philip Converse, Warren Miller, and Donald Stokes, *The American Voter*, New York, John Wiley and Sons, 1960, Chapter 10. The "Personalities" category includes those whose responses indicated that they viewed politics in terms of the personalities involved or their own immediate well being. The "Group Benefits" category includes those who interpret politics in terms of which group interests are furthered or damaged. "Ideologues and Near Ideologues" are those who are able to impose some ideological interpretations on politics.

major determinant of the respondents' choice of conception of democracy. The party was internally divided into factions, one of which tended toward doctrinaire Marxism, whereas the other was more pragmatic and accommodating in outlook. Most respondents claimed ignorance of these factions and the issues that divide them. These I refer to as Independents (though, in fact, they are merely uninformed and unconcerned): the others, following conventional usage, are the Leftists and the Autonomists.

In selecting a response to this question, Leftists would be expected to choose the Marxian conception more often than the Autonomists if ideology were significant. This turns out to be true; but the Independents, who would be expected to lie between the two factions by this logic, in fact chose the Marxian conception more than either group of factional identifiers (see Table 3.4). The Autonomist identifiers have a somewhat higher

Table 3.4.   Faction and Conception of Democracy

	Autonomist	Left	Independent
Classic	33%	31%	12%
Neoliberal	25	9	14
Marxian	42	60	74
	100%	100%	100%
$N =$	81	42	149

rate of participation than the Leftists (and, of course, the Independents), thus when participation is held constant roughly half the difference between the two factional groups disappears (table not shown). Controlling for participation has less effect on the Independents because their level of participation is low; as would be expected, most high participants were also Identifiers. Thus I conclude that Leftists are slightly more likely than Autonomists to choose the Marxian conception. Although this may be attributable to factional allegiance, it may also be explained away by reference to social class, union participation, and the like. But to do so would be to engage in the recurring temptation to overcontrol, for these are exactly the bases of factions. Consequently, it is preferable to let the differences stand: Leftists choose the Marxian conception more often than the Autonomists and less often than the Independents.

An examination of the relationships between several indices of political competence other than ideological sensitivity reinforces the conclusion that ideology does not play a large part in the choice of conception of democracy. The more knowledgeable and efficacious the respondent, the more likely he is to fall into the non-Marxian categories. When the total sample is divided into three roughly equal categories on the knowledge index, the portion choosing the Marxian conception is reduced from three out of four to less than one out of two (see Table 3.5).[46] The percentage

Table 3.5.   Knowledge and Conception of Democracy

	Low (0)	Medium (1–3)	High (4–8)
Classic	12%	12%	36%
Neoliberal	14	19	17
Marxian	74	69	47
	100%	100%	100%
N =	73	103	96

of those high in knowledge who selected the Classic conception is three times that of those in the low and medium groups; those choosing the Neoliberal, however, form roughly similar portions of each knowledge category.

The relationship between sense of efficacy and conception of democracy is similar to that just examined.[47] The portion choosing the non-Marxian conception grows with increases in efficacy (see Table 3.6).

Table 3.6.   Sense of Efficacy and Conception of Democracy

	Number of Efficacious Answers			
	0	1	2	3 and 4
Classic	10%	19%	25%	33%
Neoliberal	19	17	13	21
Marxian	71	64	62	46
	100%	100%	100%	100%
N =	63	84	76	48

[46] Respondents were asked to answer true or false to eight factual questions concerning Italian politics, and a knowledge index was obtained by totaling the number of correct answers.

[47] The index of sense of efficacy was obtained from answers to four questions designed to reflect the presence or absence of a sense of political efficacy.

Knowledge and efficacy, as has been demonstrated, are closely related to education; consequently, it is not surprising that the better educated also prefer the non-Marxian categories.[48] But an unanticipated regularity is that the percentage preferring the Classic category doubles with each education level, from 10 per cent in the lowest group to 22 per cent in the middle and 40 per cent in the highest category, those with more than five years of formal education. The portion favoring the Neoliberal conception, on the other hand, declines slightly with increases in educational level (see Table 3.7). These findings substantiate others that have demon-

Table 3.7.   Education and Conception of Democracy

	Less Than Five Years	Five Years	More Than Five Years
Classic	10%	22%	40%
Neoliberal	20	18	11
Marxian	70	60	49
	100%	100%	100%
$N =$	94	131	47

strated the explanatory power of education as a variable in political analysis.

It is thus clear that all these measures are related. Those who participate little, who are poorly educated, who know little, who rank low on sense of efficacy, and who are not ideologically sensitive chose the Marxian conception of democracy in greater proportions than those with opposing characteristics. Since this conception emphasizes democracy as a goal rather than a process, this means that a majority chose a view that did not involve participation or choice on the part of the individual member. This could mean that the leadership encounters little concern on the rank and file level for internal democracy. On the other hand, the minor-

[48] Levels of average education are low in Italy compared with the United States. In the past, few peasants or unskilled laborers received more than an elementary education (five years), and many received even less. The first two categories thus consist of those who did not finish elementary school (less than one per cent had no formal education) and those who did. The third category, "More than Five Years," groups together everyone else, including, for example, those with an additional three years or less of technical training and those with a University degree; however, there are only six of the latter in the sample.

ity that did choose the conception granting influence to the individual member includes most of the members who were high participants. It is interesting that Almond and Verba also found that high competents value democracy as a process, that is, they placed great value on elections, campaigns, etc.[49]

The evidence presented is fragmentary and limited in its applicability, and no firm general conclusions can be drawn from it. But it is suggestive in demonstrating that within one very important group of party members, democracy for those who ranked low on several indices of political competence did not involve participation or choice. It was the end product, not processes, that mattered to this group. On the other hand, it suggests that participation encourages respect for the values of participation and choice.[50]

Some Implications

What are some of the implications of the findings just presented?

Perhaps the most important is that people of low political competence can be mobilized as effectively, perhaps more effectively, by nondemocratic styles as by democratic styles of leadership, and that to many democracy is an end product, not a process. A nondemocratic style of leadership is quite compatible with many substantive programmatic orientations. Thus many aims that democrats consider desirable may be achieved as effectively by nondemocratic styles as by democratic styles of leadership. Furthermore, if in our era people of low political competence are likely to be mobilized by one procedure or another, then to insist on democratic styles of leadership among people who because of this background and general cultural norms respond better to nondemocratic styles results in either countenancing ineffective mobilization or leaving the field to the unscrupulous and irresponsible. In the light of what is known about leadership style it seems unreasonable to expect people of low political competence, authoritarian family patterns, authoritarian work and social relations, and marginal politicization to respond as well to democratic as to nondemocratic styles of leadership. Such people are likely to be mobilized quite effectively by nondemocratic styles, just as people of high competence respond well to democratic styles.

Some examples will clarify this point. In the American past, which groups have been the most effective spokesmen for lower status citizens?

[49] *The Civic Culture*, 255.

[50] Although causation cannot be demonstrated, I have suggested elsewhere that participation seems to be highly associated with increases on several indices of political competence: "Participation, Education, and Political Competence," *loc. cit.*

Big city machines, the Catholic Church, and trade unions. Which of these is actually characterized by a democratic style of leadership? In Western Europe the most effective defenders of the interests of the lower classes have been trade unions, Socialist and Communist parties, and, in some countries, the Catholic Church. Few of these organizations have, in fact, valued internal democracy highly, and some of them have frankly adopted a manipulatory style of leadership. The most effective have generally been the least democratic. Only in Northern Europe—in the United Kingdom and the Scandinavian countries—where average levels of competence are much higher and where there has been extensive experience with democratic organization over a long period of time, can claims to internally democratic organizations be sustained. Even in those countries oligarchy seems to be the rule. And the experience of Germany in this century shows how vulnerable even countries of high average competence can be if other variables are not present in the right combination.

In much of Southern Europe, where average levels of competence are much lower, the democratic mass organizations have largely been surpassed in size by others with nondemocratic styles of leadership. Within the Socialist movement, factionalism and schism have been the prices paid for internal democracy, whereas the Communists in France and Italy have made great progress among those low in competence. Studies demonstrate that in these two countries it is those who are lowest on indices of competence who support the Party.

To use as an example the country where I studied the Socialist Party, I suspect that the Italian Communist Party mobilizes segments of the Italian population that would not be mobilized by democratic styles. I also suspect that, in reality, it is not so much the leadership style of the Western European Communist parties as their friendships and foreign policy orientations that are repulsive to most American social scientists. Further, it can be argued that the Italian Communist style is at least as democratic as that of the Christian Democratic Party, although existing data are inadequate to document this statement. However, referring to voters, Almond and Verba concluded:

"Italy presents us with the curious anomaly of a political system in which the formal democratic constitution is supported in large part by traditional-clerical elements who are not democratic at all, and not even political in a specialized sense of the term. Opposed to the constitution is a left wing, which, at least in part and at the rank-and-file voter level rather than among the party elite, manifests a form of open partisanship that is consistent with a democratic system." [51]

[51] *The Civic Culture*, 160.

I am purposely leaving open the question of what the Communist Party did with the masses it has mobilized. I have stated all along that this form of mobilization is compatible with many programmatic orientations. It can be argued that the presence of the Communist Party is largely responsible for the attempts at improvements of the conditions of the masses in France and especially in Italy.[52] It can also be argued that the Communists have sacrificed the interests of the working class to the foreign policy interests of the Soviet Union. But no one denies that the Communist parties have mobilized significant sectors of the populations of these two countries.

These examples suggest that the political culture may make an independent contribution to the relationship between leadership style and level of competence. However, it is difficult to evaluate the importance of this contribution. General cultural factors undoubtedly influence the expectations of mass publics concerning styles of leadership, but it is possible that political competence is more important than political culture. People of low political competence seem to be highly susceptible to nondemocratic styles of leadership, regardless of the existence of a democratic facade or democratic norms dominating the political culture. The concept of subculture covers the situation in which particular groups such as workers or regional or ethnic minorities adhere to norms that are deviant from those of the larger culture. But our analysis of the Italian data suggests that political competence is more important than subcultural norms, for the norms of the party, shared by leaders and activists alike, encouraged internal democracy.

It seems to me that this argument has important implications for the future, implications that differ for countries in various stages of development. Since this book is concerned with industrial society I will devote my attention primarily to it. However, I would like first to point out some obvious implications for developing countries. Development is impossible without mobilization. If mobilization is crucial, then it must be achieved by whatever style of leadership is effective, regardless of the intentions or preferences of the leaders. The alternatives facing many polities probably are either ineffective mobilization by democratic means—and consequently painfully inadequate development, which is likely to discredit democracy—or nondemocratic styles that facilitate more effective mobilization. I am not advocating totalitarianism of any kind. Many alternatives to democratic mobilization fall short of totalitarianism. Undoubtedly the range of accommodations that can be made is very wide, and each polity has its own optimum solution. But the main point remains: Styles of

[52] See Joseph LaPalombara, "Political Party Systems and Crisis Governments: French and Italian Contrasts," *Midwest Journal of Political Science,* 2 (May, 1958), 117–42.

leadership need to be congruent with average levels of political competence of those being led.

Implications for the future leadership styles of industrialized polities involve projecting trends; this is a dangerous procedure because of the necessity that all things remain the same, which seldom occurs. Many variables besides political competence are involved, and changes in any of them can lead to changes in the relationship between competence and styles of leadership. I am not assuming a necessary connection between stage of development and leadership style. But, all things being equal, it is probable that the increasing competence of mass publics in industrial societies will lead to changes in leadership styles or at least to the need for such changes.[53] Industrial research suggests that more complex work, work that requires more initiative, and so on, is better performed with a democratic style of leadership. Other evidence suggests that participation, regardless of leadership style, leads to increased political competence and hence the potential for a more democratic style. And the evidence presented in this chapter suggests that high participants respect and favor conceptions of democracy that involve participation and choice. Through time, experience with nondemocratic forms of mobilization may thus increase the potential for democratic forms. Changes in the Soviet Union may reflect this trend. So does the current struggle within the Italian Communist Party. At the very least it suggests that nondemocratic forms of mobilization will involve different forms of manipulation in the future. The displacement of overt authority relationships by covert manipulation in many areas of contemporary life may be a reflection of this trend.

However, subtle manipulation is still manipulation; the advanced industrial societies are still far from achieving widespread democratic participation. This failure is much more deplorable in advanced than in developing societies, because the potential undoubtedly exists to a far greater extent in advanced societies. However, increases in education do not always lead to sufficient political competence for the individual to become an effective participant in politics. Political competence is, after all, a relative thing. Although general levels of competence may be increasing rapidly everywhere, and especially in the advanced industrial polities, the demands placed on mass publics are growing also. The levels of competence sufficient to make a man an effective citizen in nineteenth-century America, for example, are far from adequate today, and the level required is being raised all the time.[54] Even the advanced countries must run just to keep from falling behind. This, it seems to me, is another

[53] For a similar argument see Alexander Mitscherlich, "Changing Patterns of Political Authority: A Psychiatric Interpretation." Chapter 2.

[54] See Walter Dean Burnham, "The Changing Shape of the American Political Universe," *American Political Science Review*, **59** (March, 1965), 7–28.

argument for encouraging the mobilization of people of low political competence by means of intermediate structures, for these permit more informed participation since the issues are simpler and the level of competence required is lower. Thus small and intermediate-sized organizations, no matter how nondemocratically they are run, have a higher potential for democratic participation than large ones. And the intermediate structures between the individual and government present greater opportunities for democratic participation than does the governmental structure itself.

However, perhaps the nondemocratic leadership patterns that continue to exist in so many areas of contemporary life in industrial societies set outer limits on the potential of democratic styles of leadership in politics. Almond and Verba have written:

"Education, our data suggest, may lead individuals to believe that they can influence their government. . . . But education does not necessarily increase the potentiality that individuals will create groups to support them. The ability to create political structures through cooperation with one's fellow citizens in time of stress seems to be typical of some nations and not of others. It is an element of political style, not a result of educational attainment." [55]

Cultural norms and personal expectations originating in earlier periods may persist in rendering difficult or impossible the achievement of democratic styles of leadership. High average levels of political competence are thus probably a necessary but not a sufficient condition for the success of democratic styles of leadership. What seems certain is that without high political competence, democratic styles of leadership are not likely to be effective. Even those whose normative preferences are for democratic styles should therefore consider the possible utility of other styles for achieving the substantive programs preferred by liberal democrats and for promoting the higher levels of competence that make democratic styles of leadership potentially more likely of realization. There is little evidence that the existence of a democratic political system requires democratic modes of mobilization of all the subunits of which it is composed.[56] Democracy on the systemic level is quite compatible with nondemocratic (note—*non*democratic, and not *anti*democratic) styles of leadership in intermediate organizations. On the other hand, there is considerable evidence that people of low political competence cannot be

[55] *The Civic Culture*, 209.

[56] For the contrary view, see Harry Eckstein, *A Theory of Stable Democracy*, Princeton, N.J., Center for International Affairs, 1961.

effectively mobilized by democratic styles of leadership. Achievement of many of the goals favored by liberal democrats thus does not necessarily require democratic participation, but it does require effective mobilization.

Everything has its price, not in the sense that everything can be bought but rather that everything costs something. Goals and values often conflict. As Robert Dahl has stated, "We cannot maximize one goal beyond some range without sacrificing another goal." [57] In our efforts to achieve the goal of democratic participation through democratic leadership, we should not neglect the goal of effective mobilization, which today takes precedence over the achievement of other goals of democrats. We may have to settle for less than many of us would prefer. As Giovanni Sartori has written: "Man is not a winged creature. And since the beginning of history whoever ignores this elementary truth has always brought us to the brink of the precipice only to explain, after we have fallen over, that we should have known how to fly." [58] As desirable as the norm of democratic participation is to most of us, in order to achieve effective mobilization, leadership style needs to be fitted to the level of political competence of those being led.

[57] *Political Oppositions in Western Democracies*, New Haven, Conn., Yale University Press, 1966, p. 388.
[58] *Op. cit.*, 89.

4. Authority in Communist Political Systems

A. G. MEYER

Authority, as the term is used in this chapter, denotes a relationship of inequality between two or more actors measured by unquestioning acceptance of communications or compliance with decisions issued by one actor, a relationship which is perceived as legitimate by all actors involved.[1] This chapter is concerned with authority in communist systems, with emphasis on political authority.

From the outset it must be indicated that the study of authority in communist systems must be historical not only because all existing communist systems have come into being as a result of relatively recent revolutions, but also because, aside from their revolutionary origins, they concentrate their major efforts in tasks of economic, cultural, and political development. Change thus is a constant in communist systems; and authority must be examined within the context of this change.

The thesis I shall try to prove in this chapter might be stated as follows: Authority in communist systems is fluid and insecure for several reasons, among them the relatively recent revolutionary origins of these systems, the exceedingly ambitious goals they set themselves, and the drastic methods they apply in their attempts to reach these goals. Because of this insecurity, communist elites are very much preoccupied with the problem of authority and strain their systems in an effort to build up or accumulate authority. I will argue further that the communist regimes of Russia and Eastern Europe have been reasonably successful in this effort: they have achieved a good deal of legitimacy. At the same time, some of them have emerged with social structures and economic systems similar to those of Western Europe and North America and must therefore be counted among the "modern" or "industrial" or "developed" societies. Hence a chapter dealing with these selected communist systems should be in-

[1] For a more elaborate definition, see my article, "Autorität," in *Sowjetsystem und demokratische Gesellschaft; eine vergleichende Enzyklopädie,* Vol. I, Freiburg im Breisgau, Verlag Herder, 1967, pp. 546–564.

cluded in any discussion of industrial societies in general; cross-national comparisons of leadership and authority which include these communist systems are relevant. It may then become apparent that comparisons between "developed" systems may be as meaningful as comparisons between "developing" ones and that industrial societies may follow multiple and divergent political patterns.

It becomes obvious also that the communist systems of Russia and Eastern Europe are both "developing" and "developed." That means they are developing societies that have succeeded in their program of planned modernization either because communism may be a more effective method of modernization than alternative methods, or because Russia, Poland, Hungary, East Germany, not to mention Czechoslovakia (which was "modern" already at the time it became a communist system), at the time of their communist revolutions, were already far more developed than today's "developing nations." For this success, however, the communist systems paid a price which included a pattern of leadership and authority functional to a crash program of modernization. This is the so-called Stalinist pattern, which I shall briefly discuss later. Once modernization has been achieved or a certain threshold of modernization has been crossed, this structure of authority may become dysfunctional to the task of effectively managing an industrial society. Hence mature communist systems have authority problems specific to them, as we shall see at the end of this chapter.

Another prefatory statement I must make is that a strictly behavioral approach to the study of authority in communist systems is impossible, because the social scientist's access to necessary data is severely restricted in a variety of ways. The use of the vocabulary of contemporary political sociology in this chapter therefore cannot (and is not meant to) conceal the basic impressionism and intuitivism pervading it. The absence of strictly quantitative data, however, should not discourage the social scientist from making some attempts to understand different political systems and to compare them with others. Perhaps some of the statements made can later be verified or disconfirmed. Similarly, if I have used some conventional vocabulary in novel and unorthodox fashion, the suggestive value of such usage may be proven or disproven by future investigations.

Authority at the Time of the Revolution

At the moment a communist system is born, attitudes toward authority are complex, if not contradictory, since strong anti-authoritarian attitudes coexist with equally strong authoritarian ones. Communist parties coming to power profess their defiance of all previous authorities and have often given the impression that they wish to abolish all political authority altogether. The notion of the withering away of the state symbolizes this desire to replace all authority with the spontaneous self-government of the collective. To be sure, as they consolidate themselves, communist parties manifest a tendency to tone down if not reverse this initial anti-authoritarian sentiment, but it appears to be strong at the time of revolution. If it is qualified, it is only by reference to the continued need for authority in the factory: the authorities of the machine and of production processes are expected to remain, even when political authority has become superfluous. In short, communist elites justify their assumption of power by the prospect of a rapid political transformation which will abolish all but the most rudimentary and residual authority relations.

Anti-authoritarian expectations of this thought can be traced to the writings of Marx and Engels from which communist political leaders derive their beliefs. At the same time revolutionary events reinforce these Marxist assumptions by providing a free outlet for the strongest anti-authoritarian sentiments from broad masses of the population. Revolutions, by definition, are processes of authority disintegration in which the incumbent authorities are discredited. The resultant anomie is often given positive evaluation by broad masses of the population, who in words as well as spontaneous revolutionary action express their desire for a society perpetually without authority. Politically, this yearning for the reign of spontaneity expresses itself in anarcho-syndicalist activities, in the institution of "revolutionary justice" (that is, lynch law), and in the institution of the soviets. This kind of anarchism has been strong only in a few communist revolutions; but even where it was weak, the incumbent authorities had been gravely discredited for a variety of reasons.

I have pointed out that communist revolutionary ideology is anti-authoritarian in two ways: it opposes the old authorities, and it professes the aim of abolishing all authority. Yet it is also authoritarian. Communist ideology is formulated in the party's sacred texts, which every member is expected to accept as binding. The party, in turn, is proclaimed to be the institutional fountainhead of all authority: its members are, by definition, those who have mastered the authoritative doctrines; hence the organized membership is the word become flesh, ultimate authority organized as a political striking force. Furthermore, communist parties are highly authoritarian institutions. For various reasons their leaders have been inclined to stress the need for centralization, discipline, and the command principle; so much so that intraparty authoritarianism and elitism have become central elements of authoritative communist ideology itself. Finally, revolutionary communism reasserts the need for authority in its aim to establish the dictatorship of the proletariat. In doing so, communist systems proclaim a principle of human inequality, expressing itself as the class structure, according to which all polities, including their own, maintain the authority of one class to rule all others. Political inequality will disappear, according to communist theory, only when class differences themselves have been eliminated. Since this is the task of the dictatorship of the proletariat, communists, one might argue, define their authority as one which, hopefully, will liquidate itself.[2]

For the party member, this promise might possibly serve to mitigate the strain between his anti-authoritarian and his authoritarian views. Indeed, even the anarchic strivings of revolutionized masses might be curbed and subjected to doctrinal and organizational party authority with the help of the expectation that authority will liquidate itself. Yet in as chaotic and elemental a revolution as that of 1917 this was not sufficient; and in other countries, too, communist parties in the initial months and years of their rule have used other than ideological devices for the purpose of mitigating the strain between anarchy and authority. One of their methods has been to succumb, temporarily, to spontaneous and widespread anti-authoritarian sentiments, to allow them free rein, and even to voice them and incorporate them in their policies.

Perhaps the most telling illustration of this ability to ride the waves of anti-authoritarianism is the sweeping land reform carried out by all communist regimes at once after coming to power (except in cases where communist Ministers of Agriculture manage to carry out such reforms while still participating in coalition cabinets). What must be noted here is that communist ideology sharply opposes the carving-up of large landed estates into small subsistence farms; still, for the purpose of exploiting widespread, strong sentiments, the Party temporarily gives in to them. In all cases where the communists desperately tried to curb radical anti-authoritarianism (in agrarian as well as in other matters), they failed in their bid for power. For examples, one could adduce the failure of communist bids for power in Hungary (1919), in Spain (1936–1938), and in China before the rise of Mao Tse-tung to prominence in the party.

Communist parties, in the period of revolution and civil war, identify not only with the anti-authoritarianism of the masses, which the decay of previous authorities has engendered; but in doing so, they also typically voice the most sweeping expectations for a better world to come at once after power has been secured. In Russia and Cuba, and probably also in

[2] Adam Ulam, *The Unfinished Revolution*, New York, Random House, 1960, defines Marxism as a unique mixture of anarchic anti-authoritarianism and the worship of political and industrial authority. According to Ulam, this ideological syndrome neatly expresses the mood of the urban masses in the early decades of industrialization.

China and Yugoslavia, the revolutionary regimes derived their initial authority from a revolutionary euphoria they shared or professed to share with broad strata of the population, especially the underprivileged. This euphoria expressed itself in ambitious programs for the near future that appear quite utopian in retrospect.

At the time of revolution, communist parties have indulged in expectations ludicrously out of tune with reality. To the ironic bystander with his hindsight wisdom, this utopianism may appear as near-lunacy. But one must recognize that, given the chaos of revolution, civil war, and total disintegration, such "lunacy" is "eufunctional." This means that it serves to maintain at least some remnants of a social fabric and makes it possible to have at least the bare beginnings of a political system by making some leadership possible. Millennial hopes keep people going; and utopians may be the only ones left who will dare pick up the shattered pieces of the social system. Indeed, the study of revolutionary situations suggests that there may be periods of acute chaos during which only "lunatics" are likely to succeed, whereas "reasonable" men, due to their very reasonableness, may be unable to maintain themselves in control.[3]

Political scientists do not usually employ the term "eufunctional lunacy." Instead, they call it charisma. Charisma customarily is defined as a quality possessed by "inspired" leaders, by men who succeed as leaders because they are endowed with something like secular grace. Thus defined, it is regarded as one of the possible bases for authority. What I am suggesting here is a slightly more specific definition, in which "inspiration" or "secular grace" is given a content, to wit, an elite's attunement to a mass following in periods of acute anomie, during which both leaders and followers harbor millennial expectations. This definition allows us also to view charisma as a relationship rather than an attribute—a welcome opportunity, since we have defined authority itself as a relationship. Moreover, it ceases to be a term employed only for personal or dictatorial leadership; a charismatic relation can be found also between the masses and an elite, or between the masses and an organization.[4] What I am arguing, then, is that the accession of communist regimes is based on a charismatic relationship between the communist party and significant portions of the population.

[3] See, in this connection, Chapter 6 of this book. Also, Lewis J. Edinger, *Kurt Schumacher: A Study in Personality and Political Behavior,* Stanford, Cal., Stanford University Press, 1965, pp. 312–313 and, by the same author, "German Social Democracy and Hitler's 'National Revolution' of 1933," *World Politics,* V (1953), 330–367.

[4] See Irving Louis Horowitz, "Party Charisma," in *Studies in Comparative International Development,* I, 7 (1965), 83–97.

After defining acute anomie as the major precondition of a charismatic relationship, one might turn to some related questions, such as the following:

Can we make any generalizations about the relative initiative taken by either the communist elite or its mass following in engendering the revolutionary euphoria gripping both of them, which gives rise to the charisma? Is the communist party responding to mass sentiments in formulating its millennial program or does it create them? I am not sure whether verifiable answers can be given to such a question. In any event, the actual relationship is likely to be a complicated process of mutual reinforcement.

Is the charismatic relation between the party and the masses necessarily linked to charismatic relations involving the top-ranking party leader (Lenin, Castro, Tito, Mao) with either the party or the masses; and, if so, what are those links? Here, clearly, generalizations valid for all communist systems cannot be made. A different pattern emerges for each of the four revolutionary leaders named.

Not all communist systems are created with the help of charisma. In most of the East European regimes, a certain disintegration of incumbent authorities had indeed begun, and one might also be able to show that significant portions of the population indulged in highly unrealistic expectations concerning the postwar period. But neither the communist parties nor their supporters were carried away by millennial sentiments as much as their Russian, Cuban, or Chinese counterparts. The revolutions themselves were much more the result of political and military operations outside the systems than of spontaneous developments at home. To a certain extent, they were contrived revolutions.[5]

In discussing authority at the time of communist revolutions, one must be careful to observe that, charisma apart, communist parties have come to power with a degree of legitimacy ranging from one end of the continuum to the other. The respectability, as legitimate national parties, which the communists had gained in China and Czechoslovakia before coming to power must be contrasted with the utter lack of acceptance in the political cultures of Rumania, Hungary, or Russia. Among the reasons for the contrast, several come to mind easily. For instance, in China and

---

[5] These contrived revolutions have their counterparts in the contrived counterrevolutions that took place at the same time in such countries as Greece and Italy, or later in Asia and Latin America. In Greece and Italy, possibly also in France, the disintegration of previous authorities had gone far, and the charisma between the communist parties and the masses was strong. But political and military intervention from outside prevented what might have turned into spontaneous revolutions.

Yugoslavia, the communist parties were identified with the cause of national liberation and unification; they were patriotic parties or regarded as such by substantial portions of the population. In Russia, to name only one contrasting case, the communists were tainted by the accusation of being enemy agents. Again, in countries like China and Bulgaria, the parties were led by people of the majority culture, whereas in Hungary and Rumania the communist leadership came predominantly from national minorities that were hated and despised.

Another building block of legitimacy and authority is administrative experience. Here too the range of divergence is wide. Lenin, Kun,[6] and Castro were totally without administrative experience, unless one counts Lenin's skill in building and managing his political faction. In contrast, Mao came to power not only with 15 years of government responsibility behind him but also with a large cadre of veteran bureaucrats. If we compare the order and efficiency of Chinese government from 1950 to 1956 with the chaos of Soviet administration from 1918 to 1924, the disastrous consequences of this inexperience become obvious; and the authority of the Soviet regime must have been correspondingly less.

Communist Authority in the Period of System-Building

Coming to power in a revolution is rarely sufficient for establishing stable authority. For charisma, as understood here, is by definition an ephemeral relationship. Indeed, the very anomie generating it is likely to compel victorious revolutionary movements to employ ruthless and desperate methods in their attempt to master the chaos. The anarchic and anti-authoritarian strivings of workers, peasants, national minorities, and other groups, having engendered charisma, turn into disturbances as soon as the communist party sets out to govern the country. Communist parties have therefore not hesitated to suppress these strivings by the most nakedly coercive means. As a result, communist regimes soon after ascending to power have tended, by such methods, to antagonize not only their political enemies, but also their own supporters. Thus the charisma of the revolutionary period is quickly squandered; whatever authority the party enjoyed may be lost and will have to be regained, this time on a more stable basis than charisma.

I am tempted to rephrase this idea in provocative fashion: as defined in this chapter, charisma does not engender authority, except of the most

---

[6] Bela Kun was the leader of a Hungarian Soviet Republic in 1919 that lasted only a few weeks.

ephemeral kind. What it does engender is power, a relationship differing from authority in that it is founded on coercion and fear rather than on legitimacy. Authority, however, is essential for maintaining a political system, at least in the long run. Hence most communist elites, soon after installing themselves, lost whatever fleeting authority they had on the basis of charisma, thus felt themselves compelled to establish or re-establish their authority. By empathizing with communist leaders at this point of their careers, I would guess that they perceive the need for authority most urgently and pressingly: since the charisma of the revolution has all but disappeared, both the communist elite and its former mass following might be in a state akin to a hangover, in which mutual enthusiasm for the other has yielded to disillusionment, suspicion, and hatred. The more intense the charisma was, the greater the disappointment is likely to be.

In short, the loss of authority is dramatic; and the resulting crisis, already grave enough, is severely aggravated by the ever-present external pressures to which communist regimes have always been (or felt themselves to be) subject in this early period of their existence. As a result, the task of re-establishing authority must also impress itself on the communist leadership with the utmost urgency. In fact, one of the processes that have characterized communist systems in relatively early phases of their development is one that I have called the *primitive accumulation of authority*.

The primitive accumulation of authority is a desperate attempt, which must be made by many revolutionary regimes, to transform power into authority as quickly as possible. It is the creation of authority in crash program style, as if against overwhelming odds. Indeed, as I have just argued, the odds must in fact appear overwhelming. Broadly speaking, the devices available to communist elites for this purpose can be grouped under the headings of coercion, organization, persuasion, and rewards. Rewards includes the effective management of the national economy, resulting in material benefits for the population and enabling the regime to manipulate material incentives. It also includes various other manifestations of benevolence toward the population: the tolerance of diversity, opportunities for participation in decision-making processes, and a policy of limited laissez faire.

Coercion designates the extensive use or threat of punitive devices associated with the notion of the police state. Organization is meant to symbolize a generally paternalistic and manipulative pattern of relations between the party and the masses, including the attempt to subject all societal activities to centralized management through a system of bureaucratic organization encompassing the entire society. Persuasion, finally, is institutionalized in the means for an ambitious and vigorous program of indoctrination or resocialization (resocialization meaning the socialization of adults). An examination of this process will naturally lead to an examination of communist ideology.

It should be obvious that the four devices for building authority—coercion, organization, persuasion, and rewards—are not always easy to distinguish from each other. Many communist policies might be classified under two or more of these categories. Moreover, in determining the precise mix of these four categories of devices which should be applied in the primitive accumulation of authority, communist systems have experimented widely and are still doing so. These experiments appear to be guided by the following attitudes, considerations, and dilemmas: In principle, communist doctrine warns its adherents not to be squeamish in the use of power and violence. At the same time, this doctrine makes it very clear that authority is firm only when it is founded on enthusiasm, charisma, and conviction. Moreover, Lenin argued that if it lacked such genuine support, the communist regime ought to base its authority as much as possible on incentives and rewards. Terror might keep the most dangerous opponents of communism under control; but the broad strata of the indifferent or the moderately sympathetic had best be mobilized by a system of carefully manipulated rewards.

In practice, communist regimes have tended repeatedly to rely on organization and coercion rather than rewards in establishing their authority. One reason for this is that communist parties have come to power in economically backward nations that could manipulate rewards only to a limited degree.[7] Another reason for communist tendencies to rely on coercive and manipulative authority is the distrust of the masses cultivated by Lenin and his followers, and the corresponding urge, not to call it compulsion, to maintain control over them. Furthermore, the communist value system is in principle committed to egalitarianism; hence some communist leaders have hesitated to base their authority on the use of material incentives, lest the resulting inequality develop into a new class structure.

Communist leaders, moreover, appear to operate on the assumption that coercive methods of accumulating authority are indispensable, at least during the period of an initial breakthrough, which could not be achieved by more benign methods. The very term I have suggested—

[7] This is not entirely true. Communist regimes have come to power also in some developed societies, for instance, Czechoslovakia and Germany. Once in power, however, they became "satellite" regimes. That means that they found themselves tied to a stronger communist power, which exploited their economies by systematically siphoning off these countries' economic resources. Because this exploitation occurred during the crucial first years of authority accumulation, its effects were particularly drastic. In the final analysis, it forced the communist regimes of developed societies to behave as if their countries were grossly underdeveloped.

the primitive accumulation of authority—suggests the determination to make a breakthrough or initiate a crash program of authority-building. I have coined the term in analogy to a phrase used by Evgenii Preobraz-henskii, a Soviet economist of high party status, who in 1923 and subsequent years argued that the limited laissez faire policy of the Soviet regime was condemning its economy to stagnation, hence it should be replaced by a harsh, coercive, centralized program of "primitive socialist accumulation." By implication Preobrazhenskii argued that before a new order can dispense benefits or manipulate rewards it must force a drastic reorientation of the system. Many communist leaders seem to act on the assumption that this applies to authority as much as to economics.

Yet countervailing tendencies are strong even within communist parties. For one thing, the reign of Stalin has discredited terroristic methods and the entire crash program style, at least in some communist regimes, such as Yugoslavia, Poland, Hungary, and Cuba. Indeed, the revulsion against Stalinism at times seems so strong that communist leaders appear either to ignore the Preobrazhenskii dilemma or to opt deliberately for a slow accretion, rather than the rapid accumulation, of capital and authority. For such a "Fabian" approach to authority-building, suitable examples can be found already in statements and policies initiated by Lenin.

The urgency of the task which I have called the primitive accumulation of authority may become more apparent when it is seen as part of a larger undertaking faced by all communist regimes. This undertaking might suitably be called system-building. System-building appears all the more urgent and difficult to communist elites because in the period of revolutionary euphoria, when they perceive reality through the ideological gridwork of Marxism in its most millennial aspects, they do not think of system-building as a task still to be performed. Instead, they tend to assume that a new system will spontaneously emerge from the revolution, that a communist society will be born out of the ruins of the old system. Such expectations, where they are strong, soon give way to the awareness that, in fact, the revolution created only ruins and that a concerted creative effort will be required to shape a new political system out of the material at hand. Indeed, the material itself must be reshaped to be fitted into such a new system. If a thoroughly new system of institutions, structures, processes, and patterns is to be created, drastic changes must be made in the societal raw material left over from the political system of the past.

For a study of authority, the most interesting problem in this connection is the creation of a new political culture, that is, the thorough resocialization of the entire population to impart to them new views, new attitudes, new behavioral and ideological stereotypes. Culture building requires a restructuring of the whole nation's personality. It is thus a far more ambitious task than the mere legitimation of a new ruling elite or even the legitimation of a new political system.

For the purpose of this chapter, it might be well to single out those elements of culture building (or, as communists call it, of the cultural revolution) which are most closely related to the accumulation of authority. What is attempted in the cultural revolution is the retraining of all citizens for life in a communist society. The changes attempted here can be described in varying fashion: from religious to political orientation (secularization); from traditional to bureaucratic authority; from the peasant way of life to the machine age. Henry Dicks has described it as an attempt to transform oral-permissive personalities into anal-compulsive ones and argued that the former type of personality has predominated among the Russian peasantry.[8] In some countries of Eastern Europe, we might instead want to concentrate our attention on the difficulty of replacing long-engrained individualistic attitudes with collectivistic ones. In Asian countries, the cultural revolution obviously includes the attempt to substantiate rational, open-ended, autonomous, and self-reliant thinking for the imitative culture of Confucius, which prescribes specific behavior for every foreseeable traditional situation. Moreover, in all patriarchial cultures, communist re-education implies an oedipal revolution: a sharp and sudden revolt against parental authority that has been taken for granted for many centuries. In other words, communist re-education seeks the destruction of the patriarchal family, or at least its end as the focus of the entire culture. Instead, it is to serve as an ancillary institution socializing the young for citizenship and productive work within the framework of the new system.

Finally, in all previously underdeveloped countries communism seeks to effect a revolutionary restructuring of the citizens' perception of time, which is one of the most basic authorities. The peasant lives according to the authority of the seasons, the weather, the sun, and the crowing of the cock. The worker—and communist regimes regard the worker as the model—lives according to the authority of the machine; and the first machine in Western civilization, as Lewis Mumford has pointed out, was the clock. The socialization of Western man for the modern age is symbolized by the linkage of the clock with the sacred in the form of the church steeple clock that chimes every quarter hour. Such a sacred time tower dominated every town and village in late medieval Europe.

Someone recently suggested that African elites trying to modernize

---

[8] See Henry Dicks, "Observations on Contemporary Russian Behavior," *Human Relations*, V, 2 (1952), 111–176.

their countries might learn from this and speed up modernization by placing clock steeples in every village. Communist elites in the Soviet Union
and Eastern Europe have done far better than that. The universal symbol
of the new authority they have erected in all village squares and other
public places is a mast carrying a loudspeaker through which the local
radio program is continually brought to all citizens within hearing distance, unceasingly keeping them in touch with the leaders.

Incidentally, these attempts to restructure entire nations' cultures and
personalities is revolutionary not only in its ambitiousness, but also at
times in its effects or side-effects. The deliberate attempt to break down
an incumbent culture is a cataclysmic event in any society because it re-
leases pent-up psychic energies and doubtlessly creates guilt feelings of
tremendous strength, in a manner that must be described as explosive.
Currently such an explosion, or chain reaction, seems to be resulting from
the release of oedipal energy in China.

System-building and the related restructuring of authority here appear
as a disorderly process or a process engendering disorder. It also takes a
long time, even though communist regimes have shown themselves quite
impatient in this regard. Their very effort can be described as an attempt
to compress into a few decades a process of authority and personality
restructuring which in the Western world took centuries. But to the contemporary observer even a few decades may constitute a lifetime. The
point I am trying to make is that communist systems in the form in which
they first impressed themselves on outside observers, that is, in their
Stalinist form, may well constitute the system-building phase of communism. That would make Stalinism, in its Russian and East European forms,
a transitional phenomenon between the principally destructive phases of
communist revolutions and the establishment of communist societies that
are reasonably stable political systems. True, our image of the communist
system has been so colored by the Stalinist experience that Stalinism has
long been regarded as the ideal type of the communist society. When the
Western scholar says "communist system," he tends to think of the Soviet
Union between 1928 and 1956. By regarding Stalinism as the system-
building phase, I am trying to suggest that the end product of communist
revolutions may turn out to look significantly different from Russia under
Stalin.

One implication of regarding Stalinism as the system-building phase
of communism is that authority, as well as all other salient features of the
polity, are still in the process of becoming. Authority is not yet established; it is still fluid. To be sure, in Stalinist systems this fluidity is
masked by a number of seemingly constant authorities. They have appeared so stable and have proclaimed themselves so unchallengeable that

many Western observers in the past tended to regard the entire authority structure of Stalinism as equally stable. The Stalinist type of communist system was often regarded as a political order not subject to challenge or change.

The seemingly constant features suggesting this image of stability included, first, the ruling party, self-proclaimed sovereign of the Stalinist system, which at times seemed to be the most stable elite in modern history. After all, it had succeeded in eliminating all rival parties, had geared the entire system to perpetuate its authority, and grandly claimed the exclusive right to represent the nation. A second constant in Stalinist systems was the elevation of Marxism-Leninism to the status of the regimes' official ideology. The articulate doctrine as stated in official textbooks here seemed to function as the supreme authority to which even the party leadership subjected itself. A third constant in Stalinist systems was the thorough bureaucratization of life. In using this term, I have in mind the attempt made in Stalinist systems to subject all social life to planning, management, and control, through complex organization. If ever whole societies and all the structures in them conformed to the post-Weberian model of bureaucracy, they were (and are) the communist systems of Russia and Eastern Europe. And if ever a political ideology placed the Weberian model of bureaucracy on a pedestal, making it the utopia toward which the system should strive, it was the self-image of these systems, as expressed in their elaboration of "democratic centralism" as well as in their definition of socialism as the imposition of rationality on the affairs of men by means of complex organization and scientific management.

The reason for the fluidity or instability of authority in Stalinist systems was that these seeming pillars of continuity and order were stable and authoritative only formally, but not actually. The communist parties underwent sweeping changes in their leadership; indeed, it has been argued that some of them were, in fact, destroyed by Stalin. Moreover, far from having the authority of the sovereign in Stalinist systems, they were no more than ancillary structures for one-man dictatorship. There was therefore a sharp discrepancy between the theoretical hegemony of the communist parties and their factual near-impotence.

Western scholarship today is leaning toward the view that the official ideology did not function nearly as much as the supreme authority as its spokesmen claim and as was previously assumed. Precisely what the relationship between the ideology and the political systems was under Stalinism is a matter of current controversy. The point on which there seems to be the most general agreement is that it functioned to legitimize the system, hence the ideological indoctrination of the citizens was part of the effort to accumulate authority. To this I would add that it functioned primarily as a self-legitimation device; this means that with the help of ideology manipulation the communist leadership sought to convince itself of its own legitimacy and thus strengthen its own authority. One of the first requirements of authority, after all, is that it firmly believe in itself.

Bureaucratic patterns of authority, finally, are not as much of a constant of Stalinist systems as they may have appeared. For even though certain basic forms of organization and patterns of management established themselves in what might be called standardized Stalinist types, the entire administrative machinery was subject to repeated and thorough tinkering. Indeed, Stalinist systems suffered from a veritable reorganization mania. The bureaucracy was never allowed to settle down into stability.

This leads us to the most basic instability inherent in any political order devoted to system building: a perpetual tension between dynamic and static urges, between the desire for stability, orderliness, and bureaucratic rationality, on the one hand, and the equally strong need for innovation, change, and revolutionizing activity on the other. It has often been tempting to see the government administration as the agent of bureaucratization and the party (perhaps also the political police) as the source of innovation, dynamism, change, etc. Analogies with other political systems in which a similar division of labor exists between the (bureaucratic) civil service and the (dynamic) politicians may come to mind. However, in fact, the Stalinist system in Russia and Eastern Europe reduced the communist parties as well as the political police to nothing but additional administrative bureaucracies, and the conflict between dynamic and static urges pervaded all structures within the system.

Authority in the period of system-building in the communist world is made even more fluid and insecure by serious problems pertaining to the recruitment and internal structure of the elites. When discussing the elites of communist systems that are in the process of formation, it may be well, for the moment, to disregard the difference between the political elite (party and police) and the professional elites in the economy, government administration, armed forces, education, science, and cultural life. I have previously suggested that this difference is not so crucial as it has appeared to some scholars. In communist systems there is a large degree of interpenetration between political and professional pursuits. Of interest here are not the differences between different elites, but the pressing need for all kinds of elites or cadres in periods of system-building. The dearth of personnel that might be placed in positions of authority and responsibility cannot be overstated. It is all the more pressing a need in communist systems, because communist parties have usually come to power in countries that either had only a relatively small intelligentsia, or where part of the intelligentsia had been killed, had emigrated, or was thoroughly discredited by its association with precommunist systems.

Whatever the political system we investigate, the selection of personnel for elite positions must always be guided by two criteria: competence and loyalty. And the most troublesome problem for communist regimes has been the tendency for these two criteria to exclude each other. Those who were most loyal, because of their lower class status, often were illiterate or otherwise incompetent. Those who were most competent, because of their education and experience, were of dubious loyalty because of their origins in the previous elite. Hence, to use the vocabulary of Mao Tse-tung, communist systems had to choose between "red" and "expert" cadres, whereas in fact they want their cadres to be both.

It would be interesting to trace the different solutions which communist leaders, from Lenin to Mao, have tried for the purpose of overcoming this dilemma. But this would transcend the scope of this chapter. Here I will point out only that in the phase of system-building, when the communist leadership seriously embarks on industrialization and all the thorough restructuring this requires, the problem of recruiting an elite which is both competent and loyal appears far more acute than ever, and it leads to authority crises manifesting themselves in rapid and bloody turnover of elite personnel, in the mobilization of the police or the revolutionary masses against the elites, in the most vicious in-fighting within the elites, and phenomena such as those that occurred in Russia in the late 1930s, in Eastern Europe around 1950, and in China currently.

The authority crisis engendered by the crash program of industrialization and system-building is aggravated further by the related need to redefine the content and the functions of the official ideology. From an idea system which seeks to base the radical criticism of the past and millennial expectations for the future on an allegedly empirical sociological method, it must be turned into a much more conservative theory of state, in which criticism turns into apologetics and the millennium is explained away; the empirical sociology must be turned into systematic falsification of reality, and the party alone defines truth, according to the principle of *partiinost*. Such a transformation of the ideology from a stimulus for revolutionary action into a legitimation myth for a system in the process of formation is traumatic; and, since the ideology is regarded as the ultimate authority in communist systems, its transformation intensifies the authority crisis which accompanies the emergence of the system.

In the light of this crisis and the general fluidity of authority in communist systems at the time of industrialization, the institution of the dictator begins to appear as the most important factor of cohesion. He appears as the only stable authority, indeed as the one and only and therefore absolute authority. In his person, all command is concentrated. In his person, too, all conflicting elites merge. They all are subordinated to him. He also becomes the one and only legitimate interpreter of the authoritative ideology, the sole possessor of truth, in whom all ideological functions are merged. He is the chief scientist, the chief moral philosopher, and the leading practitioner in all human pursuits, the first expert and master in all fields of endeavor. To the outside observer, the praises heaped on the dictator appear as a vast public relations effort designed to endow him with what some scholars have called pseudo-charisma.[9]

The term pseudo-charisma conveys the notion that the qualities attributed to the dictator are false, unconvincing, artificial; that it springs from the imagination of public relations specialists rather than from a real leadership relation. I feel that the term easily misleads us into underestimating the charismatic qualities of the relationship between the leader and the nation. To the outsider, his near-deification may appear entirely contrived and unacceptable. Many members of communist systems, however, may find it much more believable, because in effect the leader is almost divine in his power and authority. In short, one should appreciate the real authority he acquires, both because of the roles he plays and as a result of this publicity. Pseudo-charisma thus is closer to charisma than one might at first think. Both are engendered by a deep authority crisis from which individuals or entire masses of citizens seek escape by endowing a leader (or an elite) with superhuman qualities or by allowing themselves to be convinced that he is so endowed. Thus the system-building phase, by promoting an authority crisis, also promotes the authority of the dictator. The initiator of the crash program makes himself indispensable; and the cult of the personality emerges as a typical phase of all communist rule.

It is obvious from this, incidentally, that the death or elimination of the dictator in this phase of communist rule would promote a particularly severe crisis, because he is so important an institution. He holds an extremely fluid authority structure together, and the pseudo-charisma enveloping him symbolizes his indispensability. The superhuman qualities attributed to him are not easily inherited or taken over. One might argue that the Soviet Union and China were lucky to have dictators of such

[9] The concept of pseudo-charisma is developed by Jeremiah F. Wolpert, "Toward a Sociology of Authority," in *Studies in Leadership,* ed. by Alvin W. Gouldner, New York, Harper and Row, 1950. See also Raymond A. Bauer, "The Pseudo-Charismatic Leader in Soviet Society," *Problems of Communism,* No. 3–4.

longevity. At the same time, one might also wonder whether the need for a dictator was not the result of his success in destroying all rival authorities in the first place.

Authority in Developed Communist Systems

Out of the Stalinist effort at industrialization and system-building, a number of communist regimes have emerged or are in the process of emerging as societies which in their economic productivity, state of industrialization, social structure, and living standard appear to resemble the societies of Western Europe and North America as they resemble the societies of their own pre-industrial past. Politically, they have thus far retained a character all their own. Nonetheless, we are obviously witnessing a major transformation of some of the communist systems. To summarize the implications of this transformation for authority in the communist world is the task I have set myself for the remainder of this chapter.

The implications could be stated most succinctly by saying that success in system-building strengthens the authority of communist systems and simultaneously threatens to undermine it.

The strengthening of authority can be explained by a number of factors. One is the mere longevity of the regimes, which has the effect of converting compliance with them into a habit. Any system that can maintain itself for several decades ends by being taken for granted by the citizens. Much if not most authority in the world is based on longevity in this sense.

The development of habit thus defined is speeded appreciably by the successful elimination of all alternatives to the communist system. One can observe several illustrative cases in which the authority of communist regimes grew considerably after all hopes for an alternative that might have existed in the minds of some citizens had been dashed. For instance, Western observers today point out that by building the Berlin wall the German Democratic Republic gained a considerable increment of authority. The failure of the United States to interfere in the Hungarian and Polish revolts of 1956 had similar implications and similar effects. So also did the experience of the Soviet people under German occupation in World War II, which showed them that the one alternative to communist rule was even worse than Stalinism.

The longevity of communist systems means not only that compliance with them has become a habit but also that its organizational and operational patterns may be in the process of turning into routines. In other words, the system itself gets internalized, just as parliamentary habits and Roberts' Rules are internalized by many Americans. Because of this internalization of what the communists call Democratic Centralism, it is possible for communist parties to mobilize broader masses of the citizenry into participation with the system. At the same time, participation in some cases becomes more meaningful because of a trend toward decentralized management and a rudimentary syndicalism, which we will discuss later.

One might suggest, more generally, that the strenuous indoctrination effort of communist regimes has paid off. The rank-and-file of the citizenry has internalized not only the organizational patterns of communist rule, but also the basic tenets of the ideology, especially a vague commitment to a collectivist work ethic. Any American who has traveled in communist countries will be able to confirm this on the basis of random conversations.

Additional factors in the strengthening of communist authority are the economic, scientific, and political gains made by communist regimes since World War II. These gains doubtlessly have convinced many citizens of these systems that the regimes will be able to fulfill some of their promises and that, more generally, citizenship in a communist country means membership in a reasonably successful organization, an association which both is profitable and induces pride. I believe one should connect the growing acceptance of communist ideology with these successes, because the ability of communist systems to raise living standards, dispense with mass terror, and gain prestige in world affairs, to mention only some achievements, obviously has made the ideology somewhat more plausible, not only by rendering its promises more believable, but also by enabling the party ideologists to describe the contemporary world more realistically. Indoctrination can therefore turn from a frantic resocialization into a routine, from a program of ideological restructuring into one of reaffirming established loyalties and beliefs. This, too, strengthens the authority of the ideology, because it is taken more for granted.

Many of the previous observations can be restated as a subtle but important change in the relations between the political elite and the masses of the citizens (the term "masses" is the term used in communist writing to designate all those not belonging to an elite): the regime and the masses have come to accept each other and to take each other for granted. As a result, there is not only an increase in legitimacy, but a corresponding shift in the prevailing pattern of mobilizing the citizens. The shift might be described as follows: In classifying patterns of mobilization, we can single out the style of authority as well as the principal motives it seeks to enlist. To make matters very simple, the style can be placed on a continuum ranging from authoritarian to participative: from command and dictatorship to self-government and autonomy. Among the motives the system seeks to enlist in mobilizing the masses, I shall focus on two contrasting ones: moral and material; the moral includes faith, enthusiasm, and ideological commitment; the material, the drive for material and status gain and the fear of being left behind in the race for success. A two-dimensional scheme into which these variables are placed yields four patterns of mobilization:

	Authoritarian	Participative
Moral	I. Revolutionary	IV. Utopian
Material	II. System-building	III. System-management

It can be argued that the pattern of mobilization indicated by box I has been prevalent in periods of revolutions and great leaps forward, thus in Russia in 1917–20 and 1928–31, in China in 1958–60. Combination II is typical of mature Stalinism (Russia 1938–53; Eastern Europe 1948–53). Combination III is the style that seems to be appearing in communist systems emerging from Stalinism which have achieved industrialization up to a level corresponding to that of Western European countries and have stabilized their political systems. Combination III thus is the mobilization pattern of Krushchevism, Brezhnevism, and East European Revisionism. We can recognize type IV as the stated goal of communist systems. In periods of revolutionary enthusiasm (type I), the party proclaims it as the *immediate* goals. All that is ever achieved, however, is the mobilization of selected groups from among the masses. Hence type IV turns out to be the mobilization pattern of great purges.

In this crude two-dimensional scheme of classifying mobilization patterns, the reader may miss some important variables. I am aware that reality is just a bit too complex to be fitted into four pigeonholes. All I wish to do is to suggest some differences that seem to emerge from observation.

One of the variables the reader may have missed is fear as one of the principal motives to be tapped in mobilizing the masses. I have left it out of the given scheme for two somewhat contradictory reasons: first, because all communist systems have made extensive use of fear as an enforcer of authority, hence this variable lends itself less than others to differentiation; second, because the arousal of fear through coercive or terroristic methods has been used far more extensively and effectively against elites than against the masses. For instance, in periods of mass purges, it is the masses (or select groups among them) that respond to moral or ideological impulses. But to the elites, this mobilization of revolutionary enthusiasm appears as the unleashing of terror. I must emphasize that in the past pages I have talked specifically about the authority relation between communist regimes and the masses. What is implied here is that such relations are different from the authority relations between the regime and the several elites. The differences between these two relations in communist regimes have not been studied as systematically as they might have been.

We have reached a convenient point at which to turn from the factors that have strengthened communist authority in post-Stalinist systems to those that challenge and weaken it. The point is convenient because at least some of the challenge to communist authority arises predominantly in the elites rather than the masses. I want to end this chapter by surveying these challenges.

One can note in the post-Stalinist systems of Russia and Eastern Europe a general revolt against bureaucratic authority, or at least against the overcentralized, authoritarian, punitive, and doctrinaire style of bureaucratic management established as a result of Stalinist rule. One of the motives for this revolt seems to be the need felt for innovation and adaptability in many endeavors, whether for the purpose of making the communist economies competitive in the world market, for making the entire systems competitive in the world market of opinion, or for adapting the systems to the political cultures of the nations in which they have established themselves.

In other places I have derived the impulse for this revolt from the need of mature communist systems to change from a preoccupation with system-building to one with system-management, and I have compared communist systems to large Western corporations, like the Ford Motor Company or General Motors, which have gone through analogous adjustments.[10] Whatever the motives, the fact of such a general revolt is undeniable. Paradoxically, it is directed rather sharply against the communist parties. The reason is simple: although they were often regarded as the dynamic, innovative force in communist systems, they did create the specific style of bureaucratic management against which the revolt is directed, and today they tend to be defenders of this order, if only because the party leaders regard their own authority as dependent on it. Hence the general tendency throughout the communist world today is to regard the parties and their ideological orthodoxies as conservative or reactionary forces.

[10] See Alfred G. Meyer, *The Soviet Political System*, New York, Random House, 1965, pp. 262–263.

The revolt can also be described as a conflict between rival authorities in which the party's claim to rule is challenged by competing conceptions of rationality as defined by various professional elites—economists, diplomats, scientists, artists, military specialists, and so forth.

To a lesser degree, we can also discern a revolt against bureaucratic authority in the name of a rationality as defined by the people at the grass roots, in economic enterprises, neighborhoods, communities, and various mass organizations. Who is siding with whom in this tricornered conflict between the party, the professional elite, and the masses is impossible to say, primarily because it is not a tricornered conflict at all, but a much more complicated constellation of conflicting forces; for neither the party nor the professional elite nor indeed the people in any of the European communist systems constitutes a unified political force. Instead, the political systems today have developed a markedly pluralistic substructure.

Where does this substructure come from? It is, of course, nothing but the heterogeneous society Stalinism created in its effort to promote industrial civilization in underdeveloped nations. Once this pluralistic society has been created, the social structure of industrialism begins to assert itself in the form of conflicting group interests. Just how the interests assert themselves we do not know; and even an identification of these interests is exceedingly difficult to make. We do, however, have countless indications of their existence and their self-assertion as inputs into a thoroughly bureaucratic political process. Western scholars seem to be in general agreement that they cannot be denied or suppressed, since the political elite and, indeed, the entire society have become dependent on various professional elites. This dependence very likely is mutual or reciprocal, so that the mature communist society must be seen as a complicated fabric of interdependent elites. Such a society cannot easily be governed by a centralized command system. Nor can it tolerate the sovereign abandon with which communist parties in their Stalinist phase created, changed, and abolished structures within the society.

As a result, the prime function of the political elite (communist party) is redefined from that of system-building to that of system-management, or from sovereign command to interest aggregation. Or at least this would seem to be the logical outcome of the social transformations going on. It is quite evident to long-time observers of the communist world that the party leaders find such a readjustment very difficult to make; leadership patterns that are well engrained are not easily changed. As a result, many communist leaders seem to be afraid of the very social reforms which would modernize their societies farther and make them more efficient; for they appear to believe that such reforms will jeopardize the political leadership of the party.

It is likely that communist parties' composition and structure will change in the measure to which they succeed in reorienting their leadership function to that of interest aggregation. Communist parties have always striven to be "cadre" parties. That means they have sought to include all nonpolitical elites among their members. In the past this could be interpreted primarily as a controlling device: by recruiting the society's elites into the ruling party, the party leaders could dominate these elites, organizationally, ideologically, and politically. Today the pattern in mature communist systems seems to be shifting slightly: Nonpolitical elites, including scientists, economists, specialists in military strategy, engineering, personnel management, education, medicine, and a host of other fields are being consulted by the political elite and are also being co-opted into the higher levels of the party leadership. The pluralism of elites is thus reflected in the leadership of the communist parties.

One way of suggesting the nature of this transformation is by using the language of Pareto and arguing that the successful accomplishment of the task of system-building compels the political elite to transform itself from lions into foxes. Pareto has interesting things to say about the implications of such a transformation for the entire political system and its authority structure.

Some of the challenges to the party bureaucracy, however, do not originate in the new social structure created by the party, but in older elements of the political culture that have survived through Stalinist rule, despite severe attempts to suppress or repress them. In short, the national political cultures of Eastern Europe and Russia have begun to assert themselves as rival authorities. It is not the first time they have done this; but they seem to be doing it more successfully since the death of Stalin.

Again, the reason is similar to the grounds I suggested for the social pluralism now asserting itself. The mature communist systems of Russia and Eastern Europe are faced with the task of managing their systems as efficiently as possible. They have passed through a painful period in which the party ruled by issuing commands and obtained compliance by predominantly coercive means. Even the political leaders seem to have become aware of the costliness, wastefulness, and inefficiency of this style of authority. The new pattern now emerging is one of enlisting and mobilizing existing groups, structures, and cultures, including those surviving from precommunist periods, not abolishing them.

In short, the parties are no longer as totally committed as before to a policy of destroying the national cultures they inherited. The strength of the national cultures has surprised some Western observers. It is attested by the compromises which communist regimes in Eastern Europe and Russia have made with organized religions and by the vigor of nationalist antagonisms between and within several of the communist systems. It expresses itself in seemingly trivial matters, such as specifically national forms of polite social intercourse. But multitude of trivialities add up to distinct national behavior patterns. Just as an experienced traveler may be able to distinguish Frenchmen from Englishmen at a glance on the basis of such trivialities, so also distinctions in style will mark the several mature communist systems, and there is no reason to assume that these distinctions will fail to affect the political systems.

The reassertion of national political cultures is a function also of the growing autonomy of the individual communist nations from strict Soviet control. It is not necessarily a challenge to communist party authority. On the contrary, some communist parties have shown considerable skill in enlisting nationalist sentiment and national cultural traditions for their purposes and have thus turned national political cultures into authority maintenance devices. For instance, the Socialist Unity Party of Germany appears to have succeeded in mobilizing Prussian traditions and their symbols, including even Bismarck and William II, to legitimize their own regime. Similarly, the communist regime of Czechoslovakia has been careful to continue the institution of the office of the President of the Republic more or less in the form in which it was created by Jan Masaryk and Edward Beneš. By doing so, the party (or the party leader occupying the President's office and palace) shares in the authority adhering to this office. In some East European countries, such as Poland and Rumania, even the traditional antagonism to Russia appears to have been used, in increasing measure, for the support of the local communist regimes. Still, on balance, the strength of diverse national cultures may nonetheless appear to the communist leaderships as a disturbing input, hence as a challenge to their authority.

The strain on the authority system inherited from Stalinist days is increased by a conflict of generations. On the whole, the political elites in the communist world are overaged. In this they are similar to political elites in other systems. But in contrast to many noncommunist elites, the political leaders in the communist world came to power at a younger age and have thus held their offices longer. This may intensify the generational conflict; similarly, the precedent of their accession to power at a younger age may aggravate it.

In communist systems (as in other industrial countries) this generational conflict is not only the customary challenge of the old by the young, but a clash between radically different life experiences and political expectations, creating a profound gulf of reciprocal misunderstanding and suspicion. The economic and political successes of communist regimes probably aggravate this problem. For under present circumstances, marked by a certain affluence and relaxation, the generation of young adults and adolescents no longer understands the hardships of economic depressions, war, and Stalinism. Hence they do not understand or appreciate the political style of those who went through these purgatories or the system which emerged out of them. They do not understand the political culture that arose out of these periods of hardship, and they may be prone to challenge all and any authority.

Finally, established authority in communist systems is facing the challenge of ideological "erosion," that is, a weakening of Marxism-Leninism as a doctrinal authority maintenance device. This weakening is related to all the strains adduced above, but results primarily from three developments: (1) the repudiation of Stalin and some of his policies seriously undermined the authority of the party and its ideology; (2) the breakup of the communist camp into mutually hostile systems shattered the belief that a single authoritative interpretation of the ideology could be found; and (3) the inroads on the party's authority made by many professional elites found ideological expression in the fact that party ideology is increasingly challenged in the name of science. Hence in all post-Stalinist systems, the ideology today seems to be as much on the defensive as the party itself.

To sum up: In mature communism, that is, in communist systems that have attained a level of industrialization and modernization comparable to Western Europe and North America, a conflict between rival authorities has begun in which the party and the ideological textbooks are challenged to redefine their functions within the system. Authority faces the task of restructuring itself for the task of system-management. In the process, we can expect national differences to become more apparent, so that each communist system may have to solve this task of restructuring for itself and in its own fashion. Given this process of differentiation, it may become more and more difficult to make valid generalizations about all communist systems. In that case, the peculiarities of communism may turn out to be confined to the system-building phase.

5. Heroic Leadership:
The Case of Modern France

STANLEY HOFFMANN

On the Study of Political Leadership

The study of political leadership has been the orphan of contemporary political science. Empirical studies of political life have focused on the behavior of groups rather than on the statecraft of the leaders; efforts at theory have produced a glut of typologies and models of political systems, often at a level of abstraction that squeezes out the role and impact of political leaders. Only political philosophy has continued to be concerned with the phenomenon of statecraft—under such headings as authority and legitimacy—but all too frequently without sufficient regard for empirical data. It is in the analysis of totalitarian systems and in the realm of what has been called political pathology that political scientists have paid most attention to the scars left by leaders on their countries and on the world. But statecraft is of the essence of all politics. At a time when so many regimes are nothing but a leader writ large, general and abstract frameworks and models run the risk of collapsing like sand castles whenever the leader falls. Whatever the virtues of systems theory, it is no substitute for the empirical analysis of political leadership. Indeed, when so many systems approaches appear to be based on a metaphorical assimilation of the political universe to a physical, cybernetic, or economic model, the study of statecraft may become the last refuge of political analysis.

I should like to present three remarks about the study of political leadership in general and in this chapter in particular.

1. There seem to be two different perspectives for the investigation of leadership. One is the psychological perspective: its focus is on the

Prepared for delivery at the 1966 Annual Meeting of the American Political Science Association, New York City, September 6–10. Copyright 1966 The American Political Science Association.

personality of the leader, whose behavior, beliefs, techniques, and works are studied as expressions of his personality and clues to his character. The other perspective is political: its focus is on statecraft, the way in which the leader conceives of and carries out his role as statesman, his relations with and impact on his followers or opponents. In practice, of course, the distinction often gets blurred. The study of statecraft cannot ignore the personal idiosyncrasies of the leader, especially when—if I may use a metaphor suggested by Robert C. Tucker—the leader is not merely an actor (however great) in a play but the playwright as well. The psychological perspective aims at explaining a personality through the scrutiny of political behavior: the deeds are the clues to the psyche. However, each student of political leadership must make a choice between the two approaches lest he lose any focus whatsoever, for there is inevitably some tension. Each approach pulls the analyst in a different direction: one invites him to elucidate what is always a mystery—the coils and springs of character; the other incites him to illuminate a performance. Although in both cases he examines how leadership roles are selected, defined, and played, in one the main emphasis is on the way in which personality traits shape and are shaped by these roles, and in the other the main emphasis is on the way in which those roles shape and are shaped by the polity.

My own viewpoint is the second for two reasons. One, it is a matter of training. A successful resort to the psychological perspective requires a solid and subtle training in psychology and psychoanalysis. Nothing is more irritating than attempts at playing amateur psychoanalyst: good psychologists are aware of the gaps between personality, social psychology, and political behavior; political scientists insufficiently grounded in psychology and psychoanalysis may leap imprudently over these gaps, thus producing oversimplified political analysis and crude personality studies. Two, even the most competent handling of the psychological perspective has serious drawbacks, given the current state of psychoanalytic and psychological theory. To a large extent, the leader is seen as a man driven by needs, tensions, and forces of which he is only dimly aware, toward beliefs and behavior patterns that will help him meet those needs, cope with those tensions, and appease those forces. Until psychological theory provides us with more satisfying tools, and unless political scientists learn to avoid shortcuts, the psychological approach risks being a seductive rather than productive detour. For it partakes of the fascination of adventure stories: it is the search for the missing clue and the missing link, a search in which everything revealed is treated as a sign of something concealed, and things expressed are deemed the revelation of things repressed. All too often (as in a certain contemporary approach to political philosophy) the fascination of the search induces the searchers to find in everything overt a covert meaning that makes the open record read like an exercise in deception.[1] Such a search is both risky and limited: risky, since we are reduced to hypotheses, endlessly fascinating yet tantalizingly endless; limited, because it tends to neglect the conscious part of statecraft. Leaders, especially great ones, are men who discover and exploit the personality traits and the psychological techniques required for successful statecraft, even if at the outset of their careers they were innocent of the latter and exhibited only latent or minimal aspects of the former. What traits and techniques are needed depends, of course, largely on the political circumstances—another reason for adopting the more directly political perspective, which, I repeat, involves a consideration of character whenever necessary, even if the focus is elsewhere.

2. The comparative study of political leadership will require hypotheses about the most important variables—hypotheses that will allow for the development of typologies, a first step toward theory (in few areas would the proliferation of theories unsupported by empirical evidence, characteristic of much political science, be as ludicrous). In the psychological perspective, we would expect the development of personality models. If the focus is on statecraft, we will have to find a middle ground between two extremes: case studies so descriptive that analysis and comparison would become hopeless and general propositions so "universally valid" they become meaningless. This is necessary because the study of statecraft is the study of interaction between distinctive personalities and distinctive milieux. For comparative purposes the following three variables are of special importance; they are analytically distinct, although in practice they interact continuously.

(*a*) *The style of authority in the society in which the leader operates:* political scientists, following at last the indications of the great sociologists of the past, are beginning to pay sufficient attention to this, and it is the heart of recent studies of political systems and civic cultures. The very resilience of patterns of authority in societies whose social and politcal structures are in flux points to the importance of both the ways and the views about the ways in which decisions are made, individuals and groups cooperate, and conflicts are handled. Since the study of authority patterns and beliefs about authority by political scientists is far from advanced, it is not surprising that the first efforts suffer from "globalism"—an attempt at an overview which neglects significant variations of beliefs and behavior within a given society. In the study of political leadership, one aspect is of special interest: the style of political

---

[1] This is not true of Erik Erikson's work.

authority, that is, relations (and notions about relations) of authority in the political sphere. By this I mean both the political system in the narrow sense (the pattern of power, interests, and policies) and the community at large in its dealings with the political system. Any empirical study of statecraft must investigate the relations between a political leader and the style of political authority in his society: does he express it (cf. Harry Eckstein's notion of congruence[2]), or is he trying to change it and if so from what to what? A typology of styles of political authority is a prerequisite to a typology of political leadership.

(*b*) *The nature of the political system:* (i) the institutional setup, which defines the various leadership roles, sets the limits (flexible or not) within which the leader can operate, shapes the orientations and techniques of his statecraft, provides him with (or deprives him of) various kinds of legal and political power; (ii) political legitimacy, that is, the nature of the "political formula," which consists of the way in which political leaders are selected and how power is distributed among them; and the scope and depth of consent to the political formula, which depends on how the citizens evaluate and appreciate these processes of selection and distribution. Political legitimacy is a notion that ties together the institutional setup and the various elements of what some writers call the political culture—the style of authority, the political opinions, and the social values prevalent in the community at large. A given style of authority, a given consensus among social groups about the structure of society, both rule out and are compatible with a variety of political systems; a political system, in order to be legitimate, must not only be congruent with the style of authority and based on a consensus about the social order but must express a consensus about the polity as well. A distinction that comes to mind immediately is that which exists between political leaders who operate within legitimate political systems and political leaders who do not, who come to power when the previous political system has broken down or who destroy it once in power.[3] Within each category there are other obvious distinctions: in the first group, depending on the type of political system; in the second group, depending on the kind of institutional setup and political formula the leader imposes or shapes after the breakdown.

(*c*) *The nature and scope of the taks performed by the leaders.* Here, several important factors intersect: (i) the purposes of the leader, set partly by his own beliefs, dogmas, and hierarchy of values and partly

---

[2] See his *Theory of Stable Democracy*, Princeton University, mimeographed, 1961.

[3] I hesitate to call them "illegitimate leaders," since they may possess or develop a legitimacy of their own, or "revolutionary leaders," since the word revolution carries an implication of social purpose which may be misleading.

by the circumstances in which his nation finds itself as he perceives (or misperceives) them; (ii) the economic system, social structure, and the various groups' values, which constitute the givens (yet certainly not the unchangeable givens) of statecraft; (iii) the external situation if we look at the leader's foreign policy. Depending on the question asked, various typologies can be built here. The way in which the leaders define their tasks can provide one spectrum—from pragmatic to dogmatic; the means the leaders use in carrying them out suggests another—from moderate to violent. If the question is that of the scope of the tasks undertaken, one may want to place leaders along a spectrum, from "single issue" to "the total system" (domestic and international). If one is concerned with social change, one can classify political leaders as reactionary, conservative, reformist, or revolutionary; if one is interested in the relation of the nation to the world at large, a different set of categories can be devised, etc.

I am well aware of the rudimentary character of these remarks; yet they may have at least one (negative) virtue. They suggest that the most fruitful way of studying political leadership may not be to distinguish between leadership in industrialized societies and leadership in "developing" countries. The style of authority in a given society has a way of being partly independent of the social and economic structure of that society: patterns that have been forged during a preindustrial phase live on, and indeed shape, in turn, the pattern of industrialization. The relative autonomy of politics owes a great deal to the autonomy of authority relations and to the fact that institutional arrangements and the legitimacy (or lack thereof) of a political system are the products of political forces and beliefs related to, but only partly dependent on, the economic and social systems. We all know that industrialized societies at comparable levels of development display a bewildering variety of political regimes. The same is true of the underdeveloped countries. Finally, industrialization certainly affects the tasks of statesmen, but in industrialized societies there are entire ranges of issues whose connection with the modern economy is tenuous or indirect; the ways that the economy is managed and the social groups characteristic of industrial society share its burdens and benefits are as varied as the political regimes. With underdeveloped countries it is absurd to assume either that "modernization" is the overriding, necessary concern of all political leaders or that the techniques of "political development" are so clear-cut and predetermined that they force statecraft into a necessarily small number of distinct molds. The political implications of the construct, "industrial society," or of the process, "modernization," are very few if we think of the necessary consequences, and infinitely varied if we think of the possible concomitants.

3. This chapter presents merely a few suggestions for the study of political leadership in one country—France. I am no foe of comparative undertakings, and I realize that the problem of comparison becomes hopeless when the scholar is faced with empirical studies that celebrate the uniqueness of each experience. But a confrontation of phenomena artificially made comparable by conversion into a common language that conceals essential differences is of little value. The approach that may prove most fruitful consists of accumulating empirical data that will provide not mere description but an analysis of the essential features of political leadership at given times and places. Such studies will, of necessity, focus on what appears "distinctive" (a word not synonymous with unique) at the time and place under scrutiny. But if the questions asked are of general interest for any study of political leadership, if the variables examined are significant for most investigations of statecraft, subsequent comparisons will have been made both possible and meaningful, and often, indeed, what appeared distinctive at an early stage of the scholarly process will be seen later on as characteristic of a much broader category of phenomena. It is therefore quite possible that the hypotheses presented here about political leadership in France are no more peculiar to France than, say, the behavior of parliamentarians analyzed by Nathan Leites is "peculiarly French."[4] But this will have to be determined at a later, more inclusive stage of analysis—and that more general stage cannot be validly reached through any shortcut.

The world "heroic" was suggested to me by the editor of this book, probably to avoid the heady, if largely sterile, discussions provoked by the word "charismatic." "Heroism" is a relative notion: a man who is a hero to my neighbor may be a calamity to me. Maybe it would have been preferable to speak about crisis leadership in France—the point being that whereas there are frequent crises which produce leaders whose behavior will be discussed here, not every crisis leader acts on a heroic scale. However, in some French emergencies the crisis leader makes no pretense of being unusual. What concerns us here are those crisis leaders who either see themselves or are seen by the public as different from the norm—whether their ultimate accomplishments vindicate those expectations or not. Specifically, I will concentrate on three figures and assume for brevity's sake that their exploits as well as the context in which they had to operate are familiar: Marshal Pétain, Pierre Mendès-France, and

[4] See *On the Political Game in France,* Stanford, Cal., Stanford University Press, 1959.

Charles de Gaulle. I will, in the next section, present a very *general framework* for the analysis of their statecraft. The nature, functions, and limits of French crisis leaders can best be understood by reference to the style of authority prevalent in French society in general, and in the French polity in particular, as well as by reference to the political system whose crisis brings forth the heroic leaders. In the following two sections I will put some flesh on those bones; first I will describe with more detail the *style* of "heroic" leaders, how they conceive of, establish, and maintain their authority; then I will discuss the *substance* of their statecraft: the kinds of tasks undertaken by them, and their performance in carrying out those tasks.

Heroic Leadership in France: A Framework

The French Style of Authority

The general framework is provided by recent studies of the French style of authority: here the pioneer is Michel Crozier,[5] whose extraordinarily rich and provocative work offers a sweeping interpretation of authority relations in France's bureaucracy, industrial organization, education, and political system, both in their structural aspects (how are such relations arranged) and in their cultural aspects (what are the values served by those arrangements). Major contributions have also been made by two other sociologists, Jesse R. Pitts and Laurence Wylie. Elsewhere I have tried to use their findings for the purpose of political analysis.[6] Philip Williams has also applied them in his masterpiece on the Fourth Republic.[7] Our common debt to Tocqueville need hardly be stressed.

Crozier's model is that of a system of authority relations in which each stratum, as he calls it, is isolated from other strata and governed by impersonal rules decreed by a superior authority entitled to set such rules but severely limited in its scope and means. Within each stratum there is a fierce insistence on equality which the impersonality of the rules guarantees. The joint activities of the members of the stratum are primarily negative, that is, aimed at preventing two kinds of encroachments: from outside, to protect the stratum against excessive or arbitrary acts of

---

[5] *The Bureaucratic Phenomenon*, Chicago, Ill., University of Chicago Press, 1964.

[6] In S. Hoffmann, C. P. Kindleberger, L. Wylie, J. R. Pitts, J. B. Duroselle, F. Goguel, *In Search of France*, Cambridge, Mass., Harvard University Press, 1963. See also L. Wylie, *Village in the Vaucluse*, Cambridge, Mass., Harvard University Press, 1957; and Pitts' review of Crozier in *Analyse et prévision*, SEDEIS, I (1966), 51 ff.

[7] *Crisis and Compromise*, Hamden, 1964.

external authorities; and from inside, to deny any members the possibility of taking over the leadership of the group. Such a structure of authority relations results in a society both centralized and hierarchical; centralized, since decisions are referred to higher echelons; hierarchical, since every stratum is concerned with and dedicated to the preservation of its own peculiar rank and status. Yet centralization goes along with the strict limitations of the superior's rule-making power, constantly held in check by the ruled, and within each rank there is a fierce resistance to privilege and inequality. The values served by such an arrangement are, first, what Crozier has called *"l'horreur du face-à-face"*: a dislike for the form of freedom known as participation (but also for the *face-à-face* of totalitarianism, which abolishes all freedom and turns all life into public life), a preference for independence, for as broad as possible a sphere of uninvaded private thought and action. The defense of this sphere provides the main, and almost the only excuse for occasional joint action; the perpetuation of this sphere is assured by the paucity of communications between categories as well as the combination of decision-making from above and restraints on the decision-makers' sphere of action. Another value served is what one might call a preference for homeorhetic change.[8] The word *homeostasis* implies a return to the *status quo ante* after each crisis is over; it does not apply to the French case, which is not that of a stagnant society. The word *homeorhesis* implies both the acceptance of change and the return to equilibrium after change; it therefore fits better the French polity, for there is here a pervasive dislike for the kind of change that would disturb the existing hierarchy of ranks and statuses and the existing leveling within each stratum, there is a willingness to tolerate instead either the status quo or, should it prove untenable and provoke excessive strains, the kind of change that affects the whole society yet preserves the delicate harmony of hierarchy with equalitarianism.

The origins of this extraordinary set of arrangements and values are preindustrial, a blend of feudal remnants and rebellion against feudalism. They have worked as a corset within which French industrialization has been forced and contorted. Modern France, from the Revolution to World War Two, was the product of the perfect blend of the style summarized above and a socioeconomic system which slowed down industrialization and preserved a peculiar "balance"; this blend produced what I call the stalemate society. As Crozier has shown, the French style of authority produces an alternation of routine and crisis. The absence of face-to-face relations, the distance between strata, the conception of a

[8] See C. H. Waddington, "The Desire for Material Progress as a World Ordering System," *Daedalus* (Spring, 1966), 667.

higher authority both unsharing and bound by impersonal rules condemn such authority to a mixture of abstraction and rigidity. In ordinary circumstances, the disadvantages are reduced by informal "parallel," behind-the-counter relations that violate the sacrosanct equality within each stratum and fill the gap between above and below, but this is at best a palliative, especially since the violation is covert, the link suspect. The resistance of the subordinates to their superiors and the superiors' inability to innovate result in short-circuits, that is, crises during which the normal rules of the game are suspended and changes are introduced .

Thanks to Michel Crozier, we have a convincing model of routine authority as well as change. But the model of crisis authority is barely sketched. Just as routine authority is a most peculiar mix of opposites (hierarchy and equality, dependence on and distrust of superior authority), crisis authority is a blend of extremes. On the one hand, it represents the collapse of the norm, both in a substantive sense, for it constitutes a global injection of change in a previously immobile system, and in a procedural sense, for it corresponds to a collapse of the "delicate balance of terror" which exists in routine authority relations: a sudden willingness of the strata to find a way out of crisis, a relief from stress, in a blank check to a superior who is no longer bound by the restraints and bullied by the resistance of the defensive strata. Crisis authority is a sudden reassertion of personal authority compared with the impersonal authority of routine periods—one might almost say a reassertion of aristocratic values opposed to the anti-aristocratic values of distrust and drive for impersonality.

On the other hand, crisis authority performs a *function for* the system rather than a *change of* system. In part, the way in which change is thereby introduced is often still in conformity with the basic values of France's style of authority: the avoidance of face-to-face relations and the preference for homeorhetic change, as if the authorities to whom power had been given by and for the crisis understood exactly the nature, conditions, and limits of the power delegated. In part, the structure and values of French authority relations are so firm that a crisis leader's attempt to change the style of authority away from the model described by Crozier or to produce nonhomeorhetic social change would end in fiasco. Thus crisis leadership in France has two faces. There is the cataclysmic side, which sets off French heroic leadership from crisis leadership in, say, the United States or Britain, for in those two countries the crisis is usually just a particularly strong challenge that can be handled by the normal procedures of authority, whereas in France those procedures are suspended, and crisis leadership takes on the aspects not only of a response to the challenge but of a revenge against the normal procedures.

And there is the functional side, which sets off French heroic leadership from the leadership of totalitarian countries, for next to that aspect of a revenge, there is an aspect of continuity or even complicity. During routine periods, the "parallel relations" (so largely personal) adumbrate (and help avoid) the relations that exist in a crisis: they are the shadow of crisis authority in the impersonal light of routine authority patterns. Even when that shadow takes over, the limits voluntarily observed by or forced upon crisis leaders are a glimmer of, and a promise of return to, that impersonal light in temporary eclipse. A country whose language contains no equivalents for the words statecraft and leadership but has such cold and static abstractions as *le Pouvoir* and *l'Etat* will be tempted to see in grand leadership a kind of heroic exercise in self-expression, a holiday from rules and routine, an exalting spectacle; yet that very distrust of arbitrariness which the vocabulary suggests also reminds the actor of the spectators' determination to stop the show if it should threaten to turn the audience into stage props. Crisis leadership, in order to be effective, must be more than the temporary triumph of the "parallel" procedures that exist normally behind the legal facade: it must avoid arbitrariness and somehow turn the heroic show into the impersonal rules of "total" but harmonious change. Thus the function it performs is double: crisis leadership is both the agent of social change *in* the system, and the preserver *of* the system against the mortal threat of either destruction by immobility or a change of system.

The Style of Political Authority and the Political System

These very general considerations apply, as Crozier has shown, to French political life; the alternation of representative regimes and saviors, which are "techniques of evasion" from a citizens' "participant" culture, represents, in the political sphere, that oscillation from routine to crisis already mentioned.[9] But in order to understand heroic leadership, one has to take into account several specific factors of political life.[10]

First, there are factors distinctive to the *style of political authority*. On the one hand, some of the features analyzed by Crozier in general terms are *accentuated* in the political sphere. The negative and brittle character of associations, their difficulty in cooperating and reaching

---

[9] See Crozier, p. 335 of French edition; and Gabriel Almond and Sidney Verba, *The Civic Culture*, Princeton, N. J., Princeton University Press, 1963.

[10] I am concerned with the style of political authority at the level of *national* politics, for a case can be made to show that in local politics, especially in the small *communes*, what is crisis leadership on the national level is really ordinary leadership, and vice versa—which confirms the point made above about the functionality of crisis leadership.

compromises that do more than confirm their respective statuses, are usual features of French political parties, with the partial exception of the extreme left. Especially true of French parties and interest groups is the tendency of associations to try to obtain what they want by blackmailing higher authority (hence the resort to a frequently "revolutionary" vocabularly that conceals far more limited intentions, yet reveals a general attitude toward change: all or nothing; and toward authority: a mixture of defiance and dependence). The lack of communication between strata, the distance between each stratum and higher authority, are characteristic of a political regime in which the citizens elect representatives who tend to behave as a caste of sovereign *camarades.*

On the other hand, French history and the divergences among Frenchmen concerning political legitimacy have introduced into the style of political authority three features that are *peculiar* to the political sphere. The most obvious is addiction, not merely to revolutionary talk, but to violence (to a degree considerably superior to what could be found even in industrial relations). In other words, the degree of willingness to observe the rules of the game when the results fail to give satisfaction to the claims of the "political strata" is low. Also, the long centralizing efforts of the Old Regime, the work and ideology of the Revolution, and the mistakes made by the post-1815 monarchies injected into the whole political sphere a kind of equalitarianism different from that analyzed by Crozier (unless one assimilates the whole citizenry to one of Crozier's "strata"). He is concerned only with equality within each stratum (otherwise determined to preserve its rank privileges). Authority patterns in the political sphere are distinguished by "national equalitarianism," that is, the insistence by the bulk of the population on, and the somewhat grudging acceptance by superior authority of the dogma of equality before the law, irrespective of social privileges (including, at an early stage, universal suffrage); hence the existence of *"Le Peuple,"* by which I do not mean the "presence" of the people as participating citizens in a democratic civic culture, but one important implication of universal suffrage, even for those elites and leaders fundamentally hostile to what Tocqueville called democracy: the impossibility of acting in the political sphere as if the various strata were completely isolated from each other and political decisions involved only certain select groups of society (hence a plebiscitarian component even in the most antipopular movements). The third feature is a nostalgia for unanimity and consensus—a by-product of such equalitarianism, a reaction against the curse of violence.

All those traits point in the same direction: the fragility of "routine authority." Challenged, pressured, milked, squeezed, summoned by groups that provide more stress than support, more resistance than services; surrounded by citizens used to violence, distrustful of privileges for the neighbor, yet reluctant or unable to handle their own problems; torn between widespread expectations of over-all equalitarianism and unanimity that make the constant resort to "parallel relations" highly illegitimate, and demands for particularized protection and special favors that make such resort indispensable, "routine authority" is bound to exhibit the features of excessive abstraction, unimaginativeness, distance, and sclerosis to a peculiarly large degree. In other words, the "revenge" aspect of heroic leadership is bound to be especially important. "Throughout French political history . . . there have been two 'tempers' which may be called Jacobin and Girondin: each can be found at the same time or in rapid succession in every sector of French opinion. It was the Jacobin temper which the parliamentary game left out."[11]

Second, one must take into account the *nature of the political system* itself. If we limit ourselves to the two parliamentary Republics, we can fill in the framework provided by the style of authority in the following fashion. Certain features reenforce the conclusions derived from the study of the style of political authority. The institutional setup endowed "routine authority" with a kind of anemia that goes far beyond the general weakness of such authority in Crozier's model. The number and the nature of the parties—shaped either for the mere occupation of power or for perfectly sterile opposition—the deliberative rather than representative role of a Parliament concerned with general principles rather than reform, the impotence of the cabinets, permanent stakes and frequent victims of the "game," the need to govern *au Centre* almost all the time, the multiplicity of brakes and the absence of a motor gave to "routine authority" the aspect almost of a caricature of Crozier's model. The structure of the two Republics allows one to present what the French would call a *portrait-robot* of the kind of leader who would succeed best in a system of that sort. One could christen him the nondirective leader, or the perfect broker, and compare him usefully not to executive leaders in other political systems, but to successful legislative leaders in a highly decentralized assembly such as the United States Senate. What is required is a certain indifference to policy outcomes, a tight resignation to letting events impose decisions that can then be "sold" as inevitable, instead of risking trouble by suggesting decisions which anticipate events, a Byzantine respect for ritual, inexhaustible patience for bargaining with a wide variety of groups, scrupulous observance of the dogma of equality among members of the parliamentary stratum, and of the sacrosanct

[11] *In Search of France,* p. 18.

distance between it and the electorate (that is, no appeal to the people above the heads of the parliamentarians)—in other words, a willingness to isolate oneself and one's leadership within the confines of the "House without windows" to make sure that, should one be overthrown once, one would nevertheless not be ostracized later—and, finally, the art of manipulating the "parallel relations," having in one's hand the cards represented by the key men who, behind the facade of impersonal equality, nevertheless possess the levers of influence. Smoothness, unobtrusiveness, procedural self-effacing skill, flexibility, what the French call *astuce*—a somewhat subdued brand of cleverness—these are the functional requirements of "routine authority": we recognize men like Chautemps, Queuille, Edgar Faure (until he asserted himself and dissolved the Assembly in 1955) and even Briand or Blum.

On the contrary, the institutional setup and the political formula, which were accepted by the bulk of the population, also presented features that gave to such authority a resilience which distorted the alternation of routine and crisis periods described by Crozier. Routine authority, despite its tendency toward paralysis, nevertheless functioned for a variety of reasons. The two parliamentary Republics showed a remarkable aptitude for self-preservation. The colorful deadlock of Parliaments and cabinets should not make one forget either the essential role of the bureaucracy, grinding out impersonal rules while at a distance from the public and also taking part in the game of parallel relations, or the nature of the consensus on which the Republics rested. There was, among social groups and political forces, a broad consensus for a limited state, congruent with the style of authority; now, *in most circumstances* the combination of a career bureaucracy and of a parliamentary system more adept at checking than at moving that bureaucracy corresponded exactly to what was desired. Legitimacy was conditional, in the sense that for most of those groups and forces the regime was acceptable as long as its activities left intact their sphere of independence while settling conflicts to their satisfaction. But the setup was such that this was precisely what happened most of the time. The political formula produced a political class diversified enough to appease the kind of equalitarianism characteristic of the political sphere; the setup admirably divorced equalitarianism from social reform and thus pleased most groups and parties, at the same time condemning the groups and parties that wanted change to play the "homeorhetic" game, that is, to ask for all or nothing (thus usually playing into the hands of those who wanted nothing). As a result, the political system was pervaded with a sense of legitimacy which disappeared only in major crises, those in which the conditions for legitimacy ceased to be met.

Moreover, in certain kinds of emergencies the system was quite capable of injecting for a while into "routine authority" a certain amount of efficiency. In conformity with the style of authority, this temporary closing of the ranks was essentially defensive: the Republic managed to defend itself against outside attacks, that is, against outside authorities that threatened the regime. Two kinds of techniques were used. One was attrition: attracting the enemy into the game—into Parliament—where he would spend and waste his energies and his means of action; this was gentle strangulation, and it worked against most antiparliamentary movements. The other technique was used both against such movements and also when the threat was constituted either by a foreign power or by a domestic force of subversion that operated outside the political sphere. Then the factions would agree to back a trusted parliamentarian and—again in conformity with the style of authority—burden him with the responsibility of eliminating the threat: Waldeck-Rousseau, Clemenceau, Poincaré, Doumergue, Daladier, Mollet received such temporary delegations of effectiveness.

Finally, when less extraordinary threats or strains, instead of being resolved by the political system, resulted in deadlocks among the parliamentarians, hence—given the rules of the game—in the fall of the cabinet, the system resorted to a mechanism of considerable interest, well analyzed by Williams: the cabinet crisis. It can be described as part and parcel of "routine authority," insofar as it aimed at and usually succeeded in avoiding the switch to crisis leadership, followed ritual rules which reflected the structure of the parliamentary game, and resulted in frustrating foes and defusing threats rather than giving a new impulse to society. Yet the cabinet crisis also played the role of a small change of crisis leadership, insofar as it resulted in a (temporary) resolution of the deadlock and achieved this resolution largely through "parallel relations."

Heroic Leadership: A General View

I seem to have derailed from the track of heroic leadership onto the sidetrack of routine authority. However, my point is that heroic leadership in France can only be understood by reference to its counterpart. The nature, resilience, and deep roots of routine authority explain in particular the following propositions.

1. Within the parliamentary regime there was occasional room for limited executive authority, as long as its temporary trustee respected the style and rituals of parliamentarism. But any attempt at acting in the style of heroic leadership within the confines of the regime was bound to fail: heroic leadership within would be stifled, and consequently such

leadership, if it wanted to succeed, could unfold only when the formal procedures had collapsed altogether. In the earlier period of the Third Republic, the depressing fate of Gambetta had been edifying enough. In the twentieth century, the parliamentarians' resentment of Clemenceau's wartime style was again edifyingly effective as soon as peace returned. More recently, nothing has been more enlightening than the fate of Mendès-France's premiership, unless it is what happened to de Gaulle's and Mendès' attempts at combining the style of heroic leadership with opposition to and within the Republic: both the RPF and the Radical party were turned from vehicles for their leaders' return to power into characteristically splintering and fiercely negative organizations, leading a short, nasty, and brutish life of internal excommunications and external obstreperousness, torn between job-seekers ready for absorption in the "system" and hyperbolic champions of *la politique du pire*, and reduced to proving their existence through their capacity to destroy.

2. The tension between routine and crisis authority is greater in the political sphere than in the rest of French society. The resilience of routine political authority explains why the resort to a different kind of leadership is postponed until a situation arises which breeds something like a national sense of emergency, a conviction that there is no other alternative. This, and the peculiar weakness of normal leadership, in turn explain why heroic leadership is met by chiliastic hopes which facilitate change. It is worth noting that the emergency of 1940, the greatest in modern French history, engendered not just one but two rival heroic leaders. Such an atmosphere and such hopes entail a kind of violently emotional repudiation of routine authority. On the other hand, this very repudiation of a political system and style that had offered a broad legitimacy condemns the heroic leader to a perpetual quest for a legitimacy of his own and locks him into the prison of his uniqueness.

3. Insofar as the defunct political system merely exaggerated features that resulted wholly from the national style of authority, from the desires of the "consensus groups" in society and the wishes of most political forces, heroic leadership, although free from the special limits imposed upon routine leadership by the "games, poisons and delights of the system," still collides with the limits on leadership that are inherent to that style, those desires, and those wishes.

If we try, briefly, to define the relations between French heroic leadership and two of the variables suggested earlier, the style of authority and the political system, we come to the notion of the vicious circle of French heroic leadership. Heroic leadership perpetuates the style and preserves within the political system the tension between two extreme types of authority which fight yet need each other.

Heroic leadership's relation to the style of authority literally comes out of the pattern just described, and it fits into it. Heroic leadership is the statecraft of an "outsider" who cleans Augeas' stables in such a way that Augeas does not have to do what he hates above all—getting involved, alienating what he considers his right to privacy, to independence, to (vigilant) absence. Heroic leadership comes in when change cannot be delayed any longer, that is, when there is a widely felt need for direction from above. But what such leadership provides is direction without mobilization, and the led respond with support without participation: the unwritten contract of French patterns of authority is respected, the bonds and trust of democracy *à l'anglo-saxonne* and the bondage and terror of totalitarianism are avoided. Heroic leadership is indeed a *spectacle*—the leader, an outsider who breaks in when the routine has broken down and the rituals have crumbled, has the double prestige of rebellion and prowess: he is the man who reasserts individual exploits after and against the impersonal, anonymous greyness of routine authority.

Yet the spectacle itself is part of the whole drama of French authority, for the leader's act is performed in a way that perpetuates nonparticipation—both because of his own way of turning the show into a monologue addressed to the whole people, instead of channeling the structured participation of his supporters either in totalitarian or in democratic "face-to-face" organizations, and because his insolent "personal power" confirms his adversaries in their own purely *negative* associations and in their distrust of strong leadership. As Pitts has incisively suggested, "prowess is created by the recognition of the spectator as much as by the actions of the hero";[12] equality—that constant value—is preserved, since the hero addresses himself to all the spectators indiscriminately; independence—the ultimate desire—is preserved, since prowess is a mode of "seduction," not of participation: heroic leadership is a thing to be admired (passively) or imitated (individually), it perpetuates *la peur du face-à-face*. De Gaulle did not try to organize a political force of his own until after his resignation in 1946 (and even then he called it a Rally, not a party); and Mendès-France's battle to gain control of the Radical party began only after he had been overthrown in February 1955.

On the surface it looks as if each heroic leader, although incapable of breaking the vicious circle of distance and noninvolvement, should at least be capable of violating the other chief value—the preference for homeorhetic change—because of the absence of brakes on him. At first sight the authority patterns of heroic leadership are the triumph of *le bon plaisir*, manifest both in the mass (or mock) equalitarianism of the *spectacle* and in the preponderance of the extralegal systems of parallel per-

---

[12] *Ibid.*, p. 243.

sonal relations behind the scenes, where the *decisions* are made. And yet brakes exist, for leadership (like power) is not merely an attribute, it is a relationship. There is no effective leadership without support; in French society, this banal and innocuous statement has extensive implications. Support will be facilitated if the forms of impersonality and the *respect des droits acquis,* i.e. respect for the hierarchy of ranks and statuses, are observed. Here is where the bureaucracy once again comes in: preserver of the trend behind the wild zigzags of the parliamentary fever chart, it is also the regulator and routinizer of heroic leadership. To contrast a representative and an administrative tradition[13] is a debatable way of presenting French political history, for the administrative reality behind the changing political facade is permanent; what varies is the way in which the administration operates: in "representative" periods—which are the routine—it receives some impulses and is submitted to stringent checks from a distrustful and stalemated political class; in "Savior" periods some of the checks are lifted and the impulse is invigorated (yet it always tends to translate itself into general rules). Support will disappear and heroic leadership will be pitifully checkmated if the leader should forget the formidable capacity of opposition of the various "strata" to schemes that promote the "wrong" kind of change: French society dispenses its antidotes to totalitarianism along with its resistance to voluntary participation. This explains why behind the proud facade of rule by fiat and self-inspiration, the heroic leader is often as frustrated as his despised "routine" predecessors, as obliged to coax, bargain, and compromise, to rule by "equivocation, prevarication and slow elimination of every alternative"[14] as the champions of immobilism. The edifying story of Vichy's labor policy, de Gaulle's handling of the Algerian War, the contrast between Vichy's official views of industry and the actions undertaken, the dismissal by the Fifth Republic of most of the reformist suggestions made by the Rueff-Armand Committee, the nature of educational reform in the Fifth Republic, the episode of the miners' strike in 1963 are cases in point. Heroic leadership likes to cloak itself in de Gaulle's stentorian phrase: *le pouvoir ne recule pas.* As a witty critic put it, reality is different: *le pouvoir ne recule pas, il circule.*

This impression of a vicious circle is reenforced if one turns to the relations between heroic leadership and the political system. The drama of French heroic leadership lies in its symbiotic relation to the very kind of political system it denounces—like the two mortal foes handcuffed to each other in the agony of Death Valley, in Stroheim's classic *Greed.*

[13] See Nicholas Wahl, in *Patterns of Government,* Samuel Beer and Adam Ulam, eds., New York, Random House, 1958.

[14] Williams, *op. cit.,* p. 443.

This drama takes the form of a quest for legitimacy. First, there is something significant in the determination of both Pétain and de Gaulle to be properly christened by the two Republics they were determined to lay to rest—and in the willingness of the wretched parliamentarians to sprinkle the christening waters over their assassins' brows. The parliamentarians endorsed charisma both because they sought to remind the heroic leaders of their limits by preserving "the silken thread of legality,"[15] and because they saw in these leaders a protection against would-be leaders who would have been less respectful of the French way of authority: the heralds of a single party on the Nazi model, in July 1940, and the paratroopers in May 1958. Regarding the heroic leaders, their insistence on receiving a proper delegation was, *nolens volens,* a recognition of the essential legitimacy of the fallen regimes—as if the new legitimacy each of those leaders was trying to obtain from the direct verdict of the nation would not be complete without legality, that is, the endorsement of the previous regime. Even the de Gaulle of the Resistance years, eager though he was to make a clean break with the fallen Republic, ended by reviving the Republic's parties in order to gain a full measure of internal and international legitimacy.

Second, and more important, the new regime established by the heroic leader remains plagued by the basically uninstitutionalizable character of heroic leadership. It is hard to overcome the contradiction between regular leadership and heroic leadership, since heroic leadership assumes the meteoric form of a man who comes from the depths of history to give a solo performance of patriotic prowess—and insures by his acts that regular leadership after him may well, in reaction against him, not be leadership at all. Both the Vichy regime and the Fifth Republic (the latter despite a flock of referendums) are marked by a permanent worry about legitimacy: neither the endorsement of the previous regime nor the plebiscites of the crowds seem to suffice. Both Pétain and de Gaulle have tried to find roots and solace in two arguments, yet both arguments underline the fragility of the construct. One is the "historical" legitimacy of the leader, derived from his past deeds, the other is the services rendered by the new regime itself—in other words, legitimacy is once again conditional.

Next to the problem of legitimacy, there is that of transition: of moving back from heroism to routine. Significantly, by 1943, the old Pétain, having reached the end of the frayed rope that tightened around his neck, wanted to give it back to the very Parliament that had blessed him and which he had disgraced. De Gaulle's first exercise of power ended in his

---

[15] Raymond Aron, *Democratie et totalitarisme*, Paris, Gallimard, 1965.

resignation and in a total restoration of the "routine" political system. In his second regime, of course, he has tried to build a monument that would preclude any such return to the old routine, especially through the procedure of popular election for the President; yet whether his system will do this or turn out to be a mere facade behind which a new restoration will triumph is far from clear. For the Fifth Republic to become the kind of regime that would mark a revolution in French political authority and institutions—a departure from the traditional pattern— what is required is something like the realization of Gaston Defferre's conception (largely inspired by men such as Crozier): the President would have to be the leader of a majority party or a majority coalition, thus bringing to an end the oscillation from a splintered parliamentary regime to a savior. But the prerequisite is an end to splintering, and Defferre's own fiasco suggests that France is still far from it. De Gaulle's conception is simple, fierce, and self-fulfilling: since French parties are hopelessly splintered and condemned to behaving like intensely jealous and negative "delinquent peer groups," the President must be "the nation's man." This would not really mean the end of this kind of oscillation, but it would institutionalize the savior. The trouble is that treating the parties as delinquents contributes to keeping them just that—negative associations concerned with winning power and excluding others from it—in a regime whose parliamentary features provide enough chances for deadlock to justify one's fear of either an "escalation" into dictatorship (once more heroic leadership outside of the ordinary rules of the game) or a return to routine impotence. If the parties remain unreformed, if finding a "nation's man" at regular intervals proves impossible (the notion of criteria for charisma is somewhat elusive!), all the gimmicks of the Constitution may prove useless to prevent the Presidency from fading back into the blurred blandness of Third- and Fourth-Republic Prime Ministers. De Gaulle, who in 1962 saw in the popular election of the President the sure deterrent of such a decline, in December 1965 proclaimed almost with desperation that Constitutions are mere "envelopes" and that the state of the parties made of him, de Gaulle, a continuing "national necessity." But the heroic leader cannot be made immortal as a substitute for impossible institutionalization.

Yet the problem of return to normalcy is, for the first time, less than tragic. The two Napoleons ended in national disaster, Pétain in the horrors of insurrection and invasion, whereas for reasons to be analyzed de Gaulle's regime has a chance of breaking out of the vicious circle. However, the difficulty remains evident: heroic leadership in France is too connected with the cataclysmic sense of emergency and with the notion of "total" (yet orderly and harmonious) transformation to handle easily and well a process of gradual evolution. Napoleon III tried—by a gliding descent into parliamentarism—and failed. Almost by definition, a *Gaullisme des tempêtes* looks better than a *Gaullisme de croisière*. Turning heroic leadership into a genuine and lasting political system appears as arduous as fitting such leadership into "routine" political procedures.

The Style of Heroic Leadership

The preceding remarks provide a very rough indication of the style (and dilemmas) of heroic leadership. In this section, I want to sketch with more detail some of the main features of the style.

Origins of the Leader

The heroic leader is, with reference to "routine authority," the outsider in two significant ways. He tends to be a man who has not played the game, either because he has had little contact with the political arena (an indispensable quality when the crisis that brings him to power amounts to the collapse, and not merely the stalemate of the regular regime) or, if he has been in it, because he has shown impatience with the rituals and the rules. He thus stands in contrast to a Franklin D. Roosevelt or even a Churchill. Pétain and de Gaulle fit, of course, the first category: although both had had governmental experience before June 1940, this experience merely heightened their sense of power and their distaste for the crippling conditions imposed by the Republic on the exercise of power. The second category includes Clemenceau, who was called to head the war government of 1917 precisely because he had the qualities that had made him obnoxious to his colleagues in peacetime, and Mendès-France, who had been a sharp and intransigent, if loyal, censor of the Fourth Republic until the Dien-Bien-Phu emergency brought him to power.

Moreover, the heroic leader is a man who has been a rebel against the prevalent order of things or the prevalent ideas. In other words, when those ideas are found or proven bankrupt and that order breaks down, he has the kind of prestige that fits best with French notions of authority, the prestige that comes from defiance, from nonconformity, from not having participated (in the errors of the evil way). The heroic leader is a man whose personality and behavior have shown that he has in him the necessary ingredients of such leadership: he has maintained his independence from superior authority, he has said no, he has been right when such authority was wrong, and he usually suffered for it, either through setbacks to his career or through temporary withdrawals from the public scene.[16]

And yet (here we find again the other side of occasional French willingness to lift customary restraints on leadership) there is a difference between "outness" and adventure, defiance and nihilism, being outside routine authority and being outside the over-all pattern of French authority. One turns to heroic leadership when there is no "normal" alternative; but the selection of the hero is not haphazard. Clemenceau had been in the wilderness through much of his career, yet he was a former Prime Minister and tested leader. Mendès-France had resigned with *éclat* from de Gaulle's cabinet in 1945 and mercilessly denounced the colonial and economic policies of de Gaulle's successors, yet he was in many ways a devoted servant of the parliamentary republic and of the Radical party. Pétain's military career before 1914 had suffered from his advocacy of a defensive strategy at a time when the high command was wedded to the offensive, but he had become one of the military glories, a minister and ambassador of the Republic. De Gaulle's career had known rough days for reasons inversely symmetrical to Pétain's, yet he too had tried to gain influence through the ordinary channels, not in plots against them. True, the temporary two-star general of 1940 literally stepped out of France's institutions and exerted a brand of heroic leadership pure, unbound, and self-made that is almost unique in French history; but his success in rallying the Free French and the Resistance around himself was due not just to his character and his statecraft: the rebel hero was not *n'importe qui*, he had served (however briefly) in the cabinet and had had a distinguished (if difficult) career. He was admirable, but he was also respectable. May one suggest a rapprochement between the willingness to endorse and applaud rebellion when the rebel appears not only vindicated but in other ways "notable," and the tolerance of adolescent rebellion because one knows it to be a prelude to conformity?

Beliefs

With respect to the heroic leaders' beliefs, we find some interesting common features which contrast with those of the "routine leaders" mentioned before. First, we find areas of unshakable dogmatism: a conviction of possessing a certain number of truths whose prevalence is the condition of France's salvation and the purpose of heroic leadership. Indeed, it would be worth scrutinizing the words of the three leaders for references to perdition and salvation and for expressions of a therapeutic approach to leadership, France being the beloved patient badly treated by

[16] Cf. Pétain's slow promotion before 1914, Mendes' withdrawal in 1945, de Gaulle's in 1946 and again in 1955.

puny leaders but at last to be cured by a doctor who knows exactly what is wrong with the patient and what is to be done. To be sure, each leader had his own dogmas, and each one proved capable (or had to show himself capable) of flexibility in action. Yet Pétain's austere doctrine of authoritarian regeneration through suffering and the restoration of rural values, de Gaulle's doctrine of the strong state, above factions, engaged in a permanent struggle for greatness on the world scene, Mendès-France's dogma of the primacy of economics, all contrast with the skepticism of many parliamentary Premiers as well as with the willingness of many who held principles and ideals to set them aside when in power (often with a heavy rationalization of why they had to do so).

Second, in part because of their previous experience of having been right and unrecognized, the heroic leaders' self-perception is a peculiar blend of self-orientation and identification with a cause. Self-orientation is not exactly limited to the heroic leaders—French politicians' capacity to project their personality onto the center of the stage and to discuss issues in terms of the issues' impact on their psyches is remarkable. But there is a difference between the narcissism of a Herriot or Blum and the kind of vanity displayed by the three heroic leaders. Theirs was not narcissistic but active and self-transcending, for each one saw himself as the carrier of a message greater than himself. Mendès-France, the least vain of the three, had a serene confidence in his ability; Pétain "gave his person to France in order to alleviate her misery"; de Gaulle has turned himself into a "somewhat fabulous character" whom he discusses in the third person, who is clearly the agent of destiny, and whose moves must always be carefully thought through precisely because they shape France's fate.

Third, this self-perception goes with a coldly or caustically harsh perception of the nonheroes: there is, in all three cases, an undeniable sense of superiority (expressed differently in each case). Mendès-France once confided to the deputies that France had been unlucky in some of her leaders before him. Pétain's treatment of his foes, his indifference to the personal fate of his followers, his obvious lack of sympathy for the individual members of the very elites he was trying to shore up collectively were not just symptoms of that "shipwreck," old age. De Gaulle's way of handling his own followers as instruments or part of the "heavy dough" he has to knead, that attitude of "king in exile" detected by one of his superiors at an early age,[17] the haughtiness which threw ice on the ardor of so many *Résistants* when they met him for the first time need no elaboration. We have here a clue to their personalities: they are nongregari-

[17] See J. R. Tournoux, *Pétain et de Gaulle*, Paris, Plon, 1965, p. 389.

ous men who exhibit in different degrees that melancholy quality so well described by the most self-analytic and gifted of them, de Gaulle: a propensity to solitude in the midst of action as well as in proud and bitter solace once duty has been performed. After all, is it not fitting that heroic leadership, because it is a reassertion of leadership, should be exercised by men who are by personality as well as origin distant from the pack?

Behavior

The following references to the leaders' behavior apply primarily to Pétain and de Gaulle. They are less true, or more unevenly true of Mendès-France, largely because he was operating within the constraints of the Fourth Republic; but to the extent to which they apply to him too, they show how far he had gone in trying to distinguish himself from the pattern of routine authority.

The political behavior of the heroic leaders seems, first to display a permanent contradiction. There is, on the one hand, the aspect of revenge often mentioned—the repudiation of and reprisals for the routine pattern and its servants. There is, on the other hand, the nostalgia for unanimity and reconciliation, partly tied to the revenge (since the routine pattern is blamed as divisive and denounced for having left unrepresented the "latent" general will of the French), but partly contradicted by the exclusion of the "old regime" from unanimity. The drive for consensus, however vague, mystical, or personal, is indispensable for the marshalling of support, for, as previously shown, the heroic leaders, who shun the kind of structured support that is provided by the ordinary channels (parties and established interest groups), would be at sea if faced merely with the sullen hostility of the discarded channels. The drive for punishment is, however, also necessary; it gives to the most enthusiastic supporters of the heroic leader a sense of accomplishment (as well as jobs), and it provides the new authority with an argument whenever support flags: "do you want a return to the old mess?" Hence heroic leadership always seems to have two faces: a sectarian one, which reenforces that vicious circle already described, and a Rousseauan one, both elusive and delusive, with the leader in a position comparable to Rousseau's legislator. In Vichy the sectarian face was particularly evident, yet there was a myth of latent unanimity or rather of self-evident reassertion of "natural" community structures hidden but never erased by the now defunct Republican superstructures. De Gaulle's rule offers the most clear-cut case of coexistence of the two faces—the constant flaying of the "parties of the past," and the celebration of the "will of the nation," which they do not represent. It is as if the heroic leader could establish his legitimacy only by getting the consent of the "routine authority," and by convincing himself thereafter that such authority is the abnormal, and he is the norm. Mendès-France could hardly "punish" the political forces that had fought him, yet there was an element of vindictiveness in his relations with the MRP and with right-wing Radicals, and in order to get the indispensable support of the organized channels he too resorted to the myth of unanimity, thus putting popular pressure on a restive assembly.

Second, the heroic leaders tend to behave in a way that constitutes a pointed reversal of routine authority. Even when punishment or revenge is ruled out, the heroic leader acts as the opposite of his ordinary "counterplayer." Thus, whereas the life of the ordinary Premier is absorbed by a kind of pure game of politics—defined almost entirely as a perpetual process populated by professional players—the heroic leader tries to make the public (presumably fed up with such politics) believe that he is not playing politics: they are politicians, he is a statesman (cf. Vichy's official designation as "*l'Etat* français" or de Gaulle's decision upon his arrival in liberated Paris first to "put the State back in its center, which was of course the Ministry of War" before meeting the leaders of the Resistance in the Hotel-de-Ville [18]). Ordinary politics means a method rather than a set of goals, a procedure for making (or avoiding) decisions rather than a net of decisions; therefore the leader who aims at goals and lives for decisions denies that his policies are politics. To a social scientist, politics means difficult choices among values and confrontations of ideas; the heroic leader, even when he proclaims that to govern is to choose, tends to propose to the public *his* choice as a suprapolitical course of action dictated not by necessity, as in the parliamentary style, but by the higher good of the country. De Gaulle's "interest of France," Vichy's "eternal truths," even Mendès-France's technique of *le dossier*—of facts and statistics leading to necessary conclusions by the interplay of evidence and economic science—constitute three very different approaches to "depoliti-zation": in reverse order, an economist's version, a mystical (yet basically right-wing) one, and an astutely political one. Politics also means bargaining and the public banter of horsedeals and barter. The heroic leader tries to maintain a façade of rigorous hostility to such debasing procedures, although a great deal of private trading goes on behind the scenes. Pétain, when the incessant clashes of personal cliques and clans had reached a temporary halt, liked to announce "his" decision in trenchant terms and terse decrees. De Gaulle's disdain for negotiation, his preference for unilateral offers (and vetoes) to which others must adjust and which preserve the appearance of his sovereignty, mark his handling of the Algerian war and of foreign affairs, his transfiguration of bargaining

[18] Speech in Paris, Aug. 20, 1964; in André Passeron, *De Gaulle Parle, 1962–66*, Paris, Fayard, 1966, p. 234.

into "arbitration" marks his handling of domestic ones. Mendès-France, true enough, had to bargain far more than he originally wanted to, and to an increasing extent as his time in office ran out; but it cramped his style and proved the incompatibility between the "system" and heroic leadership.

As one punster has put it, the style of such leadership (often far more than its actual substance) is caesarian—and thus totally opposed to the gentle and often unnoticeable massage administered by ordinary Premiers. Politics, for them, is a French garden of rules and regulations within which they move with caution; the heroic leader, even when he observes the unwritten rules of French authority, refuses to be bound by the "ordinary" rules of the political system. Even Mendès-France, a normal Prime Minister, tried to tell the Assembly that he had his own conception of the Executive, one quite incompatible with the rules of a game that made Premiers the mice of the parliamentary cats. Pétain, to show his dislike of the "old regime," violated outrageously the terms of the delegation he had received from Parliament. De Gaulle, in a way, went even farther, since he has proceeded to a constant reinterpretation of his own Constitution— always in the same direction—reenforcing the President's position, and often in contradiction to the letter and procedures of the text.

Ordinary politics all too often means the demise of responsibility: dismembered and buried by the too numerous occupants of power, repudiated by a temporary leader who had a variety of good reasons for wanting to appear as merely the executor of collective compromises or as the foster parent of "other people's children." The heroic leader seizes responsibility as a sword instead of hiding behind the shield of committee procedures; he deliberately puts the spotlight on his acts and claims personal authorship even for measures actually instituted below him. Sometimes such claims are pathetic as well as a bit repulsive, as with many of Pétain's punitive "decisions," actually initiated by his entourage or forced upon him by German pressures. Sometimes there is an aspect of deliberate and (again) spectacular provocation, as when de Gaulle personally took the responsibility of vetoing Britain's entry into EEC instead of letting Mr. Macmillan's application get lost in the procedural sidestreets at Brussels. The heroic leader tends to thirst for responsibility, just as the routine leader longs for absolution: Pétain's proud statement to his judges and de Gaulle's claim to all the social and economic reforms of the Liberation are cases in point.

Ordinary politics, although confined to the "house without windows," really takes place in a fishbowl, and the ratio of words to deeds is extraordinarily high. Heroic leadership certainly does not shun words, but the flow of explanations and justifications is thinner, and above all such leadership depends to an extraordinary degree on secrecy and surprise. Secrecy and surprise are necessary ingredients of the spectacle, components of prowess, ways of renewing the alertness and applause of a people whose support is needed but whose participation is unwelcome. Moreover, the very obstacles found *below* the political surface, in the resistance of the relevant "strata" to change, oblige the heroic leader to concealment and cunning, for he has to preserve the myth according to which past inefficiency came only from the paralyzing rules of the political game—the myth of heroic omnipotence—and he must be able behind the scenes to conclude the deals and wage the retreats that, if public, would make the Emperor look naked, that is, he must disguise the reality of heroic limitations. Mendès-France's "style" of steeplechase suspense in dealing with Indochina, Tunisia and E.D.C. was both "functional" in the short run and dysfunctional *à la* (rather early) *longue*, in that it infuriated the parliamentarians, who were made to look silly. Because they had to fight heavy odds in extremely constraining situations where candor could have been fatal, both Pétain and de Gaulle have resorted to ambiguity, cunning, and deviousness, often making heroic leadership into the dubious art of deceiving all groups in turn. But when similar constraints confronted "routine" leaders, they could usually not even resort to that black magic: for cunning may well be a resource of the weak, but the parliamentary premiers were too weak even to use this resource; or when they tried it, they were often not able to keep control of events.[19] "Routine authority" can best be characterized either by blustering statements in sad contrast with outcomes ("no German guns pointed at Strasbourg," "Algeria French forever," etc. . . .) or by plaintive confessions of impotence ("we are condemned to live together," "my subordinates did not obey my orders"). Heroic leadership—and this speaks volumes both about the tragic circumstances in which the French turn to it and about the limits within which the hero must operate—can best be characterized either by Mendès-France's month-long self-ultimatum for a Geneva settlement, or by de Gaulle's dazzling first words to the Algerian crowd: *je vous ai compris.*

All these deliberate contrasts, by which heroic leaders seek to differentiate themselves from routine leaders, are part of what I call the vicious circle of heroic leadership. The style of these practices is of the essence of the French style of authority. The heroic leader is the man who decides, above the hagglers, in the general interest. And by such practices, the leader tries to ground his legitimacy in deeds: routine authority was

---

[19] Cf. the sequels of Edgar Faure's devious dealings over Morocco in the summer of 1955—leading to a far more rapid grant of independence than Faure had wished—or of Guy Mollet's Suez operation in 1956.

legitimate because of what it *was;* he will be legitimate because of what he *does.*

The third aspect of the heroic leader's conduct refers to his behavior toward the citizenry as a whole, to the quest for effusive unanimity, not revenge. Here we find one feature, but one only, common to the three statesmen. It is what might be called the constant call to collective prowess. Heroic leadership is both the spectacle of the hero defying the Gods and the mobilization of the spectators' enthusiasm by presenting the hero's performance as a national undertaking. There is, for the rallying of support, a conscious attempt at promoting the identification of the audience with the character on the stage, thus wrapping his legitimacy in their complicity; yet such identification *ipso facto* evades the problem of organizing and channeling support: simply, each citizen is asked to feel like a hero. In Mendès-France's case, the quip reported by Alexander Werth [20] is eloquent enough: that heroic rush after deadlines, those swift successive confrontations with France's enemies and allies, those slayings of the domestic dragons of alcohol and "Malthusianism," *c'était du cinéma;* although it would perhaps be more accurate to switch metaphors: it was like an Olympic race, for there was in the leader's own attitude and in the behavior of his supporters something of the ardor, good humor, and grim earnestness of competitive sports (alas, it turned out to be a 500 yard race, instead of a marathon). In Pétain's antiquarians' dreamhouse, based on the Maurrassian notion that the people had had altogether too much to say in recent French history, there was nevertheless a vigilant effort at rallying enthusiasm both by the tear-jerking display of the old man's self-sacrificing stigmata, and by the beating of drums for the National Revolution, key to France's regeneration: here, the appropriate metaphor (derived from an oddly cheerful song of Maurice Chevalier) is that of the workers who rebuild the fallen house under the guidance of the wise, stern old masterbuilder. In de Gaulle's Republic, although the population is kept in a state of mental and emotional alert by the leader's incomparable sense of personal drama—the well-spaced and well-prepared public announcements, the trips, sublime or familiar, the recurrent crises—there is always an effort to present his acts as the reaching toward and the unfolding of a "great undertaking," a *grande affaire,* a "national ambition," condition of France's role in the world and of France's cure from the national itch of petty in-fighting. Here, the simile most congruent with the General's own self-image (or at least—given the man's complexity—his public version of his self-image) would be that of a modern Moses guiding his flock toward a (very misty) Promised Land.

[20] *Lost Statesman*, New York, Abelard-Schuman, 1958, p. 120.

However, the public conduct of the three men was quite different in various other respects. Mendès-France's style was fascinating because it was a heterogeneous mix between the seemingly inescapable style of French authority reflected in his perception of self and others, and his personal ideal, which is much closer to the model of democratic face-to-face discussions in a "participant political culture." There was a tension between character and convictions: on the one hand, the many himself observed, between him and his aides in particular, the kind of distance that enhances the mystery and sense of fruitful solitude around the dominant personality; his rigor and uncomprising austerity in matters of basic importance to him (such as the fight against the alcohol lobby) projected the image of a confident loner unburdened by friendships and foibles. Yet his very emphasis on *le dossier*, the simplicity of his fireside chats, his plain and flat way of stating the unadorned truth as he saw it, his preference for clear contractual relations between Parliament and Premier—as if the Fourth Republic could be turned into the British political system—pointed toward a very different political style, which his intelligence and democratic convictions admired even as his temper and training were rather unfit for it. The qualities of his temper and training contributed to his popular appeal; but those qualities and the direction of his beliefs contributed to his parliamentary downfall. Whether the citizenry was more moved by his attempt to treat them as rational human beings entitled to a faithful accounting of public affairs by their trustee than by his personality and prowess—and whether the citizenry was at all aware of a tension between the heroic activism of the harried leader and his aspirations to merely effective leadership—is impossible to know.

In the cases of Pétain and de Gaulle, however, no such tension exists. What is remarkable about their style—above and beyond Himalayan differences—is the scope and historical significance of common elements. Mendès-France, whose problem of legitimacy was simplified by the very fact that he was a regular Premier, could be satisfied with (and indeed democratically believed in) the self-evident eloquence of deeds. But Pétain and de Gaulle needed and wanted more. Conditional legitimacy based on achievements past and present is fragile. Hence the attempt at giving it deeper roots by digging, so to speak, into the archetype of the national psyche. Their style of heroic leadership represents a return to the mold or womb of the Old Regime, adapted to modern circumstances, especially to the special features of the style of political authority: a baroque version of a classic style. Here, too, we find a sense of distance between the leader and the led. The two military men, like the Radical politician, were singularly unbending and ungregarious characters. But whereas Mendès struggled somewhat against this sense, Pétain and de Gaulle have cultivated it: Pétain by developing (and letting his sycophants develop) a drooling cult of the idol who was "assuming" France's woes as a sacrificial priest; de Gaulle by following rigorously the precepts so exaltingly laid down in *The Edge of the Sword*. In both cases, there is the same repudiation of familiarity, the cult of separateness from the herd, which reproduces somehow the distance between the subjects and the King. Mendès wanted his popularity to be based merely on respect for things well done, although his precarious position obliged him to try whipping up respect with the drug of drama; Pétain wanted from the French the dependent love and anxious trust of children; and de Gaulle, cynical or contemptuous toward love, prefers consent based less on reason than on awe. Mendès tried to mitigate a sense of personal separateness and the budding personality cult that grew around him by stressing his team. Pétain and de Gaulle have tried to associate personal distance, which removes them from the crowd, with personal dips into the crowd or with personal delegations from the crowd, thus paying homage to the requirement of equalitarianism. But, as in the *bande* described by Pitts, "where all members are equal in their common subordination to the leader," [21] the result of that apparent departure from the lofty practices of the Old Regime merely confirms the purely personal, uninstitutionalized nature of leadership and the abyss between Him and Them: it is paternalism on a grand scale. In a greatly homogenized community with rapid communications, such methods of personal command and contact accentuate the contrast between impersonal administration (including the anonymity of the ministers, *commis* who serve the Leader) and personal responsibility, between impersonal immobility and personal action. They recreate the situation that existed when *le bon peuple* cursed the King's aides, saved its love for the King, and lamented: *si le roi savait*.

The natural habitat of French heroic leadership has always been monarchic: the two Napoleons established Empires; Pétain transferred and transformed his 1917 technique of command by personal presence and appeal into a pseudo-monarchy with the cramped ceremonial of Vichy's *Hotel du Parc* and the pomp of provincial tours, masses in cathedrals, dedications of symbolic trees, pictures of the Leader in every home, school children's letters to and food packages from "le Maréchal." De Gaulle (who inclines toward Louis XIV rather than St. Louis) has the rites of the press conferences, the parades, receptions, and caravans. All of them have cultivated mystery and cunning, in the best imitation of *le secret du roi*.[22] This half-instinctive, half-deliberate recreation of an old

[21] *Op. cit.*, p. 243.

[22] Secrecy—a way of preserving oneself from others' encroachments—is characteristic both of French individuals and of each "stratum." Cf Henry Ehrmann's *Organized Business in France*, Princeton, N. J., Princeton University Press, 1957.

tradition shows once again that heroic leadership has two faces: the repudiation of a certain set of rules, on behalf of personality, and the framing of personal power into a reassuring alternate set of rules. Heroic leadership is original insofar as it accepts, develops, and exploits the plebiscitary implications that were latent in the Old Regime (a regime that was once engaged in a battle against the political power of the feudal elites, just as the heroic leaders battle the political power of "routine authorities"); it is the neglect and dessication of those plebiscitary possibilities which were largely responsible for the Old Regime's decline and overthrow. At the end, the Old Regime had become anti-equalitarian and too impersonal, just as routine Republican authority became too anonymous for crises: the thirst for personal rule, which produced the leadership of a Robespierre and a Napoleon, today breeds personality cults around every potential heroic leader, however unrewarding (Pinay), chilling (de Gaulle), unworthy (Pétain), or reluctant (Mendès) his personality. Certainly, the heroic leaders' approach to *la population* [23] differs from the resolutely antiplebiscitarian "heroic leadership" of the Iberian peninsula. Yet it differs even more from totalitarian concepts of people or *Volk* (which require not just cheering spectators but structured, self-sacrificing slaves) and from the Republican notion of *le peuple* (unfortunately more a myth than an organized force). The heroic leader is neither the *peuple's* son (or rather the bourgeois' son) nor the gang leader or big brother of modern Europe's nightmares. He is a personalized King—without camaraderie or concentration camps.

A clue to the hold of the classical cast is provided by the two leaders' rhetorical style, which would also allow for a fine study of contrast with the far less self-conscious flow of Republican eloquence and with the delirium tremens and ideological gobbledygook of totalitarianism. Pétain (who rarely wrote the first drafts of his speeches) prescribed for himself a code-like simplicity and directness of style that seemed to dismiss all the impurities and excrescences grafted on the French language by the nineteenth and twentieth centuries; stark formulas worthy of medals and frontispieces were his form of eloquence—and, in a highly word-conscious nation, not the least of his appeals. De Gaulle's range is greater; whereas Pétain liked his sentences short and striking, de Gaulle indulges in long and complex phrases as if to display his incredible memory. Yet he too, so much addicted in other respects to Chateaubriand's precept of "leading the French through dreams," uses a style of eloquence closer to Corneille or Retz than Chateaubriand or Hugo: a certain fondness for archaic words, sentences that often seem translated from Latin give an early

---

[23] On *le peuple* vs. *la population*, see Emmanuel D. Astier, *Sept fois sept jours*, Paris, Gallimard, 1961.

seventeenth century flavor to speeches that are (therefore) almost impossible to translate well. The fact that both men were educated by the Jesuits, steeped in classics, and collaborated on literary projects for a while is part of the explanation—but only part: de Gaulle's speeches as a statesman differ in style from his prewar writings; the older he has become, the heavier the classic patina.

However, the Old Regime is very much of the past: although imitative resurrection always finds a response in times of emergency—for the strait jacket state described by Richelieu is the natural refuge from and remedy for intolerable centrifugal forces—it would not suffice to bring solace to the led and support to the leader, even with the full flowering of plebiscitary seeds. The Old Regime, before the "age of the democratic revolution," could afford to be nonideological, and its Kings could be just statesmen (or weaklings surrounded by statesmen). As Louis XVI's brother discovered, there are limits to mere restoration. What modern heroic leadership needs is not only the techniques of undifferentiated unanimity, which are within the realm of means, but also a grandiose sense of purpose. The heroic leader, to use Weber's distinction, must be both statesman and prophet; here his dogmas serve him well, and if his dogmas are too sketchy or too dry, he must somehow wrap them in a vision. The classicism of the statesman must be wedded to a prophetic romanticism. The literary style, to be most effective, should convey all the allusions and associations of France's golden classic age; yet the modern heroic leader must rule by the romantic resonance of his language as well as by the weight of deeds. Even Mendès, the least romantic of men, communicated a vision of economic progress, social change, efficiency, and fraternal "concert" that, in the cesspool climate of 1954, attracted those perpetual seekers after romantic causes, the young and the intellectuals. Even Pétain, flayer of ideology and foe of romantic disorder, tried to be a quaint sort of prophet: the prophet of a return to *"une francité archaïque,"* [24] the reluctant awakener of a romanticism of youth camps, physical fitness, folkloric revival, imperial duty, and agrarian utopia. And what was wartime Gaullism if not the prophecy of resurrection, the romanticism of patriotic exploits, the adventure of the ragged Resistance risking French lives against a formidable foe in order to save French honor, the epic of the unknown leader "too poor to bend," spiting the Allies in order to save France's future? If the second coming of Gaullism has seen a marked prevalence of statecraft over prophecy, the prestige of the *Rex* of 1966 still rests fundamentally on the myth and mystique of the *Dux* of 1940, and de Gaulle's foreign policy remains a remarkable blend

[24] Jean Plumyène, *Pétain*, Paris, Seuil, 1964.

of machiavellian (or rather bismarckian) tactics at the service of a vision sufficiently sweeping and remote to be termed a prophecy. But here we move from style to substance.

The Substance of Heroic Leadership

Whereas our analysis of the style of heroic leadership aimed at elucidating such leadership's relations with the style of authority and the political system, a discussion of substance aims at adding the third variable —the nature and scope of tasks undertaken—as well as at evaluating the leaders' performances in accomplishing those tasks. For convenience's sake, it may be worth dividing these remarks into two categories: external and domestic policy. The importance of external policy in all three cases justifies this division. After all, what brought the heroic leaders to power were three international crises: catastrophe in 1940, defeat in 1954, deadlock in 1958.

The Leader's External Tasks

All three heroic leaders were nationalists, if not in the sense of men for whom the nation is the highest value and the top priority (this is hardly true of Mendès-France), at least in the sense of men for whom the circumstances of the times required that such priority be put on national self-assertion. But there are other, deeper reasons as well. Heroic leadership means prowess; on the world stage, prowess and national self-assertion are twins. Moreover, for Pétain and de Gaulle, the quest for a legitimacy beyond personal deeds led, as we know, to a whole ritual that was inevitably nationalistic, insofar as it sought to remind the nation of its identity, to make its past relevant, and to reassure it of its permanence. Indeed, whether they originally intended to give precedence to foreign affairs or not, heroic leaders tend to find that a world stage of sovereign states provides the opportunities for prowess and national mobilization which the domestic scene often denies.

With respect to such nationalism, all three stand in sharp contrast (once again) with the foreign policy of the Republics, which—at least since the turn of the century—tended to put so much importance on France's alliances that they often interpreted France's national interests only in terms of her main allies' reactions. It has been pointed out most incisively [25] that de Gaulle's grating wartime insistence on national independence reacted against the third Republic's slide into excessive dependence on

[25] Unpublished manuscript by A. W. De Porte, on *de Gaulle in Power, 1964–6.*

British support, which led to national paralysis during the Rhineland crisis and again, for Blum, during the Spanish civil war. Pétain's hostility to England may have had a similar origin. In both cases, one can go back to World War One: Pétain was, in contrast with Foch, most reluctant toward France's allies, and de Gaulle was a war prisoner during the phase that saw France getting increasingly dependent on outside aid. But France's allies were not the only target: even Pétain intended to lock Vichy France in a nationalist insulation that would allow her to emulate post-1806 Prussia, to rebuild her forces, and to play a major role after having preserved her Empire and her fleet—either as a referee in a deadlocked war or as a nonnegligible and nonsubservient associate of a victorious but respectful Germany. As for Mendès-France, his acts in Geneva and Brussels seemed like defiance of the United States and a reversal of two trends which many Frenchmen saw as damaging to French autonomy: overcommitment to hopeless rearguard actions overseas, and to a scheme of European integration too beneficial to an economically stronger Germany. For Mendès-France in 1954 as for Pétain in 1940 domestic reform was the precondition for external success and the safeguard against external *effacement*.

Here the resemblance ends. A separate verdict on Mendès-France's external policy performance makes little sense. In some essential areas he acted as a "liquidator," [26] getting the best possible terms out of impossible situations (Indochina, German rearmament); what he initiated (in North Africa, in relations with Britain) did not have the time to bear fruit in "seven months and seventeen days." The conceptions were sound enough; execution, alas, was a matter of domestic politics, not diplomacy.

As for Pétain, his tragedy was a double one: incapacity to play consistently the role he had assigned to himself and to France, impossibility for the task to be performed: a bad performance of a "dysfunctional role." [27] Even within the limits of the armistice of June 1940, Pétain thought that there was some room left for external prowess. But the idea of playing Prussia to Hitler's Napoleon is an almost classic case of misapplied analogy: Hitler was not Napoleon. He was quite determined to use the rump Vichy state as an invaluable hostage, instead of letting it become a bulwark of strength. He had rightly calculated that he could have a greater hold on the French by establishing a "free zone" with a "free" government than by occupying the whole country. Consequently, even the most *attentiste* and anti-German Vichy officials found that they had to spend their time fighting off German demands and calculating what small con-

[26] Andre Siegfried, *De la 3ᵉ à la 4ᵉ Republique*, Paris, Grasset, 1956, p. 171.
[27] Lewis Edinger, *Kurt Schumacher*, Stanford, Cal., Stanford University Press, 1965, p. 272.

cessions could ward off bigger losses. Moreover, Vichy's brand of cleverness all too often led to lamentable detours from the ideal path: instead of an uncompromising stand on the terms of the Armistice, there were pseudo-machiavellian attempts at reaching the goal of French resurgence by anticipating German desires and offering "collaboration" to a victor who had not expected so much servility, however devious in intent. Tragically enough, each belated effort by Pétain to check that very trend only increased Germany's leverage, made his position ever more "dysfunctional," and led to bigger surrenders. From the conservative viewpoint of saving French physical substance, something can be said for Pétain. From the perspective of his own ambition, it is a terrifying case of misheroics careening into antiheroics. The conception was wrong, the execution worse; on both counts, Pétain's statecraft was a wretched failure. National self-assertion had led to ignominy: having endangered the national identity he had wanted to preserve, Pétain payed the price of losing whatever legitimacy he had had.

De Gaulle's external policy performance is a much more ambiguous subject, too complex for treatment here. From the viewpoint of heroic leadership, there are two important remarks to be made. One refers to the *nature and scope of the tasks* de Gaulle set for himself, in both of his periods of power. In the first period, he was after nothing less than a return of an independent France to great power status, the presence of France in postwar settlements, and the satisfaction of her security needs toward Germany. It was a fascinating mixture of a hopeless attempt at restoration and of a valiant attempt at mitigating the bad effects of the irreversible rise of extra-European superpowers. There is little doubt that the successes exceeded the failures: the purposes de Gaulle set to himself, excessive, arrogant, or downright absurd though they seemed to many of his "counterplayers," were to a considerable extent reached; some of the failures—in particular in colonial matters and in France's German policy —reflected a tendency in the "first" de Gaulle, otherwise so keenly aware of changes in world affairs, to minimize the significance of some of those innovations (such as the weakening of Empires by the war and the "devaluation" of the Franco-German conflict by the incipient Cold War and by nuclear weapons). It was as if, in pragmatically (as is his way) developing the immediate requirements of his dogma, *grandeur,* the very precariousness of France's present had led him to see a return to the requirements of the past as a prerequisite to meeting the needs of the future. The "second" de Gaulle's analysis of world trends strikes me as far more profound and provocative: the withdrawal of 1953–58 has had fascinating effects. He now had fully absorbed the lessons of decolonization and the meaning of nuclear weapons for power, peace, and politics. His new tasks are nothing less than the establishment of a new international system. Grandeur, of course, is still the goal; but de Gaulle's policy objectives adapt and reconvert "grandeur" to the changes as well as to the limits provided by the present system.[28] These objectives have not been reached yet, but the whole vision is so boldly long term that it would be rash to call it unrealistic.

In both instances there are remarkable aspects to the Gaullist *performance* itself. One often has the sense of a contradiction between conception and execution (apparently an old problem with de Gaulle); [29] the brutality of the performance detracts from the achievement of the purpose (cf. the clash between his behavior toward FDR and his purpose of a return to great power status, which required United States support; or the clash between his vision of a "European Europe" and his unilateral acts that contribute to prevent the emergence of any united Europe at all). Yet there are explanations for such contradictions. On the level of the issues, one can argue that whereas the performance is dysfunctional in the short run, it has at least a "caesarian" chance of being functional in the long term—through the effects of the shock produced by plunging a surgical knife at the right point. Behavior more functional in appearance would really have been dysfunctional: meekness toward the United States then would have resulted not in support but in dependence; European integration now would mean either a paralyzed or an "American" Europe. On a deeper level, there is another explanation: vision and performance are inseparable. For whereas the fulfillment of the vision is always distant, seldom perfect, never complete, the satisfaction of the hero and the pride of the spectators must be fed by the performance itself. When success is never full or safe, example matters more than triumph. A brilliant, even if not immediately successful act, is its own reward; the achievement is the move, not its outcome. The apparent realization of the ideal, but in a way that would entail a downgrading of the performer, would not be worth the trouble. We are in the universe of prowess. Whether such "illusionism" is "incongruent" with the present international system is a weighty matter and cannot be answered in any clear-cut way. But my own reading of the system suggests a great deal of congruence, and at any rate the performance is extraordinarily "congruent" with the French style of authority. Whereas de Gaulle, President of France, represents the authoritarian pole of the French style, de Gaulle, champion of French independence (as opposed to full participation or integration in intern-

---

[28] Cf. my essays, "De Gaulle's Memoirs: The Hero as History," *World Politics* (Oct., 1960); "De Gaulle, Europe and the Atlantic Alliance," *Int. Organization* (Winter, 1964); and "Obstinate or Obsolete: The Fate of the Nation-State and the Case of Western Europe," *Daedalus* (Summer, 1966).

[29] Cf. Tournoux, *op. cit.*, p. 390.

tional alliances and agencies), de Gaulle celebrating the art of "drinking in one's own glass while clinking it all around," de Gaulle practicing the French technique of resistance to and obstruction against would-be higher authority, accepting association but mainly of a purely contractual sort and to increase the nation's might to resist greater powers—this de Gaulle represents the other pole exactly. Domestically he tends to be *le pouvoir contre les citoyens;* outside, he is *le citoyen contre les pouvoirs:* the domestic monarch is an external *gavroche.*

The Leader's Domestic Tasks

Let us turn to domestic affairs. There are interesting lessons here about the interplay of the socioeconomic system with the political one. All three leaders have been concerned with transforming the socioeconomic system and two of them with overhauling the political; but their appeals and performances have been extraordinarily different.

The simplest case is that of Mendès-France. He came to power with a clear idea of economic reform as the key to all of France's difficulties; in his speeches he talked at least as much like a professor as a political leader. But the irony of his turbulent stay in power lies in the fact that he was never able to do more than begin. He never was the master of his time. He had been selected to cope with Indochina: this he did, and he was duly praised for it by the National Assembly. But his determination to be more than an emergency "effective leader" within the confines of "the system" proved his undoing. There was no stable majority behind his over-all program: he therefore had to try to realize it piecemeal, exploiting both different ad hoc alignments and his capital of support while it lasted. In order to get to what he saw as the core, he first had to try to get more urgent issues out of the way. Thus he spent most of his time on the foreign and colonial issues because they were altogether more pressing, even though they were ultimately dependent, in his eyes, on the economic *redressement* he was never allowed to launch. He had to hop from issue to issue instead of dealing with them according to his thread of economic reform and priority, thus giving a paradoxical impression of breathless discontinuity. This was bad enough, in that it allowed his foes to wonder "where he was going," but what was worse was that his handling of EDC and of North Africa cost him the votes he would have needed for his economic projects; with each vote of confidence forced upon him by the swelling ranks of his opponents, his majority, hence his effectiveness declined. To be sure, he was often clumsy in handling the deputies,[30] yet no amount of clever cajoling would have been of much help, for he too wanted not only to accomplish certain substantive things

[30] This point is incisively made by Peter Gourevitch in "Political Skill: A Case Study," *Public Policy* (1965).

(not so different from those his rival, minister, and successor E. Faure desired), but he also thought that the accomplishment would lose much of its worth and substance if it had to be squeezed out of the laborious, devious, and often humiliating devices of the system. Within the system, tasks could be performed in a certain way, but in the process, the performance was bound to take a frayed air and a dubious smell; yet within the system, the kind of performance heroic leadership seeks was impossible—only the style remained. To play according to the rules (as Faure did), issues had to be delayed, laminated or redefined until the cabinet's majority reached a consensus, usually at the expense of effectiveness. This is precisely what Mendès wanted to avoid; in his game, fluctuating majorities shaping issue after issue were the only tolerable alternative to the impossible ideal world in which problems could be taken up in order of intellectual importance. He thus exhausted his credit; but he got some issues settled. After him, Faure also got some issues settled; yet the way in which he did it made both the settlements and him look tarnished, and for all his skills he did not last much longer than Mendès.

Once out of power, Mendès-France's attempt to retain his charisma as a leader for times of trouble collapsed for three sets of related reasons. One, as I have indicated before, there was no room within the political system for the kind of renovated Radical party he belatedly tried to build: turning into a stern and programmatic opposition force an institution which was both a prize exhibit of "delinquent peer group" behavior and a machine for the occupation of power was a hopeless task. Two, in French society, intense hostility rose against a man whose ideas seemed to violate the French notion of change. This emanated from another tension in Mendès. On the one hand, in conformity with the idea that change is acceptable only when total, he presented his views in the most provocative and global fashion: "we are in 1788," and only a totally new approach to economic management was going to save France. On the other hand, if one looked at his more concrete suggestions, one saw that the apostle of budgetary transfers, tax reform, productive uses of resources, and colonial liberalism aimed not so much at moving France from one rather depressed plateau to a more exalted one where the hierarchy of statuses and the various strata's vested interests would be intact, but at demolishing some of those privileges and at overhauling the hierarchy. Precisely because of the nature of his plans, his stress on total change hurt rather than helped, for it sounded too much like 'uneven" total change, rather than that harmonious massive shift of the whole which leaves relations among the parts intact. Anti-Semitism in France develops only against Jewish leaders who threaten "equilibrium:" Blum or Mendès, but not René Mayer. Among marginal producers—farmers or businessmen—and inefficient shopkeepers, as well as wealthy *colons,* Mendèsisme became a *bête noire.* Mendès' conception of his task clashed with the values of French society. Three, this would not have been fatal if the electoral base of Mendès had been solid, but here was the rub: at the intersection of the economic and social system and of the political one. There was in the electorate a large mass of voters who either were, in their dissatisfaction with the regime, floating from party to party, or were supporting conservative candidates without being so committed to the parliamentary regime that they preferred those candidates to the right kind of an antiparliamentary "heroic leader," should one emerge. Yet Mendès could not count on too many of those votes, for most of this electorate was socially made of the very groups that felt threatened by him, and ideologically hostile to or skeptical of the orthodox left-wing ideology Mendès represented— for all his impatience with the "system." He was a man of the Left, and much of the floating vote or the vote that was only "conditionally Republican" was a vote of the Right. In the elections of January 1956, most of these men went to Poujade or stayed with the conservatives. Mendès' fraction was far smaller. The groups to whom Mendès appealed were largely committed to the established parties, and thereby ultimately lost to Mendès: the MRP was his enemy, Mollet's Socialists were false friends, and his own Radical candidates were, in most cases, traditional Radicals rather than faithful Mendèsistes. To sum up: what he wanted to accomplish in French society simply could not be done by a man of the Left within the French parliamentary system.

Marshal Pétain's domestic tasks were of two kinds: the establishment of a new political system and the creation of a new economic and social order. He failed on both counts, not only because of the external circumstances, nor because of the difficulty any heroic leader meets when he tries to institutionalize his personal power. There was a deeper reason: in both realms, Pétain violated some of the most important canons of the French style of authority. In the beginning, he enjoyed extraordinary advantages. He (by contrast with Mendès) could count on the support of all the forces of the Right that had become disenchanted with the Republic in the 1930s and, after many disappointments with pseudo-heroic figures, had been more or less impatiently waiting for their Godot. The collapse of left-wing parties—the suicide of the Republicans—left many of their supporters with no other resort than the old Marshal. Moreover, in two respects he was the man of the hour. At the level of ideas and values, what he proposed seemed to represent exactly the preferences of the bulk of French society, the nadir of the downward trend toward crumpled *repli* and shivering stagnation characteristic of the 1930s. His views about the right kind of social order—"only the soil does not lie"—read like the

quintessence of the stalemate society: he was going to provide the magic
that would prevent its dissolution by the evil forces of industry (labor and
big capital), urbanization, or experimentation; he was going to freeze and
embalm it both by organizing it at last for the sake of its own protection
and by purging it of all the political and social forces of drastic change.
His masochism of regenerative suffering was no more than the exaggera-
tion of a theme often heard in the 1930s: only through a period of insulation and self-concentration could France avoid the disintegration of its
cherished "equilibrium." On the level of emotions and symbols, Pétain's
own appearance and speeches suggested the incarnation of a certain
essence of France that had been submerged by the turmoils of the past
century and a half: he was the Ancestor to whom one turned to escape
from an unbearable present and a distasteful recent past, and whose
appeals—of pathos and for solidarity—spread some warmth over schemes
that were basically narrow, petty, and cold.

However, the dream of restoring and strengthening the stalemate society did indeed prove foolish.[31] Pétain literally exceeded the limits which
even heroic leadership has to observe. To be sure, his attempt at building
a corporate society with rule-making powers in the hands of each functional body, his political system purged of politicians, fitted Crozier's
model in that they intensified the distance between strata, provided each
stratum with a higher authority to save its members from *le face-à-face,*
and endowed each authority with impersonal rule-making attributes.
However, there were three major violations of the unwritten rules. First,
French authority patterns show a permanent resistance to arbitrariness.
Now, especially in the setting up of Vichy's political system, Pétain gave
revenge—purges, arrests, a mushrooming of political courts—*de facto*
priority over the quest for unanimity and gave reprisals priority over the
demand for impartiality. As a result, quick disenchantment then hostility
gripped his earlier supporters. All heroic leaders need support, for without it their aides find themselves working in a vacuum; but few leadership
groups needed a vacuum less than the amateurs—admirals, generals, businessmen, local notables long discarded by universal suffrage—Pétain put
into many of the positions from which the old political class was being
expelled. Second, in the new political system as well as in the new social
order, French equalitarianism was being trampled. As we have seen, it is
particularly strong in the pattern of political authority; Pétain's paternally
indiscriminate swims in the emotions of the crowds were not enough to
compensate for a state that seemed almost exclusively reserved for members of the authoritarian elites: the *boursier* was out, only the men with

[31] I draw here on my essay, "Aspects du régime de Vichy," *Revue française de
Science politique* (Jan.–March, 1956).

réserves were in, except for a few *arrivistes* like the ex-labor leader Belin. In the social institutions created by Pétain, elitism was the rule (this became particularly visible in the industrial Organization Committees and in the Labor Charter); but in French affairs the hierarchy among strata accompanies a desire for equality in each stratum. Vichy seemed too much like the mere triumph of the former "parallel relations" for solving conflicts, the revenge of behind-the-counter.

Third, and most serious, in the economic and social sphere Vichy violated the desire for "balanced," if total change. Pétain and his advisers did not know how to distinguish between stopping the clock—as so many elements in France wanted—and turning it back. It soon became obvious that was the regime's ideologues were after, under the name of *"retour au réel,"* was a flight to the type of social order that existed in Balzac's days. The emphasis on the kind of decentralization that would have made sense when local issues or professional problems could be treated apart from national ones, the rehabilitation of the peasantry, the rural notables, and the small entrepreneurs, the glorification of the Catholic Church, the dislike for uprooted proletarians and adventurous businessmen and civil servants (except those at the top)—all these pointed to a somnambulistic belief in the reality of the unreal, next to which Mendès' faith in the "integral rationality of reality" appears positively sophisticated, and de Gaulle's assumption that *les realités* are clear and simple to the unbiased mind seems self-evident.

Given those errors, Pétain's leadership could not escape from the following dilemma. He might set up the institutions (political and social) that his dreams required; but they would prove totally ineffective (cf. the Labor Charter, and many of his educational directives) unless they actually worked in a direction quite opposite from the one he envisaged. They would, in effect, prepare the stalemate society for the more dynamic and "concerted" experiences of the post-liberation era, instead of accentuating its static nature and its fragmentation.[32] Instead of embalming it, they would revive its circulation. Or else, sensing the resistance of economic, social, and political realities to reactionary ruminations, he might try to extend the scope and intensity of his power; however, then not only would arbitrariness escalate, but his very ideal of a state that was authoritarian yet limited to the protection of a self-ruled society would be shattered: a totalitarian Vichy would have both increased resistance and violated its own precepts. The instruments Pétain selected, such as the Veterans' Legion and the youth movements, all conformed to the pattern of emotional mobilization without political organization—and to the

---

[32] See *In Search of France*, p. 34 ff.

model of delinquent peer groups, primarily concerned with reporting misdeeds to the police, or with in-fighting, or with the defense of their own interests. Too weak to be effective, they were cumbersome enough to be detrimental. Thus here, as in external policy, Pétain set himself an impossible task; and, here again, the performance of a bad role was execrable, marked by inconsistencies, tipsy twists and turns of men and measures, and an increasing sense of drift. The old Ancestor, the living incarnation of the metaphoric "tree," was a senile man only intermittently lucid; the tree looked impressive, but it was dead.

De Gaulle's domestic leadership falls into two very different periods. In the first, he set himself three main tasks: the unification of French resistance, the initiation of measures of economic and social change designed to restore French power, and finally the establishment of a political system allowing for effective leadership. There were tensions between those tasks. The first task he performed in a way which involved a mixture of intransigence (especially during the Giraud episode) and cunning (using the parties as a means of pressure against the resistance movements), and a masterful exploitation of what could have been a fatal flaw: his very outwardness. Not being connected with any organized political or social force made him a focal point instead of a nobody: a fact Roosevelt never grasped. He had to pay a price in order to succeed: he had to remain above all factions, without any organized support all his own, bring the Communists into power, allow the old parties to reemerge, and thus encourage the resistance movements to create parties in turn. This price contributed powerfully to his failure to carry out his third task. But there would have been no possibility of even thinking about the third, or of performing the second, had the first not been accomplished.

With the benefit of hindsight, we now see that the performance of the second task marked the beginning of the liquidation of the stalemate society's socioeconomic system and associational life. The reasons why the measures of 1944–45 could be taken are numerous. The old consensus on the social order had broken down: the Resistance forces, so largely composed of foes of or dissidents from the stalemate society, were unanimously for those measures. The social groups most likely to be the victims of the reforms (essentially the *patronat)* were resigned to accept change as a substitute for the far more radical kind of purges the Left and Extreme Left were talking about. In other words, de Gaulle (who remembered the lesson later) by his moderating presence gave a kind of "homeorhetic" cast to changes which, although they stopped short of social revolution, involved the creation of a permanently interventionist state (and not only intermittently, in emergencies): a state that would guide more than protect, one that could push France away from the structures and values of the traditional social system. Finally, the traditional style of authority was respected, insofar as the measures were taken from above, involved a minimum of *face-à-face*, were mostly impersonal, and maintained equalitarianism. Indeed, it is because in one important respect de Gaulle chose to be too noninterventionist, too traditional, that his objective—social and economic reform for power—was not fully attained; this happened when he opted for Pleven's laissez faire finances over Mendès' rigor.

The goal of institutional reform was not reached at all, precisely because the role de Gaulle had chosen in order to perform his other tasks made him impotent here. As "the symbol," the champion of unanimity, and the leader above factions, he could not impose his views: the parties he had boosted and the movements he had tried to weld filled the political vacuum left by Vichy. In a familiar swing of the pendulum, they reacted against the two simultaneous displays of heroic leadership—Pétain's and de Gaulle's—by establishing a political system that was designed to be a bulwark against heroes and turned out to be a barrage against leadership. De Gaulle, condemned to solitude, chose, in conformity with his conception of the hero, to get out before being thrown out or used up— for the hero who wastes his time hanging on where he can leave no mark is a fool.[33]

De Gaulle's second exercise of power is a very different enterprise. The circumstances in which he came to power were quite different: more like Pétain in 1940, but better. Like Pétain, de Gaulle in 1958 could count on the electorate that had grown disaffected with the Republic—the mass of voters who had supported the conservatives or had swung from one party to the other and who were predominantly on the Right. But he also had the support of most of the parties: this made it both easier and almost necessary for him to play his favorite role of unifier, instead of threatening revenge and punishment. There was a large electorate available for a Gaullist party: he did not have to try, as in 1945–46, to rule above the vigilant heads of the "politicians." Nor did he at any time share Pétain's illusion that one could manage a political system exclusively with social elites: indeed, precisely because so many of those elites had been with Vichy, his own standing with and feelings for them were never very good. Also, he was able to make his various tasks consistent with one another, as they had not been in 1940–45, and to be at all points the master of his time. Now he could start with institutional reform; he handled the Algerian powder keg in a way that made it lose much of its explosiveness under the combined impact of political stability, economic expansion, and external successes, before he finally disposed of it.

If we look at his performance of what he set himself as his first task—

[33] This principle, stated in *le Fil de l'Epée*, explains much of de Gaulle's post-1958 colonial policy and his exit from NATO.

establishing at last the political system he had had in mind for so long—
we find that his statecraft has been quite ambiguous. On the one hand, by
preserving public freedoms, letting parties operate, allowing his own followers to create a Gaullist party—and manipulating the electoral system
as well as the Constitution—he has created an effective political system
for his purposes. There is an opposition to him and his style, but no determined resistance either to the man or to the Constitution; there is a Gaullist political class that provides a transmission belt between the country
and its leader—the kind of belt Pétain had been reluctant to create and
de Gaulle in 1945 had been deterred from creating by his own definition
of his task. On the other hand, the victory of the Gaullist forces is itself
largely due to de Gaulle's constant attacks on the old parties, a fact that
encourages them in their determination to avoid a perpetuation of Gaullism after de Gaulle. The Gaullist party, which is invaluable in providing
the Leader with a cooperative Parliament, is both held at arms' length
by a man hostile to all parties, and devoid of any program other than
following the leader. It thus tends to behave as the classic peer group,
primarily concerned with being "in" and with keeping all others out—
which raises the questions of the viability after de Gaulle of a party that
is far from homogeneous and of a Presidency which de Gaulle has tried
to keep tied only to the undifferentiated "people" and divorced from the
party system. For as we have seen, if the Presidency stays thus divorced,
it risks constitutional deadlock, yet if it becomes the plaything of parties
anxious to return to routine authority, it risks debasement. Whereas in
foreign affairs de Gaulle has chosen example over success, the success he
has achieved in reforming the political system may prove to be unexem-
plary after him.

One may be tempted to resolve this ambiguity by turning to his second
area of performance, the resumption of his second task of 1944–45: economic and social modernization for power. But here again we get a two-
faced answer. The liquidation of the stalemate society has proceeded, and
de Gaulle has neither hesitated to stress, in tones the prudent Fourth
Republic had shunned, the imperatives of constant (not just cataclysmi-
cally occasional) change, the need for organized groups capable of cooperative action, and the duty of "public action to guide our economy,"
nor refrained from doing what he had failed to do in 1945: hurt "established situations" and privileges by drastic financial measures in December, 1958 and again less drastically in the 1964 stabilization plan. If he has
succeeded in his role of modernizer,[34] it is partly because the ground had
been laid ever since 1945, and the wave of expansion, industrialization,
urbanization had been advancing for some years when he returned to

[34] This case is brilliantly argued by Peter Larmour, in "De Gaulle and the New
France," *Yale Review* (Spring, 1966).

power; all he had to do was to maintain the pressures, so that there would be a continuing flow of benefits to help convert the skeptics to the virtues of growth and compensate the losers. But he has succeeded also for another set of reasons. Less rash than Mendès-France, he has been careful not to destroy the homeorhetic image. When he sings the praise of change, it is because the "old equilibrium" has become untenable, and only *orderly* change can lead to a *new* equilibrium: change is but the condition of permanence. There must be progress, but in stability; industrial growth, but in financial rigor and with balanced budgets: "In France, the revolution goes on regularly, day after day, because it is accepted by the public and inscribed in law." [35] Thus the style of authority is preserved, separated from the stalemate society that had so long been its symbiotic partner. His handling of the Algerian crisis is a case in point. In order to convince a stuck and sizzling army to sacrifice the old *vested interests* of the nation overseas, of the settlers in Algeria, of the colonial army itself, he showed that an obstinate and futile pursuit of victory would actually wreck the new "equilibrium" of France; he showed that the army could find in conversion to atomic defense a far more prestigious equivalent of its imperial glories: once again total change, but in orderly harmony, was presented as the answer to both the irresistible pressure for change and the fear of changes in the hierarchy of statuses.

What serves de Gaulle so well in this double performance is his indifference to problems of class. He is not wedded to the old order, and he is ready to throw his support to whatever group is most likely to serve his goal of power: the workers in 1945, the public and private "technocrats" today. Yet his very indifference allows him to combine the notion of change-for-power with that of a harmonious hierarchy. The ambiguity in performance corresponds to a tension in the man. His vision is one of "association," of a kind of cooperative concert for growth and grandeur, very different indeed from the patterns and practices of authority in the stalemate society; yet his methods respect the old style. The State rules above the citizens, the associated groups are merely consulted, much intellectual distance between strata persists, and the behavior of each stratum toward authority still conforms to Crozier's model. Thus in France today, many of the structures of the stalemate society and the values that referred to its socioeconomic system are being abandoned, but the values that refer to authority—values which preceded the post-Revolutionary stalemate society—survive and preserve many residues from it, just as they had conserved in it residues of the feudal society.[36]

[35] Press conference, Feb. 4, 1965. Quoted in *De Gaulle: Implacable Ally*, ed. by Roy Macridis, New York, Harper and Row, 1966, p. 83.
[36] For a thoughtful discussion of the problem of change in French bureaucracy, see the July–Sept., 1966 issue of *Sociologie du Travail*, ed. by Michel Crozier.

Let us go back to the political sphere. To be sure, it reflects some of the changes that mark French society. An increase, however moderate, in "dialogues," the homogenizing impact of industrialization on a formerly fragmented economy and society, the soothing effects of economic growth and political stability have muted apocalyptic thought, calmed revolutionary talk, tamed ideological stances. This is felt throughout the political system, and it gives to most political parties a startling similarity of programs. Yet it would take an act of faith to proclaim that de Gaulle's exercise in heroic leadership will succeed in providing France after him with that synthesis so often sought between the two kinds of political systems and the two poles of authority patterns. Among the encouraging signs, there may well be the presidential elections of 1965, which tarnished de Gaulle's personal halo yet gave him an institutional blessing, in a way routinizing an excessively "charismatic" rule. Among the discouraging signs, there are the legislative elections of 1967. They have weakened and strained the Gaullist forces; they have decimated yet preserved a strategically important center; they have given back to a reviving Left that thirsts for blood its anti-Executive itch, which feeds on the Left's strength in Parliament (once again the preferred arena for the Left's exploits), on the Left's own divisions (which make pure negativism much the easiest tactic as well as the most familiar) and on the provocations of an Executive that prefers the risky exhilaration of whiplashing Parliament to the compromising attrition of reasoning with it. Thus, suspense continues. The political system remains unsettled, in part because it has its own rules, different from those of the economic and social system, and, despite all reforms, still perversely favorable to fragmentation (due to the impact of the electoral system, the tendency of old parties neither to die nor to fade, the nonsubstantive yet crucial and complex issue of the fate of the UNR after de Gaulle, the role of memories and resentments in shaping alignments), in part because the style of political authority persists. Indeed, it has changed much less than patterns of authority in the rest of society; there is less participation, less willingness to compromise and cooperate constructively, less discipline even than in the economic system; and heroic leadership takes only too fond care of that style, thus making possible by its own behavior a return to routine authority as soon as the hero is gone and as his foes, resurgent and relieved, are able to express their joy of leaping from one extreme to the other.

The Impact and Future of Heroic Leadership

Its importance has been stressed throughout this chapter. It is heroic leadership alone that can succeed in injecting massive doses of *innovation* into a national system that is highly suspicious of change and ordinarily combines tolerance for individual experimentation with social conformity. But since even heroic leadership must respect the rules of homeorhesis, and since the conversion to change requires a mobilization of national energies, a reawakening of the general will, a call to national identity, such leadership serves also as the *maintainer* of the system. When routine leaders can no longer preserve it or make change acceptable, heroic leadership saves the society by adapting it and perpetuates it by renewing it. Yet heroic leadership's importance should not conceal its disadvantages. The features of the national system which heroic leadership sustains may themselves deserve to be jettisoned, whether we think of a style of authority that impedes participation, delays, restrains, and twists economic and social progress, or of a style of behavior on the world stage that prolongs the game of national units proud of cultivating their differences. Even if one accepts these features, one cannot help noting the special flaws of heroic leadership in the French polity. First, the plague of impermanence, which drives heroic leaders into an endless and often reckless gamble for legitimacy; second, the rallying of support through magic rather than reason, the manipulation of frequently infantile needs for dependency, the creation of a civic culture in which mass hypnosis replaces organized citizenship; third, the tendency of a brand of leadership that represents one pole of a French style which juxtaposes the need for and the fear of authority, to slide into tyranny or to glide from the search for unanimity into the imposition of conformity—even if the French body politic produces its own antidotes.

Good democrats would like to celebrate at last the demise of French heroic leadership. Yet, *on ne détruit que ce qu'on remplace.* The new social system is not completed, the new style is still in limbo, the new political system is still in question. De Gaulle has written that when the traditional leadership of the old elites vanishes, the "man of character" becomes the only alternative to anonymity.[37] Whether a "man of character" can be found every seven years, and not only in emergencies, or whether the anonymous elites of routine French politics will resume their role remains to be seen. De Gaulle's inner conflict between an aspiration to political institutionalization and concerted modernization, and his instinctive, temperamental grasp of prowess-leadership which shuns institutionalization and disdains concert reflects France's own state of suspense: between drastic changes in social structure and values, and striking continuity in the structures and values of authority relations, especially political, between the so-called requirements of an industrial society, and the residues of France's pre-industrial mold, there is bound to

[37] *Le Fil de l'Epée.*

be battle. Will change defeat continuity? Will the residues prove so resilient that they will both limit the impact of industrialization and preserve the traditional oscillation in the political system? Will, as Crozier and others believe, industrialization and mass consumption bend the style of authority throughout the social and the political systems to their own need for better communications among and greater participation of all the people? Or will the old aristocratic concerns for prowess, prestige, and rank, the old clinging to independence and the fear of participation remain undefeated, at least in the political realm?

We can only raise the questions. We can also (as usual) point to some fine paradoxes. In an age in which economic progress has become a primary concern of the French, the leader who made of it the cornerstone of his program owes most of his diminished appeal to the memory of the spectacle he once gave. The leader most apparently concerned with stabilizing what he saw as the essence of France and with safeguarding the existence of the French, most adventurously strayed from what her "essence" allowed and her (if not their) existence required. The leader apparently most suspicious of dogmas, most "existentialistically" engaged in recurrent self-definition through action, without attachment to old forms of shibboleths or any other limits than the "realities" of the "situation," has been the one most aware of the unwritten rules even heroic leadership must respect to be successful.[38] French heroic leadership is like French classical theater: it never ceases being dramatic, yet the drama must follow rules. Whether such leadership is closer to the august and candid characters of Corneille, or to the devious and driven characters of Racine, is up to the reader to decide.

---

[38] Cf. the contrast between Pétain's references to the permanence of the soil, the tree, etc, . . . and the last page of de Gaulle's memoirs—a prose poem to both the permanence and the constant renewal of nature.

6. Some Psychological Aspects of Crisis Leaders

E. VICTOR WOLFENSTEIN

Introduction

It is not a new idea that certain kinds of men are attracted to and effective in crisis situations. Hero, rebel, charismatic leader: all bring to mind the image of a strong, determined man facing a chaotic and dangerous world boldly and confidently. Of course, in reality crisis leaders depart rather radically from this superhuman portrait. The men who lead in crises are, after all, men and therefore plentifully endowed with hesitancies, doubts, fears and, not uncommonly, despair. It is true that they perform unusually well under conditions when most men, even accomplished leaders, fail to meet adequately the demands of the situation; but they are not gods or even demigods.

In this chapter I will attempt to depict some of the psychological characteristics of crisis leaders that seem to facilitate their playing this kind of leadership role. The major areas of concern will be the nature of the leader's belief in his creed (his sincerity or lack thereof), his relations with other men, his orientation to goals, and his creed or ideology itself. In each case the psychodynamics as well as psychogenesis of the characteristic will be explored, primarily in terms of concepts drawn from psychoanalytic theory.[1] Particular attention will be given to the adolescent "crisis of identity" in shaping the political personalities of such men. The empirical basis for the inquiry is selected biographical materials from the lives of Churchill, Gandhi, Hitler, and Lenin. These men do not constitute, of

The author would like to express his appreciation to Alexander George, Anthony King, Erwin Hargrove, Leo Snowiss, and Robert Tucker for comments on an earlier draft of this chapter.

[1] According to psychoanalytic usage, dynamic propositions refer to the ways in which internal mental equilibrium is maintained, and are typically stated in terms of the ego's defensive reactions to incursions from the id, superego or external world. Genetic propositions refer to personality growth from birth on, and are usually stated in terms of the stages of libidinal development.

course, a systematically derived or quantitatively significant sample of crisis leaders, nor is it claimed that the materials cited validate any of the propositions offered. The task of this chapter is to suggest hypotheses, not test them; the data are included simply for illustrative purposes on the one hand, and to give the reader some idea of the kinds of evidence which suggested the hypotheses to the writer on the other. To go beyond offering hypotheses to presenting tested propositions would involve two procedures which are beyond the scope of this chapter. First, one would have to study a far greater number of crisis leaders in order to ascertain that the same personality configuration occurred in each. Then one would have to study noncrisis leaders (that is, men who lead effectively in noncrisis situations but who cannot cope with crises, such as Neville Chamberlain in contrast to Churchill) and be able to demonstrate that they do not have this kind of personality. Aside from refining for operational purposes the concepts and hypotheses presented here, these steps would be the logical procedural extension of this study.

It would be wise to dwell for a moment on the term "crisis leader" itself. For our purposes, a crisis is a situation in which a fundamental challenge has been put to an existing political and social order. This challenge must involve something more than philosophical polemic: it must, in short, be backed by substantial political (and usually military-coercive) resources. Thus a crisis situation connotes either internal or external war, and one in which the very life of the existing system is threatened. A foreign war in which the independent national existence of a country is essentially unchallenged is not, for that nation, a crisis, nor is widespread unrest within a country as long as revolutionary changes in the established political order are not being sought. In sum, we are interested in those situations which Max Weber would have considered charismatic, periods of relatively short duration in which an accepted mode of organizing power and authority is overthrown and the basis laid for a new pattern of authority or, alternatively, periods during which political movements having such goals are particularly significant, even if ultimately unsuccessful. For Britain, World War II was such a time, and for India the period preceding and immediately following independence was critical. Hitler greatly accentuated an existing crisis in German politics, and Lenin spent his life preparing for and mastering the crisis of declining Tsarism.

Needless to say, many men are involved in attempts to lead in crisis situations. Churchill was preceded by Chamberlain, Hitler by a host of Weimar parliamentarians, Gandhi was operating formally as just another leader of the Indian Congress Party, and a wide variety of factions and men were competing for power in Russia in 1917. Our interest, however, is confined to those men who lead effectively in this context on the one hand, and who produce, accentuate, and dramatize the critical character of the circumstances on the other. They are men who perceive a situation as actually or potentially critical, usually before others view it in such terms, and who quickly leap to impassioned defense of the existing order or strive to intensify the crisis to hasten the overthrow of the current pattern of political authority. Clearly such crisis personalities can exist without crisis situations, and crisis situations occur without men of this type in leadership positions. The phenomenon of crisis leadership comes into being, however, only when leadership roles during times of crisis are filled by men with crisis-perceiving and accentuating personalities.

In this chapter an attempt is made to elaborate a personality type, a model of the kind of man who is attracted to the role of crisis leadership, that role in turn being significant only when a crisis does exist.[2] In the construction of such a type, many of the characteristics that differentiate from each other men such as those being examined here are not relevant. For example, it is certainly true that no two men could be farther from each other in terms of the legitimacy they attributed to the use of violence in politics than Hitler and Gandhi. If we were examining the psychological preconditions for using violence, we would be at pains to investigate the differences between these men. Insofar as they both commanded the loyalty of a large following in a crisis situation, however, we are interested in what they might have in common which would help to explain this similarity. No two men are either totally alike or totally unlike; the question is whether the similarities or differences are more relevant to a given investigative focus.

One limitation on this study, then, is that we will be emphasizing only those aspects of the men's personalities which seem to underlie the common attributes of their political activity. Another is that, even if the propositions offered here are valid, they constitute no more than *necessary* conditions for performing the crisis leadership role. A wide range of other factors, the most obvious of which is the existence of a crisis situation, must also be taken into account if we are to arrive at the necessary and sufficient conditions for this outcome. For example, Churchill was markedly ineffective as a political leader during the years preceding World War II. Although he often held quite high office, he was not Prime Minister nor was he highly esteemed by his fellow politicians. Perhaps most important, he had virtually no following in the country at large. Yet when a fully developed crisis situation emerged, the same words which

---

[2] Lewis Edinger has stressed the need to understand personality, role, and situation in "Political Science and Political Biography," *The Journal of Politics* **26**, Nos. 2 and 3 (May and August, 1964).

Churchill had been saying for years without major positive effect were heeded and esteemed. The crisis personality was a liability not an asset until that particular role was situationally demanded. Second, as should already be apparent, we will be examining only one part of the phenomenon of crisis leadership, namely, the nature of the leader himself. This means that we are forced to set aside many, if not most, of the concerns of other students of leadership.[3] Thorough investigation of any set of variables, however, involves the relative neglect of certain others; and it may be said in defense of the present focus that, by and large, systematic studies of leadership have touched but lightly upon the personality of the leader.[4] Two of the most influential views of leadership, for example, are Weber's conception of charisma and Freud's view of the psychological group.[5] Both of these men are very suggestive about the psychological and social conditions which move men to follow a leader (and essentially both men have crisis leaders most in mind); but neither goes very far in the direction of telling us why a man wants to lead or of what enables him, in terms of his internal psychodynamics, to perform this difficult function. Yet we may fruitfully use their views as our starting point.

Ideological Commitment

On the whole, Freud and Weber perceive the general characteristics of leaders similarly, although there are variations in emphasis. And both, it may be noted, are somewhat uneasy with their subject. Weber's concept of charisma is perhaps most distinctive for its vagueness. (Its quasi-poetic invocation of a mysterious power little understood, in fact, undoubtedly helps to account for its attractiveness to later users of the term.) Charisma represents Weber's perception that the legitimating basis of political authority was often neither tradition nor law, that it had something to do with personalities and emotions, that in its pure form it seemed to be of fleeting existence, and that it did have a few generalizable characteristics. Charisma to some extent always remained outside the proper confines of

[3] For example, in an essay of this scope it would be difficult to combine Stanley Hoffman's interest in statecraft and my interest in personality without doing injustice to both. Yet there seems to be no reason why, in the long run, such approaches need exclude each other.

[4] For a review of leadership studies see Bernard M. Bass, *Leadership, Psychology and Organizational Behavior,* New York, Harper and Row, 1963.

[5] Max Weber, *The Theory of Social and Economic Organization,* New York, Free Press, 1964, pp. 359–92; Sigmund Freud, *Group Psychology and the Analysis of the Ego,* in *Freud's Works, Standard Edition,* ed. by James Strachey, London, Hogarth Press, 1955, Vol. XVIII, pp. 67–143.

Weber's usually precise and rigorous theorization, thus representing more of a challenge to his notions of authority and change than an extension of his theoretical framework. His reliance on such terms as "supernatural," "superhuman," and "exceptional" in his descriptions of charisma—terms which vaguely describe the group reaction to a leader but tell us little about why the group perceives the leader in these special terms and less about why the leader so views himself—is indicative of his dilemma.[6] Freud, too, is uncomfortable with the leader. The very fact that most of his comments on the nature of the leader come in the context of the presumed characteristics of the father of the primal horde, a man who, as Freud put it, "at the very beginning of the history of mankind, was the 'superman' whom Nietzsche only expected from the future," and that he goes on to compare the leader's power to that of the hypnotist, indicates that Freud held leaders not a little in awe, envied them their power, and feared their abuse of it.[7] Because, however, Freud was well accustomed to dealing with emotions, and especially extreme manifestations of emotion, whereas Weber was not, he penetrates rather more deeply into the nature of the "charismatic" leader than Weber did.

Both Freud and Weber, as noted earlier, are primarily interested in the effect the leader had upon his followers. They agree that the leader's continued dominance depends upon his success, that as long as he is successful his followers will believe that a powerful magical quality in some manner adheres to him, and that emotions, specifically irrational and child-like emotions, are involved to an unusual extent in the follower's response to the leader.[8] About the leader himself they both seem to believe that he is usually a sincere believer in the cause or faith he espouses.[9] Thus Weber is skeptical about classifying the Mormon Joseph Smith as a charismatic leader because he felt he might be only a sophisticated kind of "deliberate swindler." Moreover, Weber in particular stresses that when the charismatic leader fails, he "tends to think his god or his magical or heroic powers have failed him." [10]

That crisis leaders are the truest of true believers (although not necessarily in the wide range of things they advocate for strictly tactical reasons), and that they treat lack of success as a reflection upon their guiding deities or their relationship to them is well illustrated by data available on the men being considered here. Of the four men, Churchill possessed the least elaborated set of beliefs. He venerated the Anglo-American peoples,

[6] Weber, p. 358.
[7] Freud, p. 123.
[8] Freud, p. 81; Weber, pp. 358–360.
[9] Freud, *ibid.;* Weber, p. 359.
[10] Weber, p. 360.

the traditions of British political and social life (especially the monarchy, the empire, and the House of Commons), and individual and national courage. These views, in sum, represent Churchill's feelings for and perception of his family heritage. The family itself was large and widely dispersed, as English aristocratic families tend to be, but for Churchill the idea of family overwhelmingly meant three people, each of whom was elevated in his mind to a quite godly position. First, there was the Duke of Marlborough, perhaps the most brilliant politician and soldier in Europe during the latter part of the seventeenth century.[11] Second, there was his father, Lord Randolph Churchill, a clever, if ultimately unsuccessful Tory politician who in a peculiar way was the dominant influence on Churchill's early political career. Finally, there was his mother, Jeanette Jerome Churchill, an American by birth who always seemed to her son "a fairy princess: a radiant being possessed of limitless riches and power."[12] The facts and values these people embodied and advocated were the reality Churchill came to accept and the morality he honored. And when, as in the following incident, we hear Churchill telling us that he is being watched over by a special providence, it is these three deities whose presence we feel.

During World War I Churchill was stationed for a time at the front. One day he received orders to take a rather long trip from the trenches to see a visiting dignitary. After a chilling and muddy hike to and from his quarters, during which he did not get to see the man after all, Churchill was bemoaning the unpleasantness of the experience to all who would listen when he discovered that his foxhole had been blown up soon after he left on his mission. Writing about the experience later, Churchill says, "And then upon these quaint recollections there came the strong sensation that a hand had been stretched out to move me in the nick of time from the fatal spot."[13] Throughout his life Churchill felt that he was destined for great deeds, that a benevolent fate had saved him from death during the numerous occasions when he had been in extreme danger, and that all of his political actions were in the service of some great cause.[14]

Churchill's moods of exultation, which usually occurred when he felt he was at Armageddon doing battle for the Lord, were balanced by severe depressions when he was out of action and/or felt that his special

[11] Churchill's four-volume biography of the Duke bears all the marks of a work of religious devotion, as does his highly reverential biography of his father.

[12] Winston S. Churchill, *My Early Life: A Roving Commission*, New York, Charles Scribner's Sons, 1958, p. 4.

[13] Churchill, *Thoughts and Adventures*, London, Macmillan, 1942, p. 92.

[14] See the frequent allusions to this theme in Virginia Cowles, *Winston Churchill, The Man and the Era*, London, Hamioh Hamilton, 1953, for example, on pp. 121–22 and 154.

providence had deserted him. This mood was particularly pronounced after the Dardanelles incident during World War I. Churchill's advocacy of what turned out to be a military disaster led to his being dropped from his cabinet post and left him with a profound melancholia.[15] Again, once the first glorious months of his prime ministership during World War II had passed, this mood, which he termed his "Black Dog," returned with particular force. His feeling at that time is well represented in his statement to Lord Moran in September of 1944: "I have a strong feelings that my work is done. I have no message. I had a message. Now I can only say 'fight the damned socialists!' I do not believe in this brave new world." [16] And in July of 1946, just before the election which was to drop him from power, Churchill dreamed of his own death.[17] For Churchill, then, when there was a battle to be fought, he and his gods were at peace and internal harmony reigned; the overt manifestation of this harmony was a youthful exuberance, a great capacity to work, and a kind of joyous determination. When the world was at peace, however, intraphysic conflict broke out, and Churchill felt depressed, alone, and, in a very real way, dead.

Hitler, too, had a faith in a special destiny that was leading him to victory.[18] In talking about his early political work in the Rhineland, for example, he notes that on one occasion "an unpleasant presentiment" led him to abandon a course of action that would have led to his being taken prisoner by the French.[19] And throughout both *Mein Kampf* and the records of conversations during the war there are constant references to the importance of faith in the cause and the "luck" that attends the bold man or party. Moreover, Hitler's rhetoric in the canonical book he wrote for his movement is heavy with references to gods and goddesses of struggle, destiny, fate, and power—as well as to the more human "deities" of Frederick the Great and Karl Lueger, the notorious anti-Semitic mayor of Vienna. Several of the specific components which Hitler put together

---

[15] *Ibid*, pp. 202–4.

[16] Lord Moran, *Churchill,* Boston, Houghton Mifflin, 1966, p. 197.

[17] *Ibid.,* p. 306.

[18] Because psychological studies of Hitler, Lenin, and Gandhi have already been made, either by myself or by others, less space will be spent developing the empirical materials for these men than for Churchill. On Hitler see the standard biography by Alan Bullock, *Hitler,* New York, Harper and Row, 1964; and Erik H. Erikson, "The Legend of Hitler's Childhood," in his *Childhood and Society,* New York: W. W. Norton, 1963; Gustav Mark Gilbert, *The Psychology of Dictatorship,* New York, Ronald Press, 1950; and Gertrud Kurth, "The Jew and Adolph Hitler," *Psychoanalytic Quarterly,* **16** (1947).

[19] Adolph Hitler, *Table Talk 1941–1944,* London: Weidenfeld and Nicolson, 1953, p. 64.

into an ideology of will, destiny, and hatred will be elaborated later. Here let us just note that all four men thought essentially in terms of skillful individual or group action supported by some supramundane power: god, history, race, or nation. In this kind of a political world, failure is seldom attributed to error of judgment or miscalculation. If the leader has not been abandoned by his protective deity, then he has been betrayed by evil men or by the fleshly or spiritual weaknesses of his followers. Thus Hitler blamed Germany's defeat in World War I on the wicked machinations of the Jews. Germany's failure under his own leadership was attributed to the lack of will and dedication of the German people, a disgrace which could only be erased by heroic self-destruction.

All four of the men we are looking at were capable of changing position when it was expeditious to do so. Hitler and Lenin, in fact, made it a matter of principle to retain for the leadership of their movements the freedom to maneuver and manipulate. This in no way impugns, however, the sincerity of their beliefs. Lenin's constant search through the corpus of Marx's writings to justify, and often to suggest, a new course of action was not the activity of a man having only an instrumental attachment to a doctrine. Lenin used *Capital* and related works the way priests use the Bible or Koran. These were the sacred texts in which history's prophet Marx had revealed for all to see the future state of mankind and the means by which men were to achieve it. Hence Lenin's main intellectual task was to demonstrate to his followers and himself that history was on his side. All of his writings in the 1890s had as their major theme the increasing capitalization of Russian society. To give himself confidence in his revolutionary activity, he had to show that Russia was entering that phase of economic development which would make possible, in the not too far distant future, the proletarian revolution. And when he was frustrated in some political activity, Lenin did not feel that he had simply been outsmarted or that his strategy had been incorrect (although he was in fact capable of acknowledging both factors). Rather, his major response was that the times were inauspicious for such action, the ebbs and flows of history were such that success was for the moment impossible.[20]

Lenin's perception of the futility of action when history was not favorably inclined was usually accompanied by a high level of tension, manifesting itself in a host of psychosomatic complaints and substantial depression and listlessness. All three of the men so far considered, in fact, were subject to radical mood swings, ranging from extreme elation and enthusiasm combined with the ability to work untiringly for pro-

[20] Lenin's personality and politics are analyzed at some length in E. Victor Wolfenstein, *The Revolutionary Personality*, Princeton, N. J., Princeton University Press, 1967.

longed periods of time to melancholia and self-consuming rage. Even Gandhi, who in many ways achieved a more harmonious psychic integration than the other men, was not exempt from this pattern. Sadness rather than rage was his typical reaction to political misfortune, a sadness manifesting itself in self-punishing fasts and other forms of self-deprivation. Inner peace was achieved when Gandhi felt that he and his followers had acted in accord with the dictates of the "small voice within," when the Indian people were able to act in accordance with Rama's desires as enunciated through Gandhi.

Gandhi would not act politically unless he had consulted with "that little thing which resides in the heart," until he had received what is clearly comparable to, if not identical with, divine revelation.[21] Often, as before the Salt March in 1930, a long period of self-purification and religious introspection was necessary before Gandhi received the message, or inspiration, telling him what to do. He thus makes quite explicit what is only implicit in the words and actions of the other three men. God and God's word (however this superhuman force is termed by any given man) are seen as both a part of the self and as something foreign to and greater than the self which the individual is obligated to respond to and obey. In psychoanalytic terms this would be described as a particular kind of relationship between the ego and the superego. The superego, which is consciously manifested by something like Gandhi's "small voice within," represents the internalized moral standards of the individual. These standards may be more or less distant from the desires of the ego, the relatively rational, reality-oriented part of the personality which must try to satisfy not only the dictates of the superego but also the instinctual demands of the id. When the superego can be brought into close accord with the ego, the individual feels a minimum of guilt and depression and a maximum of strength and self-sufficiency as well as moral righteousness. In this condition the man has no need for the counsel, guidance, or even support of other men. He has, in a very important way, the strength of two men, both himself and his father, for the superego is formed from the identification of the growing boy with his father's strength and morality. It is the way in which the father remains alive in and important to the individual long after personal contact with the father may have ended.

In short, one would hypothesize that crisis leaders have unusually well-developed and ego-supportive superegos (although the morality that superego represents, as in Hitler's case, may be entirely foreign to our own). Their ideologies and ideological gods would then be viewed as the conscious and articulated manifestations of the superego, and hence are

[21] Again, more detailed examination of these points and the data supporting them can be found in *The Revolutionary Personality*.

indeed an integral part of the individual's personality, a sincere object of reverence. It is also clear, however, that even for these men the psychic distance between the ego and the superego is highly variable. At almost no time is the unity between the two so great that a state of genuine mania results, and rarely do the men tend to the other extreme of a truly pathological melancholia.[22] But within these limits the number of possible positions is great. When Churchill had his "Black Dog," his superego was presumably alienated from his ego. In these circumstances Churchill not only did not gain strength from this internalized representation of his father, but he was also weakened and reproached by it. The other men could similarly feel profoundly strong or very small and weak indeed. A powerful superego is a two-edged sword, an ambiguous gift at best.

What is distinctively political about this psychodynamic configuration is not its form but its content. The mood swings are in response to variations in political circumstance (although the overt content of the changes may not be what is critical to the individual) and are usually manifested in ideological pronouncement.[23] For example, after the attempted and unsuccessful Bolshevik uprising during July of 1917, Lenin found it necessary to go into hiding to avoid what he felt would be an impending death blow to his movement and himself from the Provisional Government. During this time he was evidently quite depressed, and this depression resulted in fevered and desperates notes to those Bolsheviks still active in the capital, imploring them to take care and strike quickly if and when the opportunity presented itself.[24] Lenin's mood was thus not a reaction to a private difficulty but a political distress politically expressed.

Identity Crisis and Political Crisis

If it is true that the sincerity of the leader's belief results from the interconnection of ideology and superego, then the genesis of this belief is to be found in the development of the superego. This immediately tells us that much that is important in the political character of the leader

[22] On all of these points see Freud, *"Mourning and Melancholia,"* in *The Standard Edition*, Vol. 14.

[23] The question of the reality contact or rationality of such responses is obviously raised by this formulation. The consequences for both the individual leader and his followers are likely to differ substantially depending upon the extent to which deeply seated irrational tendencies are or are not controlled. But this intriguing question, leading as it does to the impact of neurosis and psychosis on politics, must be left for another time.

[24] See *The Revolutionary Personality*, Ch. 5.

results from the experiences of the first five years of life, and in particular from the oedipal period, during which the most important bases for superego development are formed. For present purposes, however, we will not consider what little is known about the earliest life experiences of these men and focus on two aspects of their development which give a somewhat distinctive configuration to their adult personalities.

The first aspect, which has already been mentioned, is that there is an unusually intense identification with parental authority, usually the father. This is most obvious in Churchill's case. When he entered politics at the turn of the century, Churchill very consciously modeled his career and style on his father's. He dressed, sat, and attempted to speak like Lord Randolph, adopted his father's views and his father's friends, evoked his father's memory constantly in his speeches in Commons, and even attempted to justify his switch to the Liberal Party as the course of action his father would have taken had he been faced with the circumstances.[25] Eventually, identification with his father became natural and intrinsic, so that a kind of Victorian political style became one of Churchill's trademarks.

It is the belated nature of Churchill's attempt to make his father a part of himself which makes so evident the process that was taking place. In the other men the identification is somewhat more subtle. Lenin certainly did not share his father's loyalty to the Tsarist regime, but he was loyal to Marxism. Like his father he was a teacher and leader of the common man, an expert at organization, a hard and dutiful worker, an intellectual and simple and straightforward in personal style.[26] Gandhi identified much more strongly with his mother than with his father, which in part accounts for the rather singular nature of his political style. From her he took his simple cheerfulness, his fasting and vegetarianism, his maternal approach to other people's problems, and the tendency to use self-punishment as a way of exacting obedience from others.[27] Of the four men, Hitler undoubtedly worked hardest at avoiding becoming the kind of man his father was. But the veneration for strength, the blaming of personal weakness on external causes, the violence of temperament, and the rigidity of belief all appear to be aspects of both Hitler and his father— although the father probably came closer to being an archetypal "authoritarian personality" than the son. Hitler became the Führer and not a civil

---

[25] Cf. Cowles, pp. 74–93.

[26] See Edmund Wilson's treatment of this in *To the Finland Station*, Garden City, N. Y., Doubleday, 1953.

[27] Several authors allude to this phenomenon. Cf. Susanne Hoeber Rudolph, "Self-Control and Political Potency," *The American Scholar*, XXXV (Winter, 1965–66).

servant, but the two are probably not as different from each other as Hitler would have liked to believe.[28] In all cases this intense identification with parental authority gives the men a feeling that they are rightfully in positions of authority, that others owe them obedience, as a son owes a father, and that they are powerful men, as powerful as the father appears to his growing son. This analogy between the leader and the father is, of course, psychoanalysis' first gift to political science. Hitherto, however, the literature has only emphasized or debated the degree to which political authority figures are perceived as fathers, brothers, uncles, or what have you. Here the focus is different insofar as we are concerned with the leader's own feelings of fatherhood, or, more generally, parenthood, based, as we have seen, on the internalization of aspects of the parents' personalities.

The second crucial aspect of the superego development of the crisis leader is that there is a marked tendency toward fixation at an adolescent phase of development, so that these men combine something of the defiant, revolutionary character of adolescence with the self-reliance and natural authority of adulthood. In each of the four cases we are examining, the precondition for this pattern was the death of the father (and in Gandhi and Hitler's case of the mother as well) before the child had reached an independent manhood.

It is due primarily to the work of Erik Erikson that we have come to pay sufficient attention to that crucial adolescent and post-adolescent phenomenon which he terms the crisis of identity.[29] It is at this time of life, at least in many cultures, that a young man (or, somewhat less frequently, a young woman) asks himself, in the most fundamental ways, who he is. This dilemma, which is fraught with ambiguity for both the person involved and, unfortunately, those who are engaged in trying to come to some understanding of the phenomenon, results from the following questions: Psychosexually and socially, what is and ought to be the nature of the young man's relationship to his parents? In the same terms, how does he perceive and how is he perceived by the other important people in his environment? Finally, through what kind of activity (typi-

[28] See, in particular, Gilbert's treatment of this theme in *The Psychology of Dictatorship*. It should also be mentioned that there are important differences in these identificatory processes. Churchill identified directly with his father, Lenin identified with his father both directly and through an abstract ideological medium, Gandhi identified more strongly with his mother than his father, and Hitler identified with his father, as it were, against his will. These differences have important behavioral consequences but they do not vitiate the significance of what is common in the process.

[29] Erikson develops his ideas about identity in several places, but see in particular *Childhood and Society*, pp. 261–63, and *Young Man Luther*, New York, W. W. Norton, 1958, *passim*.

cally, in what vocation) is the individual going to establish for himself an independent status which will also involve satisfactory answers to the preceding questions? Because these questions are intertwined temporally, a man's choice of vocation will bear the heavy imprint of his level of psychosexual development during adolescence and young manhood. This holds for "politics as a vocation" as well as for any other kind of work. Thus in the cases we are exploring we would expect to find a connection between the relations of these men with their parents during the relevant time period, the kind of political career they selected, and the views which they upheld.

Starting again with Churchill, the intense identification which he developed with his father was not the outgrowth of a warm and easy relationship with Lord Randolph. Churchill saw little of his father during his boyhood, and the contact he had did little to inspire feelings of warmth and harmony. Churchill was a very slow learner at school, so retrograde, in fact, that his father despaired of his ability to be anything more than a soldier. Accordingly, as the boy came to the end of his public school days, his father proposed to him that he prepare for training at Sandhurst and a military career. Churchill, who even as a teenager had not outgrown his love for toy soldiers, responded to the idea with alacrity, and did not realize until several years later the insult latent in his father's suggestion.[30]

Both Lord Randolph and Winston were disappointed when the boy failed the Sandhurst entrance examinations the first two times he took them. There then occurred, in a little over two years' time, a series of incidents which firmly set the pattern for Churchill's subsequent career. Winston was visiting at home between the end of his time at Harrow and the beginning of a much needed cram course for Sandhurst. He was playing a variant of hide-and-seek with his younger brother and a cousin when he found himself trapped by his two friendly pursuers on a bridge over a deep gully. About to resign himself to inevitable capture, the youth was suddenly seized by a brilliant idea. The incident is best told in his own words:

"The chine which the bridge spanned was full of young fir trees. Their slender tops reach to the level of the footway. 'Would it not,' I asked myself, 'be possible to leap on to one of them and slip down the pole-like stem, breaking off each tier of branches as one descended, until the fall was broken?' I looked at it. I computed it. I meditated . . . To plunge or not to plunge, that was the question! In a second I had plunged, throw-

[30] See Churchill, *My Early Life*, p. 19.

ing out my arms to embrace the summit of the fir tree. The argument was correct; the data were absolutely wrong. It was three days before I recovered consciousness and more than three months before I crawled from my bed." [31]

One might think that from this experience Churchill would have learned caution and prudence. For a very important reason, however, I would speculate that the result was just the opposite, that Churchill learned that tempting death pays great rewards.

The outcome of this escapade was that, for the first time in the boy's life, his father paid attention to him! Just following the passage cited, Churchill recounts with obvious delight that his father rushed back to the family estate from a trip to Ireland, bringing with him the most famous of London surgeons. And during his convalescence Churchill was permitted to dine with his father and the family's politically important companions, to attend Commons and watch his father in action, and sometimes even to talk to his father on relatively equal terms. One would infer, then, that the message of the great leap episode, with all its suicidal connotations, was that by tempting death and punishing himself Churchill could hope to win his father's indulgence. From then on, be it in a military or a political context, Churchill would seek out the most dangerous and daring positions, hoping to gain thereby both punishment and praise: punishment from an enemy, praise from his friends. During times of genuine crisis, periods which on a broader stage recreated the situation on the bridge (most notably, of course, during the early days of World War II), this need to face danger defiantly, to risk all in the hope of gaining all, perfectly suited the needs of a nation. At other times it led to a rather grotesque searching for enemies to challenge and risks to take where none existed as, for example, in the Sidney Street episode in 1911.

There is an important additional reason why Churchill remained fixated in this posture of adolescent daring. In January, 1895, when Winston was twenty years old, his father died. Churchill believed that, at the time of his father's death, a full accord between father and son was just ahead:

"Had (my father) lived another four or five years, he could not have done without me. But there were no four or five years! Just as friendly relations were ripening into an Entente, and an alliance or at least a military agreement seemed to my mind not beyond the bounds of reasonable endeavour, he vanished forever." [32]

[31] *Ibid.*, pp. 29–30.
[32] *Ibid.*, p. 46.

It is possible that Churchill's need for the bold gesture might have diminished over time as other bases of agreement and respect were found with his father. But his father's death gave him only one model for winning the love and attention of paternal forces.[33] Moreover, Lord Randolph died before Winston was able to sort out his own feelings toward his father. There was clearly a large amount of love and admiration for the older man, but one senses a strong undercurrent of aggressive feelings as well. After all, this was the man who ignored his son for years, who thought he was not bright enough for the Bar and who was constantly reacting with disapproval and disappointment to Winston's various and sundry lacks of success. Thus with his father's death, Churchill was left with a fundamental feeling of ambivalence unresolved and, in a sense, unresolvable: with the father dead, the youth had to try to come to terms with his memory, a much more difficult task than confronting a living human being.

Thus the death of Churchill's father augmented the fixative quality of Winston's adolescent experience on the one hand and led to a combined process of internalization-externalization on the other. That is, as a result of the tendency to identify with a lost love object, Churchill went through the process, already described, of attempting to make his father's strength his own. At the same time he sought to push out of himself and maintain as an external object that part of his father which he feared and disliked. It was when he failed in this attempt, as he periodically did, that he was overcome by his "Black Dog." In psychoanalytic terms, it was only when he was able to treat the punitive component of his superego as a foreign object that Churchill was able to achieve inner harmony. When he could not find an enemy in the world around him, the battle resumed between ego and superego.

Hitler's adolescence shows a similar pattern of fixation and ambivalence, but in this case it is the love feelings for the father which were weak and the feelings of aggression which were powerful.[34] His father, Alois, had been a moderately successful civil servant who had retired in 1895 and who, during the following years, apparently fell increasingly into a pattern of alcoholic excess and quite brutal domination of his young wife and children. Adolph early showed signs of a bright, if rebellious mind, and the father was determined to make a successful civil servant

[33] Conversations with Ben Williams have been very helpful in constructing the above intepretation of Churchill's adolescence.

[34] The story of Hitler's adolescence has been ably interpreted by both Erikson and Gilbert. I am also indebted to a sensitive seminar paper by J. Peter Fiske for several insights into the meaning of Hitler's experience.

out of the boy. Even at age ten and eleven Hitler reports that he inwardly resisted his father's decision, and by the time he was twelve his resistance came out into the open. Hitler told his father he planned to become an artist:

> " 'A painter? An artist?'
> "He doubted my sanity, and thought he had not understood correctly. But when I explained it to him, and he felt the seriousness of my determination, he turned against it with all his characteristic decisiveness . . .
> " 'An artist—no; never so long as I live.' " [35]

The conditions for an independent manhood were thus made rather plain (assuming Hitler more or less accurately describes what took place, or at least reports accurately his feeling about his father's position). If Hitler were to be an artist, his father must die. And within two years, when Hitler was not quite fourteen, his father did, in fact, die. Shortly thereafter Hitler left school and spent two years at home with his mother, a time that seemed to Hitler "like a beautiful dream." [36] At the age of eighteen Hitler then set out to make his fortune in Vienna, retracing a course of action his father had performed years earlier. Within the year, however, his mother died of breast cancer and Hitler's period of aimless drifting had begun, a pattern which was to end only with the First World War.

Erikson has stressed the "unbroken adolescent" quality which Hitler conveyed to his followers. [37] Although it is possible to overemphasize this point, it does reflect the degree to which Hitler was perpetually replaying his relationship with his father and attempting to regain the lost mother. The strategy of struggle that runs throughout *Mein Kampf*—putting on a bold front against a strong but perhaps somewhat outmoded authority and using both cleverness and force to eliminate those in command— represents a continuation of the struggle against the father, which Hitler may well have viewed as ending when he and death (or destiny) overcame his father and he became master of the household. At the same time, however, the internalization-externalization pattern which we saw in the case of Churchill is also markedly present. Hitler's personal rigidity and affinity for violence are reminiscent of Alois: after all, in his own fashion Hitler did indeed become a servant of the German mother- or fatherland. Throughout the *Table Talk* we hear Hitler speaking in the voice of an aging bureaucratic official, looking forward to the days of his retirement.

[35] Hitler, *Mein Kampf*, p. 24.
[36] *Ibid.*, p. 34.
[37] Erikson, *Childhood and Society*, p. 337.

Hitler thus became like his father, a process augmented by the father's death, and he fulfilled his father's wishes for him by becoming a more successful "civil servant" than Alois. To an even greater extent than Churchill, he also found it necessary to find an evil father to fight, a satanic creature who could be blamed for all of his and Germany's problems. In the presumed conspiracy manifested in the *Protocols of the Elders of Zion* Hitler found the strong, brutal, and malicious father he needed to fight. Needless to say, it was not necessary for the Jews actually to be such a force for Hitler to view them as one.

Lenin represents something of a middle ground between Churchill and Hitler in terms of the nature of his relationship to his father during adolescence. Ilya Nikolayevich Ulyanov, Lenin's father, was a kind if somewhat austere father, who, along with his wife, dominated his family primarily on the basis of moral suasion. Lenin was a bumptious and somewhat hard to manage adolescent who appears to have been in the throes of casting off the authority of his father and his older brother Alexander when his father died just before he reached his sixteenth birthday.[38] How Lenin's development would have proceeded had nothing further of a traumatizing nature occurred in the next few years is impossible to tell, for a little over a year later his older brother Alexander was executed for his part in a futile plan to assassinate the Tsar. At one and the same time, this event created further psychic conflict for Lenin and the possibility of resolving it. By identifying with his martyred brother in his rebellion against political authority, Lenin could assert his manhood against an obviously evil paternal force and assuage the guilt feelings he appears to have had as a consequence of his brother's death. The life of political terrorism was filled with danger, however; his brother had been killed, after all, for just such activity. It was not until Lenin convinced himself of the applicability of the benevolent protective creed of Marxism to the Russian situation that he was able to proceed to actual revolutionary activity. By identifying with his father through the medium of Marx, Lenin was able to fight against his father as embodied by the Tsar.[39] In other words, Lenin, like the other two men, continued to fight the psychic battles of adolescence in the political arena. And as with the other men, a complicated pattern of internalization and externalization was involved.

Gandhi had by far the most difficult identity problem of the four men we are studying, one accentuated by a general crisis of Indian identity

[38] Lenin's adolescence and young manhood are analyzed in greater detail in Chs. 2 and 3 of *The Revolutionary Personality*.

[39] This double identification with the powerful males in his family helps to account for the great success that Lenin had in feeling at home as the father of a political brotherhood.

during the latter part of the nineteenth century. Manhood is not an easy achievement in any case, but it is particularly difficult if the conception of manhood honored by one's culture has been effectively challenged by a new one. The dilemma of the vegetarian and relatively diminutive Indian when confronted by the brawny, meat-eating, and politically dominant Englishman was great enough in normal circumstances, but Gandhi's personal situation during adolescence complicated things substantially.[40] He was a shy, secretive, and dutiful child who at an early age was tormented by feelings of disloyalty toward his parents. An attempt to eat meat in violation of parental dictates was followed by a guilty conscience and an upset stomach, and an adolescent visit to a house of prostitution led only to fear and shame. His life was further complicated by his marriage when he was thirteen. His child bride, Kasturbai, did not bend willingly to his wishes and apparently did not make him feel wanted sexually either. Then, in the midst of this crisis of masculinity, Gandhi's father died after a prolonged illness. Gandhi had been sitting at his father's bedside the night he died, but had been relieved of this duty and was in bed with his wife when his father's demise was announced. In addition, Kasturbai was pregnant at this time, and the child born of the pregnancy did not survive. Thus Gandhi at age sixteen was shouldering an almost overwhelming burden of guilt. Sexual manliness in particular and assertiveness in general were connected in his mind with the death of his father and child. There seemed to be no ready way of achieving an independent identity, and indeed it took Gandhi almost twenty years to arrive at a conception of self which allowed him internal peace.

During the years immediately following his father's death, Gandhi attempted to assert his manliness in a set of rather conventional ways for a middle-caste Hindu of that time. He studied law in England and at first attempted to transform himself into an English gentleman. This effort ended in failure and Gandhi increasingly came to adopt the ascetic practices which were characteristic of his mother. This tendency was accentuated by his mother's death when he was twenty-two. It was not until he renounced sexual intercourse at the age of thirty-six, however, that he found a way of adequately controlling the psychic conflict which had erupted so spectacularly during his adolescence. In giving up sexual activity Gandhi was foregoing manhood and accepting for himself an essentially feminine role. He would be a gentle, desireless nurse of the weak and poor, caring for them as his mother had cared for him and as he felt

---

[40] This theme is skillfully handled in Rudolph's "The New Courage: An Essay on Gandhi's Psychology," *World Politics*, XVI, No. 1 (October, 1963). The material elaborated briefly here is dealt with in greater detail in Chs. 2 and 3 of *The Revolutionary Personality*.

he should have cared for his father. In his political activity this personal solution was transformed into the practice of *satyagraha* (Gandhian non-violence), which involves placing oneself at the mercy of a powerful foe, hoping to invoke in him feelings of love, mercy, and justice for the suppli-cant.[41] By thus seeking external punishment as well as by inflicting pun-ishment upon himself, Gandhi could control the feelings of guilt which self-assertion connoted for him; but at the same time he could hope to win the esteem of the much-admired and much-dreaded political father, just as his mother had been able to do with his actual father.

Thus in all four of our cases, and it may be hypothesized for crisis leaders generally, adolescence brings with it a psychic crisis whose solu-tion serves as a model for the individual in his attempts to cope with the political crises of his adult life. But the very intensity of the crisis, linked as it may be with parental death (or perhaps more generally with other forms of separation from the parents), has a fixating quality, so that the individual tends to recognize his world and adapt well to it only when it recreates, in political form, the psychic conflict of his youth.

Emotional Independence

The other aspects of the personalities and politics of crisis leaders alluded to earlier—their relative lack of object ties, view of the world as divided into good and evil camps, and single-mindedness—all develop out of the resolution of the adolescent identity crisis.[42]

Both Freud and Weber lead us to anticipate the emotional indepen-dence of these men, their freedom from intense bonds of love or hate with other people. According to Weber, the charismatic leader "does not view his quality as dependent on the attitude of the masses toward him." [43] And Freud, describing the primal father, draws a picture of an extraordi-nary lack of constraint and emotional involvement:

"His intellectual acts were strong and independent even in isolation, and his will needed no reinforcement from others . . . his ego had few

---

[41] Another incident shortly preceding his father's death in which Gandhi begged for and received forgiveness from his father for a minor theft also helped to establish the pattern of action which underlies *satyagraha*.

[42] Here as elsewhere it should be stressed that all of the characteristics of the leader are multidetermined, both psychologically and otherwise. A condensed presentation of this kind does not allow, however, for the development of the other themes which would have to be interwoven in order to provide a more complete picture of the phenomenon.

[43] Weber, p. 359.

libidinal ties; he loved no one but himself, or other people only in so far as they served his needs. To objects his ego gave away no more than was barely necessary. . . .

. . . .

"Even today the members of the group stand in need of the illusion that they are equally and justly loved by their leader; but the leader need love no one else, he may be of a masterful nature, absolutely narcissistic, self-confident and independent." [44]

We will recognize in Weber's contention and even more in Freud's depiction of the primal father/leader that reality is being unduly bent in the direction of the leader myth referred to at the outset of this chapter. As Georg Simmel, among others, has stressed, "All leaders are also led," all power relationships involve to some extent mutual dependencies.[45] Nonetheless, several important qualities of the crisis leader are found in the material cited.

Both Freud and Weber deal only with the nature of the leader's relationship to his followers. This in itself is indicative of the fact that the kind of men we are considering do not acknowledge the existence of either superiors or peers. They have, as we have seen, an intense faith in some superhuman force to which they owe loyalty, and they often consider themselves members of a brotherhood, such as a political party or a revolutionary mass movement. But in the course of their careers they sever all ties with men who could claim to be their superiors or equals. Churchill, early in his career, accepted to some extent the direction of Lloyd George. He also accepted counsel from some of his father's old friends. In time, however, these men died or lost their political standing, and Churchill did not seek replacements for them. He was so little tied to his political brothers that he was able to switch parties twice (to rat and rerat as he put it), and once he became Prime Minister he ran the government with very little attention to the wishes of others. Lenin also at one point acknowledged the leadership of another man (Plekhanov), but only for a very short period of time. He even broke with his "blood brother" Martov when policy differences arose between them.[46] By 1903, when the Bolshevik faction had been established as an independent entity, Lenin

[44] Freud, *Group Psychology*, p. 123.

[45] Kurt H. Wolff, ed. and trans., *The Sociology of Georg Simmel*, New York, Free Press, 1950, p. 185.

[46] Because of limitations of space, the theme of political brotherhood cannot be developed here. The data of the four men suggest, however, that relations with siblings before and during adolescence is intimately involved with the ambivalent attitude that these men have about the fact and idea of equality.

was the father of his own horde. And he was quite ruthless in eliminating people from his faction if they were not willing to accept the Leninist line. Hitler and Gandhi had even fewer bonds of allegiance than the other two men. Hitler never admitted the legitimacy of another man's domination over him, and Gandhi claimed never to have found a satisfactory *guru* (teacher). Nor did either of them hesitate to sacrifice their companions to the struggle.

We have in part, then, described the "narcissism" which Freud felt was one of the attributes of leaders. As far as peers and superiors are concerned, these men have emotional attachments only to ideational representations of their fathers and/or mothers. Because so much of their emotional energy is involved in the continued working out and reliving of the adolescent confrontation with parental authority, they have little emotion, either aggressive or libidinal, available for new object ties. If they do attempt to follow the direction of another man, one of two things intervenes to destroy the bond. Either the original ambivalences which were involved in the adolescent situation reemerge in this new context, leading the man to perceive in his leader all of the qualities which he feared or hated in his father, or he finds that no living human being can compete with the godlike image of his father which has been erected in his mind.[47]

The inability to follow, of course, does not automatically connote the psychic strength to lead. This quality, as we have already seen, comes from the unusual identification these men establish with the important authorities of their early lives. And, if Freud is correct in his speculations on the subject in *Group Psychology and the Analysis of the Ego,* it is the leader's ability to convey to others a feeling for his rightful occupancy of the father's role that accounts for his hold upon his followers. But, as Freud stresses, the leader need not be emotionally involved with his followers for them to be attached to him. All four of the men had largely instrumental ties with those who followed them. They would use their followers as they were needed and could certainly become sentimental over their exploits. But the signs of deep attachment, such as grief over death or any great unwillingness to risk lives, are absent. Although the leader usually does need the emotional (as well as the physical) support of his followers, and is often responsive to their moods and desires, his ego, as Freud put it, gives away no more than is barely "necessary." [48]

---

[47] Needless to say, these are not mutually exclusive. Both were involved, for example, in Lenin's break with Plekhanov (see Ch. 4 of *The Revolutionary Personality*).

[48] No man, unless he is a psychotic, is completely devoid of object ties. What we have here described is a difference in the degree of emotional involvement between crisis leaders on the one hand and more common personality types on the other.

Two other major kinds of objects exist in the world of the crisis leader: the enemy and the oppressed. Neither of these is simply a human being or a group of human beings. Churchill fought the Nazis to protect England, Hitler sought to prevent the defilement of the German motherland by the devilish Jew, Gandhi fought against materialism and aggression in defense of an oppressed Indian spirituality, and Lenin resisted the twin forces of Tsarism and capitalism in their effort to destroy Russia and the world proletariat. To be sure, these men attached their abstractions to concrete entities against which they waged war, but it was never living people as such that they were combating.

This leads us once again to the hypothesis that these men were fighting for and against people who had been a genuine part of their lives at an earlier phase, but who were now embodied in emotionally supercharged abstractions and ideologies. All of the men we are looking at exhibit in this regard what might be termed a typical oedipal configuration: they sought to defend what was basically a mother surrogate from the incursions of a brutal father. When Germany bombed Great Britain, Churchill could with a clear conscience strike back in defense of his mother country. The latent animosity which presumably existed for the father who monopolized his "fairy princess" mother could now be expressed in a way which would not arouse the father still alive in his superego. Lenin, under the benevolent aegis of father Marx, could fight with assurance against a Tsarism that was brutalizing mother Russia. Hitler, of course, was very explicit about what he did: *Mein Kampf* abounds in examples of fancied sexual assault by Jews upon Aryan womanhood, and even when the subject matter is more governmental in orientation, the language used very frequently evokes the image of a woman in danger of being raped.[49] For Gandhi, the cultural disjunction between the English and the Indian as well as his own psychosexual development helped to establish the English in the role of the dangerous father and India in that of the assaulted mother.

In sum, the crisis leader's world is largely populated by images from his earlier life, especially from the oedipal period and its rebirth during adolescence. Although the leader connects these images to living people whom he is often able to understand and manipulate quite well, he has little emotional attachment to his contemporaries. And, as is probably already clear, it is out of these fragments of his adolescence that the leader builds his view of the world.

[49] Gertrud Kurth is particularly good in tracing the sexual content of Hitler's anti-Semitism to the circumstances surrounding his mother's death while she was under the care of a Jewish doctor.

World View

Essentially the crisis leader views his environment as divided into two warring camps. Lined up on one side with the leader are the forces of good, on the other are the forces of evil. Although there is some variation in this regard, the leader usually thinks of the conflict in which he is engaged as the last great battle before a hitherto unknown reign of peace and harmony is ushered in. His perception of the world is thus doubly split: in the present, and rigidly between present and future. A pair of quotations from *Mein Kampf* neatly depict this conception:

"He who would live, then, must fight, and he who will not do battle in this world of eternal struggle does not deserve to live."

. . . .

"Yet assuredly this world is moving toward a great upheaval. And the one possible question is whether it will turn out for the good of Aryan humanity or the profit of the wandering Jew." [50]

When the great battle was over, there would be time for building endless stretches of fine roads over which luxurious automobiles would travel from elegant town to elegant town. Museums would be built, architecture would attain new heights—Hitler himself would personally design some of the new structures. But first the race must be strengthened and kept pure, then the Aryan must go forth to do battle with the forces of international Jewry (such as the Communists, the Papacy, England, and the United States), and then at last there would be "A Germanic State of a Germanic Nation," pure, strong, and unrivaled in the world.

The pattern for the other men is markedly similar. Time after time in such works as *What Is To Be Done?*, *State and Revolution*, and *Left-Wing Communism: An Infantile Disorder*, Lenin emphasized the dangerous world in which the revolutionist lives: The Russian workers "will have to take up the fight against a monster." [51] Revolution itself is a "war which is a hundred times more difficult, protracted and complicated than the most stubborn of ordinary wars between states." [52] This cataclysmic war

[50] Hitler, *Mein Kampf*, pp. 282 and 413.
[51] V. I. Lenin, *What Is To Be Done?*, New York, International Publishers, 1943, p. 30.
[52] Lenin, *Left-Wing Communism: An Infantile Disorder*, in his *Selected Works*, Moscow, Foreign Language Publishing House, 1961, Vol. III, p. 417.

between the capitalist and the proletarian revolutionist must be fought to its bloody conclusion before the worker can proceed to create a class-less society devoid of conflict and exploitation. For Gandhi Western civilization signified "irreligion"; it was a "Satanic Civilization" which had brought a "Black Age," and India had to mobilize her spiritual power to expel it if *Hind Swaraj*, a simple and spiritual Indian self-government, were to be obtained.[53] And Churchill tells us the "story of the human race is war." [54] He subtitled the story of his early life "a roving (military) commission" and had his most effective moments politically when he spoke for the free people of the world who were threatened by the scourge of Nazism. Churchill did lack, however, a vision of the future such as that which the other men possessed. He had a genuine longing to restore the lost Victorian world in which he grew up, and, as he told Lord Moran, he did not believe "in this brave new world."

We have already seen the family plot upon which these men built their tales about the world in which they fought. But thus far we have indicated only that these men were prone to externalization, to viewing as attributes of the world around them feelings and images which were at some point internal. The mechanisms which are used to relieve internal conflict in this way are displacement, projection, and the splitting of ambivalence.[55]

The conflict these men were engaged in, as we have seen, was a political re-creation of the conflict of adolescence, an attempt to impose on a world of crisis the solution to the individual's personal crisis of maturation. These two kinds of crises are linked by the mechanisms mentioned. First, during adolescence the young man is unable to terminate his conflicts with parental authority with the parents themselves. He must thus search out other people who seem to embody their positive and negative attributes. This process of finding new objects to substitute for those we have been deprived of in one way or another is called displacement. Through displacement Lenin was able to hate the Tsar and not his father, Gandhi could fight against the British instead of his father, and Hitler could substitute the Jew for Alois. Churchill had more trouble in finding adequate objects onto which to displace his aggression for his father; it was only during the Second World War that he at last hit upon a truly

---

[53] Mohandas K. Gandhi, *Hind Swaraj*, Ahmedabad, Navajivan Publishing House, 1931, pp. 24–27.

[54] Churchill, *Thoughts and Adventures*, p. 207.

[55] The mechanisms comprise the central dynamic of the "revolutionary personality." Hence we find them less developed in Churchill, who was not a revolutionist, than in the other three men.

suitable foe. Displacement also occurs with respect to other objects. Instead of the mother, the leader seeks to gain control of or protect the motherland or some other latter day image of the mother. Moreover, he looks for an object toward which he can express his feelings of love for the father. Again, Churchill did not carry this process as far as the other men. Hitler worshipped destiny and a conception of Aryan manhood, Lenin was a follower of Marx and history, and Gandhi was a servant of Rama; but Churchill's most important object of worship remained his father.

The process just described, whereby a man worships a god and fights an opposing demon which are both representations of what was originally one object, is what we mean by the splitting of ambivalence. And because this view of the world is based upon an effort to keep separated emotions which were originally joined, an enormous strain is involved—one which the individual seeks to mitigate by reducing ambiguity. As long as he can view those around him as either good or evil, but not both, he can avoid the feeling of ambivalence which plagued him during adolescence.

Finally, as was mentioned earlier, the leader also tries to push out of himself emotions or images which cause internal disruption. This may be thought of in terms of two processes. On the one hand, the individual seeks to superimpose the configuration of his internal conflict onto the world around him. On the other, he seeks to attribute to other people or forces emotions which exist within himself. Thus he does not conceive of himself as the originator of aggressive feelings toward his foe; rather it is the enemy who is the assailant, against whom the leader must defend himself and others. Similarly, he will view his ideological gods as loving him because he sees *in* them the love he has *for* them.[56] In similar fashion his followers also come to embody something of himself. He will see them as loving him or about to betray him at least in part as a result of the feelings he projects upon them.

It is no wonder, then, that the crisis leader lives in what he perceives as a dangerous world. Quite apart from the inherent difficulty of his situation, the leader brings with him a nightmare image of the world which accentuates its conflictful character. Yet it is a nightmare which the leader can control, one which he learned to manage during and after adolescence, and one from which he can gain a certain measure of satisfaction.

[56] There is a narcissistic component to this projective trend, for an individual's gods are also a part of the self. Hence in loving them and being loved by them the individual is essentially involved in a process of providing himself with emotional support.

Single-Mindedness

There is one further attribute of the crisis leader upon which we may comment briefly; that is, these men seem possessed of a truly unusual single-mindedness. As Lord Moran puts it in describing Churchill:

"There is (in Churchill) only an extraordinary concentration on one purpose—it amounted to an obsession—on victory, whatever it might cost. It was this single-mindedness which gave him his incomparable power during the war." [57]

For most of these men, this quality can be broken down into several parts. There is first of all a terrific ability to work devotedly at their tasks. All of the men were held somewhat in awe for their penchant to work long hours without interruption. They typically were able to outlast virtually all of their contemporaries, even much younger men, in the amount of time they were able to speak, function effectively in committee, write, or administer. In part, this probably represents an inborn stamina, augmented by the development of work skills during the latency period of childhood. But in part it also is a manifestation of a kind of psychic economy: these men channel an unusually large amount of their available energies into the performance of one set of tasks. Victory or domination is what is important to them; all other concerns must be sacrificed to this one goal.

Because they are so involved in this one activity, as well as for other reasons, crisis leaders are often rather ascetic. This is markedly true of all of the men we have examined except Churchill, who had a love for the good life and social amenities which is lacking in the others. Gandhi's asceticism was for him a matter of principle, a manifestation of his religious striving and of his need for punishment. In Lenin and Hitler it is perhaps somewhat more a by-product of their total involvement in the struggle, although self-punitive implications can be found in the practices of both men. In addition, all of these men are characterized by what the Bolsheviks term "hardness": an absence of sentimentality and a willingness to sacrifice anything or anyone to the cause. We have seen that the narcissism of the leader facilitates this hardness, but it has other roots as well.[58] In particular, it represents a response to the perceived dangerous-

[57] Moran, p. 825.

[58] Nathan Leites, in *A Study of Bolshevism*, (New York, Free Press, 1953), stresses the role of hardness as a reaction-formation to homosexual impulses.

ness of the environment, a steeling of the self to defend against the blows of the malevolent enemy.

Finally, to bring us back again to our genetic starting point, the leader's single-mindedness reflects the unitary nature of the adolescent crisis of identity such a man undergoes. Unlike many men, the potential leader faces in his youth a highly interconnected psychic conflict, centering around a small number of objects and susceptible of a consolidating solution. The crisis is unusually severe, and the possibility of total failure may be as great as that of extraordinary success. In fact, successful mastery of the crisis seems to be possible only when the individual has the internal strength to control and channel emotions which for most men would prove totally disruptive. But when such mastery is achieved, through the combined action of whatever repositories of internal strength the person possesses and a certain amount of cooperation from the environment, the individual finds a way of dealing with other crises as well—at least those which present in political form the same challenge as his own intrapsychic conflict.

7. Popular Leadership in the Anglo-American Democracies

ERWIN C. HARGROVE

The study of comparative politics seems to be coming into its own. We now compare party systems, the political consequences of class systems and political culture. However, the comparative study of governmental institutions has presented problems. Forms of government seem unique to each nation. Comparisons therefore seem to be between apples and oranges: for example, between the relation of a prime minister to Parliament and a president to Congress. We discover the differences that occasion uniqueness but develop no generalizations about political leadership.

However, we talk increasingly about the "convergence" of styles of leadership in modern democracies. Journalists inform us that British national elections are becoming "presidential" contests between two party leaders. This is sometimes described as a stage in the gradual "Americanization" of English and for that matter all European democratic politics. The impact of John F. Kennedy on people everywhere has caused many younger leaders in Europe to emulate his style of vitality and appeal to youth. Political scientists write of the inevitability of the "personalization of power" in modern industrial society. It is suggested that as the old politics of class and ideological conflict declines in Europe, as television becomes the chief means of political information for the public, as parties and parliaments weaken before the executive, power will increasingly become visible to people through popular leaders and these leaders will be the chief means of engaging the political interest of publics.

In Chapter 6 of this book Stanley Hoffmann implicitly rejects the notion of convergence by suggesting that political culture has great staying power no matter what changes may take place in social and economic spheres. He implies that national styles of authority, rooted in political culture, will probably generate quite different styles of leadership in different Western democracies in the future.

Perhaps these questions provide us with new ways to study leadership comparatively. We need to get beyond the comparison of institutional roles and view the way leaders in different democracies perform comparable functions. If we can apply the notion of style of authority, as Hoffmann does, and compare leaders in those terms, perhaps we can begin to evaluate concepts of convergence by studying trends in leadership style across political systems.

This chapter deals with one aspect of style. It examines the resources in political culture that are available for political leadership by the top political executive in the United States, Canada, and Great Britain. It is against this background of resources that leadership style develops and finds its scope and limits. What resources does a leader find in public attitudes toward the office of President or Prime Minister and toward leadership and power in general? How do the generalized normative goals of the political culture, which Hoffmann calls the political formula, motivate leaders and structure the character of political competition and the aspirations of the society? What is the place in the political culture accorded to the personalities of leaders and how does this provide opportunities or inhibitions for leadership? We shall ask these questions about the office of President and the two offices of Prime Minister. We will look at popular leadership, the evolution of support for policy through the persuasion of publics by the leader. We will not look at the playing of this role so much as at the cultural resources available for the playing of the role.

This view of leadership as shaped by and shaping culture does not eliminate more conventional explanations of leader behavior in terms of institutional and party structures and patterns of social and economic interests and current policy problems. The political culture approach needs to be integrated with these other approaches. We will look at institutions and party systems insofar as they reflect the political formula and style of authority of a society. However, any emphasis on a single factor can give the false impression that this is the key factor. This claim is not made here. It is just that we cannot look at everything at once.

These three countries share a common historical and cultural background. The difference in political culture are distinguishable and yet marginal, and therefore one can infer consequences of national political culture for leadership patterns. The study of Canada is helpful for comparisons of the United States and Britain, because Canada has the parliamentary institutions of Britain and the politics of a continental North American society.

This is a pioneer venture and we will have to make do with the existing data, indicate our speculations, suggest possible relationships, and, most important, pose our questions in a way that will encourage further research.

The American Political Formula

We are accustomed to read that Americans are the most pragmatic of people, concentrating on process and leaving questions of ends open to historical change.[1] Yet others assert that the American is a moral absolutist, that we are people of the covenant who have continually sought to realize a utopia of liberty and justice for all throughout our history.[2] These assertions can be reconciled. Americans operate on both the levels of utopia and practicality, of moral fervor and expediency, out of the long-range vision and the short-range improvisation.[3]

Louis Hartz has drawn a picture of colonial America as a "Fragment" of English society, representative of middle class, Puritan England, which would later make a national ideology out of the creed of liberty and individualism of the English thinker John Locke. Jefferson was to borrow from Locke to write the Declaration of Independence.[4] With the American Revolution the national ideology was reinforced with a sense of national mission and purpose, an impetus to utopia. But this was a cautious utopia, for it celebrated that which existed, the freedom of Americans, and ever after Americans have been conservative about their liberal values. Neither reactionary nor radical had a place in the Fragment. The contests of politics have been between two kinds of individualism.

The traditional ideology of the left half of the Fragment is use of the power of government to improve the lot of the common man, but to enhance individualism not curb it. Jefferson and Jackson were the authors of this tradition and in modern times it has taken form in the Progressive Movement and the popular presidents of reform, the two Roosevelts, Wilson, Truman, Kennedy, and Johnson.

The right half of the Fragment was developed by the Whigs in response to Jacksonian political competition and brought to success by Republicans after the Civil War. It identified the fruits of capitalism with democracy and preached the myth of Horatio Alger to the people. The role of government was to free spontaneous social forces which would then realize the American dream.

[1] Max Lerner, *America as a Civilization*, New York, Simon and Schuster, 1957, p. 359.

[2] William G. McLoughlin, "Pietism and the American Character," *The American Quarterly*, XVIII (Summer, 1965), *passim*.

[3] Abraham Kaplan, "American Ethics and Public Policy," *Daedalus*, 87 (Spring, 1958), *passim*.

[4] Louis Hartz, *The Founding of New Societies*, New York, Harcourt, Brace and World, 1964, Ch. 4, *passim*.

The movement of progressive reform that opposed some of the consequences of the policy of laissez faire was not radical but actually believed in the Alger myth. The object of reform was to restore American individualism by curbing giant economic organizations.[5] The Square Deal, the New Freedom, the New Deal, the Fair Deal, the New Frontier, and the Great Society have all been movements led by presidents seeking, by many different means, to increase opportunities for individual development among certain groups in the society. Each of these presidents was driven to use presidential power and moral leadership to achieve these goals. Style in the office and sense of purpose were combined as successive progressive presidents learned from those before. Wilson took his model of the strong, preaching president from Theodore Roosevelt. Franklin Roosevelt, who knew both, imitated them and said that he wanted to be a "preaching president" like his two models. The ideals of the Fragment have been a resource for leadership in the very motivations of individual presidents. It has given a dynamic quality to their leadership.[6]

The presidents of the right half of the Fragment have also had a utopian strain to them. Herbert Hoover was the most ideological of men. He described his dream of a capitalism that would serve the needs of all as "American Individualism" and his anger at the New Deal was expressed in terms of nationalism: the American Way was being violated. This was a spiritual materialism. American conservatives are also children of the American Revolution and are thus utopians.[7]

These two halves of the Fragment have not always been clear contests between the two parties. However, since Franklin Roosevelt, the Democratic party has carried the progressive tradition and the Republican party and Republican presidents have had to face the dilemma that in an age of positive government the Presidency has become a place for progressives. Eisenhower accepted the New Deal, continued to use the rhetoric of Hoover, and failed to find a satisfactory philosophy.[8] The utopian impetus of the right always threatens to break through and overwhelm the pragmatic method, as seen in 1964 when a Republican candidate for the Presidency promised to achieve the American utopia by reducing the power of government at home.[9]

[5] Clinton Rossiter, *Conservatism in America*, New York, Vintage Books, 1962, pp. 85–96.

[6] Erwin C. Hargrove, *Presidential Leadership, Personality and Political Style*, New York, Macmillan, 1966, *passim.*

[7] Seymour Lipset, *The First New Nation*, New York, Basic Books, 1963, pp. 89–90.

[8] James W. Prothro, "Verbal Shifts in the American Presidency: A Content Analysis," *American Political Science Review*, **L** (September, 1956), *passim.*

[9] Erwin C. Hargrove, "Note on American and Canadian Political Culture," *Canadian Journal of Economics and Political Science* XXXIII (February, 1967), passim.

We are familiar with the model of American parties as nonideological brokers among diverse sectional and interest groups. This is an accurate picture, but it leaves out the fact that presidents, as party leaders, use parties as instruments by which to realize the utopian dimension. One could develop a model of party competition in terms of the dialogue between the two halves of the Fragment.[10] The left party would be that of innovation and reform, the right party one of resistance and eventual acceptance. Voters would swing their votes in one direction or the other at crucial times and the result would be bursts of governmental action followed by periods of calm.

To what extent does our knowledge of the values of party activists and the voting behavior of the American people confirm this model and this general view of presidential leadership? The Fragment ideology is a resource to motivate presidents themselves, but do they in fact move others in such terms? The evidence indicates that political activists in both parties and a relatively small proportion of the electorate share the Fragment ideology and divide along partisan lines between its two traditions. However, it does not seem likely that most voters perceive leaders, parties, and government in these terms.

A study of the delegates to the two national party conventions of 1956 shows that those in each camp share common values that differentiate them from the other camp.[11] Ideological differences were found on a wide range of domestic issues and these were generally in line with the halves of the Fragment. Democrats saw themselves as progressives, committed to equality and welfare and positive action in the economy by government. Republicans saw themselves, to a great degree, as conservatives who put greater emphasis on a limited role for government and greater confidence in the ability of spontaneous social forces to meet common problems. It was also found that these leaders could identify and support a general body of ideas and values that roughly correspond with the ideology of the Fragment.[12]

The same study compared a national sample of voters to the leaders. It was found that rank and file party supporters are much less divided on policy and ideology than their leaders.[13] The most significant divisions

[10] Talcott Parsons, " 'Voting' and the Equilibrium of the American Political System," in *American Voting Behavior*, ed. by E. Burdick and A. J. Bradbeck, New York, Free Press, 1959, p. 88.

[11] Herbert McCloskey et al., "Issue Conflict and Consensus among Party Leaders and Followers," *American Political Science Review*, LIV (June, 1960), *passim.*

[12] Herbert McCloskey, "Consensus and Ideology in American Politics," *American Political Science Review*, LVIII (June, 1964), *passim.*

[13] McCloskey (June, 1960), *op. cit.*, 418.

were over concrete "bread and butter" questions and did parallel those of the activists. Symbolic and abstract questions were not easily grasped by the rank and file to be linked to either party. All of this denies the theory that divisions within the electorate are being smothered by broker party leaders. Rather, leaders appear to be the people who keep ideologies and ideological distinctions between parties alive.

As comparison with Canada will indicate, similar competitive conditions exist between the major parties there and yet the same ideological differentiation does not occur. Perhaps the political cultures of American and Canadian political activists are different? Mass publics in the two countries could be much alike in their attitudes and yet the values of the political class in each case could shape the patterns of party competition differently.

Mass publics may believe in the Fragment ideology even though they cannot link its specific tenets to particular policies. Perhaps presidential leadership of public opinion can make clear to publics the links between historic national ideals and specific policies in a way that a public opinion poll cannot. The study summarized suggests that this is not the case.[14] The electorate fell far below its leaders in terms of acceptance of various tenets of the democratic ideology. Even when statements were accepted as valid in the abstract, people had difficulty recognizing the principle in specific applications. Those parts of the ideology that find salience for most people are those that impinge directly on personal lives and are seen in concrete ways. The basic outline of Locke is there, but it is not put in terms of general principles and linked to issues.[15]

Voting studies sustain these general conclusions about the low level of ideological thinking in mass publics.[16] Perhaps ten per cent of the voters can be said to have liberal or conservative ideologies which have a certain internal consistency in terms of issue stands. Another ten per cent can recognize the terms and link them to parties. The majority of the electorate cannot do so, nor do they show great internal consistency of issue stands. As one moves down the scale from elites to publics, information, conceptual grasp, and internal consistency dwindle rapidly. However, a majority of the electorate is able to relate parties to social groupings, such as class and interest group, and to a few policies, and these distinctions are rough imitations of the liberal and conservative positions of the better educated, more ideological, and the activist.

Presidents and political activists share a political culture and shape

[14] McCloskey (June, 1964), *op. cit.*, *passim.*
[15] Robert E. Lane, *Political Ideology*, New York, Free Press, 1964, p. 349.
[16] Angus Campbell et al., *The American Voter*, New York, John Wiley and Sons, 1960, Ch. 9, *passim.*

political dialogue and programs in terms of values from that culture. The same dynamic quality that is seen in presidential leadership can therefore perhaps be found in the motivations and actions of party leaders, members of Congress, governors and mayors, and intellectuals of both parties. Again, the problem of a viable identity is greater on the right than on the left. Ideas are very important in the elite culture. They give leaders a sense of direction.

It would not seem accurate to picture presidents or parties as appealing to the public and winning elections in these general ideological terms. Even if the appeals are made in this language, and they often are, because leaders misperceive publics, the electorate does not respond in kind. Voters seek the concrete rather than the general and they respond to specific individuals more than to ideas.

We must now turn to the Presidency itself and ask what resources for leadership exist in popular attitudes toward the office and its incumbents.

Popular Attitudes toward the Presidency

In the political world of children the president is the earliest focal point for the political system. He is seen as a benevolent figure who cares for and protects them.[17] The schools inculcate morality and patriotism through stories about the boyhoods of Washington, Lincoln, and Theodore Roosevelt. Perhaps hero worship is a necessary part of American patriotism.[18] As an equalitarian democracy, we revere popular heroes who exemplify the national experience: Daniel Boone, Thomas Edison, the Wright brothers, and our presidents are all symbols of what we take to be our greatness.

There are only a few skeletal studies on which to base a theory of popular attitudes toward the Presidency, but certain themes do appear over and over.

1. The president is highly visible to the American people, and this is a result of his institutional position. He is head of state and chief national leader. Television brings the ceremony and the political drama of the Presidency to the people. The office of president carries great public respect. The American people may be cynical about politicians in the abstract but they respect their national leaders. Even though the percentages of popular support for presidents fluctuate over time, great bipartisan majorities usually approve the presidents' conduct of their

---

[17] Fred I. Greenstein, "Popular Images of the President," *American Journal of Psychiatry*, 122 (November, 1965), 525.

[18] Dixon Wecter, *The Hero in America*, Ann Arbor, Mich., Ann Arbor Paperbacks, University of Michigan Press, 1963, p. 2.

office over the long run. People seem reluctant to view a president in partisan terms. This is perhaps due to the symbolic power of a president as head of state and president of all the people.[19] A manifestation of this is the tendency of the public to rally behind a president at a time of international crisis, even if the events reflect unfavorably upon him.

2. The president must be thought of as a warm, democratic person in order to win wide popular acceptance. The electorate seems to need this reassurance that the president cares about them.[20] A study of attitudes toward Franklin D. Roosevelt in 1949 was designed as a pilot study of American images of the ideal leader. It found that 96 per cent of the sample said that Roosevelt was a good leader and that almost 34 per cent of the reasons cited for his being a good leader dealt with his personal characteristics.[21] The largest single reason, almost 20 per cent, was "warm personal characteristics," of which the greatest specific trait was "interested in people." Personality, character, and personal competence were also cited by many as attributes they admired. Also, the category of "functional competence," which dealt with skills of leadership, emphasized personal traits like courage and intelligence. Honesty and sincerity seem to be especially important traits that people look for in a president.[22]

3. The president is evaluated in terms of his policy accomplishments. Lane's subjects were disappointed that Eisenhower had not done something about the recession or the missile gap. They saw the president as having the responsibility to initiate, whereas Congress played the passive role of disposing and representing. The president was the protector and conscience of the nation.[23] The responses to the questions on Roosevelt emphasized his policy accomplishments in terms of what was done for specific groups. Presidential acts were made intelligible in the concrete terms of everyday life. Roosevelt was not judged in terms of the contributions he made to democratic ideals or practices.

4. Certain tentative models of the ideal president can be suggested on the basis of these studies. He should be a very powerful man who is personally very human and who will champion the cause of the common man. He must be seen as personally democratic and not cold in order to be trusted. The ideal president is "honest, intelligent, and independent. He is the strong knight in shining armor, the 'Mr. District Attorney' or

[19] Greenstein, *op. cit.*, pp. 525–526.

[20] *Ibid.*, p. 526.

[21] Fillmore H. Sanford, "Public Orientation to Roosevelt," *Public Opinion Quarterly,* 15 (Summer, 1951), 191–198.

[22] Roberta S. Sigel, "Image of the American Presidency," *Midwest Journal of Political Science,* X (February, 1966), 130.

[23] Lane, *op. cit.*, pp. 147–174.

Teddy Roosevelt as folklore or television picture them; smart enough to figure out new solutions and honest and independent enough to pursue them no matter what the intimidation." [24]

5. Americans have an ambivalence about power and power holders. The Declaration of Independence condemns a king and implies that power corrupts. The weak executives of the Articles of Confederations and the first state governments proved that the absence of power can also corrupt. The constitutional office of president was thus made strong but hedged in by restraints and, since the Twenty-Second Amendment, by limited tenure. This would seem to be the manifestation of American ambivalence about power. We place great demands on executives in most of our organizations and institutions, but we also place restraints. This requires the leader to struggle for the additional power necessary to do the job. The struggle excites popular admiration and also triggers popular fear. Americans like dynamic leaders, for dynamism and innovation are national characteristics. The pioneer, the inventor, the captain of industry, and the political leader all exemplify our admiration for "the man in charge" and the man "who gets things done." We are optimistic about our ability to handle social problems and look to our leaders for solutions. But at the same time that the tempo of our national life demands strong leaders, the style of authority in the home and the school puts emphasis not on paternal power but on individual development. Americans do not like authority that threatens individual autonomy. We make secular saints out of our dead great presidents and forget the poor ones. The ambivalence is split after death. But living presidents must cope with this ambivalence. They must appear always to be more than a politician, more than an ambitious man.

The American people have been shown in polls to be very much in favor of the two-term limitation on presidential tenure. The fear of abuse of power seems to be an important reason for this.[25] However, approval of the limitation may not mean disapproval of a strong executive. The popular preference is for a strong president with limited tenure. This formula satisfies the ambivalence.

Studies of public reactions to the death of John F. Kennedy illustrate some of the points made here.[26] They reveal that the president is perceived as the head of the nation, as the protector of the nation, and as a person. The assassination brought all of these levels to an emotional pitch

[24] Siegel, *op. cit.,* p. 131.

[25] Roberta S. Sigel and David J. Butler, "The Public and the No Third Term Tradition: Inquiry into Attitudes Toward Power," *Midwest Journal of Political Science,* VII (February, 1964), 44.

[26] Bradley S. Greenberg and Edwin B. Parker, eds., *The Kennedy Assassination and the American Public,* Stanford, Cal., Stanford University Press, 1965, *passim.*

at the same time. A blow was struck against a beloved man, an office of great importance, and the nation. Such a public reaction illustrates the potentialities of the office for leadership.

The initial shock was over the death of the person. People compared it to the death of a friend or relative. People had many different personal identifications with Kennedy, either because they liked him personally or liked his policies. He was looked on as a benevolent leader.[27] To the young especially he was an ego ideal. College students commented on the great impact his youth, idealism, and vitality had on them. He was a model to emulate.[28] Something about the president's symbolic position and the public's continual exposure to him causes many people to incorporate him into their own worlds.

The great shock that people, even the nominally politically apathetic, felt about the assassination indicates that the Presidency is a focus of loyalty to the nation which seems to be deeply rooted in citizens. This loyalty, which, as we have seen, is not expressed by many people in terms of a conscious ideology, may nevertheless be there. Otherwise the popular shock at the assassination would not have been so profound.[29]

What might all this mean for resources in the political culture for presidential leadership? Since we are emphasizing prerequisites to leadership and not leadership itself we can only suggest possible links between culture and leadership style. A president can be the chief force of public education about government and policy. He has great visibility and thus the opportunity to teach and give people a sense of participation. He can be a symbol of reassurance that someone is in charge, and he can win considerable support for his actions simply because he is president. He can be the symbol of national unity and cast his policies and teaching in these terms. He can present his personality in an attractive way and win popular affection which may encompass approval of his actions.

However, each of these methods has its limitations. The public lacks political information and therefore the president must be extremely skillful in knowing how to seize public attention at crucial moments, dramatize events or his own acts, and teach the significance of acts and events to the public. Often no one is listening.[30] The American people trust a president, other things being equal, but they also tend to invest their

[27] James D. Barber, "Peer Group Discussion and Recovery from the Kennedy Assassination," in Greenberg and Parker, *op. cit.,* p. 117.

[28] Fred I. Greenstein, "College Students' Reactions," in Greenberg and Parker, *op. cit.,* p. 234.

[29] Sidney Verba, "The Kennedy Assassination and the Nature of Political Commitment," in Greenberg and Parker, *op. cit.,* pp. 359–360.

[30] Richard Neustadt, *Presidential Power,* New York, John Wiley and Sons, 1960, Ch. 5, *passim.*

optimism, their faith in good will and technique in one man. If events go against him for any length of time his popularity may sour. We ask too much and then condemn too much.

Presidential Personality

American political life has produced a rich variety of personalities: Huey Long, Al Smith, Fiorello La Guardia, Franklin Roosevelt, Dwight Eisenhower, John Kennedy, Lyndon Johnson, Barry Goldwater; just to list a few names reveals both the variety of cultural background and the great individuality. American political leaders reflect the self-confidence and vitality of American life. They shine with excitement. Perhaps a political leader takes on the vitality or lack of vitality of his culture and national myth.

It is often suggested that other polities are taking over the American emphasis on personality in politics. But more may be involved than just taking over public relations techniques and concern with the image of the leader. One can transfer techniques across cultures, but can the underlying attitudes that make them blossom in one place do so in a new place? For that matter there is much talk of the role of personality in presidential politics but very little analysis of what this implies for leadership.

Voting studies show that the candidates' personality is an important factor in voting behavior, along with party loyalty and salient issues. Most Americans have stable party affiliations which are primarily rooted in social identities. But there is sufficient fluidity in the society and in popular attitudes for elections to be won or lost on short run factors, such as attitudes toward the candidates and issues, even if party loyalties do not change in the short run. The fact that the presidential candidates run alone in a system of separation of powers surely increases this tendency.

The importance of the candidate factor varies from election to election and it is difficult to generalize about it. Presidential elections from 1952 through 1964 show that the three candidates of the Republican party had very great effects on Republican victory and defeat. The candidacy of Eisenhower gave the party an extraordinary plus factor and the candidacy of Goldwater brought the party to its lowest point.[31]

If personality is a resource for electoral leadership, the implications for policy leadership are unclear until we know what it is about personality that the voters admire. One way to evaluate the importance of personality for policy leadership is to look at the opinion polls over time and see to what extent public approval and disapproval of presidents and their policies seems related to presidential personality. With Roosevelt the one

[31] Donald E. Stokes, "Some Dynamic Elements of Contests for the Presidency," *American Political Science Review,* **LX** (March, 1966), 22.

thing that immediately stands out is public perception of the warmth of his personality. People felt he was their friend.[32] But his actions were the basis for the favorable impression. What if F.D.R. had pursued Hoover's policies? During his second term popular support for the New Deal weakened and F.D.R. was seen by some voters in a new light, as a man bent on excessive personal power.[33] Yet his personal popularity was not damaged. People still liked him, but they could evaluate the man and his actions and policies separately.[34] The polls suggest that Roosevelt might not have been reelected in 1940 or 1944 had it not been for the threat of war and then the fact of war. A majority of those polled felt that it was better he retire should war not come or should it end and said they would not vote for him in that case.[35] These findings show that personality is a resource, but only one among several and it must be reinforced by acts and events to make it effective for policy leadership.

Thomas E. Dewey was not widely liked as a person: he was seen as cold and lacking in humanity. This was a serious electoral liability.[36] No one could accuse Harry Truman of lack of human qualities, but his popularity rating oscillated more wildly than that of any modern president. For much of the time he was not seen by the electorate as a man in charge. People tended to blame him for the difficult problems of the postwar years, and his personality or his public posture in the White House gave little reassurance that he was in command.[37]

Eisenhower was liked by nearly everyone as a person. It is also clear that the electorate looked to him for strong leadership, especially in foreign affairs. He did not so much engender fears of abuse of power as occasional anxiety that he was not on top of things. His popularity fell at times due to presidential inaction.[38] What appeared to be decisive acts by the President would cause his approval rating to go up.[39]

The man Kennedy is now becoming a myth, but one study of attitudes towards the man just after his death shows that even as he was being made a hero there was not uncritical acceptance of his policies. Medicare, federal aid to education, and civil rights were discussed by his admirers in a balanced way.[40] This idealization of the man coupled with mixed feelings toward his policies was a continuous fact during his Presidency.

[32] Elmo Roper, *You and Your Leaders, Their Actions and Your Reactions, 1936–1956*, New York, Morrow, 1957, p. 24.
[33] *Ibid.*, p. 30.
[34] *Ibid.*, p. 34.
[35] *Ibid.*, pp. 38–54.
[36] *Ibid.*, pp. 111–112.
[37] *Ibid.*, pp. 115–150.
[38] *Ibid.*, p. 267; John Fenton, *In Your Opinion*, Boston, Little, Brown, 1960, p. 115.
[39] Roper, *op. cit.*, p. 268; Fenton, *op. cit.*, p. 121.
[40] Barber, Greenberg, and Parker, *op. cit.*, p. 127.

The monarchical character of the presidency may permit people to compartmentalize personality from policy just as it causes the two to blend.

The dilemma of Lyndon B. Johnson seems to be that despite great effectiveness and achievement in the office, he cannot generate the human warmth and democratic character that people require in a president. There was massive public approval of Johnson's conduct as President in the aftermath of Kennedy's death and the phenomenon of the Goldwater candidacy. However, the Vietnam war and domestic dislocations at home attendant on the war caused the President's popularity to drop to the 50 per cent mark in September 1966.[41] Events are the crucial factor here, but Johnson lacks the respect of the electorate that might enable him to use events in such a way as to win support. The evidence on this is very sketchy, coming primarily from the reports of journalists, but it appears that large numbers of people do not trust the President, find him to be an unattractive person, too much of a politician, and sleight of hand artist. He suffers from the shadow of the Kennedy personality and has to compete with an idealized Kennedy, not only in the person of the past President but in the person of his living brother. However, the idealization of Robert Kennedy not only illustrates the "star" character of American politics but that President Johnson seems unable to meet the need for warmth and reassurance which the public saw in Roosevelt, Eisenhower, and John F. Kennedy.[42]

What conclusions can we draw from all this about personality as a resource for policy leadership?

1. Personal characteristics of warmth and color are necessary but not sufficient for effective popular leadership. They must be joined to actions and policies that will meet with public approval.

2. The structure and aura of the Presidency compel that great attention be given to the personality of the incumbent. It is possible for an individual president to be "institutionalized," so that his personality becomes a reference point for the views of many citizens about policy and events.[43]

3. American voters must judge new political personalities often. This introduces an element of caprice into the system, but the "movie star" phenomenon is quite rare in contests for the Presidency. Candidates and presidents are judged as political personalities.

4. One benefit derived from caprice is innovation. The advent of fresh

---

[41] *The New York Times* (September 13, 1966), p. 32.

[42] "The Kennedy Legend and the Johnson Performance," *Time Magazine* (November 26, 1965), 30–31.

[43] V. O. Key, Jr., *Public Opinion and American Democracy*, New York, Alfred A. Knopf, 1961, p. 250.

personalities can be a strong factor for the introduction of new ideas and practices into the political system.[44]

Style and Resources

What can we conclude about resources for popular leadership?

1. The Presidents are pushed to reinterpret the American experience and American ideals for the nation and to solve problems in these terms. They are brokers in ideas. The drive to realize the American dream brings great potential dynamism to the Presidency and to the ideational culture of political and nonpolitical elites.

2. Mass publics do not participate in this ideological dimension, but they will respond to the Presidency as a symbol of national unity, national interest, and a source of help and protection. The institution has symbolic and emotional overtones which are a great resource for presidents who would lead.

3. The "strong" presidents are those who seek to lead public opinion, the "weak" presidents are those who play a passive role.[45] Weak presidents are often described as "nonpartisan" presidents who seek to be popular with all by offending no one; "strong" presidents are described as "partisan" leaders who make enemies by creating majorities for action.[46] This distinction describes weak presidents but fails to see that strong presidents must seek consensual majorities with strong support in most major groups in the population. They seek to extract support from the consensual majority they build up. The president must be more than a party leader to the public because of popular attitudes to leadership, which see him as protector of the nation rather than as a divisive force.

4. American political culture has a number of tensions and dichotomies which provide the cultural limits and resources for presidential leaders.

The president is head of state and chief politician. He is preacher and pragmatist. He must be a strong leader and yet a warm person. The office is strong, yet encircled with checks. He must innovate, yet he must take soundings and seek consensus. These tensions reflect cultural styles that are products of our history. They ensure that presidents will have to struggle to achieve. Tension is the source of creativity and dynamism in the Presidency.

---

[44] *Ibid.*, p. 253.

[45] Sidney Hyman, *The American President*, New York, Harper and Row, 1954, p. 66.

[46] Stuart Gerry Brown, *The American Presidency; Leadership, Partisanship and Popularity*, New York, Macmillan, 1966, p. 31.

The Canadian Political Formula

If the United States is a Fragment of England that had a revolution, Canada is a Fragment that did not have one.[47] The American colonists who fled to Canada at the time of the American Revolution were united by a loyalty to England and opposition to revolution. These populations were the original base for modern English Canada. The French population which was in Canada rejected the French Revolution and its ideology. Canada thus has two Fragments, neither of which has any sense of messianic destiny for Canada as a whole. The English half has for most of its history been a colonial culture. The French half has until recently been a closed society concerned with preserving its cultural integrity against the English Fragment. This section will deal only with the content of the English Fragment, because it has been the principal source of the political style of Canadian national leaders.

In concert with colonial administrators, Canadian elites created a society in which obedience to government, respect for established churches, and loyalty to empire were dominant. There was no national democratic ideology, no Jefferson, no Jackson.[48]

In the nineteenth century the various provinces of Canada developed Cabinet government by the slow, gradual process of capture of the executive power by legislatures. Cabinets developed as collections of leaders of the legislative parties. This was not done by dramatic, popular actions, and the language of governmental reform was the language of parliamentarism.[49]

Formal democracy eventually came and national political parties developed in the aftermath of Confederation in 1867. To understand the politics that developed we must look at certain traits of the political culture.

1. Although Canada is a democracy, she has been a monarchical country and not a nation of the "social compact," like the United States. Allegiance means that the law and the state have an objective reality. They

[47] Kenneth D. Mcrae in Hartz, *op. cit.*, Ch. 7, *passim*. G. Horowitz, "Conservatism, Liberalism and Socialism in Canada: An Interpretation," *Canadian Journal of Economics and Political Science*, **XXXII** (May, 1966), *passim*.

[48] Frank Underhill, *In Search of Canadian Liberalism*, Toronto, Macmillan, 1960, p. 12.

[49] Chester B. Martin, *The Foundations of Canadian Nationhood*, Toronto, University of Toronto Press, 1955, *passim*.

do not rest on contemporary assent.[50] Canadian political society has thus stressed order, loyalty, and deference to government more than popular assent. Rather than "life, liberty and the pursuit of happiness" the creed has been "peace, order and good government."

2. There has been no Canadian "way of Life" or Canadian sense of national mission. Canadian nationalism has been negative, a desire to be neither British nor American. If the American revolution opened up new springs of energy and new horizons and gave new gospels to a people, the Canadians, lacking a revolution, got no such release. They began life with a "nostalgic shove" back into history.[51]

3. Canadian political style is not generally evangelical. Whereas American political culture works on the two levels of utopia and pragmatism, Canada has only pragmatism. Canadian political leaders have lacked the drive to fulfill an abstract Canadian dream of the "good society." The central Canadian problem has been the preservation of sufficient unity for the nation to endure, thus Canadian leaders have had to be skilled pragmatists.

4. Canadian political and social values are the same as American, but more muted.[52] Social equality is desired, but with less fervor than in America. Hierarchy in all spheres of life is taken for granted. There is much less drive to improve the lot of all citizens by government action than in the United States, although, paradoxically, because there is less fear of government, the minimal welfare state is well developed.

5. Canadian society is midway between English and American society in the degree to which elite structures dominate styles of authority and the making of decisions in many different spheres. S.D. Clark maintains that Canada was the creation of business, political, religious, and cultural groups which sought monopolistic control. These groups were unable to promulgate a mass-based political patriotism. In time, these elite groups evolved from "family compacts" of the early nineteenth century into a relatively small, cohesive upper middle class with common educational and class backgrounds and strategic location in the pyramids of power in Canadian society.[53] They have dominated both major political parties. If

---

[50] W. L. Morton, *The Canadian Identity*, Madison, Wis., University of Wisconsin Press, 1961, pp. 84–87.

[51] A. R. M. Lower, *Colony to Nation: A History of Canada*, Toronto, Longmans Green, 1946, p. 135.

[52] Kaspar Naegele, "Canadian Society: Some Reflections" in *Canadian Society*, ed. by B. Blishen et al., Toronto, Macmillan, 1961, pp. 27–29.

[53] S. D. Clark, "Canada and the American Value System," in *La Dualité Canadienne A L'Heure Des Etats-Unis*, Quebec, Les Presses de L'Universite Laval, 1965, pp. 93–94.

a comparable group in America has been more open to new recruits or more dispersed among conflicting groups and the carrier of the national ideology of improvement and reform, so the articulate classes have been the carriers of the ideology of Canada as a conservative nation. The Canadian middle class has lacked interest in making its society over.[54]

This Fragment ideology and the class that carries it have shaped the patterns of party competition in Canada as in the United States. In Canada there is no "charter myth" against which progress can be measured and parties can compete. The two major parties have not divided on a right-left debate over the proper role of government. Canadian elites have had to use the power of strong central government in order to secure the western frontier for Canada, foster economic development of the nation, and ensure a minimum of national unity. There has been no group in Canada comparable to laissez faire conservatives of the American right. Positive government in Canada has been "Hamiltonian": it has favored the pragmatic use of power for concrete ends without a guiding ideology. It follows that the "Jeffersonian" impulse to use government for social improvement has been largely absent. If Canadian conservatives have not been reactionaries, Canadian liberals have not been progressives. There was nothing comparable to the American Progressive movement in Canada as a manifestation of middle class desire for widespread social reform. Canada had no "New Deal" like that of Roosevelt. The welfare state came to Canada during World War II through the expertise of civil servants working behind the scenes.[55]

Party leaders have been managers of majorities, not men inspired by visions. The major parties have seen their tasks as the promotion of national unity, especially with respect to the English-French problem and the economic development of the nation. It is not just the lack of a utopian vision in the political formula which has made for such parties. National unity has been so fragile that it has had to take precedence over all other issues. Canadian elites would not have found a left-right polarity congenial, but it is also true that such a polarity would be a luxury Canada could not afford. It has been much more important for political leaders to build bridges between sections, religions, and interests than to seek to divide them.[56]

There has been a left-right dialogue in Canadian politics but it has been between the two major parties and minor parties of protest, both

[54] *Ibid.*, p. 97.

[55] Peter Regenstreif, *The Diefenbaker Interlude*, Toronto, Longmans Canada Ltd., 1965, pp. 16–17.

[56] John Porter, *Vertical Mosaic*, Toronto, University of Toronto Press, 1965, pp. 368–369.

agrarian protest and urban, labor protest. The Social Credit and the CCF (now NDP) parties have been challenges to the prevailing values of the "establishment" of Canadian elites.

Canadian party politics have been characterized by long periods of dominance of one party. This dominance has been based on a welding together of majority coalitions of great diversity. Under Sir John A. Macdonald and Sir Wilfred Laurier, in the fifty years after Confederation the Conservatives and Liberals respectively were parties of national unity through economic development and English-French compromise. Under Mackenzie King the years of Liberal dominance in the 1930s and 1940s, and the 1950s under Louis St. Laurent, were based on the popular image of the Liberal party as the party of efficient government and social peace. The Liberal majority never had the same social bases as the Democratic party of Roosevelt. The rise of the CCF in the 1930s was evidence of this. The Liberals, the majority party of modern Canada, have based their majorities upon patchwork support in all groups and regions.[57]

Canadian prime ministers and national leaders in general have had to pursue a low-temperature style of leadership. The task was not to use conflicts for purposes of action but to dampen conflicts for purposes of victory. Canadian prime ministers have not brought a vision of utopia to their tasks. The great prime ministers have been giants of pragmatism in a political culture which has no place for heroes.

Since Confederation, Canada has had three great periods of national leadership, under Macdonald from 1867 to the 1890s, under Laurier from that time until 1911, and under King. Their styles of national leadership all had the same purpose and drew on the same strategies and tactics. If the two Roosevelts and Wilson are the American modal type of the great president, these three are the Canadian modal type. The Canadian counterpart of the weak president is not the man who will not preach to the people but the man who does, the man who puts principle over pragmatism. Usually such prime ministers have been leaders of factions within the country who have succeeded in turning a majority of the country against them. Arthur Meighen, R.B. Bennett, and perhaps John Diefenbaker fit here.

Macdonald was a genius at compromise, a man who thought with his pores, who governed in terms of management of Parliament and party and the great economic interests. His goals were to keep British North America British by joining governmental and economic power to develop Canada. The Canadian Pacific Railroad was his means and his monument. His habitual tactic was that of delay until he could see the trend and then

[57] Regenstreif, *op. cit.*, pp. 16–18; p. 24.

follow it. He was a poor executive and a brilliant manipulator. He did lead but in terms of the creation of concrete national unity, not abstract goals.[58]

Laurier, a French-Canadian who drew his ideology from British Liberalism, pursued Macdonald's objectives with the same style. Like Macdonald, he relied on his party as the vehicle of national unity, a bridge to all groups. He concentrated on the single task of settling questions quietly.[59] After his defeat in 1911 he wrote: "I am a Canadian. Canada has been the inspiration of my life. I have had before me as a pillar of fire by night and pillar of cloud by day a policy of Canadianism, of moderation, of conciliation. . . ." [60] To him Canadianism meant concrete unity, not ideals.

The nation building goal was obsolete for King and he concentrated on making the Liberal party the agent of English-French unity in the aftermath of the dispute over conscription of French-Canadians in World War I. He sought to nurture consensus by avoiding decisive action of any kind until events forced action. It was King was brought the nation through World War II in unity and successfully imposed conscription on Quebec by a tortuous process of manipulation and negotiation. King gave Canada a welfare state by sleight of hand, administrative action, and no political fanfare. Yet on the surface he was the very essence of inaction.[61]

These men had great achievements to their credit, but none of them had a vision of the "good society," only of the good Canada. They faced the same problems in the same ways. The political culture gave them scant resources for popular leadership and they had to be brokers. There was nothing in their ideological makeup or that of the political class from which they came that offered a larger vision out of which a more unified Canada might be created. Their problems were real and independent of the political culture, but the culture provided no resources for solutions, no visions.

Popular Attitudes toward the Prime Minister

The prime minister is not head of state or ceremonial leader. The governor general acts as the Queen's representative. It is difficult to tell what Canadians think of the institution of governor general, but most Canadian observers seem to feel that the Monarchy as an institution is of increasingly little interest to the great majority of Canadians. We can infer that

[58] Steven Muller, *The Canadian Prime Ministers 1867–1948*, Ph.D. Dissertation, Cornell University, 1958, p. 684.
[59] *Ibid.*, pp. 691–695.
[60] *Ibid.*, p. 331.
[61] *Ibid.*, pp. 697–700.

the prime minister does not have in his office the powerful emotional resources of a president. The prime minister is chief politician, the leader of a Cabinet team and a party. He must stand up in the House of Commons every day and face attacks from an Opposition and answer as a partisan. There seems nothing in his institutional role for him to draw on for popular support beyond the resources available to a political leader.

Canadians do not seem to have national heroes like Americans. John A. Macdonald is the Canadian George Washington but he is not revered as a myth. He is seen as all too human and his periodic drunkenness is frankly discussed by Canadians today. There do not seem to be any Canadian Davy Crocketts or Henry Fords. No military figures have become political leaders. There are few "stars" in any field except hockey.[62] Perhaps a democracy must have a strong nationalism in order to have popular heroes. Whatever the cause, Canada has a poverty of political symbols. In the summer of 1966 I asked thirty-seven young Toronto business and professional people in prominent firms and institutions, in the course of extended interviews, what symbols they thought of when they thought of Canada. A few said none. One said the flag, which is new. After the rest had paid the conventional lip-service to the maple leaf and the beaver, they talked of pine trees, lakes, wheat fields, the Atlantic coast, blizzards. No one mentioned the Prime Minister or the Queen or the government.[63]

There is a dominant theory of what Canadians want in a leader, as expressed by one of the respondents. They want to be governed without fuss or fanfare and to be left alone. Most of the respondents were critical of their fellow Canadians for not caring about government. One expressed the view that King was the ideal leader to Canadians because he managed to solve problems without involving the public. This picture is in line with the notion of Canadians as cautious, undynamic, seeking comfortable nests for themselves.

A blend of old and new attitudes toward the office of prime minister was seen in the subjects of the Toronto study. They were asked what they thought were the most important political roles of the prime minister. All of them stressed the prime minister as the leader of a Cabinet, who must get his team to govern in harmony. All mentioned the importance of sensitivity to national conflicts and the role of broker for national unity. All but two felt that the present prime minister, Lester Pearson, was a poor political leader lacking in strength. They divided on whether or not the prime minister needs to be a popular leader. Two-thirds said yes and the

---

[62] Lower, *op. cit.*, p. 429.

[63] Erwin C. Hargrove, Unpublished Interviews, June and July, 1966, Toronto, Ontario, Canada.

rest said no. The majority did not want the idealization of a prime minister, as they saw occurring with American presidents. The majority agreed that Canadian leaders usually lacked color and popular appeal and deplored it. There was a mood of despair about many of the answers. Canada seemed to be falling apart, current leadership was weak. Leaders were badly needed to give the nation unity and a sense of purpose. Yet on questions about national sense of purpose most of the respondents floundered. It was clear that the majority had a weak sense of national identity. They did not want to be Americans and were not Englishmen. Few had any notions of how English and French could be reconciled in Canada. Few had any sense of purpose for government action in the improvement of the society beyond piecemeal social measures or economic development.

These responses suggest that among these people the old broker model is somewhat discredited. It is clear that John F. Kennedy had a great influence on them. Almost all named him as the modern leader they most admired. They seemed to be groping for new styles of leadership. These responses must be put in the context of current Canadian history to be meaningful and for that we turn to the role of personality in politics.

Political Personality

Of the three party systems under consideration, the leader is most important in Canadian parties for party unity and electoral success. This is because parties mean much less to rank and file voters in Canada.[64] Neither major party has stable social group affiliations. Labor supports the NDP and business supports both major parties. Thus the personality of the leader is extremely important in the continually changing public images of the parties.

In 1957 John Diefenbaker, the leader of the Conservative party, ousted the Liberal government from office, and in 1958 Diefenbaker received a great parliamentary majority. There was talk of a new era in Canadian politics, of a new period of national development and vision. Diefenbaker campaigned on this theme, promising to develop the Canadian north, to restore the economy to Canadian hands (an implied anti-Americanism), to extend the welfare state and equality of opportunity to all Canadians. He created a burst of national enthusiasm. This was not a new thing in Canadian politics. Macdonald and Laurier had made themselves agents of a sublimated national unity. However, earlier leaders had been able to develop formulas of compromise, of integration of interests on which stable majority coalitions could be built. Diefenbaker was unable to do this. In the 1962 election his government became a minority one and in

---

[64] Regenstreif, *op. cit.*, p. 24.

1963 he was displaced by a minority Liberal government. The legacy of Diefenbaker was the fragmentation of political support and the increased support for minor parties and public alienation from both major parties.

Diefenbaker was a great campaigner who brought to national politics an evangelical, camp meeting, courtroom style of oratory from his native Saskatchewan.[65] He seems to contradict what has been said about the dullness of Canadian politics, about the lack of evangelical fervor, of the lack of national vision. There was speculation at the time of his great victory that he was bringing an end to the old broker style and ushering in a "nationalization" of politics. It was suggested that his appeal was greatest among those groups in the population who were highly mobile socially and geographically and inclined to think nationally, especially westerners and metropolitan suburbanites.[66] The theory was that a mobile, fluid society lacking stable political guidelines is likely to support a dramatic leader who makes national appeals. Perhaps a new Canadian social structure was to make possible a new kind of national leadership.

Diefenbaker sought to be a new Macdonald, to give Canada a new sense of national purpose. But his government could not develop programs to give form to that hope. It was divided on policy lines and Diefenbaker, who lacked executive skills, could not lead his Cabinet effectively.[67] Although Diefenbaker sought a new era for Canada, his personal biases were those of a man of the West, distrustful of the Canadian "establishment" of civil service and the business and financial interests of Toronto and Montreal. Yet he was not able to put politics on a left-right polarity because his own ideas were those of the small town businessmen of the past. He was a populist.[68]

Regenstreif suggests that the principal reason that Diefenbaker faded politically was that he lost the confidence of the Canadian "establishment," whom Regenstrief calls "opinion leaders": a group of perhaps five per cent of the electorate to whom much of the public looks for electoral guidance. This is interpreted as the reflection of a "deferential" political culture, more like the English than the American.[69]

George Grant suggests that Diefenbaker failed because he lacked a

---

[65] John Meisel, *The Canadian General Election of 1957*, Toronto, University of Toronto Press, 1962, pp. 155–156.

[66] Regenstreif, *op. cit.*, pp. 32, 146, 153; S. D. Clark, "Group Interests in Canadian Politics," in *The Political Process in Canada*, ed. by J. H. Aitchison, Toronto, University of Toronto Press, 1963, p. 74.

[67] Peter C. Newman, *Renegade in Power: The Diefenbaker Years*, Toronto, McClelland and Stewart, 1963, pp. 94–95; Bruce Hutchinson, *Mr. Prime Minister, 1867–1964*, New York, Harcourt, Brace and World, 1964, p. 327.

[68] Newman, *op. cit.*, pp. 179–182.

[69] Regenstreif, *op. cit.*, p. 80.

clear vision of what Canada could be. He was often at cross purposes with himself.[70] Grant concludes that the idea of Canada as a nation is now impossible, that the kind of traditional "conservatism" on which Canada was founded is impossible in a modern industrial society dominated by the liberal gospel of progress. To Grant the Canadian "establishment" is Liberal and it has sold its birthright to the United States and turned Canada into a "branch plant" society.

It is too soon to write the history of Diefenbaker or evaluate these theories. His defeat seems to have been more of a defeat for his party than for the man. He needed more time to create public confidence in the Conservative party, which had been in the wilderness for so long. Public confidence in Diefenbaker as a man continued for a time and it seems to have been his popularity that denied the Liberals majority governments in the 1963 and 1965 elections.[71] The conflict that voters faced was between the appeal of Diefenbaker as a person and identification with the Liberals as good managers of government. The Liberal leader, Lester Pearson, was not liked by a great many voters. He seemed weak and colorless. But his party was the majority choice. To vote for Diefenbaker one had to vote Conservative. This distinguishes a parliamentary from a presidential system in which voters can choose between presidential candidates regardless of party. Regenstreif concludes that had Canada had a presidential system in 1963 Diefenbaker would have been elected president and the Liberals would have captured Congress.[72] This institutional fact is a great limitation on the effectiveness of political personality in Canada. It is harder to separate a leader from his party than it is in the United States. The public may wish to punish a party or a government without punishing the leader, but this is impossible. This seems to have been true with Diefenbaker and the Conservatives. The party still had the image of a Protestant, English, Ontario party of the financial interests and there was not time to change it.

There was a genuine public feeling in 1963 that the nation required new leadership. The public seemed bored with the old leaders. The Kennedy style had impressed itself on Canadians and election surveys repeatedly received the answer that "what this country needs is someone like Jack Kennedy."[73] Canadian Gallup Polls for the years 1964, 1965, and 1966 show that almost half the electorate cannot say what they admire about Pearson or Diefenbaker.[74] A majority of the electorate would

---

[70] George Grant, *Lament for a Nation,* Princeton, N. J., Van Nostrand, 1965, p. 12.
[71] Regenstreif, *op. cit.,* pp. 41–42.
[72] *Ibid.,* p. 82.
[73] *Ibid.,* p. 80.
[74] *Canadian Institute of Public Opinion,* May 2, 1964; May 6, 1964.

like both old leaders to retire and call for new, younger leadership.[75] A series of events in 1965 and 1966, especially scandals in the Pearson government and revelations of scandals in the past Diefenbaker government, caused a public revulsion against the leadership of both old parties.

Political personality is as important in Canada in regard to the office of prime minister as it is in regard to the American president. However, the parliamentary and electoral system inhibit this factor. The office of prime minister has few of the symbolic reinforcements to leadership of the presidency. The national political formula lacks a dimension of vision for political heroes, and the political class and politically articulate upper middle classes either hold to the old Fragment ideals or have lost even these in a gradual process of Americanization. In addition to this, national political leaders are dull. This seems to be partly because so many of the Cabinet ministers come from either the corporation board room or the high civil service.[76] Mackenzie King and Lester Pearson were originally civil servants. Life in Ottawa as a backbencher is not sufficiently interesting to hold young men. Ambitious men leave for other work and return only for Cabinet posts. The political class is thus composed of "administrative politicians," to use Porter's phrase, and their style of leadership is the low temperature, colorless, broker style. This is very different from the political entrepreneurs found among American governors and senators. The character of incumbents in the two highest offices in each country reflects the different characters and recruitment bases of the respective political classes.

Style and Resources

Canada is currently in crisis. The province of Quebec, representing French-Canadians, has emerged from its cocoon of a traditional society and seeks not only modernization but cultural autonomy for itself *vis-à-vis* the rest of Canada. This centrifugal pull from the center has encouraged comparable pulls, especially from the West, and as a result a fragmented society is increasingly divided and a once strong Federal government is increasingly weak. The Canadian "establishment" of Toronto and Montreal seems to have lost confidence in itself and its way of life as an alternative to the American way of life. The English Canadian has little ground on which to appeal to the French-Canadian in terms of a common national identity. Should French Canada survive the fury of its "separatists" it too will perhaps be incorporated into North American cultural patterns. Meanwhile, however, the major parties are unable to provide leaders or ideas to either unite the nation or give it a reason for existence

---

[75] *Ibid.,* May 28, 1966.
[76] Porter, *op. cit.,* pp. 402–407.

independent of the United States. This is an old Canadian dilemma, but it seems more grievous than ever because the proportions of conflict are greater than ever.

The political class is old and tired, responding with the strategies of another day, and they are not working. Perhaps a new Macdonald will arise to bind the nation together, but perhaps Macdonald himself could not do it today, for sheer pragmatic skill may not be enough. The opportunity is present for new definitions of the national political formula, but it seems unlikely that political leaders can give a society its purpose. This must come from the society itself. The old consensus politics may be bankrupt. The politics of vision have failed for the time. It is no wonder that political leadership is weak in a society in transition.[77]

Great Britain: Political Formula

It is said that a seventeenth-century cleric asserted that "God is English," and this incorporation of the divine into the culture is characteristic of the national habit of emphasizing community and tradition. Nationalism has been particularistic and not based on abstractions. The Monarchy, the chief symbol of the past, does not stand for ideas, but for community and history. Like the common law, the constitution, the class system, and much else, it has evolved.[78] If American culture emphasizes dynamic change, English culture emphasizes adaptation within tradition.[79]

The British political formula is a product of history which has rejected few elements but has been modified and supplemented by new additions. Government is seen as beneficent. Liberty is understood as existing within community. Strong leadership is valued, but it must be diffused among power holders and consultation among elites is demanded. Government must be strong, but it is only one "corporation" among many in society. The concept of a national community demands a welfare state. And finally, all change must come by evolution and assimilation. Pragmatism is the national ideology.[80] This model of society has medieval roots. Liberal individualism is only part of the model and it has been modified in the twentieth century by a modern "corporativism." This

[77] D. J. Heasman, "The Politics of Canadian Nationhood," *Parliamentary Affairs*, **XIX** (Spring, 1966), 144–161. Bruce W. Hodgins, "The Bankruptcy of Consensus Politics in Canada," *South Atlantic Quarterly*, **LXV** (Summer, 1966), 324–344.

[78] Stanley Rothman, "Modernity and Tradition in Britain," in *Studies in British Politics*, ed. by R. Rose, New York, St. Martins Press, 1966, *passim*.

[79] Richard Rose, *Politics in England*, Boston, Little, Brown, 1964, p. 52.

[80] James Christoph, "Consensus and Cleavage in British Political Ideology," *American Political Science Review*, **LIX** (September, 1965), 631.

corporativism is seen in the character of English social institutions. England is still dominated by Victorian institutions, the civil service, the old universities (Victorian in their present form), the public schools, Parliament itself, the trade unions. The spirit of the university common room and the nonconformist chapel both reflect this corporativism of "little platoons," in Burke's phrase. English society is a honeycomb of rich little worlds, each of which overlaps other worlds but provides its members a stable sense of identity. Harry Eckstein has pointed out how the style of authority of government is mirrored in private groups.[81] Symbolic and effective leadership are separated. Leaders are given great latitude by followers, but this authority can be kept only by caution and consultation at the top.

However, within this consensus there are three distinct intellectual traditions which are important animating forces behind the three political parties: conservatism, liberalism, and socialism. Leaders have to work within these traditions and the party organizations that represent them. Ideology and party partake of the general corporativism. These three ideologies are less doctrinaire and all-encompassing than the European variety and more cohesive than American party goals. An American leader can articulate the national ideology and the party ideology as synonymous. This is not so easily done in England. The leader represents a partial group and must move outward for majority support.

The conservative tradition emphasizes hierarchy, noblesse oblige, flexibility and adaptation, leadership, national unity, and national power. The liberal tradition emphasizes individualism, reform by rational methods, and equality of opportunity. The socialist tradition emphasizes social reconstruction toward social equality, planning, and moral improvement, all to be achieved by gradualism. All three traditions exalt the pragmatic method. Each seeks to be a *via media* between liberty and authority and thus emphasizes balance in social values and institutions. Conservatives and socialists emphasize community, but for different ends, and each shares the liberal concern for individual liberty. There is both overlap and disagreement.[82]

These values are carried by the politically active and articulate in the society. A study of backbenchers in the House of Commons in the late 1950s discloses that although neither parliamentary party has great unity on issues, there is a distinct style to each set of backbenchers. The Conservatives were above all else nonideological, empiricist, flexible. Divisions within the group seemed to be over interests rather than prin-

[81] Harry Eckstein, *A Theory of Stable Democracy*, Princeton, N. J., Monograph No. 10 Center for International Studies, Princeton University, 1961, *passim.*

[82] Christoph, *op. cit.*, p. 638.

ciples. The Labor group was united by a general socialist concern with equality, welfare, and foreign policy as an instrument for international cooperation. Despite overlap of the moderates in each party it is clear that even on similar issues stands are informed by quite different traditions.[83] A study of the operational role of these traditions in British history suggests that ideology, in this sense, is a very important factor in leader actions.[84] The study of party activists is sketchy, but in his study of nominations to parliamentary candidature in constituency associations Austin Ranney finds that Conservative associations seek men of character, good education, and a general Tory tone and style, whereas the Labor groups were most concerned with commitment to the "movement."[85]

The few studies of the beliefs of mass publics show patterns similar to the United States and Canada. There is a great deal of overlap on issue positions between supporters of the different parties. The great majority of people are not "ideological" in terms of being able to say what the ideologies of the parties mean.[86] Voters support parties in terms of party images more than in regard to specific issue stands. The key to party electoral victory is in presenting an image in tune with currents of the times as manifested in voter fears and hopes.[87] However, party image and identification are much more stable in Britain than in Canada and probably more intense in Britain than in the United States. The reason is that party identification in Britain is closely tied to social class and class cleavages are greatest there by comparison.[88]

Political socialization in Britain is the most homogeneous of any of the three countries because of the fact that most people stay in the social class in which they were born throughout their lives. There are few "cross-pressures" compared to the United States.[89] Party choice does not correspond to class entirely, because from one-third to one-fourth of the manual workers have regularly voted Conservative since 1945 and much

[83] S. E. Finer et al., *Backbench Opinion in the House of Commons, 1955–59*, Oxford, Pergamon, 1961, *passim*.

[84] Samuel H. Beer, *British Politics in the Collectivist Age*, New York, Alfred A. Knopf, 1965, *passim*.

[85] Austin Ranney, *Pathways to Parliament*, Madison, Wis., University of Wisconsin Press, 1965, p. 278.

[86] Donald E. Stokes, "Ideological Competition of British Parties," a paper given at the annual meeting of the American Political Science Association, September, 1964.

[87] Jean Blondel, *Voters, Parties and Leaders*, Baltimore, Md., Penguin Books, 1963, Ch. 3.

[88] Robert Alford, *Social Class and Voting in Four Anglo-American Democracies*, Berkeley, Cal., Survey Research Center, University of California, 1961, p. 72.

[89] Rose, *Politics in England*, p. 78.

smaller proportions of the middle classes regularly vote Labor. However, these identifications are relatively stable over time. Survey data since the 1940s reveal, however, that popular images of the differences between the parties have been gradually growing less sharp, new social classes, middle and working, are becoming the chief political arbiters, and they are not interested in the old ideological appeals but in new problems of the society, like education and economic modernization.[90] It may be that a loosening of the class structure will make for a loosening of party identifications. This could have consequences for styles of political leadership because at present party leaders work within this general corporatist framework. This is a great handicap to the leader who would innovate. He must first carry his party with him and this often means a redefinition of party doctrine before he can carry new appeals to the voters. The fights within the Labor party over whether to move left or right in the late 1950s and the eventual victory of the revisionist party leadership show that a potential prime minister must first be an effective party leader.

Popular Attitudes toward the Prime Minister

British public life is rich in formal ceremony which focuses not on individual leaders like the prime minister but on institutions, and especially on ancient institutions. Each new Parliament opens with a procession of members of the Commons, led by the two party leaders, one of whom is prime minister, walking to the House of Lords. There the monarch reads the Speech from the Throne. The speech gives a preview of the legislative program ahead and is written by the prime minister, but he is a figure in the background. It cannot compare with the State of the Union message of a president. Popular reactions to the death of British monarchs seem similar to those of American presidents. When George V died in 1936 there seems to have been a universal sense of loss. People spoke of him in personal terms as a friend. Over and over it was said that the King had been a father to all the people.[91] The monarch would seem to draw to himself those impulses to national unity and personal affection which a president can arouse. This leaves the office of prime minister no great emotional power except that coming from instrumental leadership.

The P.M. is not directly elected. He does most of his speaking in the House of Commons, and thus speaks to the public indirectly. Television

[90] Mark Abrams, "Social Trends and Electoral Behaviour," in Rose, *Studies in British Politics*, pp. 141–144.
[91] Sebastian De Grazia, *The Political Community, A Study of Anomie*, Chicago, Ill., University of Chicago Press, 1948, p. 113.

appearances and press conferences are rare. In short, the office has much less institutional visibility than that of the presidency, except as the man in it makes himself visible.

It is quite clear that the prime minister can be much more powerful in his Cabinet and government than the phrase "first among equals" implies. The heavy demands placed upon modern government make collegial decision making by a Cabinet very difficult. Inevitably, increased authority is pushed up to the prime minister, but he must also delegate much authority to the wider circles of his government. He is at once more and less powerful, but the Cabinet is the weaker for certain.[92] However, it is unlikely that this could go so far as to become "Presidential" government in which each Cabinet minister would look to the premier for policy direction and the premier would exercise all the authority of the Crown. Cabinet government does not have any of the checks and balances of the presidential system. Some means would have to be found to restrain any such all-powerful P.M. in Cabinet and Parliament.[93]

Because of this accepted belief that the government is a collegial enterprise, the prime minister must hold himself in restraint. He does not go on television to announce an important measure until he has told the House of Commons. He is more limited by collegial government than a president because he spends his entire political career with the same colleagues. He can never forget that he leads a team of men who are politically strong in their own right. It is likely that he himself will be imbued with the team spirit that pervades all of British life. These influences may keep a prime minister from dramatizing himself to a degree proportionate with his actual power.

British "corporations" show a willingness to give great latitude for action to leaders, but it is assumed that such authority will be exercised with caution and in a process of collective consultation at the top. Opinion surveys find that voters want leaders who will be "strong enough to make unwelcome decisions."[94] In fact, British leaders tend to be very cautious. The "corporative" spirit requires that all interested groups be consulted on matters affecting them. The public is represented through interest groups (corporations) as well as through parties and leaders. This slows down political leaders considerably. The notion of a crusading leader who takes his case to the "people" over the heads of

---

[92] Bernard Crick, *The Reform of Parliament*, Garden City, N.Y., Anchor Books, 1965, pp. 35–44.

[93] Douglas V. Verney, *British Government and Politics*, New York, Harper and Row, 1966, pp. 63–64.

[94] Rose, *Politics in England*, p. 41.

the interests has not been a common one in Britain in the past. However, this may be changing.

The class system and the educational system, reinforcing each other, create two groups: those who are taught in home and school that they have an obligation to lead and those who are taught that they "also serve who only stand and wait." Most of the population find it natural to look up to authority and trust it.[95] Politicians are not expected to be of the people and mix with them. But whether these attitudes lead to vigorous popular leadership is another question. The great sense of trust that pervades the political culture permits leaders considerable privacy in policy-making.[96] The official justification for the tight clamps on publicity in regard to Cabinet and administrative discussions is that all within must be able to speak freely. One result is to further divorce citizens from their government. The press does not play the active part it does in the policy-making process in the United States. Top decision makers have easy access to each other and share great similarities of experience and background. They do not need the press as levers to use against each other. The path to the top in British politics does not depend upon self-dramatizing skills but rather upon impressing those above in the hierarchy. Again, changes are perhaps taking place to favor the more dramatic leader.

There is very little evidence on the attitudes of British publics toward the office of Prime Minister. The attitudes that have been cited toward leadership are not really substantiated by any great body of evidence. About all that can be concluded is that the office of the Prime Minister itself probably carries less emotional power for the general public than does the American Presidency. This is not to say that dramatic and creative leaders in the office cannot make themselves widely visible and important, as persons, to publics. Institutions and culture do not encourage personality to break through into the open but that does not mean that it does not happen. The institution of Prime Minister is perhaps defined in the minds of many British people in terms of the great historic personalities that have held the post. This is a dimension to the office that is difficult to measure but perhaps very strong. A man receives stature from sitting in the seat of Chatham, Palmerston, Disraeli, Gladstone and Churchill. However, this dimension is perhaps vivid to a relatively small number of people in the population at any given time. We must then inquire into the importance of the personality of the incumbent for his political leadership.

[95] *Ibid.*, Ch. 3, *passim.*
[96] David Butler, "Political Reporting in Britain," in Rose, *Studies in British Politics,* p. 174.

Political Personality

The margins of party competition, measured in the slight swings of percentages supporting each party from election to election, would seem to leave little role for the personalities of party leaders as factors in voter choice. This stability of party support seems to be rooted in social groupings and party loyalty. However, the old ideologies are slowly being adapted to new needs, old social strata are giving way to new and this gives an opportunity for personable leaders to make themselves the levers of electoral support and policy innovation.

That Winston Churchill could be defeated in 1945 amazed Americans. Once the war was over he was seen as a party leader, and the Tories were due for punishment as the party of depression and appeasement. Many voters seemed to want a continuation of the wartime coalition and perhaps Churchill would have been returned on this basis, but in a straight party fight there was no way to make him prime minister independently of his party.[97] This is a consequence of structure rather than culture. In the elections of '1950 and 1951 Churchill was feted as a national institution, but his own party actually based the campaigns less on him as a person than on the effort to develop a fresh image of the party.[98] The principal effect of Clement Attlee, the Labor leader in 1945, seems to have been to complement the desire of Labor supporters for a party and a man who would get about the sober business of reconstructing Britain. Attlee, the colorless former social worker, seemed right for the job.[99]

The advent of television caused the personalities of leaders to be brought into homes, and the parties began to emphasize the virtues and personal characteristics of their leaders in the 1955 election.[100] By 1959 it was becoming increasingly clear that something new was being added. The Prime Minister, Harold Macmillan, had discovered that he had a certain flair for self-dramatization. He began to exploit this by talks to the people over television and wearing arresting hats and clothes. He was able to combine the "grouse moor" image of the Tories with the newer appeals of the affluent society by combining in his public manner

[97] R. B. McCallum and Alison Readman, *The British General Election of 1945*, London, Oxford University Press, 1947, pp. 16–23, 170.

[98] H. G. Nicholas, *The British General Election of 1950*, London, Macmillan, 1951, p. 237; D. E. Butler, *The British General Election of 1951*, London, Macmillan, 1952, p. 63.

[99] McCallum, *op cit.*, pp. 93–94.

[100] D. E. Butler, *The British General Election of 1955*, London, Macmillan, 1955, p. 76.

the traditional calmness and casualness of the aristocrat with the instrumental power of a Prime Minister who presided over a prosperous society.[101] However, because of Labor attacks on the Tory "cult of personality" the party used Macmillan sparingly on television. And it is not clear that personality was an important factor in voter choice. This was seldom the answer given to polls. A 1959 study concluded that party image was much more important in the public mind than leader image. The survey results showed that for most voters the leader was seen as a party leader who was not more important than his party. Character traits of strength and culture (education, background) were thought more important than personality qualities such as warmth. However, his integrity and his concern for the welfare of all the people were thought to be important. Partisans of each party gave roughly the same reasons for liking their respective party leaders.[102]

The selection of Alec Douglas-Home as Macmillan's successor as Prime Minister seems to have hurt the Conservative party in that it reinforced a growing public concern that the party was primarily of the "grouse moor." Lord Home, the fourteenth Earl in his line, had to give up his peerage, and subsequent events, including the Labor victory in 1964, suggest that the new leader was a handicap to his party in the campaign. However, he was extremely popular with party workers in the constituencies.[103] The problem was both the inadequacies of the leader and the growing change in public perceptions of the party. When Harold Wilson became leader of the Labor party in 1963 he continued the updating of the Labor image from that of a "labor" party to that of the party of a new, modernized Britain and used himself as the vehicle for that campaign. Polls showed that Wilson, before and after he became Prime Minister, was more popular than the Labor party.[104] After he became Prime Minister, Wilson brought new techniques of public relations to Downing Street. He cultivated newspaper reporters and sought to structure the news in behalf of the acts of his government. He went on television more often than prime ministers usually do to speak to the nation. He held a few press conferences. He dramatized his narrow majority in the House of Commons by talking of governing creatively and indefi-

---

[101] D. E. Butler and Richard Rose, *The British General Election of 1959*, London, Macmillan, 1960, pp. 29–32.

[102] Joseph Tranaman and Denis McQuail, *Television and the Political Image*, London, Methuen, 1961, pp. 160–161.

[103] D. E. Butler and Anthony King, *The British General Election of 1964*, London, Macmillan, 1965, pp. 24–25, 84, 146–147.

[104] *Ibid.*, pp. 24–25.

nitely. It was quite clear that Wilson was taking a leaf from Macmillan's book and using the office to dramatize himself and policies. Was something new being added to British practices?

It is possible that a leader, either of the government or opposition, can use his personality, words, and public acts as a spearhead of innovation and public approval in a time of transition when party ideologies and images are shattering and reforming. This seems to be what Wilson has done. He has made himself a personification of the Labor party to many people.

Sir Alec Douglas-Home probably resigned as Conservative leader in 1965 because he kept receiving low ratings on poll questions that asked the public their estimate of the job he was doing as party leader. The week before he retired a poll indicated that the public regarded him as less sincere than Harold Wilson.[105] Again, in a party in transition the personality of the leader was important to the public. However, it is very hard to disentangle the public judgment on Sir Alec with the general public unhappiness with the Tories, a mood that began in the early sixties.

However, the selection of a younger, more dynamic leader did not help the Tories in the public opinion polls. Edward Heath did not seem to have the skill to make himself popular with British voters in the way that Harold Wilson had in 1963, after he became party leader. Just as the perceptions and evaluations of voters of the differences in personality between Douglas-Home and Wilson seem to have been important to the outcome of the 1964 election, so did the contest between Heath and Wilson in 1966 take on "Presidential" aspects. During the 1966 campaign the Gallup Poll asked voters which traits they would match to the two men. Heath came out poorly in comparison to Wilson. Wilson was seen as a "strong, forceful personality" by twice as many people as those who saw Heath in those terms. More voters saw Wilson as sincere, warm, and friendly and as a man to be trusted. Conservative voters never gave more than 70 per cent approval to Heath as party leader, whereas Wilson received 95 per cent support from Labor supporters.[106] It seemed clear that Wilson's personality was a matter of great interest to the voters and that Heath's was not. This could be attributed to the manner in which Wilson had governed with a majority of four: with bravado, bold statement, by the seat of his pants, and with considerable self-dramatization.

The relative unpopularity of Heath, like that of Douglas-Home, is

[105] D. E. Butler and Anthony King, *The British General Election of 1966,* London, Macmillan, 1966, p. 170.
[106] *Ibid.,* pp. 185–186, 265–266.

difficult to separate from the slump in the popular fortunes of the Conservative Party. However, the differences in public attitudes toward the respective party leaders in 1964 and 1966 as compared to 1959 suggests that personality was becoming a more important factor in the minds of voters.

Butler and King suggest that there have been changes in British campaigning practices that make British elections more "Presidential" and less a contest between two teams. Party leaders, as individuals, loom large and dominate the campaign in a way that was not true in the early fifties. They attribute this to the gradual growth of the power of the Prime Minister and the growing use of television for political broadcasts.[107] This is certainly the case but it must not be carried too far. A British general election is a much more restrained affair than an American presidential election. The British do not idealize or glamorize their leaders in a way that Americans take for granted. It was still possible for Wilson and Heath to take regularly scheduled trains as private passengers and attract little attention. One major speech a day, if that, was the usual custom for each party leader. Mr. Heath did try walking through a few supermarkets looking for hands to shake but the response and interest did not seem great. There were no bands, spotlights, cavalcades. In short, the British are a long way from making "stars" out of their leaders. Neither leader made any effort to be "charismatic." Each talked about policy in a low key style compared to their American counterparts.

The preceding survey of general elections since 1945 suggests that the personalities of leaders have become an increasingly important factor in public approval of the government of the day and in the decisions of voters. This trend, if it is a trend, is probably related to the blurring of party images, the advent of television, a loosening of the class structure, and the personalities and skills at self-dramatization of Macmillan and Wilson. However, such a conclusion stirs a bit of uneasiness because the ghosts of David Lloyd George and Winston Churchill keep pushing into view. Is the importance of personality really a new factor in British politics? This seems very unlikely. In *A Pattern of Rulers*, Francis Williams suggests that Stanley Baldwin, Ramsay Macdonald, and Neville Chamberlain at the high points of their popularity exercised almost complete dominance of the public political consciousness.[108] Polling data about public attitudes toward these men is scanty and we can only speculate. Both Lloyd George and Churchill exercised, for relatively long periods, influence over popular emotions that cannot be denied. It is

[107] *Ibid.*, p. 186.
[108] Francis Williams, *A Pattern of Rulers*, London, Longmans, Green, 1965, *passim*.

difficult to imagine the readers of the penny press for the past fifty years thinking of government in terms of "the Government" of the day or even in terms of party. Surely the great leaders have personified government to most voters.[109]

However, Lloyd George and Churchill, with their great personal need for power, with their restless, dynamic creativity, have probably not been the kind of Prime Ministers the great majority of the British people have wanted in ordinary times. The personalities and styles of leadership of Lloyd George and Churchill were very close to those of the two Roosevelts and Wilson. But, whereas American norms of Presidential leadership require the leader who is driven by a feeling of the tension between ideal and reality, by a leader who projects his own needs for power and popularity on the office, these may not be the dominant British norms.[110] Rather, the modal type of political personality in Britain may be the solid, strong, but not openly clever leader who brings stability and assurance to the nation: Asquith, Baldwin, Chamberlain, Attlee. It is an open question whether Harold Wilson belongs in the heroic or the conventional category.

Therefore, even if political personality is becoming more important in British politics or has been important for a long time, it does not follow that British leaders will act in terms of the same cultural norms as American leaders. The British may actually prefer their leaders to be more cautious than do the Americans. The British prime minister lacks the symbolic resources of a Presidential office. And a British prime minister lacks a resource like the American national myth which drives American presidents to close the gap between ideal and reality. British leaders seem to reflect little tension between ideal and reality in their actions. They work to balance opposites in harmony.

There is no one British national myth on which a prime minister can easily draw. Every prime minister speaks for his party and the political subculture within which it stands in addition to speaking for the nation. This is, of course, the case in the United States and Canada as well but more so in Britain because of the greater degree of party organization and ideological cohesiveness. The national political myth in Britain seems to be more about procedures than about substance. Tradition, pragmatism, flexibility, corporativism—these and many similar traits cannot be translated into abstract ideals of the "good society." Perhaps this helps explain why British political leadership seems to lack heroic dimensions today in a period of basic readjustment at home and abroad.

[109] I am indebted to Professor Joseph LaPalombara of Yale University for the idea that popular leadership has always been more important in Britain than conventional constitutional notions have suggested.

[110] Hargrove, *Presidential Leadership*, Ch. 1–3, *passim*.

The great periods of heroic leadership by Prime Ministers in British history have been in wartime when the diffuse, nonideological quality of British nationalism could be invoked most fully. This is much harder to do in peacetime. There is nothing quite comparable to the myth of the American Fragment.

Style and Resources

Since the early 1960s a number of intellectuals, journalists, and political leaders have cried that British society is stagnant, the people afflicted with a malaise, and many institutions of education, religion, economics, and politics are obsolete and badly need overhauling.[111] Some suggest that one of the obstacles to reform is the character of the political elite. The kinds of gentlemanly qualities that public schools, grammar schools, and the two old universities encourage are refined by a career in the House of Commons until a good deal of red blood, color, vitality, and individuality is lost. This state of affairs will not necessarily be changed by increasing social mobility into the elite. It will depend upon what models of behavior are inculcated in the educational system, the various social classes, and the early stages of socialization of young politicians. Some critics have called for a wholesale introduction of "outsiders" into the parties, Parliament, the higher civil service, and all the pyramids of power in Britain. But it is hard to imagine this or to conceive of what such "outsiders" would be like, except as people with traits lacking in Britain's present rulers. A society of greater openness and mobility may, in time, produce new patterns of leadership of innovation, direct appeals to the public, and a greater variety of leaders. But it is also possible that the present "corporativism" will continue and flourish, that rather than becoming like the United States, Britain will become more like Sweden, a holding company for gigantic interest groups that have created a politics of collective bargaining.

Certainly a people given to "muddling through," to empiricism and not theory, are at a loss when the traditional guidelines are broken down. But Britain faces very real problems and quite objective obstacles to finding new visions of the good society at home and new roles for a former imperial power abroad. Political culture provides resources for leadership in terms of stability, continuity, trust, the reliance on a political method of gradualism. However, political culture does not provide the kind of resources needed for heroic leadership in peacetime. A crisis in the balance of payments is not the Battle of Britain, but then again it may be.

All of this does not mean that problems are not solved. The method of solution is that of collegial discussion within "corporations" throughout

[111] Anthony Sampson, *Anatomy of Britain,* New York, Harper and Row, 1962, *passim.*

the whole society until government and large organized groups and bodies of citizens are prepared to shift in the direction of change. This is not done all of a sudden but occurs incrementally and almost impercertibly. A period of stagnation is followed by a period of criticism and then a period of reform. Forms may remain the same but functions change. To reform is to conserve.

Conclusion

What generalizations about political leadership can we draw from these comparisons?

1. There is a positive relationship between a national political formula and the capacity of leaders to preach a vision of the "good society" in politics. Leaders, even when they are preaching, are technicians, not philosophers. They must draw moral inspiration from the political formula and those who create it, the intellectuals and moralists.

2. Leaders do not win support from mass publics with ideological appeals but with concrete acts and words which may have their inspiration in the motivations of leaders, ideology, or national political formula. Therefore it is important to study the belief systems of leaders as well as followers.

3. Political elites and the politically articulate are the chief carriers of the national political formula.

4. The styles of leadership seen in the chief political executive are usually learned at lower levels of the political elite. An important socialization process for leaders takes place in the years of ascent to the top.

5. Different types of "modal personality" are perhaps required for the optimum performance of tasks of political leadership in the chief political executive of these and other political systems. Culture, system, and personality structure come together here and permit a union of the approach to the study of leadership advocated by Hoffmann (style of authority) and that advocated by Wolfenstein (psychoanalytic analysis). If certain kinds of personalities are valued in the playing of culturally defined political roles, there may be unanticipated consequences in leader behavior that the culture itself does not define.

6. In societies of great mobility there seem to be great popular affinities for leadership by dramatic leaders. As rigid group categories break down, people respond less to parties and ideologies associated with old groupings and more to individuals with new appeals and styles.

7. A convergence of social structures may occur in modern industrial democracies toward societies of great mobility, but it does not necessarily

follow that popular attitudes toward desired specific traits in leaders will also converge.

8. Techniques of public relations can be transferred from the politics of one nation to that of another but it is much more difficult, and perhaps impossible, to transfer to another system the underlying cultural attitudes of leaders and publics which induce the style of political appeals in the original setting.

9. It serves no purpose to impose norms and expectations about leadership on one set of leaders if they are drawn from the behavior of leaders in another system. Leaders must work within the national style of authority available to them. This is not to say that leaders cannot change the national style of authority, but this is very unlikely in a stable democracy where that style is accepted and approved.

10. The political culture approach must be integrated with other factors in the explanation of styles of leadership. It is not easy to link culture, as a background factor, with dynamic actions, but this is a good way to study trends in styles of leadership across systems.

The principal conclusion of this chapter is that styles of leadership are converging in these three countries but that institutions, culture, and problems place limits to the degree of convergence. The argument may not look far enough into the future. The great insecurities of life in complex societies have certainly brought the dramatic leader to the forefront in this century. And, correspondingly, the political party has declined in importance. This process could continue. It does not pay to be categorical about such matters. The important thing is to organize discussion and inquiry so that political scientists can examine trends across societies in the light of the kind of hypotheses presented here.

I would not want to imply a kind of cultural determinism in which the political leader is bound to act within the limits of a national political formula and cannot create new ideas and patterns. The creative genius can often break through restraining forces to change history and culture. This is probably easier to do in some societies than in others because a leader must work, in part, with the cultural resources available. However, culture is only the backdrop to leadership. It must not be confused with actual creative acts of leadership. Such acts are rare but crucial to democracy.

8. Judges and Political Leadership*

GLENDON SCHUBERT

At least since the election of 1800, which resulted in the retreat of the repudiated Federalist Party to an entrenched position in an expanded national judiciary, judges have filled important roles of political leadership in the American polity. The prevailing view among constitutional historians is that most of the leaders at the Philadelphia Convention expected that the Supreme Court would perform such a function in the emerging political system, which they were then helping to develop. And George Washington, not Franklin Roosevelt, was the first American president to pack the Supreme Court with men who could be expected to represent the interests and point of view of the political coalition which had voted him into office. There have been times when the Supreme Court has acted as a protagonist in political crises of major importance to the nation: decisions such as those relating to the extension of slavery, the income tax, and the depression [1] come readily to mind.

More recently the Court has most conspicuously led the nation by forcing to the forefront of political debate consideration of such focal issues of contemporary public policy as racial and political equality. Both native and foreign observers long have noted the importance of judicial leadership to the normal functioning of the American system at all levels of government; but the impression seems to be widespread that political judges—or judicial politicians—are a peculiar feature of political life in the United States, and that judges behave differently elsewhere in the world—except, perhaps, (1) in the Soviet Union and China now, or (2) during such other totalitarian regimes as the Nazi and Fascist dictatorships of a generation ago: and of these, the first are dismissed as pernicious, and the second as aberrational. It is true that cultural anthropologists have suggested that judicial roles are an integral (and inte-

* The author is indebted to the Social Science Research Institute, University of Hawaii, for assistance in the preparation and reproduction of this chapter.

[1] *Dred Scott* v. *Sanford*, 19 How. 393 (1857); *Pollock* v. *Farmers' Loan and Trust Co.*, 157 U.S. 429 (1895); *Schechter Poultry Co.* v. *United States*, 295 U.S. 495 (1935).

grated!) aspect of political leadership in primitive societies, but the tendency has been to dismiss such findings as probably only most remotely relevant to what one would find in industrialized societies other than the United States.[2]

In this chapter we shall undertake some partial and preliminary investigations of the hypothesis that judicial elites perform a function of political leadership in modern industrialized societies generally. Our inquiry is partial because we shall restrict our focus to comparisons among the United States and three other polities—Australia, Japan, and the Philippines—which together demark a segment of substantial scope along a postulated continuum of industrialized societies. (Of course, concepts such as industrialization, urbanization, and modernization denote continua rather than dichotomies; and moreover we should expect to observe positive intercorrelations among these dimensions, in measuring economic development in any particular sample of countries, just as we should expect that the relevant differences between even the American State of Hawaii and, say, Botswana, will also be differences in degree.)

An additional reason why our inquiry is partial is that all three of the other countries were selected precisely because of previous American influence upon the development of their lego-political cultures. Although this influence occurred in different ways and at different times, it should enhance the likelihood of discovering similar political behaviors between American and other judges. If the hypothesis cannot be supported by evidence relating to this sample of countries, it seems improbable that it could be confirmed for the much larger group of countries in which American influence on political development has been remote or absent. Indeed, one reason why Australia was selected as a country to be included in this study (in preference to such alternative possibilities as Canada or India) was the assumption that Australia is the country most like the United States on many socioeconomic as well as political and legal dimensions. As several sociologists have pointed out,[3] it may be prudent in exploratory attempts to do cross-cultural research to seek as

[2] Max Gluckman, *The Judicial Process Among the Barotse of Northern Rhodesia*, New York, Free Press, 1955; Paul Bohannan, *Justice and Judgment Among the Tiv*, New York, Oxford University Press, 1957; Paul Bohannan (ed.), *Law and Warfare: Studies in the Anthropology of Conflict*, New York, Natural History Press, 1967. Cf. Marc Galanter, "The Modernization of Law," *Modernization*, ed. by Myron Weiner, New York, Basic Books, 1966, pp. 153–165.

[3] Kurt B. Mayer, "Social Stratification in Two Egalitarian Societies: Australia and the United States," in Henry Mayer, *Australian Politics: A Reader*, Melbourne, F. W. Cheshire, 1966, pp. 30–31; Arnold M. Rose, "The Comparative Study of Institutions," in *The Institutions of Advanced Societies*, ed. by A. Rose, Minneapolis, Minn., University of Minnesota Press, 1958, pp. 3–42.

much contextual uniformity (cultural homogeneity) as it may be possible to attain, since it can be expected that at best there will be more than enough uncontrolled (and even unrecognized) variation within any societal system which one seeks to analyze and understand. Our inquiry will be preliminary in the sense that only very recently have political and other behavioral scientists begun to study the institutions and the processes of adjudicatory decision making from a cross-cultural point of view,[4] although several research projects now in process offer promise of the extension within the next several years of both theory and empirical data on comparative judicial behavior.

Ecological Description of the Sample

There are several dimensions (economic, geographic, social, and political) in terms of which we can describe and distinguish differences in the contextual parameters for the judicial system in each of the countries in our sample.

Industrialization

The United States, Japan, and Australia rank among the dozen most industrialized countries in the world; the Philippines, although it has been characterized as "the most nearly industrialized country in Southeast Asia,"[5] nevertheless ranks far behind the other three in terms of both absolute and relative measures of economic development. Indeed, our purpose in including the Philippines in this analysis is to be able to contrast judicial leadership in what remains a predominantly traditional, agricultural, rural society, with the same political function in the three modern, industrialized, urban societies—otherwise we should have little or no basis for controlling, in our analysis, whatever similarities or differences in judicial roles ought to be attributed to differences in the effect of industrial development upon political (including judicial) behavior. We shall find that such discriminations can be made at best tenuously and with minimal confidence, in the light of existing theory and available

---

[4] See, for example, Ulf Torgersen, "The Role of the Supreme Court in the Norwegian Political System," *Judicial Decision-Making*, ed. by G. Schubert, New York, Free Press, 1963, pp. 221–244; Richard D. Schwartz and James C. Miller, "Legal Evolution and Societal Complexity," *The American Journal of Sociology,* **70** (1964), 159–169; and Donald P. Kommers, "The Federal Constitutional Court of West Germany: Some Exploratory Considerations," a paper read at the 25th Midwest Conference of Political Scientists, Lafayette, Indiana, Purdue University, April 27–29, 1967 (mimeo., 40 pp.).

[5] Alden Cutshall, *The Philippines: Nation of Islands,* Princeton, N.J., Van Nostrand, 1964, p. 70.

empirical research findings; but the inclusion of the Philippines in our analysis should help to provide perspective in appraising findings about the apparent relationship between political leadership and degrees of industrial development as among the United States, Japan, and Australia.

As we mentioned earlier, we should expect indices of such industrial development to be in considerable, but by no means perfect, agreement. The United States, for example, ranks first (among the countries of the world) in gross national product, Japan sixth, and Australia twelfth; but when one notes that these ranks reflect dollar values (in billions) of 555, 47, and 16, one might well infer that the absolute are considerably more important than the relative differences. In terms of percentage of the labor force employed in manufacturing, however, the differences are much less striking: the United States, 27; Australia, 25; Japan, 14; and the Philippines, 7. Urbanization, indeed, discriminates even more sharply between the three industrialized societies and the agricultural one than do the above two economic indices: the percentages of urban population are 79 for Australia, 70 for the United States, and 64 for Japan, but only 20 for the Philippines.

Geography

Geographically, the United States is only slightly larger than Australia, and Japan than the Philippines; however, Australia contains over twenty times the land area of Japan. The United States occupies what is mostly a temperate subcontinent. Australia is either the smallest continent or the largest island in the world, depending upon one's point of view. Both Japan and the Philippines are archipelagos which include a few major and a great many lesser islands. Japan's climate is most similar to that of the east coast of the United States. The populated (largely the eastern and southern coastal) regions of Australia—the interior of which is a vast desert wasteland—have a climate that more resembles that of the southern and far western parts of the United States, but with reversed seasons, of course. Most of the Philippines is tropical rain forest. In population, the United States is far the largest, with an estimated total of about 195 million in 1965; the estimated total for Japan in the same year was almost exactly half as large, or 97.3 million. The Philippines contain only about one-third as many people as Japan; and the estimated *increase* in the population of the United States (approximately 12 million) during the first four years after the 1960 census was about the same as the *total* population of Australia.

When, however, we look at the relationship between people and land, even in the most gross statistical terms, a somewhat different emphasis is indicated. Japan has by far the highest population density, with 681 persons per square mile of territory (and the highest population density per square mile of *arable* land in the world [6]); the corresponding index for the Philippines is 272, for the United States 50, and for Australia 4. We might well expect that such sharp differences in the crowding of peoples—and this evidently bears no consistent relationship to patterns of industrial development, for the countries in our sample [7]—may have an effect upon political culture which will be reflected in political leadership styles and functions. For present purposes, however, we can only note these geographic variables as among the many which remain uncontrolled and which therefore constitute a probable source of error variance to an unspecifiable degree in the research findings upon which we shall rely for our comparison of judiciaries.

Ethnicity

The countries in our sample show considerable variation when measured by such social parameters as ethnicity, religion, and language. The United States and Australia are alike in that each was settled largely within the last two centuries primarily by immigrants from western Europe. Both were former British colonies; and both continue to reflect in many ways their long-standing ties to the United Kingdom. In both countries the aboriginal inhabitants were displaced and the remnants placed on reservations where they remain unassimilated. But until a generation ago, when many more immigrants from Europe were imported, the Australian populace—many of whom are descended from the convicts who constituted the bulk of the earliest settlers of the Australian colonies —remained a strikingly homogeneous grouping of British and Irish ethnic strains. Americans constituted both a much larger and a much more diversified blending of former European peoples; and in 1960 some 34 million (out of a total of 180 million) Americans were either foreign-born or had at least one parent who was, mostly in Italy, Germany, Canada, Poland, or the Soviet Union. There were also some 20 million Americans descended from other than European stock, including almost 19 million Negroes, less than a million persons classified by the census as orientals and Filipinos, and about half a million American Indians.

In sharp contrast, recent immigration has had very slight effect upon the composition of the populations of either Japan or the Philippines. Indeed, the Japanese people have remained relatively stable for such

[6] Chitoshi Yanaga, *Japanese People and Politics,* New York, John Wiley and Sons, 1956, p. 20.

[7] The rank correlation between the scale of industrial development (U.S., Japan, Australia, Philippines) and the sequence of these countries according to population density is precisely zero. Of course, no precise value means very much for a statistic calculated for such a small sample, but even at that it probably means as much as subjective impressions based upon the same data.

a long period of time that for present purposes it is most meaningful to characterize them as a homogeneous, indigenous populace. In the Philippines, however, there are many different ethnic groups, and these differences tend to be reinforced by their congruence with religious differences. There is an overwhelmingly dominant majority, which consists of the 90 per cent who are Malaysian ethnically, Christian in religion, and called "Filipinos." Among the minorities are the Muslims of Mindinao and pagans, including several unassimilated mountain tribes such as the Ifugao and the Igorots and the aboriginal, pygmy Negritos. There are also about one-half million Chinese, some 200,000 Indonesians, and a much larger number of "mestizos"—admixtures of Filipino-Chinese, Filipino-Spanish, and Filipino-American. Thus Australia and Japan each contains a quite homogeneous populace, although these propulations are very different from one another; the Philippines contain many small and unassimilated minorities; and the United States contains a very heterogeneous population that includes one major unassimilated minority (Negroes) and several relatively much smaller unassimilated minorities (orientals, Indians, and recently settled Latin Americans).

Religion

Australia, the United States, and the Philippines all are predominantly Christian countries. About one-third of Australia's population is claimed by the Church of England, one-fourth is Roman Catholic, one-tenth Methodist, and another tenth Presbyterian, tending to reflect whether their ancestors migrated from England or Wales (C.E. and Methodist), Scotland (Presbyterian), or Ireland (Catholic). Many of the post-World War II immigrants have been Roman Catholic workers from southern and eastern Europe, and this circumstance has been directly reflected in changes that have taken place in the Australian political party system, particularly in relation to the emergence of the Democratic Labor Party, a somewhat right-wing splinter of the Australian Labor Party.[8] About two-thirds of the populace of the United States is claimed by churches; of these, over half (about 67 million persons) are classified as Protestant (principally Baptist, Methodist, and Lutheran). The 45 million Roman Catholics constitute a much larger group than any of the individual Protestant denominations; and the Jews are a much smaller minority, although there are more Jews (5.6 million) in the United States than in any other country.

With the possible exception of parts of the Soviet Union, the Philippines is the only Christian country in Asia; and reflecting the earlier

[8] See Robert R. Alford, *Party and Society*, Chicago, Ill., Rand McNally, 1963, Ch. 7; and Paul Duffy, "The Democratic Labor Party," Ch. 29 in Henry Mayer, *op. cit.*, fn. 3.

period of Spanish colonization, the 23 million Roman Catholics clearly constitute the dominant religious group. There are also one and a half million members of the Aglipayan (Philippine Independent) Church, which is Catholic but a national church; and there are also several other minority religious groups: 1,300,000 Muslims, 785,000 Protestants, 600,000 pagans, 270,000 Iglesia ni Cristo (Church of Christ), and 40,000 Buddhists. Japan, in contrast to the three Christian countries, both experiences and tolerates considerably more diversity of and multiplicity in religious practices and affiliations. The various Shinto sects claim about 78 million followers; and the several Buddhist sects claim 65 million, which suggests the extent to which many Japanese accept (or can be identified with) two religions simultaneously: the combined total of Shintoists and Buddhists is about 50 per cent greater than the total population of Japan![9] There are also Confucian and Taoist minority groups, and about 800,000 Christians in Japan.

Language

Australia, the United States, and the Philippines also are alike in that English is the most widely used language in each of these countries. There are, of course, differences: in Australia there is no other language spoken, except among recently settled immigrants; in the United States, the only important second language is Spanish, which is spoken by Mexican-Americans in the Southwestern part of the country (and in rural areas in other states in which migrant workers have settled), by Cuban refugees in Florida, and by former Puerto Ricans now residing in New York and other cities of the Northeast; in the Philippines, however, the Spanish language tends to be a vestigial (and disappearing) reminder of the days of Spanish rule in earlier centuries. About one-third of the people of the Philippines speak Tagalog, one of nine principal Malayo-Polynesian languages, and the one which has been designated (as "pilipino") the official language for instruction (along with English) in the public schools. Japan is quite different from the other three countries, since the

[9] Other research by Professor Dator leads him to conclude that in fact, no more than 3 per cent of the populace consider themselves to be practicing Shintoists, and no more than 20 per cent are active Buddhists of any kind. And in a 1958 national opinion survey, two-thirds of the respondents replied "No" to the question, "Do you have any religious faith?" See Joichi Suetsuna et al. (Research Committee on Japanese National Character, Institute of Statistical Mathematics), *Nihonjin no Kokuminsei (A Study of Japanese National Character)*, Tokyo, Shiseido Publishing Co., 1961, Supplement p. 9. Religiosity was most highly and positively correlated with age, lack of education, and residence in the southwestern region of the country (*ibid.*, p. 478); but Professor Kuroda believes that there is no clear relationship in Japan between religion and either political or judicial decision making.

Japanese have their own language. As Yanaga has remarked, "No other major Asian country has the linguistic unity that Japan possesses. Although there are slight local variations in the vernacular, a standard language of universal currency is used and understood throughout the country." [10]

Political Culture

The four countries also vary considerably in their political institutions, styles, and cultures. The United States is a federal republic with a stable two-party system. From a functional point of view, the American political system relies primarily upon the Presidency for national political leadership, and Congress and the national judiciary afford points of political access which make it possible for minority groups to work out compromises with the relatively more extreme positions assumed by the Administration. In certain areas of policy, however, it is the Supreme Court rather than the Presidency that provides national political leadership, as we shall discuss.

Australia is a federal "commonwealth," retaining the English monarch as a permanently absentee-Sovereign, but with almost complete national political autonomy. Federalism in Australia differs from that in the United States in two principal respects: there are far fewer states and they are relatively much more dependent upon fiscal and administrative controls exercised by the commonwealth (that is, the national) government. What since just after the end of World War I had been a three-party political system has, since the Labor split of the mid-fifties, been a four-party system, with the anti-Labor coalition (the Liberal and Country Parties) controlling the Federal Cabinet uninterruptedly since 1949 and a declining labor vote—40 per cent in the 1966 elections—that is split between the Australian Labor (socialist) Party and the Democratic Labor (anti-Communist) Party. The Communists do not run in all States, and have too little popular support—less than one per cent—to affect elections directly.

Japan is a unitary country whose emperor now is limited to social functions, with a democratic constitution imposed upon the vanquished by

[10] *Op cit.*, fn. 6, p. 52. Professor Yanaga adds that "There is no other language in the world which can equal Japanese in the multiplicity and complexity of pronunciation . . . [and] the elaborate system of honorifics requires fine distinction in the use of words according to the rank and status of the persons involved in conversation or communication. This feature, which recognizes the hierarchical relationships in the family and society, hinders the development of a feeling of equality. Honorifics, however, are not confined to persons only; they apply to inanimate things as well. It is doubtful if democratization can actually take place unless and until equality is achieved in the language, and class or sex distinctions are forgotten in the speech of the people." *Ibid.*, p. 14.

the post-World War II American military government. The majority political party is the Liberal Democratic (conservative) and the Socialist Party (liberal) provides the principal parliamentary opposition to the government,[11] augmented by the Democratic Socialist Party (right wing), the Communist Party, and the Komei Party, which formed in 1964.

The Philippines, to an even greater extent than the United States, has a strong Presidential system of political leadership. Like Japan, the Philippines has a democratic constitution adopted under strong American guidance during the immediate post-World War II period. But unlike the American President, his Filipino counterpart is restrained neither by the institutional impedimenta of a federal system nor by the functional limits imposed by a stable two-party system. Political parties in the Philippines are excellent empirical referents for Lord Bryce's analogy of two empty bottles, differing only in their labels. The system of political leadership (and of opposition) is highly personalized, depending upon shifting loyalties and allegiances among politicos, and placing considerable emphasis upon a bargaining political economy; [12] the relationship between leaders and followers, however, is manipulative. The Nacionalista Party and the Liberal Party share a monopoly of the means of access to elective political office, but both are electoral coalitions of factions rather than political parties with identifiable ideologies, such as political parties in Australia, the United States,[13] and Japan.

Political Economy

We can also distinguish among the three industrialized countries in regard to their governmental expenditures and revenues (including social security and public enterprises) as a percentage of gross national product, on a politico-economic scale of governmental influence in the economy. Japan is most "socialistic," Australia ranks next, and the United States is most "capitalistic" on such a scale.[14]

[11] Yasumasa Kuroda, "Political and Psychological Correlates of Japanese Political Party Preference," *Western Political Quarterly,* 17 (1964), 47–54.

[12] Jean Grossholtz, *Politics in the Philippines,* Boston, Little, Brown, 1964, Ch. 6–7.

[13] In the opinion of Remigio Agpalo, *both* American and Philippine political parties should be classified as factional, thus distinguishing them from the more cohesive parties of Australia and Japan. James Dator, on the other hand, argues that Japanese specialists consider Japanese parties to be more factional than ideological. Of course, all parties are partly factional and partly ideological; and the statement in the text above purports to distinguish on the basis of more and less.

[14] Hayward R. Alker, Jr., Karl W. Deutsch, and Harold D. Lasswell, *World Handbook of Political and Social Indicators,* New Haven, Conn., Yale University Press, 1964, pp. 63–67. On the basis of employment by the central government and public enterprises as a percentage of working-age population, however, Australia precedes Japan, with the United States remaining in third place. *Ibid.,* p. 71.

American Influence

Australia

The directness, duration, and pervasiveness of American influence upon the development of judicial institutions and other aspects of the political systems of the countries in our sample have varied. They have been least, relatively speaking, in Australia, where American influence upon the legal system has been almost entirely ideological. The political unification of Britain's Australian colonies occurred a century after that of her former American colonies. Thus the constitutional decisions of the United States Supreme Court, particularly in regard to federalism and the commerce clause, frequently were cited with approval by the Australian High Court, especially during the latter court's first two decades, before it had had an opportunity to develop a repertory of its own precedents.[15] Indeed, the Supreme Court "was the primary model on which the Founding Fathers designed the High Court of Australia." [16] But otherwise, the American example served only to help rationalize certain policy outcomes for the High Court; the institutional structure and the procedures of other Australian courts have been patterned exclusively after English examples. And it is probably correct to say that during the period of the past twenty years, the United States Supreme Court has provided less, rather than more policy guidance for the High Court, than it did during the first four decades or so of this century.

In Japan, on the contrary, American law and legal practices have had practically no influence whatsoever *except* during the past 20 years. Japanese legal institutions, legal procedures, and—to a lesser extent—substantive legal norms were in imitation of German and French law; from the 1880s until the end of World War II. One consequence of the American military victory over Japan was the imposition of a new "democratic" constitution, which was, in effect, given to the people of Japan by General Douglas MacArthur, the American Supreme Commander. As Yanaga has pointed out, "The Preamble to the [new Japanese] Constitution reminds the reader of the ideas and language of such historic American documents as the Declaration of Independence, the Federalist Papers, the Preamble to the Constitution [of the United States], the Gettysburg Address, and even the Atlantic Charter [!]." [17] Among the "constitutional

[15] Geoffrey Sawyer, "The Supreme Court and the High Court of Australia," *Journal of Public Law*, 6 (1957), 482–508.

[16] L. F. Crisp, *Australian National Government*, Croydon, Victoria, Longmans, Green, 1965, p. 59.

[17] *Op. cit.*, fn. 6, p. 125.

changes" is an explicit investiture in the Japanese Supreme Court of a power of judicial review over parliamentary legislation and acts of the cabinet (although it should be noted that thus far, no such action of political importance has been declared by the court to be unconstitutional).[18] Probably of much greater significance is the Japanese Supreme Court's acceptance of the "democratic" idea—and practice—of judicial dissent, in explicit imitation of the American Supreme Court. The importance and the implications of this change can be appreciated only if one is familiar with the extreme extent to which Japanese culture and society indoctrinates its members in the virtues of consensus, individual deference to the views of the group and its leaders, and submission to authority.[19] Prior to the period of American military occupation, dissent on the Japanese Supreme Court was unknown. All of these authoritatively imposed American democratic innovations in the Japanese legal system were resisted, and accepted only with reluctance; and it is therefore quite understandable that American influence upon Japanese politics and law began to wane just as soon as the period of military government began to phase out. Certainly, however, American legal influence has been more direct, more recent, and more pervasive in Japan than in Australia.

Philippines

American political and legal influence have been considerably greater in the Philippines than in either Japan or Australia. The United States occupied and governed the Philippines following the Spanish-American War, and the country remained subject to American political control, except for those portions that were conquered and occupied by the Japanese during World War II, for a period of almost half a century until the end of that war. Under a series of congressional acts which purported to establish basic policies for the governance of the Philippines, both the courts and the other political institutions of the national government were patterned directly on American models and practices, which remain the forms followed today after two decades of independence. If acculturation were the only relevant variable, we ought to expect that judicial behavior in the Philippines would be most similar to that in the United States, at least in comparison to the behavior of the judges of the Supreme Court of Japan and of the High Court of Australia.

---

[18] For two of the three unimportant cases, see Masami Ito, "The Rule of Law: Constitutional Development," p. 238, n. 108 in *Law in Japan: The Legal Order in a Changing Society*, ed. by A. T. von Mehren, Cambridge, Mass., Harvard University Press, 1963.

[19] Yanaga, *op. cit.*, fn. 6, pp. 43–44.

The Judicial Systems

American

From a structural point of view, the American judiciary is the most complex. No less than 51 different systems of courts articulate with the United States Supreme Court, which at least in principle and in regard to most policy issues purports to function as a "court of last resort" for them all. There are 11 national courts of appeals, and most attempts to change the decisions of the United States district (trial) courts—of which there are about 90, with at least one in each state—are resolved at this primary appellate level.[20] Similarly, each state has an independent system of courts, and practices vary considerably from state to state in regard to the recruitment, tenure, compensation, workload, and conditions of employment of state and local judges. The most typical pattern includes one or more subordinate appellate courts and a much larger number of trial courts of so-called general jurisdiction at the level of counties or groups of counties. The trend has been toward the elimination of justices of the peace, particularly in urbanized areas, and toward the proliferation of special-function courts to work in such policy areas as juvenile crime, domestic relations, motor vehicle operating violations, and a wide variety of aspects of administrative regulation of economic activity. Non-expert civic participation in the decision making of trial courts remains a characteristic of American adjudication, but to a lesser extent in the national than in state court systems, and to a diminishing degree in all.[21] Usually trials are administered by only one judge, although in some of the most important fields of national judicial policy-making, trials are presided over by three-judge panels which are typically composed of one circuit (appeals court) judge and two district judges.

The United States Supreme Court is composed of eight associate justices and one chief justice, all of whom are appointed by the President with Senatorial approval. The Supreme Court hears oral argument, confers for discussion of the issues presented by cases, and votes upon their disposition as a single group. The Chief Justice acts as administrator for both the Supreme Court and the national court system generally. His staff agency for the latter purpose, the Administrative Office of United States Courts, is presumed to be subject to the policy control and guidance of the Supreme Court. The principal agency representing the national gov-

[20] See Glendon Schubert, *Judicial Policy-Making*, Chicago, Ill., Scott, Foresman, 1965, Ch. 2, "Judicial Systems."

[21] Harry Kalven, Jr., and Hans Zeisel, *The American Jury*, Boston, Little, Brown, 1966.

ernment in litigation is the Department of Justice, almost all of whose divisions are involved in continuing interaction with federal judges throughout the country. The Department of Justice tends to reflect more or less directly the policy views of the incumbent Presidential administration; but this is infrequently true of the Supreme Court, which tends either to lag behind or to escalate in advance of Administration—to say nothing of Congressional—views in many of the most critical contemporary fields of domestic public policy. The Supreme Court itself includes no single majority faction, but rather tends to be dominated by differing majorities depending upon whether the issue presented is one of political freedom, economic interests, or social equality. During the past decade the dominant faction has been a group of justices who have been liberally oriented on all of these issues, while other subgroups have tended to be conservative in their orientation toward *either*—but not both—political or economic policy issues.[22]

In terms of prestige and sociopolitical status, American Supreme Court justices are an elite group who enjoy the very pinnacle of public esteem, and probably they outrank the President most (if not all) of the time.[23] There have been only four instances during this century in which any justice ever resigned or retired for reasons other than those of health, and most have preferred to cling to their offices until separated from them by death, there being no compulsory retirement age. Of these exceptions, one (Hughes) left to campaign for the Presidency, and subsequently returned to the Court as the Chief Justice; the second (Clarke) was a Wilsonian Democrat who quit in the mid-twenties to work for world peace; the third (Byrnes) resigned to become "assistant president" to FDR during World War II; and the fourth (Goldberg) resigned in order to succeed Adlai Stevenson as United States Ambassador to the United Nations. One of the fundamental postulates of the American political culture is recognition of the Supreme Court's function of legitimation (or of illegitimation), for all other actors in the polity, of controversial decisions in the fields of domestic civil policy.[24]

Philippine

The Philippine judiciary is patterned directly after the model of the typical American state court system. It includes a Supreme Court, a Court

---

[22] Glendon Schubert, *The Judicial Mind,* Evanston, Ill., Northwestern University Press, 1965.

[23] In a March, 1947 National Opinion Research Center survey of 90 occupations, the Supreme Court was ranked first—and ahead of the Presidency—with an average score of 83 per cent "excellent" and 15 per cent "good" ratings. See Albert J. Reiss, Jr., *Occupations and Social Status,* New York, Free Press, 1961, p. 54.

[24] In military and foreign policy matters, the ultimate legitimizer is the President.

of Appeals, 16 District Courts located in provincial capitals, and a much larger number of local courts (justices of the peace in the rural areas, and municipal courts). For over 30 years, until the inception of Commonwealth status in 1935, the justices of the Philippine Supreme Court were appointed in precisely the same manner as were justices of the United States Supreme Court: by the President of the United States, with Senatorial approval. During this same period inferior court judges were appointed by the Governor General—himself an American chosen by the President of the United States—and confirmed by the Philippine Senate. Americans constituted a majority of the Philippine Supreme Court, and cases could be appealed from the latter court to the United States Supreme Court. Throughout this period the Philippine judiciary was an integral part of the American system of courts.

Since 1935, all Philippine judges have been appointed by the President (of the Commonwealth until 1946, and since then of the Republic),[25] with the approval of a special joint committee of the Philippine Congress. The administration of the trial courts is supervised by the Department of Justice and the Supreme Court; and trials usually are conducted by one judge, although panels of three preside over what are considered to be the more important cases. Lawyers have the very highest prestige, and they tend to monopolize leadership roles in all branches and levels of the government,[26] as well as throughout much of the economy, and in administrative positions in the universities. According to Grossholtz, "the Supreme Court is the most respected body in the Philippines"; and, "As in the United States, a justice of the Supreme Court is ranked among the highest in prestige and respect."[27] The 11 justices of the Supreme Court enter directly into current policy controversies by declaring unconstitutional (or by approving) acts of the President and of the Congress; and since the Presidency during the postwar period has assumed a relatively liberal posture, and has tended to dominate so completely the rest of the polity, the Supreme Court has offered the only principal, and a conservative, alternative to Presidential national political leadership. In the Philippines, as in the United States, the Supreme Court is the most important

[25] For a discussion of the political considerations which determined the selection of the eight justices of the peace of Occidental Mindoro Province, see Remigio E. Agpalo "Pandanggo sa Ilaw (The Politics of Occidental Mindoro)," *Philippine Social Sciences and Humanities Review*, 28 (1963), 458–461.

[26] Throughout the past half century, for example, almost three-fourths of the members of the Congress have been lawyers, irrespective of whether the regime has been colonial, commonwealth, or republican. See Robert B. Stauffer, "Philippine Legislators and Their Changing Universe," *Journal of Politics*, 28 (1966), 580.

[27] Grossholtz, *op. cit.* fn. 12, p. 126.

legitimizer in the political system,[28] except (of course) for the national electorate.

Australian

Although Australia, like the United States, has a federal constitutional structure, there is only a single system of courts, as in the Philippines and in Japan. The judicial systems in four of the six states include supreme courts appointed by the incumbent state cabinets and a miscellany of local and municipal courts. In the two most populous states there is also an intervening level of courts for the trial of more important cases. Trials of the most important cases in each are conducted by a single state supreme court justice, and appeals from lower courts usually are decided by panels of three supreme court justices. Juries are used only in the more serious criminal cases, and usually only in the most important civil cases, as in the United States. The size of supreme courts ranges from four justices in Tasmania, the least populous state, to over a score in New South Wales, the most populous.

The High Court is the only national court of general jurisdiction, and its seven justices are appointed by the federal cabinet. There is no compulsory retirement age for High Court justices (as there is for all other Australian judges and for all Philippine judges). Although the High Court does conduct some trials—always through one of its justices, and usually in cases that are conceptualized as raising constitutional issues of national-state or interstate relations—mostly it decides appeals through panels of three or five justices. Such appeals come from decisions of the state supreme courts, from trials conducted by a High Court justice, or from some other commonwealth court, such as the Federal Bankruptcy Court or the Commonwealth Court of Conciliation and Arbitration, which has specialized functions to resolve disputes involving labor and management in the field of industrial relations. It is also possible to appeal decisions of the High Court itself to the Judicial Committee of the Privy Council in England; and when they have disagreed, the Privy Council almost always has taken a more conservative position than the High Court. The effect of retaining Privy Council appeals as a political device for slowing down the rate and direction of economic development and of social change may have also been to detract somewhat from the prestige of High Court justices. Nevertheless, the social status of the justices within Australian

---

[28] "The impact of the court is seen in the constant references of legislators and executives to the constitutionality of legislation they are attacking or defending." *Ibid.*, p. 127.

society is at least as high as that of their American and Philippine counterparts.[29]

The three most populous states (New South Wales, Victoria, and Queensland, which together include about four-fifths of the populace) retain in practice (though in Victoria not in theory) the English system of the bifurcated bar; all High Court justices invariably have been chosen either directly from among the leading barristers (a relatively small and influential elite in Australian society) of those three states, or else from those states' supreme court justices (themselves drawn exclusively from the respective state bars).[30]

Japanese

The Japanese judicial system still owes much more to its nineteenth-century Franco-German models than it does to the postwar political "reforms" mandated by American military authorities.[31] As in the Philippines, all Japanese courts are national courts. But in sharp contrast to the Philippines (and to Australia and the United States as well), the status of lawyers in prewar Japanese society was relatively low, and although it is improving, the prestige of the legal profession in Japan remains markedly lower than in the other three countries.[32] Judges have more prestige than lawyers generally, but this has been because of the respect accorded generally to government officials, and not because of their legal training.

One apparent reason for the relatively low esteem given to lawyers is found in one of the most characteristic features of the Japanese culture: the extraordinarily high value that is placed upon the avoidance of open conflict in small groups and the acquiescence of all relevant parties to

[29] Upon his recent retirement after 35 years on the High Court (and as Chief Justice during the last dozen of these years), Sir Owen Dixon was widely acclaimed in Australian newspapers and periodicals as the greatest living common-law judge in the world. Even state supreme judges rank at the very top of the occupational social status scale: see Athol A. Congalton, "Methodology of Research into Occupational Prestige," *Australian and New Zealand Journal of Sociology,* 1 (1965), 128; and cf. A. F. Davies and E. Encel (eds), *Australian Society: A Sociological Introduction,* New York, Atherton, 1966, especially Ch. 3, "Class and Status."

[30] If they have not already been knighted, all High Court (and many supreme court) justices are so distinguished after receiving their judicial appointments.

[31] For a more detailed description of the Japanese judicial system, see John M. Maki, *Court and Constitution in Japan,* Seattle, Wash., University of Washington Press, 1964, pp. xv–xlvi.

[32] Takaaki Hattori, "The Legal Profession in Japan: Its Historical Development and Present State," pp. 111–152 in von Mehren, *op. cit.* fn. 18. Cf. Charles E. Ramsey and Robert J. Smith, "Japanese and American Perceptions of Occupations," *American Journal of Sociology,* 65, (1960), 475–482.

decisions which are reached consensually.[33] To reach such decisions requires a considerable amount of negotiation and mediation, extending to the most detailed and minute aspects of what in many other cultures (for example, the American) would be considered personal behavior, as well as to what a Westerner more readily would recognize as a social or political issue. But there has been no Japanese tradition—as there have been in the Philippine and American political cultures—that lawyers have a special set of roles to play in negotiating nonlitigational settlements of most economic and political disputes. Neither has it been true in Japan, as it has in all three of the other countries in our sample, that litigation itself is a specialized structure for the functioning of mediation and negotiation as primary decision-making processes, since only a small proportion of either civil or criminal cases that are docketed with courts ever persist to the stage where they are resolved by a formal decision of a trial judge.[34] Instead of being the quasi-monopoly of the bar, conciliatory roles in Japan are the very warp and woof of the social structure.[35] Consequently there is, as Yanaga has remarked, "an amazing lack of litigation in Japan." [36]

Before World War II the Ministry of Justice supervised the activity and the assignment of judges, but one of the American reforms intended to strengthen the judiciary was to transfer this authority to the Supreme Court, which now carries out a diverse array of administrative functions through its Legal Training and Research Institute. Under the present system, the Supreme Court is supposed to make "rules" (that is, policy) specifying procedures and practices and other aspects of judicial administration generally for the lower courts, for attorneys, and for procurators (public prosecutors), although the latter remain also under the administrative control of the Minister of Justice. The Supreme Court's Legal Training and Research Institute provides a two-year course of instruction for all (mostly university graduates) who have passed the national bar examination; at the end of their training candidates select either the judiciary, the procuracy, or the bar for their legal career.[37] Thus judges,

[33] Professor Agpalo points out that the same compulsive need for manifest harmony is true of the Philippine *political* culture.

[34] The same comment applies also, of course, to the United States, but to a lesser degree. *Op. cit.* fn. 20, pp. 79–80.

[35] Takeyoshi Kawashima, "Dispute Resolution in Contemporary Japan," in von Mehren, *op. cit.*, fn. 18, pp. 41–72.

[36] *Op. cit.* fn. 6, p. 362.

[37] Hakaru Abe, "Education of the Legal Profession in Japan," in von Mehren, *op. cit.*, fn. 18, pp. 153–187. Cf. Joseph Zelan, "Occupational Recruitment and Socialization in Law School," (a mimeographed paper presented at the Meeting of the American Sociological Association, Chicago, Illinois, August, 1965); and Seymour Warkov, *Lawyers in the Making*, Chicago, Ill., Aldine, 1965.

prosecutors, and attorneys now all receive a common professional socialization; [38] and since attorneys were trained before the war primarily by the apprenticeship method and under much looser standards than were judges or prosecutors, the present method of training constitutes another effort to upgrade the status of the bar.

The Chief Justice of the Supreme Court is, like the Prime Minister, appointed by the Emperor; [39] the other justices of the Supreme Court are appointed by the Prime Minister on the advice of the Cabinet. There are fifteen justices, of whom usually five were lower-court judges, five were attorneys, and the remaining five are persons with other relevant governmental or educational experience (as procurators, diplomats, or law professors), in accordance with the prevailing practice, under an informal rule. They are appointed for indefinite terms, subject to recall by an adverse vote at popular referenda which are held at the next general election of the House of Representatives and (in principle) decennially thereafter; and they are subject to compulsory retirement at the age of 70. The recall proviso means little, however, since the next general election to the lower house of the Diet comes so soon—within two or three years—after appointment that it is hard to see how the electorate very often can be informed to act on any rational ground other than partisanship; and most Supreme Court justices already are past the usual Japanese retirement age (which ranges, depending upon the position, from 60 to 65) at the time they are appointed. Hence only a small minority of Communists and some Socialists seem to register a protest vote, either at the premature initial referenda or against those few justices who enjoy that rare combination of longevity and early appointment which makes it possible for them to seek popular consent to their continuing tenure after a decade or more of service. The Supreme Court is divided into three five-justice panels, and most cases that are appealed to the court are decided by one of these panels, although major questions of policy are decided by the "Grand Bench," consisting of all 15 justices. The justices are assisted by 30 research officials who are themselves judges with extensive trial or appellate experience in the lower courts; they are assigned to the Supreme Court for terms averaging about five years, and it is noteworthy that the combined total of Supreme Court justices and research officials —45 persons—is precisely the size of the *Daishinin,* the prewar predecessor of the present court.

[38] For a study of the political behavior of Japanese law students, focusing upon their status as a potential political elite, see Yasumasa Kuroda, "Agencies of Political Socialization and Political Change: Political Orientation of Japanese Law Students," *Human Organization,* 24 (1965), 328–331.

[39] The Cabinet nominates to the Emperor a Chief Justice, while the Diet nominates a Prime Minister.

Before the war there was also a Court of Administrative Litigation, inspired by the *Conseil d'État* and the French system of relatively inexpensive and widely available suits by citizens against public officials; but A. V. Dicey's shade must have worked through the American military officials who persuaded the Japanese to keep faith with the Anglo-American principle of the separation of executive and judicial powers, by abolishing this court.

There are 8 High Courts, each consisting of from 7 to 64 (in Tokyo) judges; and on the prefectural level of government, there are 49 district and family courts and their 235 branches. There are also some 570 summary courts. Juries are not used in Japan, although they were tried briefly and then abandoned during the 1920s; the summary trials are presided over by individual judges, and so are most trials in the district courts, although what are considered to be more important cases are decided by three-judge panels, as are appeals from the high courts.

A Model of Decision-Making

Our conception of judicial decision making postulates a model in which there are three classes of variables: input (independent), conversion (intervening), and output (dependent), as suggested by Fig. 8.1.[40] Our par-

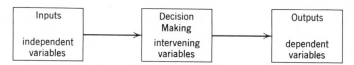

Fig. 8.1. Types of variables in the policy-making process.

ticular concern in the remainder of this chapter will be with the processes of decision making which convert the inputs of judicial systems into policy outputs. The patterning of these relationships, as they are hypothesized to interrelate in the model, is depicted in Fig. 8.2.[41]

The three input variables upon which our analysis is based are modernization, political impact, and legal culture. Two principal indices of modernization are (1) the persistence of traditional cultural components and (2) the extent and rate of industrialization. We hypothesize that these factors are highly negatively correlated, so that countries which are low

[40] For more sophisticated versions of this figure, see David Easton, *A Framework for Political Analysis*, Englewood Cliffs, N.J., Prentice Hall, 1965, p. 110; and cf. *op. cit.*, fn. 20, p. 106.

[41] For a more detailed development of the theory of the conversion process as depicted in this figure, see Schubert, "Human Jurisprudence," (forthcoming).

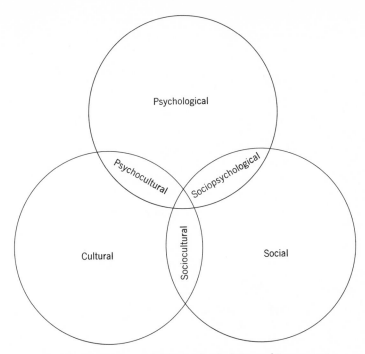

Fig. 8.2. Conversion variables in the decision-making process.

on the first and high on the second will be on one end of a scale of modernization, and countries which are traditional and nonindustrialized will be at the opposite end of the scale. The socioeconomic data we have previously examined indicate that on the modernization scale, the countries in our sample are ordered: (1) the United States; (2) Japan; (3) Australia; and considerably behind the others (4) the Philippines.

The political impact variable is based on the index, influence of the American political system, which ranks the Philippines as most similar to the United States, Japan next, and Australia least similar of the countries in our sample. The third variable is legal culture, which uses similarity to the English (common-law) legal system as an index, and scales our sample in the sequence Australia, the United States, the Philippines, and Japan.

There are three conversion variables, and also (as Fig. 8.2 indicates) three types of interaction between pairs of the conversion variables, in which we are particularly interested. Decision making is defined as the field in which all three variables interact together. Following the notation of the figure: (1) the *cultural* dimension measures variance in the substantive content of norms (laws, customs, and myths); (2) the *sociocultural* variables relate to institutional roles, and to regional, language, ethnic, educational, and class attributes; (3) the *social* variables deal with group interaction, social structure, and interest aggregation; (4) the *sociopsychological* variables are concerned with the socialization and recruitment of decision-makers, interest articulation, and the representation of interests through political party identification and affiliation, (5) the *psychological* variables measure the perception, cognition, and attitudes of individual decision-makers; and (6) the *psychocultural* variables concern individual roles, ideologies, and such attributes of decision makers as religion.

The output or decisional variables can also be classified as psychological, social, and cultural. The psychological output variable measures the individual and group preferences of decision makers (that is, their preferred outcomes), as inferred by analysis of their decisional behavior. The social variable deals with the legitimation and illegitimation of the decisions of other actors; in the case of judicial elites such as supreme court justices, it is concerned with the approval or disapproval of the acts of lower courts, attorneys, litigants, legislators, chief executives, bureaucrats, etc. The cultural variable measures the changes that take place in norms as a consequence of the decisions under analysis.

The available empirical studies of judicial decision making from a behavioral point of view are far from adequate to support an analysis of the scope specified by our model. We can, however, say something about the relationship between judicial attributes and attitudes and decisions and the feedback effect of these decisions upon political parties and leaders, public opinion, legislative and administrative policy, and private groups and organizations. Such findings will be at what we might denote as the *manifest* level of analysis. But we are concerned also with a *latent* level of analysis, in which we attempt to link economic, legal, and political development to the leadership roles of judicial elites, which we can trace through an examination of differences in judicial styles and functions. This will be an even more dubious task than the manifest analysis, partly because the latent variables are broader and less amenable to operationalization and partly because the fragmentary empirical data available are certainly no more sufficient for the latent than for the manifest analysis.

The Judicial Elites

Sociocultural Variables

When we examine such sociocultural attributes of decision-makers as region, class, occupation, education, and ethnicity, we are asking to what extent our elite is representative of the population in regard to whom it acts.[42] When we ask such a question in a comparative survey of judicial elites, we are asking which are relatively more, and which relatively less representative of the political societies from which they are drawn.[43]

Region. In Japan the metropolitan areas are overrepresented on the high (appellate) courts, but not on the Supreme Court. There does not appear to be either an urban or a rural bias in the supreme courts of the other three countries. In Australia there is a pronounced regional bias in representation on the High Court, since all High Court justices have come only from the three most populous states—roughly in proportion to their respective populations. In the Philippines, the southernmost and second largest island (Mindanao) has been conspicuously denied any representation on the Supreme Court.[44] No regional bias is apparent in either the Japanese or the American Supreme Court.

Class. Throughout the period since the establishment of the United States Supreme Court, the justices have tended to come primarily from either (initially) the gentry or (thereafter) the professionalized upper middle class, although this no longer appears to be true since Earl Warren became Chief Justice a dozen years ago: a majority of the incumbent court was raised in middle or lower-middle class homes. Similarly, most High Court justices in Australia now come from middle and lower-middle class families, with fathers and fathers-in-law who were clergymen, merchants, or solicitors (rather than upper-class barristers). A majority of the Philippine justices were born in upper-class families of large landowners, or in upper-middle class families with fathers who were lawyers, physicians, businessmen, or small landowners; about a third had lower-middle class origins, and only one came from the laboring class.

Familial ties—both patrilineal and through marriage—appear to be particularly important in the selection of Japanese Supreme Court justices, who are related by marriage to persons important in universities, government, business, and the nobility, and about in that order of sig-

---

[42] Unless the contrary is explicitly stated, the time periods covered by the empirical studies, upon which the remainder of this chapter is based, are as follows: Australia (1951–61), Japan (1950–60), the Philippines (1946–66), and the United States (1946–65).

[43] For a discussion of some of the difficulties which suggest caution in inferring, from available data, the universe parameters for the political societies of which judges putatively are more or less representative, see: Erwin K. Scheuch, "Cross-National Comparisons Using Aggregate Data: Some Substantive and Methodological Problems," and Erik Allardt, "Implications of Within-Nation Variations and Regional Imbalances for Cross-National Research," *Comparing Nations: The Use of Quantitative Data in Cross-National Research,* ed. by R. L. Merritt and S. Rokkan, New Haven, Conn., Yale University Press, 1966, pp. 169–199 and 337–348.

[44] Mindinao has failed also to supply any Presidents.

nificance. Of the fathers of Japanese high court judges, almost a third were upper or upper-middle class (professionals, governmental officials, or big businessmen), which is grossly overrepresentative of the proportion of these occupations to the employed-population base which existed during the first decade of this century, when most of these judges were born; but it is also true that the proportion of fathers who are professionals is much smaller and the proportion of those engaged in white collar jobs or in small businesses is much larger than for the most nearly similar group (state supreme courts) of American judges. Upper-class bias in judicial representation appears to be greatest in the nonindustrialized Philippines, probably next in American appellate courts, except for the contemporary Supreme Court, then Japan and Australia, with the United States Supreme Court now least biased in terms of the social class origins of the justices.

Occupation. All the judges were male lawyers. American Supreme Court justices are mostly lawyer-politicians with experience primarily at the federal level; occasionally law professors or corporation lawyers are chosen, but the "promotion" of state judges is rare, although this occurred once under Eisenhower and there was then some evidence of a trend to use brief appointments to the lower federal judiciary as an interim, "qualifying" stage in the recruitment of men who perhaps had already been earmarked for appointment.

In Japan the custom of adhering to the quotas allocated when the Supreme Court was first organized in 1947 appears to be well established; as a consequence, five of the justices are career judges, five others were attorneys, and the remaining five are men "of learning and experience" (supervising procurators, or on the Tokyo University law faculty, or lawyer-bureaucrats).

All the Australian High Court justices during the period studied were barristers with extensive experience; but only three had as much as a year or more of prior judicial experience, and only one had a primarily political career, although one other had unsuccessfully sought party endorsement as a potential senate candidate.[45] Several had considerable administrative experience. Most of the Australian justices had spent most of their adult lives, prior to appointment to the High Court, in professional legal positions.

---

[45] Throughout the High Court's history, there have been only three other justices, or a total of about one-fourth (6/23) with such prior judicial experience. In sharp contrast, there have been ten others with definite partisan alignment, for a total of over half (12/23). The Dixon Court (1951–61), therefore, was hardly typical in terms of these two parameters since it was relatively *over*represented with prior judicial experience but *under*represented with political party men.

In the Philippines, almost half of the Supreme Court justices had prior judicial experience,[46] although the proportion now is less than it was during the colonial and commonwealth periods, while the proportion with bureaucratic experience has been increasing, and is now about half. About one-third had experience as government lawyers, and almost half had done some law school teaching, although usually on a part-time basis in evening classes. Over half also had experience in private practice. But in the land where politics has been described as the "national pastime," less than a third of the Philippine justices had had political careers, and of these a majority had reached the Supreme Court only after "retiring" from politics by serving in the lower courts or in the bureaucracy, although a contrary trend is apparent in recent years. However, if we posit a continuum ranging from "primarily partisan political" careers at one extreme, and careers as nonpartisan legal technicians at the other extreme, it seems clear that American justices are most political, Philippine justices come next, then the Australian High Court justices, and the Japanese justices are least politicized.

Education. Two-thirds of the justices of the United States Supreme Court are graduates of both universities and law schools of high standing, and the other third are graduates of universities and law schools of average status. In the 1920s and 1930s, when these justices were completing their formal education, it was much less common for young Americans to complete six or seven years of university work then it is today; and in their level of educational attainment Supreme Court justices differ markedly from the general population of their age group.

All of the Japanese Supreme Court justices also were university graduates, with almost three-fourths of them from the Imperial University of Tokyo, the highest ranking in the country;[47] indeed, a majority were graduates of that university's law school. Unlike law schools in the United States, however, those in Japan offer instruction at the undergraduate level; and although today graduation from the Supreme Court Legal Training and Research Institute approximates the level of educational attainment corresponding to graduation from an American law school, no such alternative was available until after World War II. The third of the justices who had been professional attorneys received their

---

[46] Since 1950, with one controversial exception (S. M. Sikri, in 1964), *all* appointees to the Supreme Court of India have had previous experience as High Court judges. George Gadbois, Jr., *The Paramount Judiciary in India: 1937–64* (Duke University, Ph.D. dissertation in political science, 1965, p. 127.

[47] An additional 10 per cent graduated from the Imperial University of Kyoto, which ranked next in prestige. A 1964 survey of a national sample of High Court judges showed that 58 per cent had graduated from Tokyo, and 14 per cent from Kyoto.

technical indoctrination in legal skills in a decentralized system of officially sponsored apprenticeship training, while the justices who had been attorneys went through what was generally much less rigorous private apprenticeship training.

Of the Australian High Court justices, five were graduates of the University of Sydney, three of the University of Melbourne, and the other of the University of Queensland, all with degrees of LLB or LLM; in addition, six of them had BA or both BA and MA degrees.

Apparently all of the Philippine Supreme Court justices were graduates of both universities and law schools. Over half of the justices did their undergraduate work at Catholic (Jesuit or Dominican) universities, a quarter at the public University of the Philippines, and the rest at other colleges or universities. Over half went to the University of the Philippines Law School,[48] however, with another quarter attending the (Dominican) University of Santo Tomas Law School, and the balance elsewhere. Moreover, a third of the justices completed postgraduate master's or doctor's degrees in law.

The data will not support qualitative judgments concerning the relative merits of law degrees in different countries, to say nothing of their adequacy for preparing law graduates for roles as supreme court justices in these differing political cultures; but a scale of the quantitative data just summarized indicates that educational attainment tends to be highest in the nonindustrialized Philippines, with the United States next, then Australia, and Japan—where the status of both lawyers and judges is lowest among the countries in our sample—least.

Ethnicity. Throughout American history, the ethnic background of American Supreme Court justices has been overwhelmingly—over 90 per cent most of the time—British-Irish, with a few (mostly matrilineal) tracing their ancestry to other Western European countries. Several of the recent justices appointed to the Supreme Court's "Jewish" seat [Cardozo (Spain), Frankfurter (Austria), Goldberg (Russia)] constitute the most diverse array of unBritishers ever to gain access to the Court; but the incumbent, Fortas, is English. There have been no justices with ancestors coming from Asia, Africa, or Latin America. In Australia, all of the High Court justices appear to have been British-Irish in their ancestry. All of the Japanese justices were of Japanese ancestry. In the Philippines, where greater ethnic diversity is recognized, over half of the justices were Tagalog and Ilongo, corresponding to about one-third of

---

[48] This is the only American-style law school, and the trend has been in its favor, in the training of Supreme Court justices, of whom in 1964 ten (out of 11) were its alumni. Most recent Presidents of the Republic also studied both as undergraduates and at the law school of the University of the Philippines.

the population; and the two other largest ethnic groups—the Cebuano and Ilocano, with a combined population greater than that of the Tagalogs and Ilongos—were represented by only one-sixth as many justices. Since half of the six presidents of the Republic have themselves been Ilocanos, it appears that other considerations than at least diffuse consanguinity have been determinative in the selection process. Evidently, the Japanese and the Australians, with ethnically homogenous general populations, have had homologous justices. Biased representation, in favor of a dominant majority or of dominant minorities, has occurred in the ethnically more heterogeneous United States and Philippines, respectively.

Institutional Roles. There are wide differences in the postulation of institutional roles, as among the countries in our sample, but the available data will support only a single example. In the United States Supreme Court, justices are expected to participate in all decisions unless precluded by illness or the custom regarding putative bias, which each interprets for himself; but there is no expectation that each will write an opinion in every decision. The opinion for the Court is assigned to one of the associate justices or to himself by the Chief Justice; and any other justice is permitted to write an additional opinion if he so chooses, but considerations of workload, clientele reaction, custom, and tactics[49] tend to militate against his doing so very often. On the Australian High Court, the Chief Justice decides who will participate in each decision; but the expectation is that each participating judge will give his individual opinion to justify (or to protest) the decision. Contrary to his successor, Barwick, Chief Justice Owen Dixon set a Stakhanovite example for his colleagues by participating in 35 per cent more decisions than the average for the court; and he and two other justices constituted a majority of most of the panels (at frequencies of occurrence that exceed chance, with high statistical significance) so that the effect necessarily was to bias the court in favor of the policy preferences of these three persons. Japanese Supreme Court justices are expected to participate in all decisions of the five-justice panels to which each is assigned; but Chief Justice Tanaka never participated in the decisions of Petty Bench I to which he was nominally assigned, and it therefore functioned with only four justices throughout the decade of his tenure. By thus interpreting his institutional role as Chief Justice as requiring his participation only in *en banc* decisions of the whole court—thereby presumably allowing him

---

[49] Alexander Bickel, *The Unpublished Opinions of Mr. Justice Brandeis: The Supreme Court at Work,* Cambridge, Mass., Belknap Press, 1957; and Walter F. Murphy, *Elements Supreme Court Strategy,* Chicago, Ill., University of Chicago Press, 1964.

more time for his administrative tasks—Tanaka biased the panel in a more *liberal* direction by his persistent nonparticipation, since he himself was (as we shall see) a leading *conservative* member of the court.

In the United States, the justices of the Supreme Court frequently interrupt both the attorneys presenting oral arguments and each other, for they often join in a spirited group discussion of the issues presented for decision. In Japan there is much less questioning by the justices and practically no give-and-take between them and the attorneys, with the justices (as one observer put it) "sitting like Buddha" until the lawyers complete their prepared statements. It should be recalled, in this regard, that in this sort of situation the United States Supreme Court typically is the *larger* group, with nine justices, while the panel of the Japanese Supreme Court has only five. Moreover, after the justices have conferred and a group decision has been reached on the merits of the substantive policy issues, at least one justice dissents in a majority of the American Supreme Court's cases; however, dissent is quite rare—the rate is less than one per cent—in petty bench decisions in Japan. But when the Grand Bench of all 15 justices assembles in Japan, conference discussions become livelier and dissent vastly more frequent: almost 50 per cent in recent years, which is not only nearly as great as the current rate for the United States Supreme Court, but also extraordinarily high when one takes into account the considerable difference in the social consensus norms of the two societies.

One might hypothesize that the consensus norm is felt to be most obligatory in the smaller groups (petty benches) which must interact most frequently and intimately, while the effect of mixing the three smaller groups together is to magnify for each justice his sense of individual identity so that he is enabled to lose himself in "the lonely crowd" of the Grand Bench. Alternatively, however, it should be noted that cases deemed by the petty benches to be controversial tend to be bucked on to the Grand Bench, and there is also a corresponding specialization in the casting of rationales with the larger group exercising the function of manipulating constitutional norms. But whatever the explanation for the high rate of dissent in Grand Bench decisions, it is *signified* very differently in the process of group decision making than in the American Supreme Court, where discussion of cases at the group conference follows a strict order of seniority (starting with the Chief Justice) and voting follows the reverse sequence (with the Chief voting last). In Grand Bench conferences, both discussion and voting are informal. It appears that the consensus norm still has the effect of inducing the Japanese justices to seek to sublimate oral expression of their disagreement when in direct face-to-face contacts, at the same time permitting them to articulate it in writing.

In Australia, the rate of dissent in High Court decisions is about 25 per cent, and it appears to bear no relationship to the size of panels. Far from encouraging consensus, the effect of the norm which emphasizes individual expression—and oral articulation—of opinions is to encourage —in both a psychological and a statistical sense—the likelihood of dissensus.[50] There was a sharp increase in the average group rate of disagreement in opinions, from 42 to 60 per cent, when one justice who was almost 70 and another who was 72 retired and were replaced by men in their mid-fifties. In both the period before and the one after this change in personnel, Chief Justice Dixon wrote the opinions with which other justices agreed most: in each period, five of the other justices were in closer agreement with the Chief Justice's opinions than those of anyone else, and Dixon was the second choice of the remaining justice. There was least agreement with the opinions of the only Labor justice, McTiernan, during the first period; but even greater disagreement was evidenced during the second period in regard to the opinions of one of the new justices, Menzies, who had been affiliated with the anti-Labor Young Nationalists Organization and the Liberal Party. In the Philippines, dissent in voting occurred in less than 3 per cent of the decisions in 1954, although it was considerably higher—almost 30 per cent—only half a dozen years earlier, shortly after independence became effective and at a time when societal dissensus was high because this was a period of postwar reorganization and protests against wartime emergency powers actions.

Sociopsychological Variables

Partisan Affiliation. In the United States, the political party affiliations of Supreme Court justices are not secret, but neither do they appear to have more than a modest bearing upon whether justices vote as liberals or as conservatives. In recent years there have been six Democrats and three Republicans, reflecting the predominance of Democratic Presidents during the past three decades; only one of the Republicans (Chief Justice Warren) has been among the more liberal members of the Court, but two of the Democrats (Clark and White) were among the more conservative, which shows that there is a slight tendency for Democrats (4-2) to be more liberal, and Republicans (1-2) to be more conservative on the Supreme Court, just as in the American electorate generally.

Less than half of the Australian High Court justices were identified with political parties, and of these, two were Liberals and the other was

[50] From a methodological point of view, the relatively greater adequacy of opinion data, for the High Court, makes it preferable statistically to carry out analyses of attitudinal and ideological differences by examining interagreement in opinions; voting data are used to make similar analyses of the United States Supreme Court because there the votes provide the more complete index to interagreement and disagreement.

one of the only two Labor justices ever appointed to the High Court. Both of these Laborites were appointed in 1930; since 1932, Labor Governments have been in office only during the eight years of World War II and the immediate postwar period (1941–49). Only one vacancy arose during that period, and this appointment went to the Chief Justice of Queensland (who had been a state supreme court judge for over 20 years), reportedly because of his willingness to accept the assignment— "the Bench as a whole being very reluctant"—to represent Australia as President of the International Military Tribunal for the Far East in the trial of Japanese General Tojo and other "war criminals." In general, Labor Governments have been at a disadvantage, because there is an immediate hue and cry of "packing the Bench" if the appointment of a lawyer with Labor affiliations is proposed; the Liberal-Country coalition government, however, is on solid ground when it appoints nonpartisan barristers or state supreme court judges, the overwhelming majority of whom are ideological partisans of anti-Labor governments in any event.

In Japan the political party sympathies or identifications of Supreme Court justices are a *de facto* secret, and what they may have been for the justices in our sample is not known; neither does it appear that prior partisan affiliations of the former attorneys and men "of learning and experience" are accessible data, and it might be presumed that there are no such affiliations for the career judges. However, the survey of High Court judges included a question which asked the respondents which political party they voted for in national elections, and three-fourths of them replied, showing that 34 per cent support the conservative Liberal Democratic Party, 18 per cent the right-wing socialist Democratic Socialist Party, 10 per cent the Socialist Party, and none the Communist Party. These data suggest that probably a majority of Japanese appellate judges are supporters of the majority (that is, the Liberal Democratic) national party, and a substantial minority support the opposition socialist parties— although it should be noted that the proportion of judges supporting the more central Democratic Socialist Party is larger than the proportion supporting the left-wing and principal opposition, the Socialist Party.[51]

When the responses of these Japanese high court judges to the ideological parts of the questionnaire were compared to their partisan preferences, it was found that the scale (ranging from liberal to conservative) was as follows: Socialist voters, independents, nonrespondents to the question on party support, Democratic Socialists, and Liberal Democrats. In other words, judges who vote for liberal parties also support the gen-

---

[51] In the last two elections since the formation of the present party system, the Liberal Democratic Party has polled about 55 per cent of the popular vote, the Democratic Socialist Party only 8 per cent, the Socialist Party 28 per cent, and the Communist Party 4 per cent.

eral policy position with which the party is identified; conversely, judges who vote for conservative parties support the kinds of policy outcomes consistent with such a choice of parties. It seems likely that the nondisclosure of the political party preferences of Japanese Supreme Court justices is another instance of the effect of cultural norms which encourage the sublimination of the overt symbols rather than the actual elimination of ideological disharmony.

For the three industrialized countries, partisan affiliation of judicial elites is most conspicuous, and probably most important, in the United States. It might be hypothesized, however, that if the principal opposition parties in Australia and in Japan were to organize governments within some reasonably proximate future period, then the question of partisan affiliation of High Court and of Supreme Court justices might assume considerably more operational significance for staffing these courts than appears to be present under the prevailing circumstances of extended one-party dominance.

Group Affiliation. No systematic data on the social and interest group affiliations of either the United States or Japanese Supreme Court justices appear to have been published. In the survey of Japanese high court judges, one-third did not answer the question on group affiliations, and one-fourth stated that they were members of no such organization; but 42 per cent replied positively, and of these almost all mentioned bar associations and other organizations that were appraised as ranging ideologically from middle-of-the-road to moderately conservative; not one judge mentioned a liberal organization. Similarly, a survey of American state supreme court justices did not yield a single designation of such conceivably relevant liberal organizations as Americans for Democratic Action, the American Civil Liberties Union, the National Lawyers Guild, or the American Veterans Committee; the organizations mentioned were, in addition to bar associations and business groups, invariably conservative ones such as the Sons of the American Revolution or the American Legion.[52]

In the Philippines, however, five of the thirteen justices who were members of the Supreme Court during all or part of 1964 were members of the tiny (Philippines) Civil Liberties Union, as had been several other justices appointed during the preceding decade; almost all of the incumbent justices belong also to Philconsa (Philippines Constitutional Association), a much larger national civic group organized in the 1960s. Many of the Philippine justices also were members of upper-class social clubs and of both domestic and foreign professional associations. Two of the three most recently appointed Australian High Court justices each

[52] Stuart S. Nagel, "Off-the-Bench Judicial Attitudes," in Schubert, *op. cit.*, fn. 4, pp. 46–47 and fn. 31.

had been president of his state's bar association shortly before his recruitment to the court; three had had extensive military service; and four were active as directors of business corporations, either immediately before or subsequent to their service on the court. Each of the nine Australian justices belonged to several conservative, upper-class social clubs. It is notable that the justices in the nonindustrialized Philippines seem to maintain much more liberal, and also more professionally diverse, group associations[53] than do the judges in any of the three industrialized countries in our sample, although it is possible that the availability of systematic data concerning American and Japanese Supreme Court justices might necessitate modification of this inference.

Recruitment. Group associations do have a great deal to do with the recruitment of Japanese Supreme Court justices, which is based upon three parallel ladders of professional escalation. The preferred route for career judges involves such steps as graduating from the Tokyo University Law School, thereby gaining membership in the correct school clique (*gakubatsu*); an outstanding record as a student in in-service training at the Legal Training and Research Institute; successive appointments as assistant judge, district judge (particularly in Tokyo), high court judge, president of the Tokyo District Court, president of the Osaka High Court, and president of the Tokyo High Court. At one of the early stages of the judge's career he should seek an assignment as one of the Supreme Court's 30 research officials; and at a later stage appointment as president of the Legal Training and Research Institute can take the place of, and will doubtless be perceived as more prestigious than, a court presidency. But the first claim on a vacancy on the Supreme Court in any of the five professional-judge positions belongs to the president of the Tokyo High Court. For the attorney positions the route lies through leadership in the most important bar associations; and of the first eight lawyers appointed to the Supreme Court, seven had been presidents of either the Tokyo or the Osaka bar associations, and the other had been chairman of a major committee of the Japanese Federation of Lawyers. Of course, not all of those who could claim appointments to the Supreme Court wish to do so; the court is, after all, considered by the Japanese to be a political institution of distinctly secondary importance; and to accept appointment as a justice implies less money,[54] more work, and a duller life. Procurators

[53] It has been suggested that this is due to their common socialization at the liberally oriented University of the Philippines.

[54] When Abe Fortas resigned in 1965 his senior partnership in one of the largest and most affluent Washington law firms in order to become a member of the United States Supreme Court, it was reported that he was giving up an average annual private income of about $150,000 in exchange for a judicial salary of $39,000.

and diplomats work their way up the bureaucracies of the ministries of justice and foreign affairs, respectively; and law professors should rise through the academic bureaucracy of either Tokyo or Kyoto University.

In neither Australia nor the United States is the recruitment of justices hierarchically systematized as it is in Japan. Five of the twenty-one justices appointed to the American court during the past three decades have been "promoted" from the Department of Justice (where they had been, variously, Attorney General, Solicitor General, or Deputy Attorney General), but certainly no such custom as the earmarking of a "Department of Justice position" has emerged or even seems likely. The selection process has become institutionalized, in recent years, to the extent that the Deputy Attorney-General—who supervises the dispensation of federal judicial patronage generally—functions as an official clearing house for developing dossiers on all candidates whom the President wishes to consider for possible appointment; and a standing committee of the American Bar Association provides evaluations, nominally in terms of the professional qualifications of candidates.[55] Senate Judiciary Committee hearings on Presidential nominations afford a forum through which groups opposed to the preferred candidate—such opposition almost invariably is on ideological grounds—can attempt to block the appointment; only rarely have nominations of Supreme Court justices been withdrawn from or denied confirmation by the Senate, although some celebrated near-misses have occurred, such as Louis Dembitz Brandeis and Felix Frankfurter, both of whom were misperceived by the lunatic conservative fringe to be wild-eyed radicals.

In Australia appointments are made by the Cabinet and presumably the Attorney-General often has more than an *inter pares* voice in the decision, but what is known about how individual justices have been picked suggests that the selection process is even less—indeed, much less—clearly articulated than in the United States. What is clear is that the selection of justices in the United States and Australia and the Philippines alike is a highly politicized process, and one which is subject to even more flexibility than, say, the recruitment of members of the cabinet in any of these three countries. In Japan it is very different, as Dator has so well stated:

. . . [T]he whole legal profession, including the lawyers, can be considered to be more nearly a different manifestation of a single bureaucracy than a separate "branch" of the national government. The educational background of the judges,

---

[55] See Joel Grossman, *Lawyers and Judges*, New York, John Wiley and Sons, 1965; and Harold W. Chase, "Federal Judges: The Appointing Process," *Minnesota Law Review*, 51 (1966), 185–221.

prosecuting attorneys, and defense attorneys is essentially the same as that of the Foreign Service officers and the higher civil servants. . . . Moreover, the social background of each of these five elites also is essentially the same. In addition, each had to pass similar, governmentally-administered examinations in order to reach their positions. Subsequently, they have each approached their tasks in an essentially legalistic, nonpartisan, completely serious, and very competent way. They have been strengthened in this approach by in-service training and apprenticeships, each patterned on the same basic model. The result is that they all have been socialized into roles which sharply distinguish them from non-elites, but which has resulted in an administrative and a judicial elite made up of virtually interchangeable parts. Thus, it might be said that the administrators and judges are all bureaucrats, merely concerned with different aspects of the polity.[56]

Attitudes. Several studies of United States Supreme Court justices confirm that, at least in recent decades, there has been considerable consistency in the structure of both their individual and group attitudes toward the major issues of public policy that have confronted them for decision, including political freedom, fair procedure for criminal defendants, the right to privacy, civic equality, legislative reapportionment, governmental regulation of business, and the unionization of labor. Several justices—at the present time there is a majority on most of these issues—have supported in both their voting and their opinions positions which, in the framework of the American political culture, are liberal; some others have tended to take a conservative position on the political issues but a more moderate position on the economic issues; and still others have been moderate on political issues but conservative on economic ones.

Parallel inquiries, using similar methods, indicate that although policy issues vary from country to country, some are close analogues, if not duplicates, of American issues; and there appears to be similar high structure in the attitudes of justices irrespective of the policy content of issues. The votes of Japanese Supreme Court justices in fair procedure decisions, which involve claims of criminal defendants, form a very consistent scale. In the one year for which data are available (1948), the votes of the justices of the Philippine Supreme Court form a marginally consistent scale in regard to the issue of civil liberties generally. Very few cases raising issues of fair procedure or any other aspects of civil liberties are decided by the Australian High Court, which instead is mostly concerned with aspects of economic policy, including many aspects whose counterparts used to (but no longer) reach the United States Supreme Court. Two major scales were attributed to the High Court, one of which

[56] Dator, *op. cit.*, 438.

was tentatively identified as an attitudinal dimension of individualism-collectivism, and the other as pragmatism-dogmatism.

Intensive studies also have been made of the values espoused by justices in their writing. For example, a content analysis of all of the opinions written by one American justice (Robert H. Jackson) shows that he supported: civil liberties claims against the national government, but not against state governments; regulation of business by both the national and state governments, but at the same time defending the virtues of free enterprise and denouncing the vices of organized labor; states' rights; restraint in Supreme Court policy-making; deference to policy-making by the Administration and by Congress; and a significant degree of negative deference toward litigants before the Court.[57] It was concluded that Jackson was a nineteenth-century liberal in his attitudes, which meant that in terms of the contemporary American political culture, he was one of the most common type of conservative: the usually well-educated (although Jackson was not formally so), upper-class professional whose model of the American political economy finds a better fit in Bryce—or even Tocqueville—than in what is often today called the Great Society.

A similar type of study has been made of essays written by Kotaro Tanaka during the first year of the American military occupation, a few years before he became Chief Justice of the Japanese Supreme Court. Content analysis showed that he particularly favored natural law, order and harmony, spiritual life, humanity, absolute justice, the Emperor, democracy, truth, reason, and orthodoxy; he disapproved of anarchy, naturalism and epicureanism, dictatorship and fascism, positivism, chauvinism, professional politicians, power politics, and Marxism. Although several of these values reflect—not unnaturally—his concern for political exigencies of particular moment at that time in Japanese and world history, the portrait that clearly emerges is that of a spiritually oriented[58] Japanese conservative whose preference for order over freedom is overwhelming. And as Danelski has pointed out, a number of Tanaka's central positive values—the Emperor system, orthodoxy, and the feeling of shame—are the very ones emphasized in the Court's rationales for such leading decisions as those of the Grand Bench in the Fukuoka Patricide and the *Lady Chatterley's Lover* cases.[59] Chief Justice Tanaka and those other justices whose attitudes were similar to his functioned as spokesmen

---

[57] Schubert, "Jackson's Judicial Philosophy: An Exploration in Value Analysis," *American Political Science Review*, **59** (1965), 949.

[58] Tanaka became a devout Roman Catholic convert at about the age of 37.

[59] For an English translation of the opinions accompanying these decisions, see Maki, *op. cit.*, fn. 31, pp. 3–38 and 126–155.

for the traditional values of Japanese culture, in the face of the heretical and dangerous liberal currents that were sweeping Japanese society as a direct consequence of American military conquest—a war that was over— and of the assault of American influences upon the Japanese way of life— a war that was still in process, with some of its battles being fought in the Japanese Supreme Court.

Psychocultural Variables

The principal psychocultural variables in terms of which we can compare the judges in our sample are ideologies and the attributes of religion and age. Age seems to be better conceptualized as a psychocultural characteristic (rather than, for example, as a psychophysiological one) for present purposes, because his age is useful as an index to the cultural milieu in which a judge was socialized: persons a generation apart are apt to undergo very different experiences of acculturation in societies which are undergoing rapid industrial change and development.

Religion. Throughout the history of the United States Supreme Court, two-thirds of its justices have been affiliated with high social status Protestant religious organizations (Episcopalian, Presbyterian, Unitarian). The establishment by custom of a Jewish seat (beginning in 1916) has been mentioned previously; and with some minor and brief discontinuities, there has been at least one Catholic on the Court since the 1890s. The other justices have been affiliated with low social status Protestant denominations. A survey of the decision making of state Supreme Court justices showed that Catholic judges tended to vote more liberally than Protestant judges, but there were too few Jewish judges to make possible meaningful statistical comparison; and both Jewish and Catholic judges were conspicuously underrepresented on the state supreme courts, with only 11 per cent of the positions compared to 40 per cent of the claimed proportion of communicants in the populace.[60]

Although, as we noted, it is known that Chief Justice Tanaka is a Catholic, the religious affiliations of the other Japanese Supreme Court justices in the sample have not been identified. The survey of Japanese high court judges indicates that the overwhelming majority (over 70 per cent) identified themselves as Buddhist, most specifying a particular sect but many others indicating only the generic category (and frequently with the volunteered comment that the affiliation was strictly nominal). Only 2 per cent claimed to be Shintoists, but 9 per cent stated that they were

---

[60] Stuart S. Nagel, "Ethnic Affiliations and Judicial Propensities," *Journal of Politics,* **24** (1962), 95–104. Cf. Sheldon Goldman, "Voting Behavior on the United States Courts of Appeals, 1961–1964," *American Political Science Review,* **60** (1966), 381–382.

Christians and 12 per cent stated that they had no religious affiliation. This suggests that Christians (who comprise only one per cent of the populace) are greatly overrepresented—and recall that the Chief Justice of the Supreme Court himself was a member of this tiny Christian minority—among Japanese appellate judges; many other groups (and especially those affiliated with the various Nichiren sects, and all of the "New Religions") are greatly underrepresented.

In the Philippines over 90 per cent of the Supreme Court justices during the past three decades have been Roman Catholic, and only four others (two Protestants, a Mason, and a member of the Philippine Independent Church) have reached the court since the end of the Colonial period (during which American protestants had predominated). Almost the opposite is true in Australia, which had two Roman Catholics—both appointed by Labor governments—and seven Protestants (of whom at least two were Anglican and at least one was known to be Presbyterian) on the High Court during the 1950s.

Age. Age is of particular importance in discussing judicial leadership, because supreme court justices in the countries in our sample were mostly old men even *before* they were appointed to their respective courts. Most supreme court justices, when we think in terms of average age of their court groups, are products of a world that lies a full half century in the past and can be experienced only vicariously through historiography by the political generation that is coming of age in their country. This is what was at issue in President Roosevelt's attack upon the Supreme Court in 1937, which proved to be a great watershed in the development of American constitutional policy. But that was 30 years ago; and now the Supreme Court again is crowded with a majority of elderly men: Hugo Black (80), Chief Justice Earl Warren (75), William O. Douglas (68), and Tom Clark and John M. Harlan (both 67); the average age of this group at the times they were appointed was only 52, but their present average is over 70. The addition of the four most recently appointed, younger members of the court brings the present average down to about 63. The average age of Australian High Court justices during the 1950s was about the same, 61.

In Japan, however, the average age *at the time of appointment* has been 61, which is a direct consequence of the hierarchical career ladders that have been established, as Danelski has explained. Men leave the three ladders only when they reach the compulsory retirement age for the position they then are filling; for presidents of high courts, this is 65; for procurators, 63 or 65; for Tokyo University professors, 60; and although there is no such limit for attorneys in private practice, their average at appointment has been 62. Since Japanese Supreme Court

Justices themselves are compelled to retire at 70, the recruitment and tenure systems operate to assure a high rate of turnover among a group of men who are almost without exception sexagenarians. The effect of this squeeze on judicial age is not likely to be the assurance of an orderly transition to a relatively more liberal court in any proximate future, however. As Danelski has pointed out:

> . . . [T]hings are probably going to get worse before they get better. The reason is that if appointments are made much as they are now, the men coming to the Court in the next ten years will have been born around 1910. Unlike some of their predecessors, they will not have had the experience of the liberal World War I period and the early Taisho Democracy in their backgrounds. In interviews with retired justices and high court judges, the importance of this period of modern Japanese history often came up, especially in regard to the genesis of their liberal ideas which, in some cases, they wrote in Supreme Court [dissenting] opinions.[61]

In the Philippines, the average age of Supreme Court appointees was 46 during the Colonial period and 49 under the Commonwealth. During the past 20 years the trend has been toward the appointment of older men, and the average age of new justices increased from 57 years (in 1948) to 65 (in 1964). So now the average age of supreme court justices is in the sixties in all four countries of our sample. The United States and Australia, without a compulsory retirement age, from time to time have a few septagenarian justices, and a much greater *range* of ages represented at any given time on their highest court than does Japan. But this cuts both ways: one of the Australian justices in the sample had been appointed at the age of 38 (McTiernan, the Laborite), and among incumbent American Supreme Court justices, Douglas was appointed at 41, Stewart at 43, and White at 45. The Japanese Supreme Court differs from the others also in that internal debate and discussion within the group by justices representing differing generational points of view is impossible when all are of the same generation and advanced age group. This homogeneity of viewpoint doubtless tends to reinforce the many other factors, which we already have noted, that combine to make conservative ideology dominant among the Japanese justices.

[61] *Op. cit.*, p. 17. Danelski's hypothesis seems to be explicitly (albeit partially) confirmed by Dator's finding that among the high court judges whom he surveyed, the judges in the thirties and forties were more liberal than those in their sixties, but the fifty-year olds were the most conservative of all. Judges who were in their fifties in 1964 were born during the decade 1905–1914, and they were the political generation that came of age just as militarism displaced constitutional democracy in Japan and in the other Axis dictatorships during the 1930s.

Ideology. Beginning only a few years ago, John Kennedy's appointment of Arthur Goldberg to the Supreme Court meant that, for the first time in its history (and perhaps for the first time in the history of *any* national supreme court), a majority sympathetic to political liberalism controlled the Court; a different majority, sympathetic to economic liberalism, had been created half a dozen years earlier in 1956, with the appointment of William Brennan (since Clark voted liberally on economic issues but conservatively on political ones).[62] But there was a strong minority of liberals on both issues beginning in the early 1940s, and of course there had been occasional minorities of one or two for a much longer time.

On certain fundamental aspects of political equality, the Court began to produce consistently supporting majorities even during World War II. Among the policy components of this growing and increasingly dominant ideology of egalitarianism have been racial equality (through the elimination of the white primary and of restrictive covenants which precluded access to decent housing; and the assistance of Negroes to gain access first to higher education, next to public education generally, and then to a wide variety of other public facilities on an integrated basis); civic equality (for Americans residing abroad); voting equality (through insistence upon state legislative reapportionment); and equal justice for indigent persons accused of crimes (through assurance of the right to counsel, the right to be protected against conviction on the basis of testimonial compulsion, and the right to gain access to public records needed in order to appeal convictions). More recently the Court has given considerable emphasis to the right to privacy of persons living in an increasingly urbanized and mechanized society. The Court also has given some support to those citizens in local communities who have sought to resist the increasing efforts of various sectarians to use the public schools as an instrument for imposing their private faiths upon captive audiences of children. In every one of these policy areas, the Supreme Court not only has provided leadership: it has provided the *only* national political leadership in initiating and in encouraging political, economic, and social changes of fundamental significance for, and impact upon, American society.[63]

In none of the other countries in our sample does the highest court play any such role as that which we have just described. Both the Austral-

---

[62] *Op. cit.* fn. 22, Ch. 5.

[63] To the extent that Congress and the Presidency have become involved in some—by no means in all—of these policy sectors, it has been with evident reluctance and only to the extent that their participation has been forced by sequences of events set in motion by earlier actions of the judiciary—particularly the federal courts—under the stimulus of the Supreme Court.

ian High Court and the Philippine Supreme Court have from time to time undertaken the negative function of blocking the Administration from carrying through proposed programs (by "exercising the power of judicial review," as lawyers like to put it). The American Supreme Court used to do the same sort of thing, and particularly during the seventy-odd years from the end of the Civil War until the Roosevelt reforms that began in 1937; but the conservative function of blocking or slowing down social change is a very different activity than the liberal function of initiating such change. The Japanese Supreme Court, which thus far has not carried out either of these functions, plays the much more passive role of very limited political leadership, which is exercised in the main by supporting the government in its current programs. It is, of course, quite understandable that the Japanese Supreme Court should do this, given the almost complete homogeneity of general policy orientation which characterizes both the real political leaders in the government and a majority of the justices as well.[64]

It is apparently in the Philippines, rather than in either of the two other and industrialized countries, that the substantive content of judicial ideologies most closely resembles what has been attributed to American Supreme Court justices. In 1948 almost 70 per cent of the cases in which the Philippine justices divided related either to civil liberties, economic policy, or to other restraint of governmental activity; and the corresponding proportion in 1954 was 80 per cent. Samonte analyzed these decisions in relation to the predominant occupational background experience of the justices, and he found that those who had been politicians were consistently most liberal on all three policy issues. Those with a public rather than a Catholic education tended to be particularly sympathetic to civil liberties. Bureaucrats were liberal in regard to restraint of the government but conservative on economic issues. Prosecutors were conservative toward both civil liberties and governmental restraint. Professors were economic conservatives. And those with previous judicial experience were the most conservative of all, in their reluctance to exercise "judicial

[64] Norway also has a system of one legal education but diverse governmental activities based upon it. As Ulf Torgersen has commented, "This system once introduced, seems to have had certain consequences. The common education has led to a certain amount of solidarity and understanding among people from highly varied walks of legal life, and the interchange of personnel between the various organizations in which the legally trained man works has tied the professional subcultures together. More specifically, the judges, who to a considerable extent have been recruited from the administration, tend to feel loyalty to the [government], and are somewhat reluctant to act against the government when faced with the problem of determining the legality of some measure." *Op. cit.,* fn. 4, 228–229.

review" to restrain the Administration[65]—a finding that will give little comfort to those political conservatives who cherish the notion that a requirement of extensive previous judicial experience is the best way to stack courts which will checkmate liberal chief executives and legislatures.[66]

In the Philippines, as in the United States, about one-third of all decisions in which the supreme court divides involve issues of civil liberties. Such questions rarely reach the Australian High Court; hence—as with the Japanese Supreme Court—these justices cannot be differentiated on this basis. But two scales, one involving primarily different aspects of economic policy and the other a psychological dimension, were identified, and when these are related to over-all patterns of voting agreement and disagreement, the nine Australian justices can be classified as follows: the solitary Laborite is a collectivist; the other appointee of a Labor cabinet and two of the other justices are pragmatists; three of the justices are individualists, taking a position opposite to that of the Laborite; and the remaining two—Chief Justice Owen Dixon and one of the two more recent appointees—are dogmatists. Considering the differing stages, directions, and magnitudes of development of the American and Australian societies, it seems likely that one would have to go back to an earlier period in the history of the Supreme Court, certainly before 1937 and probably before the jurisdictional changes of 1916 and 1925, to find better correspondence between the substance of value content of the American and Australian justices, respectively.

Danelski has noted that in his analysis of the Japanese Supreme Court he was unable to identify systematic expression of either political freedom or political equality, subcomponents of liberalism that have been

---

[65] A recent flurry of such decisions by the Philippine Supreme Court, against the Macapagal Administration, provoked in turn a much milder kind of feedback from the President than that experienced by the American Supreme Court three decades ago. Macapagal desisted from launching an open political attack upon the justices, instead merely expressing his disagreement with their judgment. But other American Presidents (and among them, Jefferson, Jackson, and Lincoln) had attacked the Supreme Court long before Franklin Roosevelt; and the available data do not suggest that either the Philippine or the Japanese Supreme Court has as yet produced a Marshall or a Taney—which is perhaps to say that the political cultures in those countries have not yet (at least) provided a need for the kind of aggressive leadership which so often has characterized the interpretation by American Chief Justices of their political roles.

[66] Cf. John Schmidhauser's finding that those justices with previous judicial experience were the ones *least* inclined to follow precedents: see his "*Stare Decisis*, Dissent, and the Background of the Justices of the Supreme Court of the United States," *University of Toronto Law Journal*, 14 (1962), 194–212.

important in the policy leadership of the American Supreme Court. But neither, as we have seen, do these issues assume importance in the leadership of the highest court in Australia. For the Japanese Supreme Court, on the basis of analysis of a large sample of fair procedure cases, involving claims of criminal defendants, it appears that about half of the justices were relatively liberal, and the remainder were split equally between moderates and conservatives. Chief Justice Tanaka was the third most conservative member of the group on this issue consistently throughout the ten-year period covered. As a consequence of the preponderance of relatively liberal justices, over half—about 60 per cent—of these appeals to the Supreme Court were successful; but it should be remembered, of course, that a very much larger number of appeals—90 per cent, just as with the American Supreme Court—were considered so unmeritorious that they were rejected by research officials without even reaching consideration by the justices or they were disposed of by petty benches without being decided by the Grand Bench. Hence our use of the adjective "relatively" liberal, for these were presumably the cases that presented the very strongest claims of what American lawyers would term the denial of procedural due process of law.

It is also notable that in a selected group of cases, chosen to illustrate the typical patterning of values in the Japanese Supreme Court's decisions during 1948–60 (which is largely the same period that Danelski's analysis covered), only one (involving a claim of police brutality and a coerced confession) out of seventeen civil liberties cases was decided liberally; half of these cases dealt with fair procedure, and the other half with political freedom.[67] The responses of high court judges to Dators' survey showed that the item on which the Japanese most clearly were more conservative than American or British respondents was one which read: "Unrestricted freedom of discussion on every topic is desirable in the press, in literature, and on the stage." Eighty-five per cent of the Japanese judges disagreed.[68] When we recall, however, the pervasiveness of the consensus norm in Japan, it is easy to understand why very few Japanese judges could bring themselves to opt for unlimited freedom of speech.

Decisional Outputs

The preceding discussion illustrates in many ways how, from a psychological point of view, decisions of courts consist of an aggregation of ex-

[67] Maki, *op. cit.*, fn. 31.

[68] In a similar survey, a majority of American judges *agreed* with the statement. See Nagel, "Off-the-Bench Judicial Attitudes," in Schubert, *op. cit.*, fn. 4, p. 34.

pressions of individual preferences among policy alternatives; if we choose to focus our attention upon the characteristics of the aggregations rather than upon those of the individuals who do the preferring, then we can speak of group preferences, which brings us closer to the legal (and lay) concept of what an appellate court decision signifies. From a sociological point of view, however, a court's decisions are important not primarily as outputs for the court, but as inputs for other groups of people who are affected by them. Our focus has been upon processes of decision making, and our data do not extend in any systematic way to the legitimizing (and illegitimizing) consequences of the decisions of the courts in our sample, for such other political actors as lower court judges, attorneys, litigants, and other government officials, to name only a few of those typically concerned. Neither do our data permit us to examine systematically how the prevailing patterns of dominant norms, in each of the countries sampled, were modified because of not only what the courts decided, but also what other actors did in response to these judicial decisions; and from the point of view of social anthropology, such knowledge would be indispensable to a really comprehensive cross-cultural analysis of comparative judicial behavior.

Our present task is to explore rather than to exhaust the subject; and so we suggest that the judicial role of norm (not *law*) production is a facet of judicial leadership that merits further exploration. As Wolfson has observed:

Judges, leading clergymen, some business leaders and military men, and a small band of university professors and college heads are representative of ["ideology-makers" as a] group . . . [and] it is as final arbiters on national issues and as producers of political, social and moral norms that they stand out from the rest of their peers. . . . [T]heir norm-producing activities must be to some extent forced upon them owing to their high professional status in the community. Among the ideology-makers, judges and clergymen predominate as they are professional norm-makers.[69]

At the manifest level of functional analysis, we have examined some of the relationships among attributes and attitudes of judges and their decisions, and we can now note briefly some of the ways in which the decisions function as a form of norm-feedback for the very actors (among others) who are the principal sources of the judges' own inputs. In 1959 the Japanese Supreme Court made two decisions which attracted unusual —for that court—publicity. One of these involved an appeal from the conviction of seventeen (out of twenty original) defendants for the mur-

[69] Hugo Wolfsohn, "Ideology Makers," Ch. 4 in Mayer, *op. cit.*, fn. 3, 76–77.

der of three persons killed in a train derailment that many persons believed to have been engineered by the Communist Party in Japan. On the day that the court's decision was to be announced, thousands marched on Tokyo to lobby with the court and demand a reversal of the convictions, and thousands of other persons were massed just beyond the cordon of 3000 police who surrounded the Supreme Court building to protect the justices. Under these circumstances the court remanded the case for re-trial; and the Socialist Party issued a public statement approving the court's action. Soon thereafter, however, the Socialist Party changed its tune, and issued a statement saying that it would campaign against all justices who had participated in a unanimous decision upholding the continuance of American military bases in Japan.[70] This announcement was significant, of course, for its ideological implications, rather than as any serious threat against the personnel of the court. A large number of other groups and organizations also took public stands in regard to the court's decision in this case: among those supporting the Supreme Court were the Japan Wounded War Veterans' Association and the National Association of Towns and Villages; those in opposition included the General Council of Japan Labor Unions and the Jurists' Council for Research on the Security Treaty.

In the United States, where Supreme Court Justice Felix Frankfurter's notorious preference for law clerks trained at Harvard (where he had been a professor for a quarter of a century before joining the Court) was noted in the doubtlessly irreverent but indubitably felicitous designation of these young men as the "happy hot dogs," most students of the Court are convinced that Justice Frankfurter was much more concerned about how his opinions were received at Harvard than at Yale.[71] Similarly, in Japan individual justices appear to make their decisions and write (or fail to write) opinions with feedback to and from *their* reference groups in mind. As one Japanese Supreme Court justice—and as it happens, a former professor—remarked to Danelski in an interview, he often wondered what his former colleagues thought about his judicial work, and he was therefore gratified when, after having sent (for example) a dissenting opinion of his to such an old friend, the other professor expressed his complete agreement with it.[72]

---

[70] The opinions of the justices in this, the Sunakawa Case, are reported in Maki, *op. cit.*, fn. 31, 298–361.

[71] See Jack W. Peltason, *Federal Courts in the Political Process*, New York, Random House, 1955, p. 72, n. 20.

[72] Cf. Mark De Wolfe Howe (ed.), *The Holmes-Pollock Letters*, Cambridge, Mass., Harvard University Press, 1941, 2 vols., and *The Holmes-Laski Letters*, Cambridge, Mass., Harvard University Press, 1953, 2 vols.

Judicial Styles and Functions

Finally, at the latent level of functional analysis, we are concerned with the fundamental impact of differing stages of economic and political development [73] upon the manner in which judicial leadership is expressed through varying styles and functions. Style is expressed by the manner in which the court reaches and communicates its decisions. A group of justices whose members are representative of a broad spectrum of the attributes, attitudes, and ideologies which characterize the society; who produce norms that are "open compromises, openly arrived at"; and who articulate their disagreement in dissenting and concurring opinions and votes; such a court is itself a democratic society in microcosm, and it can therefore be viewed as an interpretive model of the larger political society with which it interacts—and vice versa.

For the countries in our sample, the scale of democratic style among highest courts is the following: the United States, the Philippines, Australia, and Japan. This scale of democratic style has a very low (rho = .2) correlation with the modernization scale of socioeconomic development for these countries (United States, Japan, Australia, and last the Philippines). We earlier suggested two other possible hypotheses: (1) that differences in the behavior of justices in different countries might be attributed, at least for this sample, to differences in the extent to which they accept the institutions and norms of the British legal culture; and (2) that differences might be due to differentials in the extent of American influence upon their political development. The democratic style scale correlates somewhat better (rho = .4) with the legal culture scale (Australia, United States, Philippines, and Japan), but it clearly correlates best (rho = .8) with the political impact scale (United States, Philippines, Japan, and Australia).[74] On this evidence, we must conclude that American influence upon political development in these countries is more closely associated with a democratic style of judicial leadership than is either acceptance of the British legal culture, or industrialization and socio-economic modernization.[75]

[73] Alker et al. classify the United States as the most highly developed nation in the world on their scale of economic and political development, with Australia also classified in the fifth stage as a "high mass-consumption" society, Japan in the fourth as an "industrial revolution" society, and the Philippines in the third stage as a "transitional" society. *Op. cit.*, fn. 14, pp. 296–298.

[74] The corresponding correlations of the political impact scales are .4 with the socioeconomic scale and −.2 with the legal scale; between the socioeconomic and legal scales, the correlation is zero.

[75] Several non-American readers of a draft of this chapter have informed me how

Our analysis distinguished three primary functions of judicial leadership: policy *initiation, resistance,* and *legitimation.* We found that during the period of the 1950s, a time for which the research studies upon which we have relied overlap, only the United States Supreme Court played a conspicuous role of initiating policy leadership. Both the Philippine Supreme Court and the Australian High Court—apparently in that order—played the more negative role of resisting policies that were initiated by other national political leaders. The Japanese Supreme Court acted only to legitimate the policies initiated by the country's political leaders; it seems clear that the Japanese justices have considerably less stature as political leaders themselves, both compared to other justices in our sample, and also compared to other actors in the Japanese polity.[76] The scale of judicial leadership *functions* is, therefore, the United States, the Philippines, Australia, and Japan. But this is the same as our scale of judicial leadership *styles;* and therefore it has precisely the same correlations with the scales of socioeconomic development, legal culture, and political impact. In terms therefore of both the styles and functions of political leadership by judges, our findings indicate that it is political impact rather than legal culture or socioeconomic development, and explicitly it is the extent to which other polities resemble the American, that best accounts for the observable differences in judicial behavior between the highest judicial elites in Australia, Japan, and the Philippines.

    ✿   ✿   ✿   ✿   ✿   ✿

Acknowledgment

For support of and assistance in my research in cross-cultural study of judicial behavior, I am particularly indebted to: the Institute of Advanced

---

chauvinistic they consider this, one of my major conclusions. In particular, Professor Blackshield considers the sentence (denoted by this footnote index in the text) perverse; and Professor Agpalo believes that indigenous liberal political forces, which resulted also in the Revolution of 1896–1901, provide an independent and better explanation for the democratic elements in Philippine political—including judicial—style and functions.

[76] Dator has pointed out that, particularly as a consequence of the influence of Anglo-American lego-political concepts and practices that were introduced during the military occupation, Japanese Supreme Court justices may—he might well have said "must"—be experiencing considerable conflict concerning their individual and collective roles. The foreign (that is, American) cultural norms tell them to be individualists, to defend human freedom and dignity, to dissent when they disagree, and to declare acts of the Parliament to be unconstitutional. But their own traditional culture conveys a very different message; and their status level, as governmental officials, remains below that of even the higher civil servants in the bureaucracy. Judges are, as Dator has remarked, "the one major Japanese elite which has not yet settled into a comfortable position within the Japanese political and social system."

Projects of the Center for Cultural and Technical Interchange between East and West, University of Hawaii; the Social Science Research Institute of the University of Hawaii; and the Asian Studies Center of the Office of International Programs of Michigan State University.

This chapter constitutes an attempt to synthesize, and is therefore based primarily upon three papers that were presented at the panel on "Judicial Leadership" of the American Political Science Association's 62nd Annual Meeting in New York City on September 10, 1966: David J. Danelski's "The Japanese Supreme Court: An Exploratory Study," Abelardo G. Samonte's "The Philippine and American Supreme Courts: A Comparative Study of Judicial Attributes, Attitudes, and Decisions," and my own "The High Court and the Supreme Court: Two Styles of Judicial Hierocracy." I have relied upon all three of these papers to such an extent that I make this general acknowledgment of my indebtedness, in lieu of any attempt to cite them in detail in the preceding discussion. I have made similar use of an earlier and somewhat different version of Dr. Samonte's paper, which he presented under the title "The Philippine Supreme Court: A Study of Judicial Attributes, Attitudes and Decisions" at a seminar meeting of the Comparative Judicial Behavior Group of the Institute of Advanced Projects, Center for Cultural and Technical Interchange Between East and West, University of Hawaii, during the summer of 1965; and also of an article by James Allen Dator, "The Life History and Attitudes of Japanese High Court Judges," *Western Political Quarterly*, **20** (June, 1967), 408–439.

I am grateful, for their many helpful comments upon an earlier version of this chapter, to the following people: to my collaborators, Professors Danelski (Yale University), Dator (Virginia Polytechnic Institute), and Samonte (Philippine Executive Academy); to my University of Hawaii colleagues Theodore L. Becker, Yasumasa Kuroda, and Robert B. Stauffer (all of the Department of Political Science) and Forrest R. Pitts (Social Science Research Institute); and to several gracious friends, including Remigio Agpalo (University of the Philippines), Anthony R. Blackshield (University of Sydney), George H. Gadbois, Jr. (University of Kentucky), Gene L. Mason (University of Kentucky), Walter F. Murphy (Princeton University), and John Sprague (Washington University).

9. Political Careers
and Party Leadership

JOSEPH A. SCHLESINGER

In this chapter I am interested in the relationship between the characteristics of political parties and the careers of their leaders.[1] Since the assumptions on which this analysis rests depart radically from the attitudes of my coauthors toward political leaders I shall briefly discuss the differences.

My basic assumption is that ambition for public office motivates political leaders. It follows that the activities of political leaders are directed by what they must do to achieve office: they adopt policies, form alliances, and indeed create political organizations to the extent that such actions aid them in achieving their office goals. Obviously leaders must provide others, certainly the voters in a democracy, with good reasons for letting them attain and hold office. Thus, in my view, the leader-follower relationship is a rational exchange of values in which followers barter their support for political decisions to their liking.

My approach, which focuses upon office as the goal toward which politicians strive by employing rational calculations, is closest to the approach used in much of economic theory. Unlike the psychologist or sociologist, who is properly concerned with uncovering the complexity of motives which underlie behavior, the economic theorist seeks to hold the most critical motives constant. Thus it is self-evident that men strive to attain economic goals (such as increased income) from a diversity of motives. Nevertheless there are useful economic theories that pay no attention to the reasons why men want to increase income, but develop instead the logical consequences which follow from the assumption that men do. Similarly, the ambition perspective leads us away from asking why men want to gain public office toward what they must do in order to gain office.

The "economic" perspective on politics has already been applied to the behavior of political parties, most successfully, naturally enough, by econ-

[1] By the term "leader" I mean here simply those men who hold or seek public office in the name of the political party.

omists. Schumpeter [2] stated most effectively the argument that political parties adopt policies to gain office, not the reverse, and that the system in which parties compete for popular support provides the controls, if any, upon their behavior. Anthony Downs [3] expanded this argument into a more refined theory of party behavior.

For the political scientists, however, the theories of Schumpeter and Downs have an important weakness. Both start with political parties that are organized, cohesive teams whose members are united in the pursuit of a single goal, control of government. They then extend the concept of cohesive organization to government itself. But in so doing they ignore the complexities of party and governmental organization which derive from the conflicting ambitions of office-seekers and officeholders. Yet the logic which accepts as its basic premise that parties are office-oriented would seem to lead to the proposition that party organization emerges and takes its characteristics from the distinctive ways in which individual party leaders pursue their office goals.[4]

Considering the range of disciplines among social scientists, it is probably the political scientist's responsibility to offer the simple but crucial proposition that parties do not, after all, establish the goals which give rise to their existence. It is the state and its peculiar structure that establish the prizes of office for which parties strive. In every representative democracy, at least, it is the state's multitude of offices which indicate the stages of advancement or failure in a politician's career.

Once we accept this proposition, its consequences for the study of party organization become obvious: we must examine parties within the context of the complex of offices they have organized to capture. The various rules, formal and informal, which define the routes of political advancement, as well as the party system which defines the relative chances of each party to gain office, must shape party organization. Revolutionary organizations whose objective is to alter the state or pressure groups whose objective is to influence the state's policies without capturing office can often be studied as distinct entities. But organizations competing according to a given set of rules for control of a given set of institutions cannot be understood without knowledge of those rules and institutions.

---

[2] Joseph A. Schumpeter, *Capitalism, Socialism, and Democracy* (3rd ed.), New York, Harper and Row, 1950.

[3] Anthony Downs, *An Economic Theory of Democracy, New York,* Harper and Row, 1957.

[4] For a more complete discussion of the relations between forms of ambition and party organization see Joseph A. Schlesinger, "Political Party Organization," in *Handbook of Organizations*, ed. by James G. March, Chicago, Ill., Rand McNally, 1965, pp. 764–801.

The concept that parties are office-seeking organizations shaped largely by institutional arrangements, which is my view, is not universally held by political scientists. Many who readily acknowledge the seeming office-orientation of certain political groups, especially in the United States, are convinced that parties "really" represent class or group interests and therefore are issue-oriented rather than office-oriented. Among political scientists of this persuasion Maurice Duverger has undoubtedly been the most influential. Duverger's comprehensive theory of parties [5] follows from the assumption that all the important characteristics of party organization derive from group and class interests or from ideology, the world view of a particular group or class. [6] For Duverger, then, American parties appear to be office-oriented organizations only because they represent the same bourgeois, middle-class interests and can therefore dispense with overt ideological expression.

It is doubtful if any amount of investigation will determine the correct view of parties. To me, at least, at this stage of our knowledge, the weight of historical evidence indicates that in political organizations which have a good chance of capturing public office, the office drive predominates. Duverger sees the mass-based party and its elaborate organization of nonofficeholders as the inevitable products of universal suffrage whose purpose is to subsume office-seeking within doctrinal goals. Yet in all representative democracies major political parties have inevitably drawn criticism not for the pursuit of principle at the cost of office, but for their stubborn pursuit of office even at the cost of program. [7]

I would certainly assert, then, that the office-seeking view of parties is at least as valid for purposes of comparative analysis as the ideological view. Indeed, for these purposes I would say there is much to recommend its preferment. The comparative study of parties has been hampered by the great variety of organizations, including pressure groups and totalitarian governing agencies, to which the term "party" has been applied. The office-seeking view, by focusing upon the goal of elective office, restricts the term to organizations which compete according to an accepted set of political rules for political control which is clearly delimited by an

[5] Maurice Duverger, *Political Parties*, New York, John Wiley and Sons, 1954.

[6] Much debate has centered on the term "ideology" and whether or not it has declined in any or all of the various meanings attributed to it. See, for example, the exchange by Joseph LaPalombara, "Decline of Ideology: A Dissent and an Interpretation," and the reply by Seymour M. Lipset, "Some Further Comments on the 'End of Ideology,'" in the *American Political Science Review*, LX, 1966, 5–18.

[7] Such pursuit was also largely responsible for Robert Michels' famous critique of the German Social Democratic Party, whose appetite for office was whetted by the limited representative institutions of Kaiser Germany. Robert Michels, *Political Parties*, New York, Free Press, 1949 (first published 1915).

established set of institutions. I recognize that for those who prefer the ideological view of parties the restrictive nature of the office-seeking definition destroys its usefulness. Yet I would argue that the compulsion to seek an all-inclusive definition of parties blinds us to the great varieties and types of political organizations and the crucial distinctions which should be made between them. My office-seeking definition of parties may well be based on personal preference alone; I prefer to think, naturally, that it is based on valid historical and empirical reasons. Modern political parties, after all, developed within the framework of representative institutions as office-seeking organizations; within that framework, and with interesting variations which I shall discuss later, these office-seeking organizations persist and function.

Political Parties and Political Opportunities

If we accept the office-seeking view of parties, then for comparative study we must devise techniques for analyzing the ways in which different political systems structure opportunities for office.[8] Yet does not this focus upon office and office careers pose difficulties for systematic comparison? A country's office structure is, after all, very much the result of its own peculiar history and customs. An American congressman is not a replica of the British M.P., and membership in the British House of Lords is certainly not equivalent to membership in the American Senate. Admittedly, the structure of offices which marks the careers of American politicians differs from that which allows us to plot the careers of politicians in Great Britain and France. If parties are organized to capture offices, are we not restricted in our analysis to the description of particular institutions?

I would suggest that we can compare and measure careers across systems as long as we place our emphasis upon opportunities and ask questions about the universal characteristics of political careers. For example, we can compare the number of political opportunities in various systems. The number of political opportunities within a system is critical to both the generation and the satisfaction of ambitions. The number of offices

[8] To assert that party organization reflects the structure of political opportunities is not to deny that parties, in turn, affect the opportunity structure. Certainly the developments which took place in British party organization at the end of the nineteenth century transformed greatly the process of becoming prime minister. In the United States, parties early captured the Electoral College, which presumably was to choose the president. At the same time, the differences between American and British parties reflect the different methods by which the two countries choose their chief executives. Clearly parties and institutions affect each other.

of significance and the frequency with which they become available to new men define for the ambitious their sense of chances for advancement. Only if it holds the promise of adequate opportunities for advancement can any organization retain the services of its potential leaders.

In most organizations we can observe the multiplication of high offices combined with assurances of turnover. The multiplication of university provosts, vice presidents, and chancellors alongside those old standbys, presidents and deans, is a counterpart of the multiplication of corporate vice presidents (ranked) and chairmen of the board alongside the company president. Here the level of opportunity can be maintained or raised either by expanding the number of positions or by increasing the turnover among their holders. The promotional system is assured by limiting tenure within offices and by setting forth rigid retirement ages. Such turnover is made feasible by establishing comfortable pensions.

In terms of specific offices, an elective office structure is less readily expandible than the corporate organization or the appointive bureaucracy. There are limits to the size of parliaments. Even in a presidential system only a few executives can be directly elected. It is true that within legislative bodies, whether of the British or American variety, gradations of office are established which are significant in defining the structure and level of opportunities. The British Parliament, for example, has a hierarchy of front and back benchers, and positions more or less close to the principal cabinet posts are well defined. The United States Congress has its hierarchy of committees and committee chairmanships which show consistent tendencies to proliferate. In other words, the core of elected leaders can and does develop a structure of opportunities which refines even more the chances for political advancement.

At the same time, the number of men who attain significant elective positions, as well as the pace of change critical to the sense of expectations, are measurable quantities, comparable from system to system. Let me propose a simple measure of the level of political opportunities, the "opportunity rate" for a particular group of offices. Its virtue is that it provides a number which can be meaningfully added to others. The universe of significant offices is not necessarily clearly defined. Thus we need some flexible measure which can tell us, for example, what the level of opportunities is in the United States if we look simply at national offices, but one which can also readily be used to include significant state and local positions as well. The measure must also provide us with totals which can be compared not only within a political system, but also across national boundaries.

The measure is based first upon the calculation of the frequency with which new personnel are elected over a significantly long period (long enough to encompass more than spurts of active competition among parties which may produce sporadic highs in turnover) or the number of elections for the given set of offices within a given time span. I have chosen 12 years as the standard period because it is a common multiple of most set office terms. For any political body therefore we can calculate the typical number of chances to hold office, to be, for example, a member of the British Parliament or the United States Congress over a typical 12-year standard period or generation.

In Table 9.1 we have the opportunity rates for the American House of Representatives and the British House of Commons. Since the American House has fixed terms of two years, the number of elections in a 12 year period is a direct product of the six regular elections times the number of seats (column *D*). For the British House, with variable timing, the number of seats has been multiplied by the average number of elections in a 12-year period.

The results show that in a 12-year generation there are 610 chances to be one of 435 congressmen and 558 chances to be one of 620 members of parliament. The turnover rates for the two chambers are not substantially

Table 9.1. Opportunity Rates for the British House of Commons Compared with the United States House of Representatives

	Average No. of Offices	No. of General Elections	No. of Personnel Changes	Personnel Turnover Rate (B/A)	Ave. No. General Elections in a 12-Year Period	Opportunity Rate (C × D)
	A	B	C	D	E
U.S. House[9] (1914–1958)	435	9509	2228	0.234	2610	610.74
British House[10] (1919–1964)	621.3	7455	2142	0.287	1944.67	558.12

[9] Joseph A. Schlesinger, *Ambition and Politics: Political Careers in the United States*, Chicago, Ill., Rand McNally, 1966, p. 40.

[10] I am indebted to Paul Dawson for the calculations of turnover in the British Parliament.

different. What reduces the opportunity rate for the British Parliament is the longer time typically between elections. Of course the per capita chances of becoming an M.P. are considerably higher in England because of its smaller population.

Yet calculating the chances for the lower houses of the two legislatures hardly exhausts the total number of political opportunities in either country. Chances for other offices can be added to these already calculated. Thus using the same method, we find that in the United States there are 93.50 chances to become a Senator and 136.07 to become a governor within a 12-year period. If these chances, along with those for U.S. Representative, are taken to be the significant universe of political opportunities, then there are a total of 840.31 chances to attain an important office every 12 years in the United States. And we can continue to add other offices. If we add minor statewide elective posts such as lieutenant governor, attorney general, and secretary of state, then the total number of significant outlets in the United States rises to 1273 every 12 years.[11]

In assessing the total number of opportunities in a political system, some account must be taken of multiple officeholding. Obviously when one man holds several offices other men's chances are reduced. In this respect wide differences exist among political systems. There is little multiple officeholding in the United States. Of course the federal constitution does not permit a man to hold both congressional and executive office, but there is no national law which prevents him from being a congressman and a state executive or legislator or mayor at the same time. It simply is not done. On the other hand, the ethos of the parliamentary cabinet system is more conducive to multiple officeholding. Whereas only some members of the British Parliament retain local offices, France has many conspicuous examples.

As may be seen in Table 9.2, joint officeholding is fundamental to the French career structure. One-third of the deputies elected in 1956 retained some local office which they had held before being elected to the Chamber for the first time. One out of four deputies added a local office after becoming deputies. And these were not minor posts: 177 were mayors and 25 were presidents of the departmental *conseil général.* Thus one-third of all the presidents of the governing bodies of France's departments were also deputies, most having attained the position after becoming deputies.

Although such joint officeholding in France and elsewhere on the continent has been noted as providing a measure of local influence in centralized unitary states, it should also be seen as severely restricting

[11] J. A. Schlesinger, *Ambition and Politics,* p. 50.

Table 9.2.   Joint Officeholding in France
(*Based on the Chamber elected in 1956*)

	Per Cent of Deputies
A. Offices Held Prior to Deputy and Held Concurrently (total: 33.8 per cent)	
Municipal Council	25.6
Mayor	16.3
General Council	21.2
President of General Council	0.8
B. Offices Added after Becoming Deputy (total: 25.7 per cent)	
Municipal Council	5.7
Mayor	13.4
General Council	10.9
President of General Council	3.4
N of Deputies:	595

opportunities in the political system.[12] Ambition as a control on the behavior of political leaders is enhanced by the orderly distribution of expectations. The fact that the advancement of one man opens up his position to others is critical to the development of a network of ambitions. The restrictive quality of the French system is exacerbated because deputies not only retain local offices which would otherwise be available to others, but also gain additional, more important, local positions.

Political Parties and Political Careers

A measure of all of a country's political opportunities does not, of course, differentiate among political parties. Yet it is as a Democrat or Republican, Labourite or Conservative, that one becomes a congressman or M.P. The parties have relative shares of political opportunities. By providing multiple routes to political leadership the parties also expand the general sense of opportunities for the ambitious. For if only one man at a time can be prime minister, the leaders of competing parties retain their expectations.

If party organizations are built around the political office careers of their leaders, then we must also develop measures of partisan careers which can be compared across systems. The five countries I have chosen

[12] For example, see W. J. M. Mackenzie, "Local Government Experience of Legislators," *Public Administration*, 32, 1954, reprinted in J. Wahlke and H. Eulau, *Legislative Behavior*, New York, Free Press, 1959, pp. 272–280.

for comparison are all developed democracies with similar representative structures whose constitutional similarities and differences are widely known: the United States, Great Britain, Canada, and Australia, all English-speaking democracies, to which I have added the French Fourth Republic. The United States, Canada, and Australia are federal in structure; they have states or provinces which provide a significant intermediate and to a degree an independent career outlet for politicians. All but the United States have cabinet systems, in which it is assumed that the leading members of the executive will also be members of the legislature. The United States is a presidential system in which the executive is explicitly excluded from membership in the legislature. The leaders whose careers I have examined are roughly comparable across the five countries. They are first, the members of the lower house of the national legislature elected at some point during the 1950s,[13] and second, the members of the body called the cabinet for each country in some significant period of the twentieth century.[14] I shall use arrival in the lower house and the achievement of cabinet status as two benchmarks in political careers which may reveal distinctive characteristics of political parties.[15]

[13] The data on legislative careers come from a single legislature in each country. The specific legislature and the principal sources of information on it are as follows: The United States House of Representatives—elected in 1956; principal source— *Congressional Directory*, 1957, Washington, D.C., U.S. Government Printing Office. Great Britain—House of Commons elected in 1959; principal source—*The Times, House of Commons, 1959*, London, The *Times* Office. Canada—House of Commons elected in 1957; principal source—*Canadian Parliamentary Guide*, 1958. Australia— House of Representatives elected in 1954; principal source—*Commonwealth Parliamentary Handbook*, 1957, Canberra, Commonwealth Public Library. France—Chamber of Deputies elected in 1956; principal source—*Who's Who in France 1957–58*, Paris, Jacques Lafitte.

[14] The data on cabinet members cover a period of years. The particular years for each country and the principal sources are as follows: The United States Cabinet, 1900–1958; principal sources: *Who's Who in America* and the *National Cyclopedia of American Biography*. Great Britain, cabinets from 1922–1960; principal sources: David Butler and Jennie Freeman, *British Political Facts, 1900–1960*, London, Macmillan, 1963; also *Who's Who* and *Who Was Who*, London, Adam and Charles Black. Canada, cabinets from 1921–1957; principal sources: *Guide to Canadian Ministries Since Confederation, 1867–1957*, Ottawa, Public Archives of Canada, 1957; also *Who's Who* and the *Dictionary of Canadian Biography*. Australia, cabinets from 1946–1957; principal source: *Who's Who in Australia*, Melbourne, 1938 and following. France, cabinets from 1947–1958; principal sources: Phillip Williams, *Crisis and Compromise: Politics in the Fourth Republic*, Hamden, Conn., Archon Books, 1964; also *Who's Who in France*.

[15] There are several notable statistical studies dealing with the backgrounds of the legislatures and cabinets under study here. On Britain there is W. L. Guttsman, *The British Political Elite*, London, Macgibbon and Kee, 1963; Philip W. Buck, *Amateurs and Professionals in British Politics, 1918–1959*, Chicago, Ill., University of Chicago

It is true that neither the lower houses nor the cabinets under consideration enjoy exactly the same political position in one country as in another, although the differences may be revealed by their different career structures. In terms of relative importance in the political system, it is not always easy to define where a particular institution stands. Thus if we were to rank the lower houses according to the legislative power they must share, the American House of Representatives would be least important because of the powerful Senate. On the other hand, compared with the legislatures of the four other countries the American House enjoys a measure of independence possible only to a legislature free of the cabinet system. Similarly, the American cabinet is both more and less important than other cabinets due to the separation of powers. I shall not, however, attempt here to estimate the importance or influence of the different bodies.

Concerning the party systems of the five countries, the emphasis upon opportunities provides us with a simple method of classification: the number of parties within a system which are realistic routes to significant office.[16] The four English-speaking countries have two-party national systems, by which I mean that only two parties have good chances at gaining control of the national government. In the United States one pursues a political career as a Republican or Democrat, although minor parties have occasionally provided some outlet. The Labour and Conservative parties dominate British politics, although the Liberals manage to maintain a small group in Parliament. In Canadian national politics, Liberals and Conservatives have run the government in modern times despite persistent strength of other parties in the provinces. The Social Credit Party and the CCF have controlled provincial capitols without ever being able to translate such power into national strength.

Press, 1963; Peter G. Richards, *Honourable Members: A Study of the British Back-bencher*, London, Faber and Faber, 1958; F. M. G. Willson, "Routes of Entry of New Members of the British Cabinet, 1868–1958," *Political Studies*, VII (1959), 222–232; as well as Austin Ranney, *Pathways to Parliament*, Madison, Wis., University of Wisconsin Press, 1965. On Canada there is John Meisel, *The Canadian General Election of 1957*, Toronto, University of Toronto Press, 1962; Margaret A. Banks, "Privy Council, Cabinet and Ministry in Britain and Canada," *The Canadian Journal of Economics and Political Science*, 31 (1965), 193–205; Allan Kornberg and Norman Thomas, "Representative Democracy and Political Elites in Canada and the United States, *Parliamentary Affairs*, 19 (1965–66), 91–102; F. A. Kunz, *The Modern Senate of Canada, 1925–1963*, Toronto, University of Toronto Press, 1965. On Australia, S. Encel, "The Political Elite in Australia," *Political Studies*, IX (1961), 16–36; and *Cabinet Government in Australia*, Melbourne, Melbourne University Press, 1962.

[16] For another simple but highly suggestive scheme for classifying party systems see Robert A. Dahl, *Political Oppositions in Western Democracies*, New Haven, Conn., Yale University Press, 1966, pp. 335–338.

In Australia the Labour and Liberal parties control national politics, although the Country Party has shown persistent regional strength among farmers and can usually gain some seats in the government in alliance with the Liberals. In contrast, government in the French Fourth Republic was always a coalition of the leaders of several parties. The Socialists (SFIO) and Radical Socialists were usually well represented in the cabinet. The MRP, the Catholic center party formed after World War II, was very important in the earlier days of the Republic but lost considerable strength as it turned conservative toward the end of the Republic. The Independents reflected the development of effective organization among French conservatives and tended to dominate government of the right.[17]

Two aspects of legislative careers can be easily measured and compared from party to party. One is the age at which men are first elected to the legislature. Note that I do not mean here the age of the members of a particular legislature, which would be affected by the varying seniority and longevity of parties. Since our concern is with the process of advancement, the age of achievement better defines differences in the ways parties and party systems control careers. The age factor, as I have defined it, is critical to the very definition of career. It states the range of opportunities available to a man; it also relates his political career to any other career he pursues.

Among the five systems and thirteen parties I have examined there are sharp differences in the ages at which men are first elected to the lower house (Table 9.3). The youngest are the British Conservatives,75 per cent of whom were first elected before middle-age (45 years). The oldest are the Canadian Conservatives, 53 per cent of whom were first elected after they were 45 years old. The age at arrival in the legislature points up two important aspects of a political career: (1) how much of a prior career a man can have had before legislative service, and (2) how long a future he can have in politics. A party which brings men into the legislature at an older age coinciding with the peak of their performance, which is probably around the mid-forties, has had to take them from some other career. That it to say, it is unlikely that a man can break into a national legislative body in his late forties because his law practice has failed or because he is suddenly unemployed. He must be someone who has developed a claim for preferment. In contrast, the man who emerges in politics in his late

---

[17] The Communists, although they always had one of the largest blocs of seats in the Chamber, were never, after 1947, a part of government. There were, of course, other parties of varied sizes and importance in France which had a share in government, such as the center UDSR or the right-wing Gaullist group, the RPF, and later the Social Republicans.

Table 9.3. Ages at First Election to Lower House of the National Legislature
(*Percentages*)

Ages	United States (elected 1956)			Canada (elected 1957)			Australia (elected 1954)			Great Britain (elected 1959)			France (elected 1956)					
	Rep.	Dem.	Tot.	Cons.	Lib.	Tot.[a]	Lib.	Lab.	Tot.[b]	Cons.	Lab.	Tot.[c]	C.P.	SFIO	RAD.	MRP.	IND.	Tot.[d]
65+	1.6	1.4	1.5	0.0	1.0	0.8	2.2	2.0	2.7	0.0	0.0	0.0	2.0	1.0	1.8	1.3	1.0	1.8
60–64	3.6	1.4	2.4	7.4	8.6	7.4	0.0	2.0	0.9	0.0	1.6	0.8	1.4	1.0	3.5	2.7	3.0	2.0
55–59	6.6	5.9	6.3	7.4	6.8	7.0	10.8	2.0	7.1	3.1	7.9	4.9	3.9	2.0	7.0	2.7	8.0	4.5
50–54	14.4	11.5	13.1	20.1	13.4	14.4	6.5	14.0	10.7	8.9	12.2	10.1	4.6	14.2	10.5	5.3	16.8	10.0
45–49	20.6	13.2	16.4	16.5	12.5	15.2	15.2	24.0	21.4	12.8	23.2	17.4	13.9	21.3	8.8	14.9	15.8	16.3
40–44	20.6	22.3	21.8	13.8	20.2	18.3	28.3	20.0	22.4	19.6	18.5	18.7	17.1	24.6	24.6	17.6	28.7	21.7
35–39	18.6	26.5	22.5	19.2	14.4	17.1	21.7	20.0	20.5	25.8	17.7	22.3	22.2	24.6	22.8	36.5	9.9	22.0
30–34	12.4	15.5	14.1	11.9	20.2	16.7	10.9	14.0	11.6	19.6	10.6	16.3	30.3	8.2	14.0	14.9	15.8	18.0
25–29	1.6	2.3	1.9	3.7	2.9	2.7	4.4	0.0	2.7	8.8	7.9	8.5	4.6	3.1	7.0	4.1	1.0	3.7
20–24	0.0	0.0	0.0	0.0	0.0	0.4	0.0	0.0	0.0	1.4	0.4	1.0	0.0	0.0	0.0	0.0	0.0	0.0
	100.0	100.0	100.0	100.0	100.0	100.0	100.0	100.0	100.0	100.0	100.0	100.0	100.0	100.0	100.0	100.0	100.0	100.0
N	194	219	413	109	104	257	46	50	112	352	254	625	152	98	57	74	101	595

[a] Includes 44 members of other parties.
[b] Includes 16 members of other parties.
[c] Includes 19 members of other parties.
[d] Includes 113 members of other parties.

twenties or early thirties has had little time to develop a prior career. He may have inherited political advantages, but it is not his external accomplishments which are most relevant. At the same time his total political career is potentially fuller and of longer duration.

The second aspect of the legislative career which can be measured and compared is that of prior officeholding. Either a legislator has or has not had some public office before election to the legislature. Every democratic system provides a multitude of elective and appointive positions which men interested in public life may hold. It seems reasonable to infer that when a man holding a public office is elected to a legislature, some relationship exists between these two factors. Again there is a great range of difference among the 13 parties I have examined (Table 9.4). The least prior officeholding occurred among the British Conservatives, who had only 24.3 per cent. Since they were also the youngest legislators it would appear reasonable to conclude that their lack of office experience is related to their youth. But note that the legislators with the greatest amount of prior office experience were the American Democrats (73 per cent), who also were first elected to the legislature at a relatively early age (67 per cent before age 45). Thus age and prior officeholding appear to be independent measures of political parties and legislative careers.

The second measure, the amount of prior officeholding, is a useful indicator of a significant aspect of party organization: the extent to which a party is controlled by its public officeholders. The problem, of course, is one of long standing in the study of political parties: how free is the elected official of direction by an organization external to government? What I am suggesting is that a simple indication of control within a party is the extent to which career advancement rests upon obtaining public offices. This argument derives from the assumption that we are dealing with governing parties which seek public office and have public officials among their membership, parties which are imbedded in the structure of political opportunities. Therefore, when such parties frequently bypass obvious officeholders to advance men outside of politics, they must have organizational foci independent of the opportunity structure. If, for example, the American Republican Party were always to nominate for president the Willkies and the Eisenhowers over the Vandenbergs and Tafts we could assume the external groups played an important role in the party. Because the Republicans and not the Democrats nominate the Willkies and Eisenhowers, I infer, on balance, that the Democratic Party is more strongly controlled by its public officeholders. Although I believe that in the long run all democratic governing parties are controlled by their officeholders and that therefore political careers in democracies tend to derive from public officeholding, differences among parties within and across party systems can be discerned.

Table 9.4. Prior Office Experiences of Legislators

Offices	United States (elected 1956)			Canada (elected 1957)			Australia (elected 1954)			Great Britain (elected 1959)			France (elected 1956)					
	Rep.	Dem.	Tot.	Cons.	Lib.	Tot.	Lib.	Lab.	Tot.	Cons.	Lab.	Tot.	C.P.	SFIO	RAD.	MRP.	IND.	Tot.
Local elective	13.1	11.7	12.3	31.3	26.7	27.0	14.9	20.0	17.7	22.3	36.8	27.8	19.7	45.9	31.6	32.4	37.6	28.9
Provincial legislature[a]	33.8	38.5	36.5	9.8	8.6	10.6	17.0	25.0	21.0				13.2	34.7	35.1	14.9	41.6	23.8
Provincial executive[b]	2.0	1.3	1.6	1.8	2.9	2.3	6.4	6.7	6.4				1.3	4.1	0.0	0.0	1.9	0.7
Law enforcement	28.2	35.3	31.2	8.9	5.7	6.1	0.0	5.0	3.0									
Administrative																		
National	5.6	7.4	6.5	0.9	4.8	2.3	4.3	11.7	7.3	5.1	2.7	4.6	1.3	13.3	26.3	9.5	7.9	9.6
Provincial	6.6	4.8	5.6	3.6	3.8	3.4	8.5	6.7	6.4									
Local	4.0	3.0	3.5	8.0	2.9	4.9	2.1	6.7	4.8									
No office experience	31.3	24.6	27.8	49.2	51.3	52.2	59.6	40.0	50.7	70.2	58.5	65.5	68.4	38.8	31.6	47.3	34.7	50.9
N	198	231	429	112	105	263	47	60	124	352	258	630	152	98	57	74	101	595

a For France this is the Conseil général

b For United States, statewide elective executive positions. For Canada and Australia, provincial or state cabinet membership. For France, president of the Conseil général

The precise nature of prior officeholding, as distinct from the mere fact of having held office, is less readily comparable among political systems. Nevertheless, all of the party systems under study have some local elective offices which can be compared: the city councillors and aldermen in the United States, the British urban councillors, and the French municipal councillors. In addition, the three federal systems have well-marked intermediary legislatures and executives at the state or provincial level which are comparable. In France the department has a general council which is elective, and although its powers are markedly fewer than those of an American state legislature, it does represent an intermediate stage in the structure of government and in the structure of political careers. Thus for our purposes we can describe the council as equivalent to the American or Canadian state or provincial legislature. Because the levels of British government are less neatly arranged, there I have considered all offices below the national level as local elective offices (Tables 9.4, 9.5).

By combining and comparing the two measures of age and prior officeholding we obtain a fourfold grouping of parties which can serve as a model of the relation between types of party and types of political careers (Figure 9.1). The model points up two characteristics of parties: (1) the extent to which a party is *hierarchic,* by which I mean that advancement is regular and gives the appearance of being controlled by some organized group, in or out of public office, the extent to which it is *open,* that is, advancement is irregular and does not appear to be controlled by organized groups and (2) the extent to which public officeholding is the base of party organization. We also obtain four model types of parties: (1) the open party, organized primarily around public elective offices; (2) the hierarchical party, predominantly office-based; (3) the hierarchical

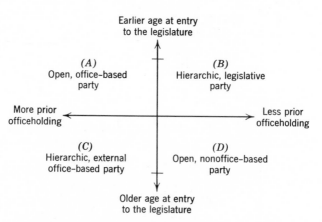

Fig. 9.1. The relation between careers and party structure
(based on attainment of national legislative office).

party whose organization is strongly rooted in the legislature; and (4) the open party whose organization is not primarily based in public offices. I will discuss each type and, using the two measures of age and office-holding, relate each of the 13 parties to one of the four models (Figure 9.2).

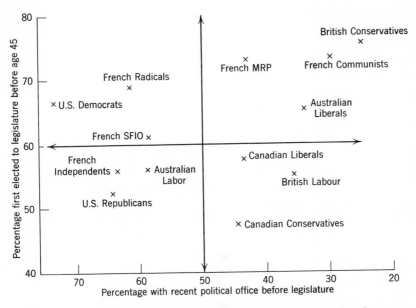

Fig. 9.2. Career structures of political parties in five democratic political systems (lower houses of national legislatures).

In the upper right-hand quadrant *B* we find the hierarchic legislative party. In this party legislators arrive early, with little experience at other levels of government. Because they lack experience both in government and elsewhere, these men are most likely to advance by achievement within the legislature. Conditions are thus set up for a party organization stratified within the legislature and preoccupied with its legislators' fates. The ability of such parties to bring young men without independent office experience into the national legislature is a measure of the closed quality of the party.[18] Note here that we are decribing stable organi-

---

[18] An assumption underlying my analysis is that national legislative office is, for each of the five nations, a prestigious position for which many men strive. Our expectations about both age and prior office experience vary considerably according to the office. Therefore, the inferences I am making here about the kinds of parties falling in each of the quadrants would not necessarily be the same if the leaders examined were in provincial legislatures or city councils.

Table 9.5. Last Office Held Before Election to Lower House of the National Legislature
(*Percentages*)

Office	United States (elected 1956)			Canada (elected 1957)			Australia (elected 1954)			Great Britain (elected 1959)			France (elected 1956)					
	Rep.	Dem.	Tot.	Cons.	Lib.	Tot.	Lib.	Lab.	Tot.	Cons.	Lab.	Tot.	C.P.	SFIO	RAD.	MRP.	IND.	Tot.
Provincial legislature	26.2	25.2	25.6	7.1	4.8	6.8	8.4	13.4	11.2				15.1	27.6	31.6	16.1	36.7	21.7
Provincial executive	1.1	0.9	1.0	0.9	1.9	1.5	6.4	6.7	6.3				0.0	3.1	0.0	0.0	1.9	1.0
Local elective	7.6	6.5	7.0	23.3	23.8	22.2	8.5	13.3	12.0	21.3	33.7	25.8	13.2	18.4	10.5	18.9	18.8	14.1
Law enforcement	18.2	28.6	23.8	2.7	3.8	2.8	0.0	5.0	3.1	0.7	0.0	0.6						
Administrative	11.1	11.6	11.4	10.7	9.5	9.2	10.7	20.0	13.4	2.3	1.6	2.2	0.0	8.2	14.0	6.8	3.0	5.4
Upper house national legislature		0.4	0.2										1.3	1.0	5.3	1.4	3.0	2.7
No recent office	35.8	26.8	31.0	55.3	56.2	57.5	66.0	41.6	54.0	75.7	64.7	71.4	70.4	41.7	38.6	56.8	36.6	55.1
Total	100.0	100.0	100.0	100.0	100.0	100.0	100.0	100.0	100.0	100.0	100.0	100.0	100.0	100.0	100.0	100.0	100.0	100.0
N	198	231	429	112	106	263	47	60	124	352	258	630	152	98	57	74	101	595

zations with some history. A new party, drawing upon essentially new sources for its leadership, could, of course, exhibit similar characteristics.

When we classify the 13 parties according to the measures of age and office experience, four fall in the hierarchic legislative cluster: the British Conservatives, the French Communists, the Australian Liberals, and the French MRP. Of these, the MRP alone represents the new party which brings in younger men without previous office experience. Both the British Conservatives and French Communists are much older parties, yet their legislators are at the extremes on both youth and little office experience. I need not belabor the hierarchic nature of both parties. Their restrictive character is reflected not only in the predominance of youth among their new legislators but also in the very small proportion (only slightly above 10 per cent) of older starters, those 50 or above. With few exceptions, then, these parties hold little opportunity for men who have not risen within their parliamentary ranks.

Of course the Communists and Conservatives play very different roles within their respective party systems. The Communist Party, for most of the Third and Fourth Republics, was only a part-time player in the parliamentary game, a role conducive to the development of hierarchic legislative organization. What is remarkable is the ability of the British Conservative Party to develop such an organization within the context of competitive politics. The Australian Liberals, falling within the quadrant, probably can be said to have tendencies in this direction.[19]

Moving to the upper-left quadrant *A* we find the combination of youth and experience among a party's legislators. The most reasonable explanation of this combination is a party organization built around public offices and open for advancement to public officeholders. Although it may seem paradoxical to conclude that youth in one instance is related to a closed hierarchical organization and in another to a more open party, the explanation lies in the concept of the office-based party. In such a party the officeholder has influence and is able to use his office to advance. When he can do so relatively early, before middle-age, we can conclude that the party is open, that is, incapable of confining men in offices if they wish to advance, regardless of their age.

The parties falling in this quadrant are the American Democrats, the French Radicals, and marginally the French Socialists. The Radicals have already been described as the most American of French parties. Within their respective systems both parties have been the principal vehicles used by political careerists. Toward the end of the Third Republic the Socialists

---

[19] Those offices which were held by members of these parties are shown in Table 6.5. None of these parties is completely cut off from lower office experience, with approximately one-quarter of their members having had a local office.

began to replace the Radicals as the pivotal party in the French party system, a process which they completed in the Fourth Republic.

In all three parties, the offices held most frequently prior to election to the legislature were at the intermediate level of government. One in four Democratic congressmen came from a state legislature. (An additional 29 per cent came from some kind of law enforcement position, a fact peculiar, as far as I can determine, to American politics.) Some 30 per cent of both the Radicals and Socialists came from a departmental council. What is most interesting is the unimportance in all three parties of local elective office as the final steppingstone to the legislature, although both the Radicals and Socialists had extensive local office experience. These findings refine our picture of the open, office-based party: young men advancing to national prominence from office to office, through an organization sensitive to the importance of gradations of officeholding to the process of promotion.

In the lower left-hand quadrant *C,* the predominance of older, experienced legislators within a party gives us a picture of a hierarchic organization which is nevertheless office-based. Although the party's intermediate officeholders can become legislators, they must wait their turn. In this quadrant we find the American Republicans, the French Independents, and marginally the Australian Labourites. Of all 13 parties the Independents advanced the fewest young men to the legislature; only 27 per cent were under 40. The Republicans were next; only 32 per cent of their new legislators were under 40. At the same time, the experience of the men promoted by the Independents and the Republicans was much like that of the legislators in the preceding category: experience at the intermediate level of government. In the Australian Labour Party some 20 per cent of the new legislators came from state parliaments, a higher figure than for any other party in Australia or Canada. (It was also the only party for which administrative office was a significant path, 20 per cent, to promotion.)

Of course, there is nothing in my data which indicates why or how hierarchical organization is maintained. British Conservatives may choose young men for parliament and American Republicans may choose older officeholders either because an oligarchy makes these decisions or merely because of the sense of propriety held by their membership. My evidence indicates simply that these parties do behave and promote men differently from other parties in their own systems and elsewhere.

In the lower right-hand quadrant *D* the predominance of older legislators without much office experience gives us the picture of a party organization which is open but not conspicuously office-based. Within such a party, men can presumably advance at any age from anywhere.

External accomplishments and therefore external groups can play an important role.

The three parties in this category are the British Labour Party and the two national Canadian parties. For the British Labour Party, the trade union is naturally the important external source of personnel. In all three parties the public officials most likely to advance to the legislature are local officials. Whereas all three parties had a low percentage of new legislators with office experience, all three ranked first in promoting local officials. Of course, given the structure of British government, there was no question of finding intermediate office experience among Labourites. What is remarkable, however, is the importance of local officeholding in the two Canadian parties and the relatively small part played by provincial offices in careers leading to the national legislature. In this respect, the two Canadian parties appear to be far less affected by the federal office structure than either American party or the Australian Labour Party. Such findings refine our picture of the open party which is not office-oriented. Not only could the Canadians and Labourites come to national prominence at an older age and from nonoffice posts outside the office structure, but even when they had had prior office experience they had not needed to use a stepladder of offices to the legislature.[20]

Party and the Attainment of Cabinet Status

The second benchmark in the development of political careers which can enlighten us about party organization is the attainment of cabinet status. The relation between legislative and cabinet office is, of course, more clearly defined in the cabinet systems than in the American presidential system. The intermediary legislative positions which lead to the cabinet have been worked out most finely in the British Parliament, with its host of whips, parliamentary secretaries, undersecretaries, junior ministers, and ministers outside the cabinet. The picture of the House of Commons, then, as containing an assembly of about 20 cabinet members

[20] The inability of the two major national Canadian parties to suppress minor parties, in contrast to the situation in the United States, has been a matter of some comment. See, for example, John Meisel, "The Stalled Omnibus: Canadian Parties in the 1960's," *Social Research*, **30** (1963), 367–390. The reason, I suspect, lies in the different career structures of the two countries as revealed in these figures. In Canada federalism combined with a cabinet system at the provincial level provides meaningful long-run career outlets for indigenous provincial parties. Significant elective careers for any length of time are not possible at the state level in the United States. Thus the national two-party system crushes state third parties in the United States because it provides no outlet for their leaders, whereas it is unable to do so in Canada.

and a mob of backbenchers is hardly accurate. According to one estimate, 25 per cent of members of parliament from 1918 to 1955 had held some leadership post.[21] Indeed, if one views parliament from the perspective of ambition it is evident that hopes and expectations must be widely spread there and that discipline may well result from the orderly outlets provided for ambitions. Such arrangements have not been worked out as completely in the other legislatures under consideration. In Canada, for example, only in 1943 did the cabinet make provision for parliamentary assistants. Nevertheless, career data can give us more detail about the relation between legislative and cabinet office and, when broken down by parties, can hopefully be related to the inferences reached in the analysis of legislative officeholding.

The most obvious question which the data can answer is, how much legislative experience do cabinet members have? The classic picture of the parliamentary system is a cabinet emerging from among the party's legislators. If anything distinguishes the cabinet from the presidential system it is the distinctive careers of cabinet officials and chief executives. The varied paths to the presidency and its cabinet contrasts with the restricted legislative route to cabinet ministries.

If we take the number of years spent in the lower house by cabinet members, it is evident that the classic view applies primarily to the British system (Table 9.6). More than half of the cabinet members in both British parties spent ten or more years in the Commons. One in four Conservative cabinet members came from the Lords, but half of these had been in the Commons. Less than ten per cent of the ministers of both parties had less than five years in the Commons. The picture is of full parliamentary apprenticeship before major advancement.

The classic picture, however, fits none of the other parties or party systems studied. The French Independent Party approaches the model most closely; most of its cabinet members had between five and nine years experience in the Chamber of Deputies. For most of the other parties, one-third or more of the cabinet members had less than five years of legislative experience. Of the French Socialists, 32 per cent had less than one year in the chamber; the same proportion held for the French MRP. True, the MRP was a new party which came to power rapidly in postwar France. But the Canadian Liberals, a party which governed Canada for 22 unbroken years, promoted over 35 per cent of their cabinet members after less than one year in the House of Commons.

When a significant proportion of a party's cabinet members has spent less than five years and some even less than one year in the legislature,

---

[21] Buck, *Amateurs and Professionals*, p. 47.

Table 9.6. Years in Lower House Before Attaining Cabinet Post
(*Percentages*)

No. of years	Canada (1921–1957)			Australia (1946–1957)			Great Britain (1922–1960)			France (1947–1958)				
	Cons.	Lib.	Tot.	Lib.	Lab.	Tot.	Cons.	Lab.	Tot.	SFIO	RAD.	MRP.	IND.	Tot.
20+	5.2	0.0	2.0	0.0	0.0	0.0	11.9	11.5	11.7	4.6	0.0	5.0	0.0	1.7
15–19	5.2	5.9	5.5	0.0	0.0	0.0	15.6	16.4	15.9	9.1	4.0	0.0	8.3	4.9
10–14	15.5	15.4	15.4	4.2	10.5	8.0	23.9	27.9	25.3	13.6	20.0	5.0	4.2	9.9
5–9	36.2	18.8	25.9	29.2	15.7	20.0	12.8	22.9	16.5	9.1	32.0	15.0	62.5	32.3
1–4	19.0	18.8	18.9	33.3	21.0	30.0	4.6	6.6	5.3	31.8	20.0	45.0	8.3	28.9
0–1	17.2	36.4	28.7	4.2	10.5	6.0	5.5	1.6	4.1	31.8	8.0	30.0	4.2	15.7
Upper house	1.7	4.7	3.5	29.1	42.3	36.0	25.7	13.1	21.2	0.0	16.0	0.0	12.5	6.6
Total	100.0	100.0	100.0	100.0	100.0	100.0	100.0	100.0	100.0	100.0	100.0	100.0	100.0	100.0
N	58	85	143	24	19	50	109	61	170	22	25	20	24	121

it is hard to accept the legislature as the base for their advancement. The legislature may be the formal last step, but the routes to the top begin to look much like those in the presidential system: government administration, state or provincial offices, posts in industry or with other pressure groups.

Although these figures show that there are more paths to the cabinet than might have been supposed within parliamentary systems, we cannot deny the legislative tie. For none of the parties in parliamentary systems was the parliamentary route irrelevant. For none, except the MRP, did less than one-third of their cabinet members arrive with fewer than ten years of legislative experience. This contrasts with the American cabinet, less than 20 per cent of whose members have any congressional experience and less than 10 per cent of whom come directly from congress. Undoubtedly a more sophisticated analysis would reveal variations among the types of cabinet posts and the routes leading to them. One might expect, for example, that the true positions of party leadership such as the office of prime minister would be more likely to go to experienced parliamentarians. Cabinet members brought in with token legislative backgrounds might be expected to head technical ministries or ministries related to strong interest groups, such as the ministry of agriculture. The examination of the formal group, the "cabinet," may encompass two different types of party leadership.

In relating the analysis of careers leading to the cabinet to our analysis of legislative careers, it becomes clear that the party system is the important variable at the cabinet level. In Britain, Canada, and Australia the experience and the ages of new cabinet members tend to be similar for the parties within each system, at least more so than was the case for new legislators. The greatest differences among parties of the same system are those between the American Republicans and Democrats and among the principal French parties. In the United States, institutional factors which would bring the parties together at the cabinet level are lacking. In France, despite the cabinet system, the peculiar multiparty system of the Fourth Republic undoubtedly permitted greater individuality among parties in their promotional procedures.

When we look at the ages at which men first attain cabinet status (Table 9.7), these are highest in the United States, where the route to the cabinet is independent of the legislature.[22] With respect to the ages of

[22] Since careers leading to the American Cabinet are at least formally very different from those leading to cabinets in parliamentary systems, the inclusion of these figures in a single table may appear to be the comparison of unlike things. But I am not comparing cabinets as such; rather I am measuring and comparing opportunities for political advancement. The differences between the ages at which men typically attain

Table 9.7. Age at First Membership in the Cabinet
(*Percentage*)

Ages	United States (1900–1958)			Canada (1921–1957)			Australia (1946–1957)			Great Britain (1922–1960)			France (1947–1958)				
	Rep.	Dem.	Tot.	Cons.	Lib.	Tot.	Lib.	Lab.	Tot.	Cons.	Lab.	Tot.	SFIO	RAD.	MRP.	IND.	Tot.
65+	6.2	14.0	9.7	7.8	3.4	5.3	0.0	0.0	0.0	8.8	13.3	10.4	0.0	0.0	0.0	8.3	2.4
60–64	26.3	9.3	18.7	17.2	9.2	12.5	0.0	11.8	4.2	5.9	18.3	10.4	18.2	0.0	5.0	4.2	5.0
55–59	13.7	14.0	13.9	12.5	10.0	11.1	12.5	17.6	18.7	20.4	25.0	22.2	0.0	20.0	0.0	16.7	11.5
50–54	18.8	28.2	22.9	20.3	23.9	22.4	25.0	17.6	18.7	27.2	18.3	23.9	13.6	40.0	10.0	29.1	26.2
45–49	21.2	26.6	23.7	15.6	27.3	22.4	33.3	29.5	29.2	16.5	8.3	13.5	22.7	12.0	20.0	33.3	24.0
40–44	12.5	6.3	9.7	21.9	20.5	21.0	25.0	5.9	18.7	11.6	15.0	12.9	31.9	16.0	35.0	4.2	18.1
35–39	1.3	1.6	1.4	4.7	5.7	5.3	0.0	17.6	8.4	7.7	0.0	4.9	13.6	12.0	30.0	4.2	12.2
30–34	0.0	0.0	0.0	0.0	0.0	0.0	4.2	0.0	2.1	1.9	1.8	1.8	0.0	0.0	0.0	0.0	0.6
Total	100.0	100.0	100.0	100.0	100.0	100.0	100.0	100.0	100.0	100.0	100.0	100.0	100.0	100.0	100.0	100.0	100.0
N	80	64	144	64	88	152	24	17	48	103	60	163	22	25	20	24	121

new cabinet members, the British system is closest to that of the United States; Canada falls in the middle, and France and Australia have the youngest cabinets. In Australia only 4.2 per cent of the new cabinet members were 60 years or older when first appointed. This contrasts with over 28 per cent of the new American personnel.

By comparing the ages of new cabinet members with those of new legislators we gain a more refined picture of the relationship between cabinet and legislative office. In Figure 9.3 we see two extremes, the British Conservative Party, for which there was a sharp difference between the two age distributions, and the Canadian Conservative Party, for which there was little distinction between the two. A simple measure which we can apply to all of the party systems and the parties within them is the total difference between the two age distribution arrays, age at entrance to the legislature and age at cabinet status $(a-a' + b-b' + c-c' + \ldots)$. If the two distributions are the same the result will be zero; if the two never overlap the total difference would be 200.

As we can see in Table 9.8, the parties and party systems vary considerably in terms of the index of differentiation between legislative and cabinet careers. The classic character of the British cabinet system is revealed by its high index, 102.1. Thus although the Labour Party had older legislators than the Conservatives, both parties had nearly the same index of differentiation. The lowest indices of differentiation were those of Australia (62.8) and Canada (63.3).

The greatest differences between parties within systems were in the United States and France. Of course the construct is quite artificial for the United States, since there is little relationship between getting into the House of Representatives and becoming a member of the president's cabinet. The French Radicals and Independents here appear to behave much like the two British parties. The MRP and the SFIO reveal the least differentiation, for the MRP possibly because of its brief history.

If we relate our earlier findings on legislative careers to the indices of differentiation, we can see the extent to which our earlier inferences about party organization are supported. Using the classifications of Figure 6.1, let us project the index of differentiation for each type of party. For the parties in the upper quadrants (A, B) there is a greater possibility of higher indices. The legislators in these parties start earlier; therefore their cabinet leaders can arrive later. The opposite is true for the parties in the

---

any two offices in the same system are a measure of each office's relation to the aging process. If, for example, there were no differences in the ages at which men attained all offices, if the ages of attainment of such offices as state legislator, congressman, governor, senator, and president in the United States were simply randomly distributed, then there would be little structure to political careers.

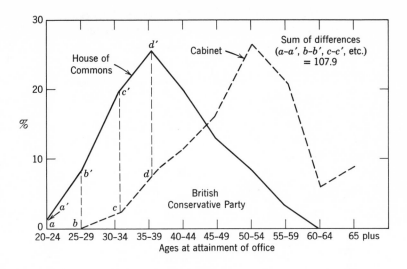

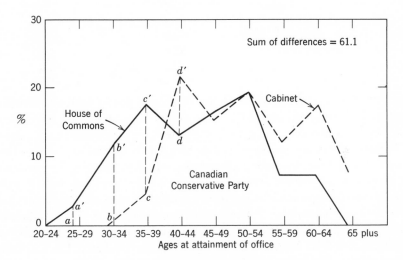

Fig. 9.3. The index of differentiation between legislative
and cabinet attainment.

bottom quadrants (C, D), because their legislators get a late start. But in addition to the arithmetic possibilities, there is the hierarchic factor, which implies a greater degree of age differentiation for the parties in B and C. The parties in category B therefore should have the highest index of differentiation, the product of youth and hierarchy. Those parties in category D should show the least differentiation: the late start of their

Table 9.8.   Index of Age Differentiation between
Attainment of Legislative and Cabinet Status

	Index	
Great Britain		102.1
Conservative	107.9	
Labour	109.2	
Australia		62.8
Liberal	76.8	
Labour	68.8	
United States		98.3
Republican	79.4	
Democrat	117.6	
Canada		63.3
Conservative	61.1	
Liberal	63.6	
France		68.9
Independent	94.2	
Radical	91.4	
MRP	59.0	
SFIO	51.8	

legislators lessens the likelihood that the open party without an office base will distinguish markedly between its legislators and its cabinet members. For the remaining two categories our expectations are mixed.

To what extent are our expectations fulfilled? Both the British Conservative Party and the Australian Liberals have high indices, as we predicted for hierarchic legislative parties. The French MRP does not, but we have already noted its peculiar characteristics. Both the Canadian Liberals and Conservatives in category *D* have, as we expected, low indices of differentiation. The British Labour Party is, however, out of place; its index of differentiation is as high as that of the Conservative Party. One explanation, supported by most of the literature on British parties, is that the Labour Party has been developing more like the Conservative Party.[23] It is therefore probable that our measures reveal the party at two stages of that development. Presumably the same measurements taken ten years from today would find younger Labourites entering parliament, the result of hierarchic organization.

In the upper left quadrant, both the French Radicals and the American

[23] Robert McKenzie, *British Political Parties*, 2nd ed., London, Mercury Books, 1963.

Democrats had high indices of differentiation, as we projected. The office-holding character of their organizations, inferred from the careers of their legislators, is reinforced by the distinction in the ages of lower and higher officials, a status distinction based on the office structure. The French Socialists, on the other hand, had a lower index of differentiation, which we could not have predicted. Perhaps, as in the case of the MRP, its accession to power in the Fourth Republic was too rapid to reveal signs of differentiation. But note, in any event, that its place in quadrant A is marginal, and we should expect its behavior to be the least clear.

The parties in the lower left quadrant allow the widest range of speculation. The late start of their legislators suggests a low index of differentiation; but they are also hierarchic, promoting officeholders in sequence, thereby making disinctions possible. Both the American Republicans and Australian Labourites had low indices of differentiation for their respective systems, probably because of the age factor. The French Independents, on the other hand, showed as much differentiation as the Radicals, despite the later start of their legislators. In this sense the Independents constitute the model hierarchical organization which is office-based, combining offices outside and inside the legislature.

Conclusion

In terms of their leaders' careers, then, the thirteen parties which we have examined show distinctly different structures. The differences have no obvious relationship to the parties' ideological positions; and political institutions, while providing the framework for political careers, can apparently support widely variant approaches to capturing the same offices. At the very least therefore the evidence supports my initial assertion that the office-seeking view, by leading us to examine parties as instruments for political careers, can help us to distinguish among parties.

Whether these distinctions have any significance for the ways in which parties behave within their respective systems is certainly a matter for further theoretical and empirical investigation. I hope I have at least demonstrated that the various career perspectives within a party, for example, the hierarchical and the office base, provide a measure of the tensions within an organization which are bound to affect its response to the tensions generated by competition with other parties. It is true that the party teams formulated by economic theorists have now become less orderly. Yet it seems reasonable to conclude that the ways in which they respond to the tensions of party competition will to a large extent be determined by the very different ways in which these teams come together.

10. Political Parties and the Recruitment of Political Leadership

LESTER G. SELIGMAN

The growing literature on political leadership continues to refine our conceptions of this elusive subject.[1] One conclusion deducible from the literature is that the understanding of leadership is enhanced when it is viewed in its group and organizational contexts. This is applicable to political parties which have a special organizational role in the emergence, maintenance, and change of political leadership.

The critical contribution of political parties to leadership is their strategic role in the structure of political opportunity. The latter refers to the various chances offered members of social strata to enter and compete for specific political roles. The political opportunity structure also includes the sources and resources of leadership and criteria of leadership selection as well as the rates of circulation. These are powerful determinants of leadership role behavior. The selections made by the channels of political mobility are no less important to the functioning of the system than the roles that those selected are expected to perform. Indeed, the gap between leadership recruitment processes and the needed and expected capacities of leadership is a major problem in many political systems today.

Work on this chapter was derived from my research on leadership recruitment in the United States and in other countries. I was impressed early with leadership as an organizational product, as well as its influence on organization. While working on this chapter, I discovered that it shared a good deal of affinity with the contributions of Sam Eldersveld (*Political Parties: A Behavioral Analysis*, Chicago, Ill., Rand McNally, 1964) and Frank Sorauf (*Political Parties in the American System*, Boston, Mass., Little, Brown, 1964). I am happy to acknowledge that I found their perceptive contributions of great value. I wish to express my appreciation to Michael King and Kim Chong Lim, graduate assistants, for their helpful criticism and suggestions.

[1] Kenneth F. Janda, "Towards the Explication of the Concept of Leadership in Terms of the Concept of Power," *Human Relations*, 13, No. 4, 345–363.

Much current theory about political parties attaches primary importance to the role of parties in the recruitment of political leadership.[2] For some, the functions of nominating and electing candidates for political elective office are attributed exclusively to political parties. Were this always their primary or only contribution, the comparative analysis of political parties would be simpler. However, as our comparative perspective broadens we recognize that political parties are complex organizations with *many functions* in diverse political systems and leadership recruitment is but one.

The thesis of this chapter is that the comparative role of parties in the recruitment of political leadership, may be approached as the product of the interaction between the internal organization dynamics and diverse party environments as mediated by the structure of political opportunity and political risk. Recruitment is a facet of the exchange between the party organization with the polity and the society.

In the interaction between the large-scale organization and environmental influences can be found the explanation for various types of political parties today. We shall proceed to show what effect environmental and organizational variables have for the strategies by which parties organize the recruitment of candidates, using the diagram below to indicate the basic units of our analysis. The lines of interaction in reality are *not* sequential, however. Patterns of interaction interrelate these variables, as I will attempt to indicate.

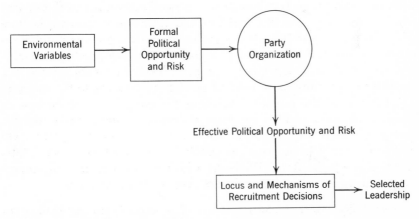

[2] See E. E. Schattschneider, *Party Government,* New York, Holt, Rinehart and Winston, 1942; R. McKenzie, *British Political Parties,* New York, Praeger, 1963, 2nd ed.; Anthony Downs, *An Economic Theory of Democracy,* New York, Harper and Row, 1957. Joseph Schlesinger "Political Party Organization" in *Handbook of Political Organizations,* ed. by James March, Chicago, Ill., Rand McNally, 1965.

Comparative analysis of political parties in the industrialized nations is still not very advanced. It may well be that further progress will result from the comparative analysis of industrialized and preindustrialized systems because such comparison focuses on change and transition.[3] This task is especially difficult today because of limited knowledge of new and varied species of political parties within the newer nations. Current conceptual models of political parties which derive primarily from observations of political structure in modern, industrialized Western nations do not fit many of these parties. For example, it is customary to begin with the number of parties—one, or two, or multiparties—and infer from this many characteristics of the political system. This method requires, for tenability, that the systems compared share minimally a common level of economic and political development and cultural integration. The contexts may then be taken as "givens." The same approach is of doubtful value in comparing industrial and pre-industrial systems, or even the range of pre-industrial systems.

Another example may be given of the limited value of Western generalizations about political parties applied to newer parties. A prevailing generalization about parties in industrialized systems is that the cohesion of party organization and the coherence of party ideology go together. When applying this hypothesis to developing countries, it is found that even within the context of Africa, political parties that might cluster together on the basis of ideological coherence exhibit considerable variation in degree of organizational cohesion.[4]

The corrective to such culture-bound generalizations lies in theory that includes more *environmental* variables and their effects than we have so far considered. A starting point might be how party goals and processes are constrained *by* the social and political structure, followed by an analysis of the "feedback" consequences of party behavior for the system. We may find that the number of political parties is secondary to the structure and problems of the polities (including the competence of citizens as Barnes emphasizes) and the processes of organizational decision making. Thus in a system with fragile national integration, political parties will behave differently from parties in political systems where national integration is at a higher level. We begin with the fact that the most important political parties in the world are large-scale organizations.

[3] Joseph La Palombara and Myran Weiner, ed., *Political Parties and Political Development*, Princeton, N.J., Princeton University Press, 1966.

[4] James Coleman and Carl Rosberg, eds., *Political Parties and National Integration in Tropical Africa*, Berkeley, Cal., University of California Press, 1964, p. 4.

Political Parties: A Comparative Model

Although many implications of large-scale party organization have been treated, the *organizational processes* within parties deserve more attention. How a party, as an organization, makes decisions is not easily analyzed because parties are complex organizations which do not conform to prevailing models of organizations. In referring to American political parties, Eldersveld has stated:

". . . it must be recognized that parties do not possess many of the conventional attributes of the bureaucratic system. In particular, the bureaucratic prerequisites of impermeability, depersonalized human regulations and rule enforcement, precise allocation of obligations, duties and roles, discipline and sanctions, even low circulation of personnel, are found wanting in most party structures. We sense that the Republican and Democratic parties are structually different from General Motors, the Catholic Church, the AFL-CIO, or the Farm Bureau. How they differ is the task of empirical theory and research." [5]

Although conventional bureaucratic models do not fit the varieties of political parties, insight drawn from many organizational examples may be used in an exploratory way.[6] Our starting point is that political parties have many functions, a representative group of which includes the following: (1) leadership recruitment—the function of recruiting candidates and political office holders; (2) mass membership recruitment—whether the party membership is open or restricted; (3) party as an object of political identifications, which include ideological, social, and psychological identifications; and (4) party as an agency of government and a channel of access to decision making.

The several functions of party are at once competitive and complementary. Thus nominating and electing legislative candidates and/or choosing members of the government's executive may fulfill some political party functions but are costly to other functions. For example, the nomination of certain leaders with potential for great electoral support may result in the loss of some ideological principle.

Cleavages and conflicts are endemic to large-scale party organizations

[5] Samuel Eldersveld, *Political Parties: A Behavioral Analysis,* Chicago, Ill., Rand McNally, 1964.

[6] Thus an organizational model of a volunteer organization, may be highly relevant to some party organizations. For example, David L. Sills, *The Volunteers,* New York, Free Press, 1957.

because organizational components or subsystems with specialized tasks or parochial interests respond differentially and autonomously to their environments.[7] These organizational components are of various kinds: (1) hierarchical and rank differentiations of positions; (2) stratifications of participation, leadership, activists, and rank and file; (3) specialized functional units, for example, organization, fund raising, public relations; (4) ethnic, religious, linguistic groups, generational or age-graded associations, attached interest groups;[8] and (5) factions and cliques that form over ideological differences or charismatic attachments.[9] These differentiated units, designed as means toward party goals, have their own biases, autonomous purposes, and organizational requirements, often at variance with general party goals. This is the well-known organizational phenomenon of goal displacement. Each one of these party suborganizations protects and maintains itself, behavior often most evident in the sponsorship and promotion of leadership aspirants. Such autonomous tendencies create egregious problems for party cohesion and consensus.

For these reasons the community of interest within large-scale parties may not be taken for granted; it is not a "given," but a product of tradition and such processes as hierarchy, bargaining, coercion, co-optation, and competition with other parties, associations, and institutions. In the face of these centrifugal influences, to treat political parties as political unities by definition (as we often do) is a dubious assumption. The curve of organizational solidarity is an undulating one that varies with time and context. On close examination, the unity of political parties is only a balance between environmental and intra-organizational influences. The term "aggregation"[10] is less descriptive of the process than it is of the magnitude of the task of coalescing the numerous competing and complementary influences which bear upon the mass political party.

The Intervening Variables—Political Opportunity and Political Risk

Between the party organization and the political system stand two factors that have direct bearing on the recruitment of leadership: the struc-

[7] Richard L. Simpson and William H. Gulley, "Goals, Environmental Pressures, and Organizational Characteristics," *American Sociological Review* XXXVI (1962), 334–51; Herbert Kaufman, "Organization Theory and Political Theory" *APSR*, LVIII, No. 1 (March, 1964), 5–14.

[8] M. Duverger, *Political Parties*, New York, John Wiley & Sons, 1954, p. 152.

[9] Raphael Zaritzky, "Party Factions and Comparative Politics: Some Preliminary Observations," *Midwest Journal of Political Science*, I (Feb., 1960), 27–61; see also Henry Ehrmann, "Direct Democracy in France," *APSR*, CVIII, No. 4 (Dec., 1963), 901.

[10] Gabriel Almond and James Coleman, *The Politics of Developing Areas*, Princeton, N.J., Princeton University Press, 1960, pp. 38–44.

ture of political opportunity and political risk. Political opportunity has two facets: formal opportunity and effective opportunity. Formal opportunity refers to the explicit legal barriers to entry of political aspirants for political leadership roles. Effective opportunity refers to whether conditions, motivation, and resources are present and/or available to those aspiring to leadership roles. Political risk refers to the extent of the losses in status, income, and influence when a person loses political office. Formal risk is the legally defined loss and effective risk is the real deprivation. The balance between opportunity for attaining office and the rewards and risk of office determines the incentives for political recruitment.

The formal opportunity and risk structure filter those in the social structure that are not denied political entry and ascent to leadership roles. *Effective opportunity is determined largely by the party system, the sponsors and gatekeepers to leadership recruitment.* Effective political opportunity is an output of the party to the system. The party system allocates resources important to those who seek political roles. Moreover, directly and indirectly the party system socializes political leadership motivation.

Political Party Organization, Goals, and Environment

By the term "environments of political parties" we do not "refer to a collection of systems and organizations external to the one we are studying. Instead we view the environment as it affects the organization which we are studying. By environment, we focus on those inputs which bear on goal setting and goal attainment within the organization. These elements form, for the organization, its task environment." [11]

Political parties which pursue numerous goals are subjected to many environmental pressures and must satisfy demands made by the general community as well as their own members. They confront more complex pressures than associations with few goals and little or no need to satisfy community expectations. "Organizations which must adapt to a wide range of pressures will differ in internal characteristics from those which face a narrower range of pressures." [12]

In response to this environmental pressure, this kind of party organization will show a strong concern for grass roots involvement. Such organi-

[11] R. Dill, "The Impact of Environment on Organizational Development," in *Concepts and Issues in Administrative Behavior,* Sidney Mailick, and Edward H. Van Ness, Englewood Cliffs, N.J., Prentice Hall, 1962, p. 96; David Easton, *A Framework for Political Analysis,* Prentice Hall, 1965, Ch. V.

[12] James D. Thompson and W. J. McEwen, "Organizational Goals and Environment," in *Complex Organizations,* Amitai Etzioni, New York, Holt, Rinehart and Winston, 1961, p. 177; William R. Dill, *op. cit.* pp. 94–109.

zations enlist broad rank and file membership to stabilize their position in the community. This type of party organization tends to be relatively decentralized or to have an elaborate organization at its periphery to articulate with citizens.

Fluid membership and highly permeable boundaries are other characteristics of organizations with many goals and active environmental exchanges. Large organizations, whose survival is contingent upon sensitive responsiveness to their environment, must be relatively open to membership, or they risk isolation and sectarianism.

With these organizational properties in mind, the environmental factors which impinge upon political parties can be considered. These environmental influences may be regarded as structural aspects of the system that limit, condition, and influence party organization and behavior. They are: (1) the degree of national integration; (2) the electoral system and its norms; (3) the degree of monopoly or competition among political parties; (4) the extent to which the parties are an instrument of stratification and channel of mobility; and (5) a situational variable, the existence or absence of crisis.

Our concern is with the function of leadership recruitment, which is an outcome of organizational reconciliation of party internal components, each with its own goals. These subunits, with considerable variability, share a community of interest with the party as a whole. In selecting leaders, the party organization is an active arena for those competing influences, creating what Schlesinger has called the multinuclear party. Recruitment and selection reflect the organizational complexities of political parties.

Environmental Factors

The Degree of National Integration

National integrations may be defined in various ways. Coleman and Rosberg use a two-dimensional definition:

"(1) political integration, which refers to the progressive bridging of the elite-mass gap on the vertical plane in the course of developing an integrated political process and a participant political community; (2) territorial integration, which refers to the progressive reduction of cultural and regional tensions and discontinuities on the horizontal plane in the process of creating a homogeneous territorial political community." [13]

[13] Coleman and Rosberg, *op. cit.,* p. 9.

Integration is often more clearly defined negatively, that is, by the degree to which cultural and social cleavages impair national solidarity. Societies that are subdivided by long-standing ethnic and religious differences have been called plural societies. Many of the developing nations approximate this category. In such divided systems, the political party is an agency for "making" citizens, catalyzing the change from parochial loyalties to national loyalty. The political party does this in several ways. One of the most important is the opening of its ranks to mass membership. In West Africa, "The most important mechanism to reduce the conflict between ethnicity and national integration is the nationalist party." [14] Party identification may be a substitute attachment during a transitional period when ties to village and tribe are being loosened. In many newer states political institutions do not earn more than superficial loyalties from their citizenry. Political institutions have not worn down cultural separatist tendencies. Western governmental forms are but a superficial graft upon deeply rooted custom and values.

Despite a longer history there are varying degrees of national integration among Western nations, too. In many Western industrialized nations, cultural, religious, and linguistic divisions are still of importance. In Belgium, political cleavages reflect and constitute the "fault lines" of religious, linguistic, and economic cleavages. French, German, Italian, and Austrian politics today reflect persistent historical cultural differences. Yet historic, ethnic, and religious differences are overlapped by cleavages that derive from industrial and agrarian social stratification. Over time, social mobility, new issues, and generational changes have worn down some of these older cleavages, and national consciousness is more deeply rooted among the citizenry. Resting on this bedrock, political parties are devoted to promoting the interests of associated groups. Political parties may assume the civic attachments of the citizenry as a "given," more or less firmly rooted, even though they are now and then subjected to stress.

Electoral System and Party Competition

The electoral system is an important structural feature of a political system. Stability and regularity in the electoral system (for example, a presidential election every four years; no president may serve more than two terms in succession) are firm expectations which condition the behavior of political parties. Among other structural certainties are electoral procedures and rules (elections and/or nominations will take place without violence). Parties are strongly influenced by such electoral rules. Three components of the electoral system will be discussed: 1. method

[14] Immanuel Wallerstein, "Elites in French-Speaking West Africa," *Journal of Modern African Studies*, III, No. 1 (May, 1965), 7.

of electoral scoring; 2. norms of political competition; and 3. the extent of political competition.

Methods of Electoral Scoring. Another important structural determinant is the method of electoral scoring—such as single member constituencies with plurality systems, single member districts and runoff elections, or proportional representation. ". . . electoral methods tend to influence such factors as party solidarity, electoral alliances, and dependence of candidates on party organization. One possible effect . . . is the apparent tendency of plurality and majority systems to produce a geographic concentration of a given party's voting strength and the contrary tendency of PR to create a wider dispersion of its electoral support." [15] These scoring methods limit party strategies and influence many aspects of party behavior. Thus Zaritzki evaluates the effects of electoral system on the degree of factionalism in various parties. [16]

These structural certainties dynamically influence parties and are, in turn, reciprocally influenced by the parties. A two-party system is not merely a product of an electoral system, but also contributes to the consensus and stability which supports such an electoral system and indeed may bring it into being.

The Norms of Political Conflict and Competition. The electoral system relates also to the general norms and institutionalized practices governing political conflict and competition. In many new nations politics is regarded as warlike conflict which must result in total victory or total defeat. In game theory terminology, politics is viewed as a zero-sum game, in which there must be total victory for one party and total loss for the other. Such systems are "high risk" systems because political losses result in the severe deprivations in status and influence.

In mature democratic systems, political opposition is institutionalized, partial, and transitory. The opposition criticizes policy but does not challenge the legitimacy of the system. Only rarely does opposition polarize and rigidify. [17] Characteristically, opposition parties are institutionalized as in England or the United States. They are potential coalition partners and hence are never too polarized in their opposition because many shared values underlie policy differences.

In mature democratic systems, political conflict is constrained by accepted rules of the game which serve to diminish political risk. Most

---

[15] John G. Grumm, "Theories of Electoral Systems," *Midwest Journal of Political Science,* II, No. 3 (Aug., 1958), 375–76.

[16] Zaritzki, *op. cit.,* pp. 37–41.

[17] Giovanni Sartori, "Opposition, Control, Contestation," *Government and Opposition,* I, No. 2 (Feb., 1966), 149–54; Robert A. Dahl, "Reflections on Opposition," *Government and Opposition,* I, No. 1 (Nov., 1965), 7–24.

political defeats do not preclude further opportunities for political entry. Political gains and losses are both of moderate magnitude, a fact which does not discourage many from competing for political office.

Political Competition and Monopoly. The degree of political party competition or monopoly may be a structural as well as behavioral characteristic of the environment. In some countries the political monopoly by one party is stipulated in law which bars competition. Other systems permit open entry and party competition. Between these two extremes range the various political systems of the world.

Competition between or among parties varies in level, quality, and durability. First, there are various *levels* of political competition. Some parties are unable to nominate candidates for all public offices and offer candidates for local offices only. Other parties have candidates for parliamentary contests, but not for local contests. Second, competition varies qualitatively. Some small, intensely ideological parties nominate candidates only intermittently yet compete ideologically with vigor. Third, competition varies because the risks in competitive loss are variable. In some systems the failure of a political party to win a plurality means only a lesser role in a governing coalition. In others electoral loss is tantamount to exclusion from the political system.

Competition varies also in degree from ongoing, durable, and close competition to one-sided contests, dominated consistently by one party. Lesser parties include many types: those with no expectation of winning, but hope for opposition status; [18] other minority parties compete only for a place in a hoped-for governing coalition, like the Socialist party in Germany in recent years; and others compete to gain a majority.

The degree of competition and monopoly has a direct bearing on recruitment. A permanent minority party with little hope or expectation of gaining a majority and governing will choose a leadership proficient in opposing but lacking experience and/or capacity for governing. Such minority parties tend toward purism and sectarianism; their candidates are more concerned with expressing ideological integrity than with winning the broadest spectrum of popular support. In contrast, a party with expectations of governing will select candidates with the skills, abilities, and resources to win and to govern. The party will calculate more strategically about winning and will attract more of the politically ambitious, who will seek the party as an avenue to political advancement.

The degree of competition and monopoly also affects political turnover and the circulation of leadership. Electoral competition (when it results in alternation) assures that some officials will be turned out and new ones

[18] Grumm, *ibid.*

introduced. This expectation of turnover therefore fosters incentives to political mobility and the pursuit of the political vocation. Moreover, competition reduces political risk because it protects the displaced by cushioning the losses in the event of political defeat, so that they may continue to compete. In contrast, political monopoly has difficulty in institutionalizing succession and permits turnover only by violence and purges, with the displaced subject to sharp reductions in status. Under conditions of political monopoly, political risk is very high.

Political Parties as Channels for Mobility

The role that political parties play in determining the social and political status of individuals, groups, and organizations is an environmental factor that greatly influences the power of party. If political role is significant in determining social status (as it is in many developing systems and increasingly so in developed systems), then the power of political parties will be greatly enhanced. Thus the monopoly in allocating economic and social resources distinguishes single parties or the continually dominant party in a multiparty system from parties in a competitive party system.

With the advent of independence in the new nations, many new positions are created in the governmental bureaucracy and party apparatus. The dominant party controls access to these positions by its control over the associations and positions which are the sources of leadership. This control is an important aspect of what is called "the primacy of politics," which includes governmental centralization, broad state control of economic life, and control over *both* the opportunities and resources needed for social and political mobility.

"The primacy of politics means that the ladder of career advancement for the elite is concentrated in directly political positions. Political posts become a primary source of income, both licit and illicit, and the possibilities of successful private enterprise are early conditioned by political influence. This means that students are attracted to political careers, whether in state or party, and in general many students tend to see educational training as a step to higher-level, non-technical posts. These posts are doubly attractive; as posts of national service they are worthy of high social approval, and they are also highly rewarded in a material sense. The material rewards do not contradict the sense of virtue in national service. Rather they legitimate recompense for the high career risk of political activities." [19]

In the new states the belief in more equalitarian social and political

[19] Wallerstein, *op. cit.,* p. 17.

opportunity is a keystone of the nationalist ideology. The state promises new opportunities to its citizens as retribution for the discrimination experienced under colonial rule. The nationalist vision promises the fulfillment of new collective and individual social, economic, and political status. The primacy of party (and politics) is related to the level of economic development. National income is low and steeply stratified in its distribution. In less developed countries the scope of political control is very broad, so that the resources for political participation, including skills in organization and access to communication, are highly restricted. In consequence, there is a large gap between the *formal political opportunity structure*, with its legal promise of abundant opportunity for participation, and the highly restricted *effective political opportunity*.

One party not only controls the channels to political status, but occupational career paths course through party affiliation and loyalty to the regime. The party allocates jobs, licenses, loans, subsidies, and other economic resources for which no competitive suppliers are permitted.[20] To be in good favor with state or party bureaucracy is imperative to improvement in income, status, and influence. Since outside the control of the party political and social opportunity are severely restricted, the costs of political deviance are very great. This control over both social and political mobility gives party and regime their commanding role.

In the history of Western industrialized nations, political parties contributed to opening new channels and widening existing channels of social mobility. Indeed, political parties were formed to facilitate the collective mobility of classes and subcultures. Thus working class parties were formed so that laborers could use their numerical strength at the ballot box to gain economic policies in their collective interest. Political parties also provided collective escalators for individual mobility; the principal beneficiaries of such collective mobility were middle-class individuals.

Although political parties were instrumental in upward mobility in the Western industrialized nations, there were great variations among nations in this regard. Party routes are more significant in Great Britain, Weimar Germany, the Scandinavian countries, or Republican Italy than in France.[21] Moreover, in Western systems political parties are but one of several channels of mobility. The cumulative adoption of achievement

[20] Otto Kircheimer's statement is relevant here: "There is a substantial difference between parties that initiate, purvey, and receive services and obligations while government agencies are confined to purely technical functions, and parties that merely strive to impose alternative claims on governmental bodies that retain an appreciable range of discretion in the adjudication and balancing of conflicting claims," in "The Party in Mass Society," *World Politics*, X (Oct., 1957–July, 1958), 290.

[21] Mattei Dogan, "Political Ascent in a Class Society: French Deputies 1870–1958," in *Political Decision Makers*, ed. by Dwaine Marvick, New York, Free Press, 1961, p. 76.

criteria has made partisanship and party activity less important to the attainment of occupational positions.

As Western parties become large scale and bureaucratized, they draw leaders primarily from their own ranks. In part, functional specificity of roles incident to bureaucratization makes this necessary. Seniority in the service of the party, another bureaucratic criterion, becomes a basis for candidate and party leader selection. Moreover, seniority as a criterion ensures party loyalty and protects the prevailing status stratification in the party. At the same time, the existence of autonomous associations, interest groups, and occupational structures makes available leaders who may be co-opted from nonpolitical positions of prestige.

"To the extent that political parties do not form their own cadres, they chiefly recruit their representatives and their leaders from the social elite, that is, from universities, higher administration, union federations, the army, churches, the bar, the press, the medical profession, the engineers, the landed aristocracy, the rural squirearchy, financial circles, and large-scale industry. . . ." [22]

Parties play a leading role everywhere in legitimating and institutionalizing the paths of political careers. The more bureaucratized the party the more prescribed are these paths, the more narrow and limited are the characteristics of those who pursue them. The more diffuse are party roles, the more variegated are career paths and more diverse the people selected thereby.

Situational Variables—Crisis

Crisis situations have an immediate and direct impact on political leadership recruitment. There are several kinds of crises—bargaining, internal security, legitimacy, and external threat.[23] Crises have been neglected in the comparative analysis of parties, although acute and chronic crises cause many structural and behavioral changes in both developing and developed political systems.

Under crisis conditions the role of political parties as articulators of interest groups and public opinion becomes subordinated to the party function of governing. Minority and/or opposition parties become eclipsed by the urgent need for national consensus. In crisis periods, the executive exercises complete authority and political parties become government instruments for mobilizing public opinion and administrative agent for political control.

[22] Dogan, *op. cit.*, p. 82.
[23] Lester G. Seligman, "Leadership: Political Aspects" forthcoming in the *New Encyclopedia of the Social Sciences.*

Exigencies of crisis occasion the breakdown of established methods of recruitment. Personalities that would be overlooked under normal circumstances come to the fore. The significance of these changes is that the innovations of crisis often become accepted and institutionalized, as the chapters by Hoffmann and Wolfenstein indicate.

Bargaining and legitimacy crises often arise from recruitment policies. Serious gaps between formal and effective political opportuinty for some elements of the population—those "left out" or those whose representation has been sharply diminished—may generate acute bargaining and legitimacy crises. Student protest movements, the demands of ethnic minorities, and functional groups for representation are characteristic examples.[24]

The Leadership Recruitment Function of Political Parties

Party Systems: Political Opportunities and Political Risk

Political parties interact with the aforementioned environmental variables to generate types of party systems. La Palombara and Weiner have distinguished between hegemonic and turnover patterns of party recruitment.[25] In the hegemonic patterns, the same party or coalition of parties holds a dominant position for a long time. Turnover patterns indicate alterations of parties in power and generate such expectations.

The full leadership recruitment tasks of parties include the following: (1) the nomination of candidates for public office—parliament, state, and local elective officials; (2) the selection of officials for executive positions; and (3) the selection of party organization officials. Throughout this chapter, we shall refer only to the selection of parliamentary candidates. In every system, the leading party's selection of candidates is tantamount to their election to public office. Because of this, these several levels of political roles may be linked together, forming regular career patterns of advancement, or they may be separate career ladders.

The recruitment function of parties may be described as the way in which parties select a team, drawn from their own leadership, membership, and/or the groups and organizations in their environment, that is acceptable to their organization and public constituency. Recruitment is accomplished by two general strategies: (1) attracting individuals and groups to the rewards of office or (2) changing the rewards of office to

[24] William Kornhauser, "Rebellion and Political Development," *Institute of International Studies*, General Studies Reprint #143 (1964).

[25] Joseph La Palombara and Myron Weiner, "The Origin and Development of Political Parties," in *Political Parties and Political Development*, ed. by La Palombara and Weiner, Princeton, N.J., Princeton University Press, 1966.

attract aspirants to leadership. The first method is employed when supply of aspirants is sufficient for the demand. Rewards are modified when the supply of aspirants is insufficient.

The complex, large-scale, multipurpose organization offers several channels of access for its partisans and its politically ambitious, as Joseph Schlesinger has shown.[26] Each level and functional group can be a source for leadership and a step in the path toward a political career. "Push-pull" mechanisms operate to supply leadership to the organizational components. The push is supplied by the politically ambitious, and the pulls by the organizational needs for leadership that will advance and protect its interests and give expression to its aims.

The large-scale party provides resources for advancement and cushions political risk for its leaders or sets limits on their losses. Party organizations provide campaign organizations, finances, and propaganda for their leaders. This is especially true where the party list system is employed. Of equal importance are the supports party organization may provide the candidates and leaders in the event of defeat. Thus in Germany, because of the Socialist Party's "prolonged failure to gain federal office," major or middle level politicians "have a good chance to find berths with financial and status rewards in the top echelons of state governments." [27] Political parties furnish political positions within the party and may assist in securing private positions for defeated candidates. If candidates are demoted and downgraded, the party provides for them when their usefulness has diminished.

The organization of recruitment in political parties will be discussed on three levels of interaction: (1) party and its environment, (2) intraparty relationships, and (3) party and its relationship to the candidates.

Single Party. Single party regimes assume exclusive rights to nominate candidates for government offices. For example, the Egyptian constitution of 1964 specifies that a single organization, "the National Union," has exclusive authority to nominate candidates for the National Assembly. In the Ivory Coast no African could be elected without the endorsement of the PDCI.[28] Since the single party does not have external opposition, recruitment offers high stakes of prestige and power for the party as a whole and for each party component. Each faction battles for recognition of its own leaders. The party calibrates the power of its various factions and subdivisions by the relative ranks of its leaders.

[26] Joseph Schlesinger, "Political Party Organization," in *Handbook of Organizations,* ed. by James G. March, Chicago, Rand McNally, 1965, p. 776.

[27] Otto Kirchheimer, "Germany: The Vanishing Opposition," in Dahl, *op. cit.,* p. 251.

[28] I. Wallerstein, *op. cit.,* p. 16.

Relieved of competition from other parties, single parties have the task of controlling the total political environment instead. Each political resource—money, organization, mass media—may become an instrument of potential threat and must be controlled. In contrast to a competitive system, in which parties regard themselves as representing only a segment of the nation, the single party regime sees itself as synonymous with the *entire* people. Consequently, the ruling party must attempt to enlist all significant subcultures and groups that may have potential as bases for autonomous and rival leadership. The complete control over statuses which are or may become paths of political mobility is essential to the maintenance of authority by the single party.

For the system as a whole, the single party offers less political opportunity and higher political risk than parties in a competitive system. The single party, although it tries to be broadly representative, affords proportionately fewer places and draws its leadership from a narrower base than all the parties combined in a competitive system. The single party regime through its control over the channels of mobility is less compelled to compete for personnel with other occupational spheres; consequently, there is less incentive for the party to broaden political opportunity.

In the single party the political career and political roles are very risky because there is "no place to go" outside the party. Only through the party can a political career be achieved, and dismissal from the party is oblivion, purgatory, or worse. High political risk and high rewards attract the ambitious and compel their compliance.

Competitive Party Systems. We shall use the United States to illustrate recruitment politics in competitive systems. In party organizations operating under the primary system, party officials are legally prohibited from recruiting candidates. Thus new suborganizations arise to solicit, encourage, and sponsor candidates. Some of these organizations are assimilated into the party organization; other organizations are peripheral to the party organization. Among the internal ones are factions derived from generational differences, urban-rural divisions, economic interest, and ideological or programmatic divisions. Interest groups that are linked in various ways to the party also serve as vehicles for candidate recruitment. Finally, there is a miscellaneous group of candidates who are a peculiar, self-recruited mixture and who are instigated into candidacy by social cliques or occupational associations.

The potentiality of competition from another party, the absence of hierarchy, and the open competition within the party prevent ideological cohesion among candidates, for "every group is in business for itself." The intraparty conflicts are less contests for status *within* the organization than they are competition by autonomous groups for political influence.

Indeed, so diffuse are organizational roles that party organization resists analogies to bureaucratic models completely. The boundaries of party organization blend into social and economic associations, thereby making it difficult to decide where the boundaries of one begin and the others end. The recruitment processes in these parties reveal the looseness of party structure and its high permeability by environmental influences.

Political opportunity is expanded by: (1) competing parties, (2) the plurality of suborganizations within the party which may sponsor political careers, and (3) provision for defeated candidates made by the groups and components of the parties.

Organizational Loci of Recruitment Decisions

Several methods are employed by political parties to manage the recruitment of leaders according to the locus of the decision: (1) interest group allocation, (2) devolution to local branches, and (3) centralized selection.

Interest Group Allocation. Interest group allocation is practiced where parties try to ally with several major interest groups. The party is pluralistic, caters to diverse and heterogeneous interests, and achieves unity only by coalition of several interest groups. A bargain is struck with various interest groups, a condition of which is their right to select a definite number of candidates.

This method is employed where the electoral system makes it disadvantageous for interest groups to become political parties and where their position in society gives interest groups autonomy from governmental control. Through this method of collective bargaining the party becomes a broad political front whose ideology has sufficient generality so that various interest groups may legitimate their efforts by identification with it.

When the party is a governing party, interest group allocation includes leading government officials plus the party bureaucracy and the interest groups. The dominant party in Mexico, the PRI, employs this method. "Interest groups are currently organized into three 'sectors' of the party—labor, agrarian, and popular—the last as a catch-all category. PRI nominations to elective posts, which are normally equivalent to election, are allocated to the sector strongest in the constituency to be represented." [29]

Specifically, interest groups play a variety of roles in candidate recruitment: (1) sponsorship, (2) veto, (3) exclusive franchise, and (4) candidate socialization. *Sponsorship* by interest groups includes instigating candidacy and providing organization and financial resources for candidates.

[29] Martin C. Needler, "The Political Development of Mexico," *American Political Science Review*, LV, No. 2 (June, 1961), 309.

Interest groups with *veto power* have the power to block a candidate from receiving approval. *Exclusive franchise* involves an allocation to groups to designate and sponsor a candidate exclusively, without further approval. Finally, interest groups that *socialize candidates* are those that provide a career channel for candidate aspirants.

Devolution to Local Branches. Western political parties vary greatly in their degree of centralization and decentralization. The decentralized parties are associated with a federal political structure. For some time it was usual to contrast the British party system (an example of centralized party organization) with the American system (a federal and decentralized structure). Recent empirical research has dissolved this polarized conception. Austin Ranney's study of British parties [30] indicates that despite the formal requirements for approval of party candidates by central headquarters, many candidates are, in fact, chosen by local constituencies with pro forma approval by central party headquarters. The American party system, because of its federalism, vests a good deal of autonomy in state and local party organizations. As a result, the party system is described as a loose league of state, county, and municipal organizations. The requirement that candidates be residents of their localities gives local organizations great power over selection processes.

The method of devolution has several effects: it gives considerable autonomy to local branches, which enables the party organization to be close to its members and respond flexibly to the demands of its diverse membership. This was exemplified in French parties during the Fourth Republic. Candidates for Parliament were chosen by each departmental constituency, thus giving considerable local measure of autonomy. The rank and file have a level of organization through which they can be heard. Candidates solicited through local branches can remain beholden to a local constituency and, in turn, can be beholden to central party organization for their governmental effectiveness. Candidates are chosen for their ability to compete with opposing parties in a locality, not for their consistency with national leadership.

Furthermore, the method of decentralization enables the party to tap subcultures directly by choosing candidates who are of various subcultures. At the same time decentralized party organization may act as a "brake" on the political advancement of candidates recruited in this manner, because it requires them to achieve broader appeal as a condition of advancement.

Centralized Selection. Centralized selection is a method whereby a party central committee or a committee especially established for this

[30] Austin Ranney, *Pathways to Parliament,* Madison, Wis., University of Wisconsin Press, 1965.

purpose designates candidates. Parties that centralize candidate recruitment are those with explicit ideologies and bureaucratized organizations. Branch and constituency organizations and interest groups play a minor role. This method is widely employed among single parties of the new states and is also employed in Western industrialized regimes. Both major German parties, CDV/CSU and the SPD, choose candidates in this manner.[31] The wishes of local branches are taken into account, but the party insists upon ideological conformity, and centralized selection ensures this. The centralization of authority means that the party bureaucracy plays an active role. There are contending groups, but they engage in a kind of palace politics around the central committees of party government. Recruitment of leadership is not representation from below but is the selection of people who are above all loyal and trusted by central leadership. The politics of recruitment resembles bureaucratic competition rather than electoral competition.

Party Organization and the Individual Candidate

The three predominant organizational patterns of recruitment that we have indicated use certain selection mechanisms to enlist individuals for political office and political roles.[32] These mechanisms of selection are: (1) self-recruitment, (2) sponsorship, (3) conscription, and (4) co-optation.

Self-Recruitment. This refers to the mechanism wherein the individual is the initial and primary instigator of his candidacy. Self-recruitment is elusive since it is not easy to separate self-initiation and the covert social support that makes it possible. It is only a matter of degree that distinguishes self-recruitment from group sponsorship as a mode of recruitment. The purest form of self-recruitment is the unaided aspirant in search of followers. Such types are rare. The self-recruited is a residual category distinguishable by the relative absence of visible, manifest collective support.

Sponsorship. This is by far the most common method of selection. Sponsorship makes the candidate the agent of interest groups and organizations. Sponsorship may be used to draw recruits from within an association or may be used to co-opt individuals of high status to shore up party strength.

[31] On the centralization of German parties see Lewis J. Edinger, "Continuity and Change in the Background of German Decision-Makers," *Western Political Science Quarterly*, **XIV**, No. 1, Part 1 (March, 1961), 19–20. I am grateful to my colleague Arthur M. Hanhardt, Jr., for enlightenment in this matter.

[32] Lester G. Seligman, "Political Recruitment and Party Structure," *American Political Science Review*, **LV**, No. 1 (March, 1961), 77–86. Compare with the findings of Frank Sorauf in another context. *Party and Representation: Legislative Politics in Pennsylvania*, New York, Atherton Press, pp. 107–20.

Conscription. In this type a candidate is drafted to run for office or is appointed to political posts and accepts the discipline of the group that chooses him. The conscript is not an office-seeker; his loyalty to the party obligates him to accept the draft of his services.

Co-Optation. This mechanism invites and enlists established political influence into party leadership in order to strengthen party organization and/or mass support. Co-optation is widely employed by groups and associations that are linked to parties as well as by organizational components of parties. It is used extensively, because very often those co-opted, no less than those whom they join, profit by the exchange.

There is a lack of empirical evidence about the frequency with which these mechanisms are employed in various parties. All four mechanisms are doubtlessly employed at various times by political parties. However, hypotheses that define probabilities for the employment of these mechanisms are warranted.

The Outcomes

Organizational patterns of recruitment tend to become rigid and resistant to change. These organizational patterns tend to bias the types of persons chosen. Every party produces certain preferred types who are trained and apprenticed in the prescribed patterns of political career. Thus the Swedish Social Democrats required local government experience of its aspirants for Parliament, a requirement which ensured slow ascent and circulation and protected the status of the old guard.[33]

The large-scale party tends to resist responsiveness to new leadership.[34] Bureaucratic succession and appointments by consensus rather than open competition are the most common processes of leadership selection. Moreover, in both competitive and authoritarian systems if one party has long tenure in power its selections perpetuate themselves. The familiar old guard, the notables of service, is a feature in all party systems. Thus we have been reminded that political parties, whose historical role was that of preventing a closed group of officials, may become the means to achieve such a result.

It is no surprise that crises develop when the leadership becomes estranged from environmental demands and parties must co-opt leadership from the ranks of the successful and those with prestige. Under such crises conditions, parties invite lateral entry to introduce new blood. Changes in

---

[33] Jean Meynaud, "The Parliamentary Profession," *International Social Science Bulletin,* XIII, No. 4 (1961) 520; Nils Stgernquist, "Sweden," in Dahl, *op. cit.,* p. 139.

[34] Duverger, *op. cit.,* p. 163, *passim.*

patterns of recruitment may then result which later modify the structure of internal party components, the interdependence among organizational units, and exchanges with environmental demands.

Parties have a dualistic relationship to the political opportunity-risk structure. They may, like democratic competitive parties, broaden opportunity by opening new avenues for elements of the population hitherto left out. In the same vein, parties may augment political risk (as do single party regimes) by denying access to other statuses for defeated aspirants or those in leadership roles. Parties may also cushion the defeated and the rejected, opening avenues to other positions to prevent sharp losses in status.

Conclusions

To concretize our analysis, some research we have conducted may illustrate one pattern of interaction. We analyzed the rise of the Democratic Party in the state of Oregon, with emphasis on the emergence of a new corps of leadership aspirants.[35] The findings may be summarized as follows. Considerable economic growth in the late 1940s stimulated migration of young lawyers and others with political ambition into the state. Economic expansion enhanced occupational status from which channels of political mobility could be used. At the same time, a young native political generation had come of age, now eligible for political activity. These environmental changes contributed to the emergence of a group of new political leaders in the following way. The Democratic Party had been a minority party faced with difficulties in regularly filling the nomination ticket. The direct primary system (an electoral factor) made candidacy relatively easy, and the looseness of party organization combined to enhance political opportunity. Political risk was lessened because political defeat often *enhanced* occupational success and the investment in competition for political office was not very great. The loose party organization in each constituency made it easier for interest associations and other groups to sponsor candidates. Internal factional battles (organizational factor) in the Oregon Democratic Party refracted the national issues that gave the Democratic Party its identity in those years and enabled the local party to distinguish itself from its rival, the dominant Republican Party. Thus environmental changes affected party recruitment because party organization, electoral system, the formal and effective political opportunity-risk structure were amenable to such responsiveness.

[35] L. Seligman, "Political Change: Legislative Elites and Parties in Oregon," *Western Political Science Quarterly*, XVII, No. 2, June, 1964), 177–187.

We have attempted no more than an approach toward parties and their recruitment role. Our premise has been that a comparative theory should include the pre-industrial systems as well as the industrial systems, and that light will be shed on industrial systems by this contrast.

The large-scale organizational character of parties is ubiquitous, however various its specific forms. Yet too little is known about party organizational processes, including the methods of leadership recruitment. The recruitment function may be seen as an exchange with environmental variables mediated by political opportunity and political risk. Organizations reconcile these influences through various patterns of organizational decision making: centralization, interest group allocation, and devolution to local branches.

In selection of leadership, political parties play a special and sometimes exclusive function. The question we have been asking tacitly is why, despite cultural and environmental differences, the large-scale political party in many diverse environments appears to generate some similar roles and role behaviors, yet the functions of political parties in political systems are so varied. In the answer to this question lies the fruitfulness of exploring leadership in its organizational contexts and as an organizational product.

11. Political Systems, Styles and Personalities

HAROLD D. LASSWELL

The study of political leadership in industrial societies carries us beyond the investigation of individuals to the analysis of political systems and styles. Beside referring to the leadership of individuals like Franklin D. Roosevelt, we speak of the leading role of groups of Virginians, like Washington and Jefferson, in early American politics; of Republicans as the leading political party after the Civil War; and of the doctrines of democracy and welfare as among the leading perspectives in modern politics. Obviously our first problem is to clarify the meaning that we intend to attach to the concept of leadership.

Political Leadership: A Stable Pattern of Effective Initiative for Decision

If a term is to be useful in studying politics it must be defined as a pattern of interaction; politics is, after all, part of social process, and "social process" is a term for all the ways that human beings affect each other. Leadership is a leader-follower pattern. Consider the following.

If two people see an approaching landslide simultaneously and jump out of the way, there is no advantage in seeking to identify one or the other as a "leader" or "follower." However, if A perceives the slide before B and shouts, thus drawing B's attention to the danger and permitting B to get off the highway, it makes sense to say that A led B. Suppose A had no time to notify B and simply shoved him out of the way. Should we refer to this as a leadership relation?

Our analysis of the landslide episode suggests that a leadership pattern can be identified in any interaction in which *orientation is given and received*.[1] Consider situations in which "political" identity is beyond debate. No competent person denies that Lenin, Churchill, and Roosevelt

[1] See H. D. Lasswell, "Conflict and Leadership: The Process of Decision and the Nature of Authority," in *Ciba Foundation Symposium on Conflict in Society*, ed. by A. V. S. de Reuck and Julie Knight, London, J. & A. Churchill Ltd., 1966, pp. 210–228.

were playing leadership roles in national and transnational politics. Unquestionably they influenced orientation in the decision process of bodies politic. At the simplest level they affected the attention of participants. Unquestionably, too, decisions often entailed the use of coercive measures directed against particular individuals or entire nations. Some of these coercions, like *A*'s shove of *B*, can in retrospect be perceived as contributing to the immediate welfare of the target. Other coercive acts were aimed less to protect the welfare of the target than to advance the value position of a group on whose behalf the coercion was used. Roosevelt joined in coercing Nazi Germany primarily for the benefit of beleaguered Englishmen and threatened Americans, two nationalities with which Roosevelt felt identified and whose security demands were important to him. In identifying leadership in politics we take more than a single incident into account, since we are concerned with *relatively stable patterns of effective initiative for decision.* By the term "political role" we mean a stable pattern of participation in political process. For instance, in a given committee it is conceivable that during a selected period, every member will play the role of "leader" with equal frequency (hence most of the time everyone will be a "follower"). In the context of a large body politic it is, of course, wildly improbable that, if we consider the career line as a whole, every adult will play a role of equal weight.

The leadership relation is broad enough to include all degrees of temporory or permanent dominance and subordination or voluntary and involuntary involvement. The dominance may be authoritative and controlling, as when higher courts overrule lower courts or when a cabinet officer modifies the decision of a bureau chief. For examples of involuntary and unlawful dominance and subordination we think of criminal gangs who force "protection" payments from shopkeepers and residents.

When we referred to the leading part played in contemporary politics by doctrines that justify democracy and welfare, the direct reference was not to individuals, groups, or organizations. A "perspective" is a subjective event which can be described introspectively or by inference from the behavior of others. A "doctrine" is a pattern of abstract perspectives, such as the general statement that "the goal of the body politic ought to be the realization of human dignity on the widest possible scale"; or more specific statements, such as "a proper function of government is to guarantee to all citizens at least a minimum degree of welfare" (for example, of income, education, medical care). In the contemporary world community these beliefs are part of the political system of many nation states.

A Problem Orientation Toward Leadership

After clarifying our working conception of political leadership as a stable pattern of effective initiative for decision, the next step is to ask what we want to know about it.

One question is scientific: How is leadership to be explained? What consequences does it have?

Another is historical: What are the trends in national, transnational, and subnational patterns of leadership?

A further question is projective: What are the most probable future manifestations of leader-follower relations?

There is an additional task, which might have been mentioned first: What is the overriding value goal with respect to whose realization leadership studies are made?

Finally, in this list of five tasks pertinent to the problem of leadership, what policy alternatives will probably contribute to the realization of the postulated goal at the least cost and lowest risk?

Clearly this collection of studies is primarily scientific in the sense that each writer challenges himself to advance the current stock of knowledge about the place of leadership in politics. It would, however, be a mistake to suppose that the other four intellectual tasks receive no consideration or that no contributions are made to their accomplishment. Some of the studies are basically historical, and all must unavoidably deal with the description of recent and remote events as primary data. Projections are rarely explicit; nevertheless it is impossible to touch on a subject as important and fascinating as the alternating cycle of leadership in France without conveying some intimation of what the future holds.

Most of the writers are personally committed to the overriding value goal commonly associated with "human dignity," a conception that includes a voice in the decision processes of the body politic. Hence implications are continually drawn for the clarification of the nature of effective leadership in popularly governed states. It is not within the primary scope of this book to devise or evaluate a set of policies for the cultivation of democratic leadership in advanced industrial societies. Nonetheless it is obvious that the challenge is alive in the minds of the writers, for example, in connection with the forecasts commonly formulated in the name of psychoanalysis.

The foregoing comments have been intended to show how leadership studies are perceived in the frame of reference of a comprehensive methodological approach to politics. The suggestion is that an adequate approach is *problem-oriented*, hence aware of the five intellectual tasks referred to in terms of goal, trend, condition, projection, and alternatives.

The recommended approach is also *contextual,* since it deals with politics as part of the social process to which it belongs and with which it is in perpetual interaction. Such an approach must also be *multimethod,* since it utilizes all available methods of model building, data gathering, and processing. In short, the recommended method for studying leadership, as for investigating any phenomenon, is *configurative.* The approach is problem-oriented, contextual, and multimethod.[2]

Implied in what has been said is the view that the political process is "psychological," in that subjective events are invariably included in all interactions in politics and society. However, politics is not exhausted by the psychological dimension of the relation between leaders and those led, since behavioral *operations* as well as *perspectives* are always involved. Furthermore, if the context of the social process is to be kept in sight, the microacts of politics must simultaneously be classified as part of the macroacts that we identify as sufficiently stable regularities to be called an *institution.* Institutional practices, in turn, are open to the combined macro- and microanalysis that characterizes them as relatively specialized to major *value* outcomes: power, wealth, respect, etc.

In investigating political leadership, political scientists are problem-oriented toward the institutions of government, law, and politics, or, more generally, of decision. Leadership patterns are part of the "political culture" of a given body politic, that is, the stable patterns of interaction in situations relatively specialized to decision. The term "personality" refers to the stable patterns exhibited by a person when his interactions in every type of situation are taken into account. "Political personality" is a convenient label for personalities who are relatively specialized to the decision process. Note that "culture" includes the forms of personality developed within it, not excluding the subcultures in distinctive territorial and pluralistic settings. As indicated before, a political "role" is the pattern of participation displayed in a political arena.

The Range of Personality Studies

At this point it may be serviceable to glance at the strategy of some researches intended to clarify the place of psychocultural factors in politics.

1. A prominent political figure is analyzed in order to discover the significance of his main political role in the context of his whole personality system.

---

[2] The term "configurative method" was employed by the writer in *World Politics and Personal Insecurity,* Paperback Reprint, New York, Free Press, 1965; see also H.D. Lasswell and A. Kaplan, *Power and Society; A Framework for Political Inquiry* Paperback Reprint, New Haven, Conn., Yale University Press, 1963; *The Future of Political Science,* New York, Atherton Press, 1963.

Alexander and Juliet George studied Woodrow Wilson in the hope of throwing light on why Wilson moved into active politics and explaining some of his leading characteristics as a politician.[3] Stimulated by hypotheses derived from psychoanalysis, they called attention to the significance of Wilson's relationship to his father, noting the inner necessity for overreacting against any subsequent authority figure who reawakened incompletely resolved unconscious conflicts. More recently Arnold Rogow examined another national figure, James Forrestal, from a similar point of view.[4] Forrestal did not enter the arena of conventional politics by seeking election. Nevertheless, in his career as an appointed official, Forrestal exhibited an intense commitment to power—a drive that eventually led him to self-destruction when his future seemed in eclipse. The development of Forrestal's severity in dealing with himself is intelligible when seen in the light of his early family orientation and his attempts to overcome discordant dispositions within himself by the mechanisms of repression and suppression.

2. Selecting an official structure of government, investigators have undertaken to describe and explore the relevance of the prevailing distribution of personality systems in the structure.

The traditional literature of political science contains the following types of assertions about offices (official organs of government) and personality: (*a*) personality characteristics influence the degree to which a leadership function is performed by a given structure; (*b*) personality differences are modified by exposure to an official environment; (*c*) government structures are selectively attractive to different kinds of persons. Today's political scientists are attempting to verify the truth of these propositions with the aid of more dependable methods than have been present in the past. It is also hoped that the validity of pertinent generalizations can be established by exploring current situations.

For example, one hypothesis is that elected legislatures reflect their constituencies; we should therefore expect to find the same distribution of personality characteristics among legislators and their constituents. However, another hypothesis is no less common: elective public office is more attractive to some forms of personality than others; hence representatives should differ from their constituents. The most common assertion about political personalities is that they excel in self-confidence, even to an extreme degree resembling paranoia. Assuming that paranoid tendencies include intense leadership demands, the implications are clear: "paranoids"

[3] A. L. George and J. L. George, *Woodrow Wilson and Colonel House*, New York, Day, 1956.
[4] A. A. Rogow, *James Forrestal: A Study of Personality, Politics and Policy*, New York, Macmillan, 1963.

will search out the organs of government; moreover, among all the organs of government those structures excelling in leadership potential will be most attractive to paranoids.

An early study of the legislature and electorate of South Carolina reported no shift toward psychopathology among legislators.[5] On the contrary, according to the psychological tests used in the research, legislators could be called more "reality-oriented" than their constituents. In recent years the National Institute of Mental Health has financed field surveys of the mental health status of whole populations in selected urban and non-urban areas. Researches now under way should provide us with the best information yet obtained on political participation, for it will be possible to connect at least some personality features with voting and office holding. Meanwhile, data tend to support the hypothesis that alleges a direct connection between high self-confidence and success in politics.[6]

3. Selecting nonofficial arenas and roles, political scientists have explored the distribution and significance of personality.

Although political bosses may occupy no official position, it is plausible that they are more power motivated and proficient than persons who occupy more formal posts. Frequently, however, not power but wealth may be the principal value outcome pursued by a boss. Biographical studies may identify other value objectives, such as gratifications derived from the exercise of skill in manipulating public affairs, as the principal value outcome sought by some bosses. A distinction between "gain" and "game" bosses has been made on the foundation of a study of American politicians.[7] The "gain" bosses often come from immigrant families who were "looked down on" by established families. From the standpoint of the upper respect classes such politicians might engage in "corrupt practices." As a rule, however, this did not lead to inner conflict, since family and friends were glad to benefit. Because the boss who originated in upper-class circles usually deviated from the "ideal type" of his class, he might be expected to show more evidence of inner stress.

Closer to the boss type, under some circumstances, is the vigorous leader of an opposition party. In such a context the personality factor is cast in high relief if it can be shown that the leader resisted policies and

---

[5] J. B. McConaughey, "Certain Personality Factors of State Legislators in South Carolina," *American Political Science Review*, 44 (1950), 897–903.

[6] For example, in a forthcoming study Brent M. Rutherford (of Northwestern University) has compared the leaders selected by the patients in the wards of the Elgin State Hospital in Illinois with the patients as a whole in regard to psychiatric diagnosis and prehospital leadership in the community.

[7] A. A. Rogow and H. D. Lasswell, *Power, Corruption, and Rectitude,* Englewood Cliffs, N.J., Prentice-Hall, 1963. Ch. 2. In this book see the chapters by Samuel H. Barnes and Lester Seligman.

strategies that in all probability would have led to governmental authority. Lewis Edinger's analysis of Kurt Schumacher carries conviction because of the careful attention that Edinger gives to the opportunities that Schumacher turned down.[8] Contemporary psychocultural interpretations are used to help explain why this outstanding Social Democrat was unwilling to take less intransigent positions.

A particularly attractive line of inquiry focuses on the revolutionary boss who must face the situation created by the successful seizure of power; hence the interest in Lenin, Mussolini, Hitler, Mao, Sukarno, and the leaders of movements for national independence.[9]

4. In viewing career lines as a whole, comprehensive models have been proposed to account for politically oriented personalities and to identify predispositions that facilitate the performance of one role rather than another.

The "political man" is a theoretical construct emphasizing the intensity and realism of the individual's commitment to the pursuit of power (a strong disposition to modify others to one's will).[10] In this context it must be stressed that "functional" theories of political man are not to be confused with "conventional" office holders. The aim of a general theory of "the political man" is to explain a phenomenon that may be found in any society. In some societies inculcated lack of ambition for individual distinction may result in few if any "political men" corresponding to the power model. However, the theoretical model is always helpful in calling attention to what is absent as well as present in a given body politic.

Individuals differ in the political roles that they find most congenial and in which they succeed. Hence it is possible to identify the predispositions of "agitators," for example, and to distinguish them from "administrators" or "theorists." A practicing psychoanalyst used his study of Martin Luther to generalize about the manner of man who becomes a great ideological innovator.[11] A fascinating though unresolved question concerns the truth of the hypothesis that the innovator experiences in more acute form the intellectual and personal conflicts current in the larger setting; hence his symbolic creations resonate with particular effectiveness among his contemporaries.

[8] L. J. Edinger, *Kurt Schumacher: A Study in Personality and Political Behavior*, Stanford, Cal., Stanford University Press, 1965.

[9] In this book see Alfred G. Meyer's analysis of Communist leadership and the depth interpretations by E. Victor Wolfenstein.

[10] H. J. Eysenck, *The Psychology of Politics*, London, Routledge and Kegan Paul, 1956; H. D. Lasswell, *Psychopathology and Politics* (Paperback Reprint with "Afterthoughts: Thirty Years Later"), New York, Viking Press, 1960; *Power and Personality* Paperback Reprint, New York, Viking Press, 1962.

[11] E. H. Erikson, *Young Man Luther: A Study in Psychoanalysis and History*, New York, Norton, 1958.

5. By focusing on a particular structure or role, researchers have sought to describe the style of political behavior that occurs and to relate style to psychocultural factors.

That the environment provided for each member (and for the entire membership) of an organ of government can influence political style was demonstrated for the Connecticut legislature by James D. Barber.[12] The conception of political style is not simple, since it characterizes a pattern of many components. There are, for instance, distinctive strategies employed by members of a legislature in dealing with leaders and followers on the floor, in committee meetings, and in the constituency. These strategies include discernible modes of communication and negotiation. They are accompanied by and interact with images of the self, with value demands in the name of the ego as a whole and of ego components with which the individual is identified, and with ways of thinking about the past, present, and future (with particular reference to coming elections). Barber obtained many hints of the manner of man who achieved one style or another.

In an important analysis of a series of interviews with German lawyers, Walter Weyrauch succeeded in formulating some highly suggestive hypotheses about the dynamics and style of lawyers in general as well as in contemporary Germany.[13] Among many significant points, those relating to basic perspectives on the law are notable. Traditionally the German lawyer expresses and defends the institutional system of a highly stratified, not a mobile, society. Weyrauch indicates how this affects the role of law in a body politic that formally speaking is now committed to the values and institutions of freedom.

6. Considering the elites of a body politic or a political system as a whole, investigators have undertaken to identify the styles of leadership characteristic of each and to isolate the factor combinations that account for the results.

Most elite studies describe the predispositions of official or unofficial leaders by examining previous environmental exposures. One of the most

[12] James D. Barber, *The Lawmakers; Recruitment and Adaptation to Legislative Life*, New Haven, Conn., Yale University Press, 1965. Style is a central category in several chapters of this book, especially in the chapters by Erwin C. Hargrove, Stanley Hoffman, and Alfred G. Meyer.

[13] Walter O. Weyrauch, *The Personality of Lawyers; A Comparative Study of Subjective Factors in Law, Based on Interviews with German Lawyers*, New Haven, Conn., Yale University Press, 1964. Glendon Schubert examines the flow of supreme court decisions by the body as a whole and by each Justice in order to characterize the perspectives that find expression during particular periods. The performance profile may, as Schubert points out, be shown to be related in various ways to personality structure and culture conditioning. A similar analysis could be made, in principle, at every layer of the office networks described by Joseph Schlesinger in this book.

prevalent factors referred to is "culture," in the sense of exposure to somewhat distinctive styles of life, such as "peripheral or nuclear communities" (for example, "Alsace Lorrainers" versus "midi"), upper, middle, or lower, class family and rearing ("large landholding," "small farmer," "farm laborer"), or particular interest groups ("specific school," "specific industry"). Because of the lack of data it is not, as a rule, possible to characterize the distribution of personality patterns.[14]

7. Concentrating on a cross section defined by age (or "stage" of development from birth to death), inquirers have explored the factors that affect political orientation.

In some ways the most promising approach to the assessment of political personality, role, and situation is by examining age groups, particularly pre-adults. The dependence of the "constitution" of a body politic on the successful formation among the young of the appropriate "character" has been a major emphasis in traditional political theory. Today research on the socialization of the young (or of strangers) can be conducted on a transnational scale. We have already seen how a relatively simple exploratory investigation can draw attention to a problem whose importance is conceded by any competent observer. Fred Greenstein reports that many elementary school pupils are explicitly identified with a political party, a finding that seems to indicate how American political institutions are able to shape the perspectives on which their smooth continuation depends.[15]

Even this cursory review of types of research by political scientists has provided many indications that students of politics often step outside the limits of their field as conventionally defined. They do not, of course, fail to feel responsible for investigating Franklin D. Roosevelt rather than John D. Rockefeller, Albert Einstein, or leaders in other fields of private activity. Subject to important reservations, this is a reasonable limitation, for other specialists are presumably better qualified to understand the subtleties of leadership in business, science, and the remaining sectors of society. In turn, political scientists are likely to be relatively well-equipped to comprehend the nuances of influence in the political process.

[14] Research on developing societies has thrown psychocultural factors into high relief. See the emphasis on "empathy" in D. Lerner, *The Passing of Traditional Society*, New York, Free Press, 1958; on "achievement" in D.S. McClelland, *The Achieving Society*, Princeton, N.J., Van Nostrand, 1961; on various mechanisms in E. Hagen, *On the Theory of Social Change*, Homewood, Ill., Dorsey Press, 1962. Consult especially the volumes edited by Lucian W. Pye and James S. Coleman in *Studies in Political Development*, Princeton, N.J., Princeton University Press, 1963. For bibliographic guidance to research on elites see Carl Beck's forthcoming volume in Lasswell, Lerner, and Pool, editors, *M.I.T. Studies in Comparative Politics Series*.

[15] F. I. Greenstein, *Children and Politics*, New Haven, Conn., Yale University Press, 1965. S. M. Lipset is projecting a series devoted to world youth in politics.

The reservations cursorily referred to are by no means trivial. With ample justification, political scientists often set aside the limits on the study of "government, law, and politics," as these terms are ordinarily understood in the United States. Since our task is comparative, we do not and cannot wisely limit ourselves to the "conventional" usages of any single society. In comparative research we find that institutions are similar in the degree to which they perform equivalent functions. Hence the professional political scientist takes responsibility for choosing a set of "functional" definitions. These definitions may point to political leadership in situations usually assumed to be outside the realm of government. Political scientists may then examine or encourage the examination of leadership in industry, the family, the school—in fact, in every institutional component of society.

The Distinguishing Features of Industrial Society

In recent years the attention of political scientists interested in leadership and other political phenomena has to an increasing degree turned outward toward Asia, Africa, and Latin America, where former colonies are demanding freedom and where the descendants of ancient empires are seeking to revive their former glories in the arena of contemporary world affairs. The key symbols of the time are national "independence," "development," or "growth"; however diversified the details may be, it is generally understood that these demands signify a determination to universalize the civilization whose distinguishing feature is science and technology.

Among political scientists one consequence of studying transitional government, law, and politics has been "the self-reference effect," the tendency to reexamine the self in the context of newly perceived likenesses and differences. We are in the process of increasing our self-knowledge, hence our renewed concern with leadership in highly industrialized societies.

Part of the problem is to achieve a clearer conception of what is meant by a highly industrialized society. The term "industry" emphasizes the institutional patterns specialized to production; among these the distinctive institutional practice appears to be ready application of scientific knowledge to the choice of energies and materials. From the age of steam we have moved rapidly to technologies based on chemistry, electromagnetism, and nuclear physics.

If we are to locate the role of politics, we must operate with a systematic conception of industrial society. A fundamental way to begin is by outlining a comprehensive model of social process, wherever it is; then the task is to distinguish the significant features of an industrial society.

Table 11.1.   Social Process

Man → Striving to optimalize preferred outcomes (values)
   → employs institutional practices
   → affecting resources

The generalized map (or model) in Table 11.1 calls attention to the inescapable features of any context in which human beings interact with one another, whether in the world as a whole or in a national or subnational community. As scientific observers we can identify the culminating events in the stream of interaction; for example, as political scientists we focus on victory or defeat in votes or fights (the power value). The institutional practices specialized to voting or fighting are "government, law, and politics"; further specification indicates that buildings, locations, and weapons are among the resources mobilized in the power process.

A relatively refined definition of power outcomes (decisions) is that they are outcomes that importantly affect the values at stake in the social context under consideration; also, they are expected to be enforced by using severe sanctions against any deviant. The outcome itself is the giving, receiving, withholding, or rejecting of support. Table 11.1 is a dynamic model since it presents human beings taking initiatives or reacting in ways that they perceive as most likely to yield net advantages in terms of all preferred outcomes (values). Not only power values are sought; hence our model must be specified to include a set of categories to be employed by scientific observers in classifying all outcomes. In addition to power (P), for instance, there is enlightenment (E), which refers to the giving, receiving, withholding, or rejecting of knowledge. Since scientific knowledge plays a conspicuous part in industrial societies, this will be of particular interest to us. On the list is wealth (W), which refers to claims to goods and services; well-being (B), or health, safety, and comfort; skill (S), or opportunity to require and exercise excellence in specific operations; affection (A), or intimacy, friendship, and loyalty; respect (R), or recognition; and rectitude (D), or opportunity to worship and act responsibly.

Table 11.2 amplifies Table 11.1 as a guide to more detailed inquiry into pre-outcome, outcome, and post-outcome sequences of interactions.

Each category can be applied to each value of the list given above $(P\ E\ W\ S\ B\ S\ A\ R\ D)$ or to all. For instance, perspectives refer to values, and so do situations.

How can this map be utilized to formulate a working model of industrial society? Industrialism is partly characterized by institutional practices that employ impersonal sources of energy (nuclear, electromagnetic,

Table 11.2.   Social Process (Amplified)

Participants
   with varying *perspectives* (expectations, demands, identities)
     interacting in *situations* (organized, unorganized)
       controlling various *base values*
         utilizing *strategies*
           to optimalize values *outcomes* (*P E W B S A R D*)
           and *effects.*

---

and so on) in production. Typically these practices introduce a complex pattern of new and interdependent situations related to production. Initially, man-machine combinations are applied to raw resources (mining, agriculture, etc.). They are then adapted to the processing of partly finished resources and to the dispersion of the finished product for use in further production or consumption. Societies are industrialized when they have achieved a self-sustaining flow of capital accumulation for expanding production utilizing scientifically based technology.

The situations that the new technology brings into existence provide a common focus of attention for all who work in each; in turn, this tends to establish perspectives of common identity, expectation, and value demand. Sometimes demands are precipitated by a sense of deprivation in the work relationship itself; hence arise protests and programs for obtaining higher wages, shorter hours, and better working conditions.

Industrialism is usually introduced at locations close to raw resources or markets; new locations attract or conscript labor, providing sites for mines, power plants, construction work, or manufacturing. Typically, urbanization is stimulated, since workers abandon farming or herding operations, which, in turn, affects family life. Unless advanced planning occurs, the workers are often separated from their families. In advanced industrial societies, however, these separations are less frequent, partly because urbanization and the changes that accompany it transform family institutions by emphasizing the primacy of the small nuclear unit over the extended family and kinship groups of traditional culture.

Whatever disturbs the family-kinship structure of traditional society is likely to modify the class and caste system of the established order. Instead of directing respect almost exclusively to elders, new respect institutions emerge in which workers' trade union officials, foremen and submanagers, owners (or controllers) and top managers become the recipients of awe or ridicule. Although the hierarchy of economic life in an industrializing country may be laterally recruited from the ascriptive hierarchies of an earlier time, the carry-over is usually incomplete. Hence greater opportunity exists for individuality, for the attaining of self-respect based on personal achievement. Money income increases independence (if the market does, in fact, supply commodities), and typically allows women, young people, low caste, and other low-respect strata to perceive themselves differently, thus paving the way for being seen differently by others.

Crucial to the rapid expansion of advanced industrialism and of mobility is the establishment of educational institutions that modify the skill capital of individuals and of the social aggregate. Reading, writing, and arithmetic make accessible to the individual a range of new economic opportunities; and intermediate, secondary, and advanced education not only increases job capability but furnishes background to the people who pursue knowledge as an end in itself. This goes beyond the transmission and exercise of skill to enlightenment, which includes redrawing the individual's map of knowledge by work done in laboratories, field expeditions, and libraries.

It was, after all, the fusion of an emerging scientific view of man and nature with practical know-how that accounts for the fabulous dynamics of advanced industrial societies. Today, for example, scientific research is an activity carried on for its own sake by many men and women, young and old, who respond to the challenge of overcoming the clouds of ignorance that stand between man and knowledge of his habitat in space and the fundamental laws of life. The base values required to permit thousands of scientists to devote themselves to the advancement of knowledge (enlightenment) are supplied in modern societies as a result of the cumulative acceptance of the overriding myth that "research pays," whether the payoffs are in terms of production, military preparedness, health, or comfort.

Whatever changes the stream of daily human adjustments to one another or to nature is bound to modify the prevalent standards of responsible and nonresponsible conduct, hence to alter the observance, interpretation, or even the accepted source of ethical norms. The industrial societies of the European World have developed from societies in which religious institutions played a major role in defining and applying ethical prescriptions. It is commonly said that an outstanding feature of industrial societies is the spread of secular perspectives, an institutional change usually attributed to a confluence of several factors. Industrialism is ideologically pro-scientific, since science is perceived as the Aladdin's lamp of technological innovation. The scientific view of the world is usually described as tentative, exploratory, and empirical, rather than dogmatic, expository, and dialectical. The rise of modern science and technology was repeatedly attacked in the name of religion by the top elite of ecclesiastical hierarchies. In the eighteenth century the churches combined with the landed nobility of France to fight a revolution whose ideologists felt great admiration for scientific enlightenment. In the twentieth century a similar coalition tried to block the Russian Revolution; and although the prestigious churches of the West have largely accommodated their doctrine to the findings of science, the sects that cater to the less advantaged strata of society continue to mobilize hostility to the "atheism" or "agnosticism" of science.

The Political Features of Industrial Society

At this point we turn to the institutional features of industrialism—government, law, and politics—on which we are chiefly focused. If we glance at the world arena in which highly industrial societies operate, the outstanding characteristic is not change, but absence of change. Long before the rise of industrialized bodies politic, the institutions of war and preparation for war were the most fundamental facts. Since they shared a common expectation of violence in a divided world, the powers engaged in the making and remaking of coalitions by a strategy of defending or improving their position (in terms of power, wealth, respect, and other values). Modern science and technology have increased the degree of interdependence while simultaneously increasing the realism of the expectation of violence. The authoritative and controlling elites of industrial nations have thus far refrained from introducing institutional changes that would substitute a unified world for a divided world and transform the institution of war into institutions for policing civil order. Presumably this is to be explained by examining the perspectives of elites as they actively engage in the decision process. Research will probably demonstrate that the policy of innovation is perceived as affording more net deprivations than indulgences to those who are responsible for promoting, accepting, and giving effect to the policy.

When described at any cross section in time, the highly industrial nations exhibit a wide range of differences in their internal institutions of power. In fact, the diversity is so great that there is no present agreement on a political model that summarizes the characteristic features of a hypothetical entity called the political system of a highly industrial society. A few reminders will corroborate the point.

In regard to the structure of organized arenas, the following conditions exist. In the United States, for instance, the scope of government is far less inclusive of the whole of society than it is in socialist countries. The governmental sector varies in the degree of centralization—decentralization, a difference partly expressed in the contrast between féderal and unitary institutions. At the national level, the United States has a relatively deconcentrated government enshrined in the formula of a coordinate, tripartite separation of authority. In the Soviet Union, however, decision-making authority is highly concentrated in a dual governmental and party hierarchy.

Comparative political analysts emphasize differences in the degree of competition permitted in the stirring up of public dissent, especially by organizing political parties and in the range of promotional activity permitted to pluralized associations or individuals. Contrasting degrees of legal protection against public officials are given to individuals and associations.

In demonstrating the theme of diversity, stress is laid on the carry-over into industrialized society of political predispositions and institutional practices that are deeply entrenched in the culture of each society. In 1917 Lenin dreamed of dispensing with a trained officialdom; once in power he quickly took steps that culminated in consolidating a bureaucracy far more comprehensive and authoritarian than that which existed under the Tsar. The social-democratic and the anarchistic strands in the ideology of the revolutionary leadership led to the proclamation of democracy; yet the Revolution soon resumed the practice of autocratic or despotic power. In Great Britain the evolution of popular government was continued, and in many ways perfected, with the advent of advanced industrialization.

It is possible to identify cyclical fluctuations in a political culture. Stanley Hoffman has delineated such a pattern in the alternation of heroic leadership with the trading style of governmental and party institutions which were expected to sustain the status quo among the segmented components of French society.[16]

The most obvious difficulty in attempting to generalize a model that adequately characterizes the political system is the urgency and the dynamism of industrialization. Part of the task is to find an approach sufficiently flexible to bring out the timing of phenomena. Evidence is plentiful, for instance, that quantitative description of the changing social and political processes can narrow the relevant issues. Gross national product per capita is a convenient indicator of industrialization since it is only possible to achieve high levels of production in a large country by using science-based technology. Many indications show that advanced industrialization economies must stimulate and permit high levels of mass consumption (partly as a means of forestalling political division and conflict). We may therefore classify the nation states of the world in five groups of societies: "High Mass Consumption," "Industrial Revolution," "Transi-

[16] See Stanley Hoffman, "Heroic Leadership: The Case of Modern France," Chapter 5.

tional," "Traditional," and "Traditional Primitive" societies.[17] The complexity of the task of identifying a distinctive political model is indicated when we note that the United States, Luxembourg, and New Zealand, for example, are bracketed together in the first group; the USSR, Italy, and Mexico in the second; Turkey, Ghana, and Peru in the third; Haiti, India, and China in the fourth; and Uganda, Burma, and Nepal in the last.

The trend data permit correlations to be made that point strongly, if not conclusively, toward various causal explanations. For instance, the "high mass-consumption" societies are all bodies politic having a popular form of government and—with West Germany as a possible exception—having a history of considerable devotion to institutions where power is widely rather than narrowly shared. Evidently the leadership role has been performed with sufficient effect in these communities to allow and to encourage industrialization by consent, rather than by coercive imposition.

In a relatively confused and rapidly shifting context scientific inquiry can sometimes be focused on promising problems by setting up a developmental construct designed to characterize the principal features of the past ("from what") and a possible, if not indeed probable, future ("toward what"). Can we identify the factors of political relevance that appear to be closely connected with techno-scientific institutions? With these in mind can we identify significant political developments likely to achieve stability as industrialization continues to spread? Consider the following consequences of the new technology.

1. *Interdependencies increase.* This means that whether we examine localities, nations, or the world as a whole we find that technology increases the extent and the magnitude of mutual influencing.

2. *Expectations of interdependency rise.* The present point is that people quickly or slowly become aware of the fact of interdependence.

3. *Expectations concerning the possibility of control increase.* Mutual influencing seems to indicate that people can deliberately affect what goes on; hence more people become aware of the possibility that they are being deliberately influenced by others and that they themselves may be able to join the game.

4. *Demands to participate in the influencing process increase.* Changed patterns of expectation provide an image of the self as a potential initiator of influence on others. This increases the likelihood that individuals will demand of themselves that they become effective) and that they will de-

---

[17] B. M. Russett and H. R. Alker, Jr., K. W. Deutsch, H. D. Lasswell, *World Handbook of Political and Social Indicators,* New Haven, Conn., Yale University Press, pp. 294–298.

mand of others that they permit it; also, they are more likely to try to make themselves effective in specific situations in the social process.

5. *The individual ego becomes identified with other egos as the range of exposure to situations increases.* Interdependence is a result and an occasion for participating in new situations and in widening the range of exposure to new experience. As new people are met—fellow workers, residents, sportsmen, and so on—the individual ego develops more complex images of how other people feel and think (we say that he empathizes with them); he also perceives himself as resembling other people in various ways, thereby achieving a common identity (by including the symbols that refer to others as part of the self). He also achieves negative identification with others and excludes them from the primary ego. "They" are "foreigners"; "we" are "American."

6. *The media of public communication play a particularly important role in providing images of the context and in mobilizing collective action.* In preindustrial societies an influential part is played by oral networks of communication that spread news, gossip, and rumor about the world beyond the horizon of direct observation open to most individuals. With the invention of movable type and its application to printing, literacy became more widespread; hence books and other printed media played a much larger part in reaching young and old than handwritten manuscripts. Scientific technology has not eliminated oral networks; it has, however, utterly transformed the media of print and supplemented them with media of instantaneous dissemination. From the earliest years, young and old are exposed to an unceasing barrage from television, radio, newspapers, and books. In every nation the images of reality are largely dependent on these exposures. This is true of the images of authority and control—that is, of all value-shaping and sharing processes and institutional practices. Public media are the instruments through which the perspectives and operations of thousands or millions of people are mobilized (or immobilized) for collective action.

7. *The operation of modern society calls for interlocking personnel in organized and unorganized situations that reach from the smallest locality or pluralistic group to the most inclusive national or international context.* Interdependence requires interlocking personnel; that is, an interdependent society cannot rely entirely on public media. Primary (face-to-face) relations are essential if perspectives and operations are to be coordinated among government services, industrial plants, medical facilities, schools, or among the units in any other sector of society. The face-to-face relations may be incidental to appointed bureaucracies, elected hierarchies (and co-archies), or of informal grouping. The interlocking contact may be part of a legislating function (prescribing); or perhaps it may relate to

other outcome functions in the power, wealth, or any other value process.

8. *Science and technology favor sudden innovation, diffusion, and restriction.* The social process is always the scene of some degree of innovation, hence of diffusion and restriction. Science and technology institutionalize innovation and thereby increase the likelihood of new and abrupt change. Inspired by ideas for new research and development, scientists and technicians initiate research programs on scales both large and small. As with nuclear and space science, the projects often involve extensive reallocation of man and materials and the exploitation of new locations. Technology creates new industries—the automobile, oil, electronics, and so on.

9. *Science and technology create a data-rich civilization,* since the storage, retrieval and processing of data is a necessary condition of modern research and development.

10. *Science and technology increase the values at the disposal of scientifically trained persons and organizations.* Knowledge has no limit; the larger the sphere of knowledge the greater the surface in contact with the unknown. Hence the "knowledge dynamism" of an industrial society.

Among implications for the power process are the following.

1. *The consequences for the power process of the factors intimately connected with industrial society are contradictory and depend on the factor configuration in which they appear.* If, for example, we consider whether the principal impact is toward wider or narrower power sharing, the significance of the time relation among various factors is especially evident. For instance, it may be asserted that the computer, which has an unlimited potentiality for data storage and retrieval, is most economically applied in a single gigantic system, and the centralization of data carries with it the invasion of individual and group privacy for the benefit of centralized power.[18] Intelligence and appraisal functions, when implemented by the new technology, will put central agencies at a great advantage and foster the erosion of initiative and of realistic self-confidence everywhere. In a world where the expectation of violence continues, the boundaries set by the divided world put the only effective limit on centralization. In a divided world arena computers will be utilized, not by the authorities of a unified globe but by the central agencies of the principal states, who will presumably employ them to maintain power at home and abroad. Internally this signfies an effective narrowing of power and a tendency to approximate the garrison-police form of politicized society.

[18] See A. Westin, *Science, Privacy, and Freedom,* New York, Columbia University Press, 1966.

These tendencies are not necessarily destined to succeed, it may be argued, since the internal institutions in many polities foster counterdispositions. Hence the demand to share power may lead to effective demand from all party and pressure group leaders, as well as scholars, for access to any comprehensive system of data handling, with the result that opinions critical of official views can be realistically justified. The strength of equalitarian tendencies can be partly demonstrated by noticing the tenacity with which popular government has thus far survived among the "high mass consumption" states.

2. *The fate of popular government will depend in no small measure on whether the net impact of those who function as leaders can mobilize the symbols, operations, and resources capable of acting realistically and promptly to maintain democratic public order while adapting institutions to obviate destructive changes.* Although we have indicated that the future cannot be assumed to be a foregone conclusion, it is not difficult to identify several factors that make for destructive outbursts and erosions of democratic public order: (*a*) The proliferation of new situations multiplies territorial and pluralistic groups having distinctive experiences, hence distinctive identities, value demands, and expectations; such a development multiplies the particular interests that are championed in the body politic, precipitating conflicts that undermine public order and security. (*b*) The expectation that control of social institutions is possible diminishes the propensity of the population to acquiesce patiently in deprivations; hence in times of adversity conflicts quickly develop that undermine settlement by persuasive assent. (*c*) Sudden innovations are likely to carry with them abrupt deprivations of territorial communities and especially of pluralistic groups who, for instance, suffer obsolescence of skill, loss of a respected place in society, loss of capital or income, family disruption, anixety or depression, or disturbing provocations to unethical conduct; such crisis deprivations predispose toward destructive action. (*d*) If the scientists and technologists gain respect and other value indulgences, many of them are likely to take a noninvolved, manipulative, and impatient attitude toward people as a whole, thus undermining acceptance of the democratic ideology. (*e*) If young people are expected to assume full adult responsibilities later and later in life, there may be failure to identify with the responsibilities of a mature adult and a cumulative sense of alienation that undermines the capability of the public order to mobilize "the minds and hearts" of the body politic for public service in either crisis or intercrisis periods. (*f*) If the growth of opulence in an industrial society decreases the willingness of parents (and parent surrogates) to endure direct encounters in which ambivalence is met and conquered by firmness and love, the capability of human beings to achieve identification may be diminished.

Leadership in the Political Process

The critical role of leadership in affecting the structure and function of politics in industrial society has been intimated in the preceding analysis. As a guide to the study of leadership in industrial or indeed any society a generalized model is needed. Table 11.3 provides this model of a stable leadership.

Table 11.3.   A Stable Leadership Relation

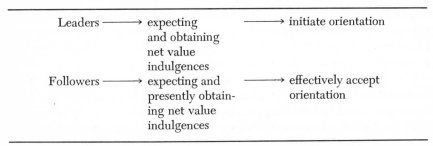

Any comprehensive explanation of a leadership relationship will account for what both leaders and followers get out of it. Presumably anyone who takes an initiative affecting the orientation of others expects to be better off by taking this initiative than by not doing so. Similarly, anyone who effectively follows an initiative expects to be better off.

Table 11.4 paves the way for the analysis of the leadership pattern in political situations by outlining seven decision outcomes. Since we are chiefly concerned with the pattern of leadership in political situations, Table 11.4 draws attention to the several outcomes that taken aggregately are the decision process.

Table 11.4.   The Decision Process (Outcomes)

Intelligence ⟶ Promotion ⟶ Prescription ⟶ Invocation ⟶
Application ⟶ Termination ⟶ Appraisal

The model can be used to identify structures specialized to each function and individuals whose role is specialized to each. Overt and covert "intelligence" agencies can be found in government; also the role of some members of a committee may be the intelligence task of informing the others about recent or prospective developments. "Promotional" activities are carried on by political parties; some individuals may emphasize the promotional role in committees. "Prescribing" occupies legislatures; and in a committee one person may be much involved with formulating general rules of procedure. In the whole body politic "invocation" is exemplified in the function of an arresting officer, who must provisionally characterize the relation between a concrete situation and a prescription. Complaints— also an invoking function—may be the self-selected province of particular committee members. "Applications" are final characterizations of a concrete state of affairs in terms of prescription, as when a court decides for the plaintiff or the defendant. Similarly, a committee member may be accepted as the last word on certain types of controversies. The "terminating" function may be exercised by an agency charged with locating and eliminating obsolete prescriptions or by an individual who is charged by a committee with reviewing and revising obsolete rules.

The "appraising" function may be the province of a commission to investigate and report on successes and failures in foreign policy or of a committee member who characterizes committee policies in similar terms.

The seven categories outlined in Table 11.4 can be used to construct a political systems model. From historical and contemporary studies of government, law, and politics, we know that in a given body politic changes of a given magnitude in one function are likely to precipitate changes in all the other functions. For example, news of external threat (intelligence) may precipitate promotional programs in favor of more armament; legislation may follow; the legislation may be invoked to inaugurate administrative action; administrative applications may occur; old legislation may be terminated; appraisals may be made of past policy. Actually, changes may be initiated anywhere within the system; moreover, they may precipitate immediate consequences anywhere within it. A completely worked out model would emphasize these interdependent routines by showing arrows that point in both directions between every two functions.

A systems model is complete when it includes the perspectives of the participants in sufficient detail to show that practices are continued as long as the effective participants in the decision process expect to be relatively better off by adhering to routine than by departing from it. This point is made in Table 11.5 which expresses the expectations that must be sustained by the results that come from continuing to play a leader or follower role. The extent to which a given structure in the decision process, such as a legislature, is able to maintain an established degree of leadership depends on the expectations of all concerned that they are better off by continuing than by changing. A corollary of the analysis is that when effective decision makers change their expectations of net advantage, they support changed patterns of leadership.

Table 11.5 provides a more refined model of the leadership relation in politics.

The outline expands a long question about leader-follower interactions: Who, with what perspectives, interacting in what arenas, with a given value asset and liability position, employing which strategies, influences what outcomes, with what effects?

Within the frame of reference provided by Tables 11.3 to 11.5 it is possible to locate researches of various degrees of scope. The macro-studies may explore the differential recruitment of leaders and followers in industrial democracies or totalitarian powers and disclose the sources in terms of culture, class, and interest groups. Microstudies can bring personality variables into the picture, supplementing the first approximations of the macrostudies by data that permit a wider range of explanation, projection, and policy management.

For microstudies, in particular, we need more formal conceptions of various categories than have been called for before. Clearly the term "act" is fundamental to an interaction analysis. A very general definition refers to it as a sequence of subjective and nonsubjective events (perspectives, operations) engaged in by an "actor" and regarded as a completed pattern by the scientific observer or by the actor. It is important to note that the observer must apply his own conception of pattern as an aid to discovering how the "actor" perceives completion and how such perspectives condition the completed act. The observer may regard an act of "voting" as complete when the ballot is marked; the actor may think of the act not as "voting" but as an economic transaction that is completed only when he collects his pay for putting some marks on paper. Unless the scientific observer is aware of the voter's conception of what he is doing, he will select irrelevant factors to explain the direction and magnitude of the interaction.

Formally, then, a completed act is defined as a sequence of events passing through "impulse" to "subjectivity" and "expression." To bring out its relationship to the maximization (optimalization) postulate we may add the phrase "terminating in gratification." This extension underlines the "dynamic" dimensions of the sequence, indicating that the initial "impulses" are so patterned that they are followed by one set of subjectivities rather than another and that the selective factor is "pointing" toward "value indulgence" rather than "value deprivational" events.

No one act is alone in the context of all the acts of an individual. Various degrees of facilitation and conflict occur; hence the mechanisms by which conflicts are resolved are peculiarly important.

If a voter must choose between going to the polls and having a haircut, he may complete one or the other act with little intensity of feeling. This is rejection of completion *a* by *b*. If a voter is deeply involved in the

Table 11.5. The Leadership Relation in Decision Process

Participants	Perspectives	Arenas	Base Values	Strategies	Outcomes	Effect
Leaders	Value demands	Organized	Value assets	Coercive	Alignment	Value
Followers	Expectations	Unorganized	Value liabilities	Persuasive	(won, lost,	accumulation
	Identities			Symbols-resources	noncommitted)	enjoyment
					Pivot, initiative	Institution
					(function)	initiation
						diffusion
						restriction

Table 11.6.   Conflicting Acts

IMPULSE	SUBJECTIVITY	EXPRESSION
⟶	⟶	REJECTION
⟶	——	
⟶	⟶	SUPPRESSION
⟶	——	
⟶	⟶	REPRESSION
⟶	—	
⟶	⟶	RESISTANCE
——		

election but a business obligation suddenly presents itself, he may or may not go to the polls after a struggle that ends in dismissing the suppressed alternative from his attention. A voter may have a tremendous urge to kill one of the candidates; and this may precipitate a terrific conflict with demands on himself to act in law abiding fashion. The vivid conflict may be ended in repression; the person may not allow himself to recall his intense blood lust. Subsequently his impulses to kill public authority figures can be aborted at the presubjective level (resistance).

In this connection the term "personality" can be employed to designate the stable patterns of acts exhibited by a person. In modified psychoanalytic terminology the subjective and expressive patterns are the "ego"; the channels established by repression and suppression are the "superego"; the earlier impulse channels are the "id."

More salient to our task is a mode of describing personality that emphasizes the value-institutional orientations and the mechanisms (inner strategies) by which acts are interrelated. In this frame of reference we describe individuals according to the intensity of their effective demands for power and other values (including the specific institutional patterns involved) and the strategies by which conflicting impulses are dealt with.

The examination of collective processes requires a somewhat amplified model in order to put the relevant factors in researchable perspective. The general outline of the social process dealt with value-shaping and

Table 11.7.   Conflicting Collective Demands

————————→	Rejection
———————	
————————→	Suppression
————	
————————→	Repression
—	
	(Resistance)

sharing; it did not, however, expand the institutional components by putting the strategies of conflict resolution into focus.

A collective demand is *rejected* if after the outcome phase there is little attempt made to continue the effort to influence decision in favor of the blocked alternative. A demand is *suppressed* when a moderate degree of coercion is successfully used to put a stop to further public promotional activity. A demand is *repressed* when further support is not tolerated publicly or privately. *Collective repression* is not necessarily as deep as individual repression since individual repression, strictly defined, relegates the repressed impulse to the out-of-conscious, where it is prevented from reappearing at the full focus of waking attention by the anxieties generated by the defense mechanisms of the superego.

The analysis makes it clear that the processes of any system of public order may receive relatively distinctive patterns of support. Some are positively incorporated in individual superegos (consciences) and may vary among subcultural, class, and interest groups. The same prescriptions may be vigorously opposed and persistently evaded in some local, class, and interest groups. And the prescriptions may be assessed with little effective involvement according to simple expediency. (The relationships are among *ego, superego,* and *id; mores, countermores,* and *expediencies.*)

The revised model calls attention to the complex factor-combinations that sustain the leadership aggregate of any body politic, indicating the range of demands, expectations, and identifications that provide pockets of support for a leadership relation. No large-scale community has yet been fully enough described to enable political scientists to demonstrate these "pockets" or predispositions and to show how the leaders are related to them. On the basis of the usual sources of historical and contemporary information, it is at least possible to assert that some leaders are specialized to "mores" predispositions (such as those who appeal to established religious identities and standards), to the "countermores" (such as the "criminal" and "irresponsible" elements), and to "expediences" (such as leaders who are loosely identified with several groups).

Similarly, we can provisionally identify the strategy of action most congenial to leaders. Some of them exacerbate conflict among and within groups, holding firmly to positions that can neither be *compromised* nor *integrated*. In a compromise solution the parties to the arrangement can identify their gains and losses in relatively definite terms. An employer-employee controversy, for instance, can terminate in a contract that turns down demands to cut hours of labor, although hourly wages are increased. An integrative solution, in contrast, provides an acceptable result that cannot be clearly perceived by the parties in terms of "wins" and "losses." The labor-management contract may sidestep wage and hour demands by instituting an inquiry into profit sharing, efficiency ratings, and pensions.

The amplification of a political systems model ultimately requires the inclusion of personality variables as well as those of culture, class, and interest. For instance, a drop-off in the recruitment of the brightest and most ambitious members of a rising generation can be expected to contribute to the decline of any political structure. A "leadership crisis" may be deferred for several years, but such long-term factors are among those that research is concerned with bringing into the open. Many of these interconnections are given prominence by researchers who focus on particular organizations.

If the influence of personality factors is to be convincingly shown, the limitations of other factors must be indicated. This is the problem that gives particular interest to the study of political careers. As previously indicated, Edinger's analysis of Schumacher is a good example, since the author examines the political situations in which Schumacher operated at successive stages of his career and demonstrates that Schumacher acted "rigidly" by continuing his policies in the face of high political costs. Rivals for party and national leadership often took more flexible views. Clearly Edinger makes a strong case for the relevance of searching for "personality" factors in explaining Schumacher's intransigence.

The Strategy of Continuing Observation

The advantages of continuing observation of the leadership function are pertinent to each of the five intellectual tasks relating to the problem-oriented approach. The goal model, for instance, can be respecified as knowledge expands. Initially it is enough to say that leaders ought to be chosen from individuals whose egocentricity is not so great that it seriously interferes with their capacity to empathize with other people. If our understanding is to grow, it must be possible to give operational meaning to "egocentricity" and "empathy." The development of appropriate tests requires research; the validation of tests depends on having access to "real world situations."

The most immediate advantage to be obtained from continuing observation is in the description of trends in time and space. It is important, for example, to learn that tension and unrest are on the increase in the middle echelons of military and civilian officialdom and that regional offices are focal points of internal friction that find partial expression in "bureaucratism." Such information is obviously important for policy purposes. However, the immediate question is scientific: What factor combinations explain the situation? The analysis of promotion rates may show that the middle ranks are advancing less rapidly today than they did ten years ago. Or if this is not true, a simple macroanalysis of the "time spent away from headquarters" may indicate that mobility has dropped considerably. This gives a clue for microanalytic researches by interview or participant observation of selected samples to discover whether the decline in mobility affects the value gratifications realized on the job. It may be that when officials are immobilized at headquarters, they obtain less satisfaction from performing a leadership role than when they dealt directly with workers and clients in the field. Many of the most ambitious, well-balanced, and competent members of the service may transfer from it, leaving relatively conflicted personalities to compete with one another in marshaling discontent.

Continuing observation clearly provides a body of information for projecting the probable sequence of future development and for devising appropriate policies. It is not always recognized that continuing observation provides an important opportunity for scientists to modify their own policies of investigation in ways that contribute to the advancement of knowledge. We have emphasized the factor-combinations that account for the style and impact of leadership; hence the importance of field researches, and especially of field studies that attempt to explore scientific hypotheses in unfolding situations. The strategy of prototyping is, in fact, somewhat different from the strategy of experimentation in a tightly controlled situation or of correlation studies. Prototyping is appropriate when the scientist is able to enter the situation and to innovate partial controls as a means of evaluating hypotheses.[19]

[19] R. Rubenstein and H. D. Lasswell, *The Sharing of Power in a Psychiatric Hospital*, New Haven, Conn., Yale University Press, 1966, especially pp. 268–273.

In connection with leadership problems, prototyping is a promising strategy of knowledge, since it permits institutional practices to be pre-tested before they are targets of controversy in major political arenas. Many innovations can be initiated and evaluated for the purpose of un-derstanding and modifying leadership relations in industrial societies. By prototyping it is feasible to examine in selected situations the impact and the modifiability of the factors closely tied to scientific and technological innovations. It is practicable to explore the scope of interdependency and especially of awareness of it and the growth of expectations concerning the possibility of influence, and of demands to exercise influence. Changes in the identification of egos with one another and in the relative effect of direct experience and of experience with mass media are within the range of researchable phenomena. The consequences of sudden innova-tion and of computerized data systems, as well as of the prominent role of scientists and engineers, are inviting lines of investigation.

It is to be emphasized that the politically significant context can be described by methods that vary in "intensiveness," depending on the com-plexity of the observational technique that is used or the length of contact between the scientific inquirer and the events in his field of observation. The records of voting behavior by electorates or other decision structures can be obtained with comparatively little effort and utilized in building up a micropicture of politics. The techniques employed in processing the data may be much more complicated than those used in gathering it. Survey interviews call for more intensive contact with the scientific oper-ation at the data-gathering phase; and more intensive interviews, tests, or participant observation are even more elaborate modes of data gather-ing.

In connection with several scientific operations it may be necessary to supplement the layman-like knowledge common in the culture by periods of prolonged training. For many purposes a short course can supply all the information required. Psychoanalytic psychiatry, on the other hand, calls for long professional preparation. Efficient research often depends on teams composed of specialists in many skills, since it is rare that political scientists will acquire an elaborate double competence. Hence it is rec-ognized that interdisciplinary approaches depend on cooperation, and particularly on the willingness of those who use contrasting skills and rather different theoretical models to communicate with one another.

A striking example of the problem involved is communication between psychoanalytic psychiatrists and political scientists. The most stimulating approach to the study of psychocultural factors in politics is provided by psychoanalysts. We classify psychoanalysis among the intensive methods of scientific observation since it requires professional training, relies on distinctive procedures, and depends on a protracted relationship between analyst and subject. The interview brings into the open data about the finer patterns of culture, since it encourages the recall of experiences from early as well as recent years of exposure to the culture, class, interest, and personality environment. The value orientations and the mechanisms revealed in the analytic situation are, in varying degree, representative of the cultural context.

The psychoanalyst's frame of reference is the personality system; the political scientist, by contrast, is primarily focused on group systems. Hence the political scientist begins by examining the decision process as disclosed by publicly available information, and he moves with ever-increasing intensity of observation and analysis to the study of more detailed features of the context, including the selective influence of personality variables on perspectives and operations. Psychoanalysts, if they pool their case reports, can move toward more knowledge of the collective practices affecting the growth of personality and, in return, are influenced by personality. Thanks to the division of labor in the intellectual community, it is not necessary to postpone an understanding of personality until an elite corps of scientists comes into existence whose professional training includes both psychiatry and political science.

More immediate results can be obtained by encouraging some psychiatrists to interest themselves sufficiently in the political process to formulate tentative hypotheses inspired by the data available to them in psychiatric situations. Some political scientists can obtain enough knowledge of psychiatry, including psychoanalysis, to comprehend these new hypotheses and to explore them within the limits of the observational procedures to which the political scientist is accustomed (or traditional procedures may be modified to make them efficient). Psychoanalysis is (1) a set of theoretical models principally designed to explain mental health and disease and (2) a set of procedures specialized to obtaining and processing data. The most distinctive procedure is a combination of "free association" by the patient and "interpretation" by the analyst. Although the procedures of psychoanalysis have been transferred to other situations than the interplay of physician and patient, the distinctive theory of psychoanalysis is chiefly designed to make sense of the experience of participants in the traditional setting.

Nevertheless, the psychocultural hypotheses generated by psychoanalysts or inspired by psychoanalysis are amenable to research that obtains data by the use of procedures that differ from those employed in the traditional doctor-patient relationship. The time-cluster of factors in the political context constitutes a self-contained frame of reference, even as the physician's frame of reference is a self-contained field of observation.

Why are psychoanalytic models of personality development of any interest to political scientists? The conception of personality can be generalized as a dynamic model in which impulses of "love" are competing with impulses of "aggression." The significance of culture, including political culture, is that it provides an environment that affects the relative intensity and timing of effective expression of these rival dispositions. The most challenging hypothesis of all is that civilization as we know it is incapable of achieving permanent freedom from aggressive crises of such urgency that they threaten civilization (to say nothing of the survival of the species).[20] The essential point can be simplified by asserting that civilization demands repression of aggressive impulses; but such repression cannot be completely successful.

Examine the way in which Alexander Mitscherlich (Chapter 2 of this book) employs the basic model, to raise questions about the stability of industrial societies. Reference has been made to the diagnoses of "alienation" that are frequently heard in "industrial" and especially relatively "opulent" societies like the United States. The essential difficulty is traced to a failure that can be partially formulated as an early failure of repression, suggesting that civilization itself is insufficiently incorporated into the personality systems formed by exposure to higher industrialism. Mitscherlich suggests that comparatively successful incorporation can occur in *a situation in which ambivalence toward a significant person* is resolved by sacrifice on one side and intensified love in response to the sacrifice of destructiveness.

How can the studies of political socialization be influenced by such a model? The construct is highly suggestive of hypotheses that can be explored by political scientists acting in conjunction with other students of socialization. It is recognized by Mitscherlich that the basic model must be amplified to refer operationally to early patterns of interaction in the social environment and *carefully timed*. This is indicated by the point that early toilet training may not be affected by opulent industrialism, even though later experiences may be changed in disorganizing ways. Can it be shown, for instance, that mothers diminish their demands on the child to sacrifice; hence, since no great sacrifice is made, the mother also diminishes the love that she gives the child? Is it true that ambivalences must be worked out toward *one* person (such as the mother) rather than overcome by exposure to a peer *group* environment that insists on sacrifices of extreme aggressivity in return for respect and other positive indulgences? Furthermore, how does exposure to the remote environment as represented in mass media programs affect development? Do displace-

[20] Formulated explicitly by Freud in *Civilization and Its Discontents*, London, Hogarth Press, 1949.

ments onto political symbols (partisan, governmental) diminish the demand for (need of) giving (or receiving) love or aggression in the immediate environment?

The essential point to be stressed is that every context constituted by an observer and his field is an independent frame of reference. It is not to be assumed that because the same symbols, for example, "love" or "aggression," are used in the clinic and in describing party negotiation the "same" factors are being studied. Certainly they are not being described by the "same" operational indices, since the political observer cannot make use of prolonged free association without disrupting the phenomena which it is his task to explain. It is not necessary or useful to think in terms of "reducing" political contexts to psychoanalytic contexts, any more than it is necessary to "reduce" psychoanalytic phenomena to electrochemical contexts. However, it is important to retain the frames of reference of the community decision process and to reexamine these macroevents by micromethods, not for the purpose of doing away with the macroevents but as a strategy of disclosing finer factor-combinations that can multiply the range of policy alternatives open for coping with them.

A continuing program of observation designed to provide an adequate flow of information for intelligence and appraisal purposes about the leadership function in advanced industrial societies will find a place for research approaches of the kind that have already been pioneered. There will be a place for studies of prominent figures; and there will be ample room for researches that take off from an official or unofficial structure of government. Models of power-centered personalities will gain more immediate significance as they bring out the distinctive cluster of value priorities that distinguish various patterns of conventional leadership. Studies that focus on structures and roles will continue to highlight the changing or permanent styles in politics and add to our knowledge of the relevant psychocultural dynamics. Despite the diversified environments generated in industrial society, homogeneities may emerge in the elite aggregates of power that will set them apart in some degree from the elite of other value-institutional sectors of the social process. In particular, researches will focus on the age and grade differences that distinguish the newest generations from their predecessors.

As political science learns to make yet fuller use of the macro-micro and intermediate methods of gathering and processing data, of identifying the factor combinations that comprise a given political institution, and of accounting for the value indulgences and deprivations sought and realized, the decision processes of mankind will be better understood in terms of system, style, and personality. A problem-oriented political science will proceed with full awareness of the diversity and interconnectedness of the several intellectual tasks related to goal clarification, trend description, analysis of conditions, projection, and policy commitment. The challenge is to establish leadership structures in advanced industrial polities that exercise an aggregate impact on the tension and unrest generated by dynamic industrialism—structures that guide collective initiative toward the realization of at least a minimum system of public order. Such a task can be tackled at every level with some prospect of contributing to the whole. No one can foretell the precise lines along which the ever-shifting balances of power—territorial, pluralistic—will momentarily settle, or at what particular location in the context of world or national process a pivotal role will fall to a specific person, style, or structure.

12. Leadership: An Interdisciplinary Bibliography

LEWIS J. EDINGER
AND DONALD D. SEARING

The literature on leadership is vast and encompasses numerous disciplines. The following annotated bibliography is not intended to be exhaustive, but selective. As a guide to further reading about political leadership in industrialized societies, it is for the most part limited to works in English published over the last two decades. It emphasizes the interdisciplinary nature of such studies and differences as well as similarities in theory and method.

The arrangement of the bibliography divides these studies into those dealing with leadership groups or elites and those focusing on individual leaders. Under each of these major headings, further subdivisions identify general theoretical and methodological studies and investigations of particular actors in national and subnational settings.

Leaders Studied as Collectivities

Some General Approaches

1. Aron, Raymond, "Social Structure and the Ruling Class," *British Journal of Sociology*, **1**, 1 and 2 (March, 1950), pp. 1–16, 126–43. An attempt to synthesize Marx and Pareto by combining "class" and "elite" sociology and relating elite characteristics to their contextual setting in social and political systems.
2. Bachrach, Peter and Morton S. Baratz, "Two Faces of Power," *American Political Science Review*, **56**, 4 (December, 1962), pp. 947–52. An assessment of the assumptions and methodology of stratification and pluralist approaches to the study of community power which includes suggestions for a fresh approach to the study of power centering around the concept of "the mobilization of bias."
3. Beck, Carl and James M. Malloy, "Political Elites: A Mode of Analysis," Unpublished paper presented at the Sixth World Congress of the International Political Association, Geneva, September 15–21, 1964. Beck and Malloy explore concepts and approaches to the study of elites and present an elite typology.
4. Beck, Carl, *et al.*, *A Survey of Elite Studies* (Special Operations Research Office,

The American University, 1965). A summary of theoretically and substantively oriented studies, including an extensive bibliography categorized by geographical area.

5. Bell, Wendell, *et al.*, *Public Leadership: A Critical Review* (San Francisco, Cal.: Chandler Publishing Co., 1961). A review of works on elite background, attitudes, and behavior, with particular reference to American community power studies.

6. Bendix, Reinhard, "Social Stratification and Political Power," in Reinhard Bendix and Seymour Martin Lipset (eds.), *Class, Status, and Power: A Reader in Social Stratification* (New York: Free Press, 1953), pp. 596–609. The relationships between politics and social stratification are studied in contexts of Marxian analysis; retrospective investigations; totalitarian movements; and social background and psychological approaches to elite analysis.

7. Bendix, Reinhard and Seymour Martin Lipset, "Political Sociology," *Current Sociology*, 6, 3 (1957), pp. 79–169. A review and bibliography which includes a critical discussion of the assumptions and findings of various elite studies.

8. Bottomore, T. B., *Elites and Society* (New York: Basic Books, 1964). A review and critique of elite theory from Mosca and Pareto through C. Wright Mills which also examines the roles of intellectual, economic, and political elites in modernized and modernizing societies.

9. Brinton, Crane, *The Anatomy of Revolution* (rev. ed., New York: Vintage Books, 1960). A study in comparative historical sociology which considers leaders of the American, English, French, and Russian revolutions in terms of socioeconomic recruitment patterns and the functionality of various types of leadership in different contexts.

10. Burnham, James M., *The Machiavellians: Defenders of Freedom* (Toronto: Longmans, 1943). A critical discussion of Pareto, Mosca, other elite theorists, and "machiavellianism" in light of democratic theory.

11. Clifford-Vaughan, M., "Some French Concepts of Elites," *British Journal of Sociology*, 11, 4 (December, 1960), pp. 319–31. A discussion of French elites and of the normatively oriented approaches to their study employed by recent French observers.

12. Dahl, Robert A., "A Critique of the Ruling Elite Model," *American Political Science Review*, 52, 2 (June, 1958), pp. 463–69. Dahl analyzes difficulties inherent in what he calls the "ruling elite model" and its application and proposes his issue analytic approach as a means of judging a model's "fit" in particular cases.

13. Dahl, Robert A., "The Concept of Power," *Behavioral Science*, 2, 3 (July, 1957), pp. 201–15. A methodological contribution to the conceptualization of power, defining it in relational terms and expressing these in symbolic notation.

14. Dahl, Robert A., "Hierarchy, Democracy, and Bargaining in Politics and Economics," in S. Bailey (ed.), *Research Frontiers in Politics and Government* (Washington, D. C.: Brookings Institution, 1955), pp. 45–69. A treatment of problems involved in the study of power, decision-making processes, values, and political participation.

15. Edinger, Lewis J. and Donald D. Searing, "Social Background in Elite Analysis," *American Political Review*, 61, 2 (June, 1967), pp. 428–445. A methodological exploration of some assumptions in the social background approach to elite studies which suggests a research strategy for increasing the usefulness of background variables as predictive indices.

16. Etzioni, Amitai, "Dual Leadership in Complex Organizations," *American Sociological Review*, **30**, 5 (October, 1965), pp. 688–99. A functional analysis of the roles of instrumental and expressive leaders in complex organizations that fuses the "Bales-Parsons" small group model with organization theory.

17. Friedrich, Carl J. (ed.), *Authority* (Cambridge, Mass.: Harvard University Press, 1958). A collection of essays discussing authority as a general concept, a historical phenomenon, and in its relationship to particular sociopolitical problems.

18. Gibb, Cecil A., "Leadership," in Gardner Lindzey (ed.), *Handbook of Social Psychology*, Vol. II (Cambridge, Mass.: Addison-Wesley, 1954), pp. 877–920. A discussion of conceptual problems in the study of leadership in small groups, emphasizing an interactionist approach.

19. Gouldner, Alvin W. (ed.), *Studies in Leadership* (New York: Russell and Russell, 1965). A reissue of a 1950 symposium which includes a useful introduction and sociopsychological studies of elite-elite and elite-mass relationships, leadership typologies, and leadership styles.

20. Hemphill, John K., *Situational Factors in Leadership* (Columbus, Ohio: Ohio State University Press, 1949). A sociopsychological approach to the study of leadership which employs questionnaire responses to delineate the interaction between behavior and situational factors in small groups.

21. Janowitz, Morris, "The Systematic Analysis of Political Biography," *World Politics* (April, 1954), pp. 405–12. A review of the Hoover Institute (RADIR) Elite Studies, including a useful discussion of the social background approach in elite analysis.

22. Lasswell, Harold D., "The Selective Effect of Personality on Political Participation," in Richard Christie and Marie Jahoda (eds.), *Studies in the Scope and Method of "The Authoritarian Personality"* (New York: Free Press, 1954), pp. 197–225. A review of some of the literature of political leadership studies bearing upon the interrelationships between political structure and character structure and including a statement of some of Lasswell's own concepts and his approach to the problem.

23. Lasswell, Harold D., *et al.*, *World Revolutionary Elites* (Cambridge, Mass.: M.I.T. Press, 1965). A new edition of a number of the Hoover Institute RADIR studies which includes theoretical chapters on Lasswell's developmental approach and comparative analysis of elite social background and recruitment in four political systems.

24. Mannheim, Karl, *Man and Society in an Age of Reconstruction* (New York: Harcourt, Brace and World, 1940). A seminal sociological study in elite theory which analyzes elite recruitment, composition, behavior, and modes of influence in modernized societies.

25. March, James G., "An Introduction to the Theory and Measurement of Influence," *American Political Science Review*, **59**, 2 (June, 1955), pp. 431–51. A discussion of problems in the study of influence which defines the concept, builds a decision-making model on these foundations, and considers measurement techniques as well.

26. Marvick, Dwaine (ed.), *Political Decision-Makers* (New York: Free Press, 1961). A collection of original essays on current elite theory and research, including analyses of leadership recruitment and socialization patterns in six political systems.

27. Matthews, Donald R., *The Social Background of Political Decision-Makers* (Garden City, N. Y.: Doubleday, 1954). Presentation of a widespread approach

to elite analysis, including a review of some of the relevant theoretical literature and case studies.

28. Meisel, James H., *The Myth of the Ruling Class: Gaetano Mosca and the "Elite"* (Ann Arbor, Mich.: University of Michigan Press, 1958). A critical evaluation of the elite theories of Gaetano Mosca and those of related writers.

29. Meisel, James H. (ed.), *Pareto and Mosca*. (Englewood Cliffs, N. J.: Prentice-Hall, 1965). A collection of essays analyzing the works of two of the most prominent elite theorists, which includes noteworthy contributions by Meisel, Parsons, and Timasheff.

30. Mosca, Gaetano, *The Ruling Class* (trans. Hannah D. Kahn, New York: McGraw-Hill, 1939). Originally conceived as an attack on Marxian class analysis, Mosca's interdisciplinary approach is executed in the context of a philosophy of history treating the interplay between society and polity.

31. Nadel, S. F., "The Concept of Social Elites," *International Social Science Bulletin*, 8, 3 (Autumn, 1956), pp. 413–24. A treatment of conceptual problems in elite analysis which categorizes and synthesizes much of the relevant literature.

32. Olson, Mancur, Jr., *The Logic of Collective Action* (Cambridge, Mass.: Harvard University Press, 1965). An interdisciplinary study of the link between an implicit social science theory of motivation (which underlies elite studies among others), and the theories of group behavior constructed upon it.

33. Ortega y Gasset, José, *The Revolt of the Masses* (New York: W. W. Norton, 1957). This philosophical analysis of social organization trends in modern mass societies holds that changing elite recruitment patterns are profoundly altering the political cultures of many nations.

34. Pareto, Vilfredo, *The Mind and Society* (4 vols., ed. Arthur Livingston; trans. A. Livingston and Andrew Bongiorno; New York: Harcourt, Brace and World, 1935). Pareto's influential contributions to elite theory are scattered throughout this comparative and inductive approach to sociological theory.

35. Parsons, Talcott, "The Distribution of Power in American Society," *World Politics*, 10, 1 (October, 1957), pp. 123–44. This critical review of C. Wright Mills' *Power Elite* discusses several important questions relevant to elite analysis at the total system level.

36. Polsby, Nelson, *Community Power and Political Theory* (New Haven, Conn.: Yale University Press, 1963). Growing out of Dahl's "New Haven Study," this critical examination of other American community power studies rejects the homogeneous social class model as unsupportable by the evidence and opts instead for Dahl's heterogeneous pluralist model.

37. Ross, Ralph Gilbert, "Elites and the Methodology of Politics," *Public Opinion Quarterly* (Spring, 1952), pp. 27–32. A critical review of the Hoover Institute (RADIR) elite studies.

38. Russell, Bertrand, *Power: A New Social Analysis* (London: George Allan and Unwin, 1938). A discussion of various forms of power and the problems they present from the point of view of a social philosopher.

39. Schulze, Robert O. and L. V. Blumberg, "The Determination of Local Power Elites," *American Journal of Sociology*, 63 (1957–1958), pp. 290–96. The results of positional and reputational approaches are compared for the community of Cibola.

40. Seligman, Lester G., "Changes in the Presidency and the Conception of Political Leadership," *American Sociological Review*, 20, 6 (December, 1955), pp. 706–12. A discussion of the leader's staff or organization as a neglected leadership variable, substantively focusing upon the American Presidency.

41. Seligman, Lester G., "Elite Recruitment and Political Development," *Journal of Politics*, **26**, 3 (August, 1964), pp. 612–26. The elite recruitment process in new nations is discussed with reference to elite legitimation, paths of power, elite representativeness, and its relationship to political change.

42. Seligman, Lester G., "The Study of Political Leadership," *American Political Science Review*, **44**, 4 (December, 1950), pp. 904–15. A review of some of the more important problems for political leadership in modernized societies and of some of the recent leadership literature.

43. Sereno, Renzo, *The Rulers* (New York: Praeger, 1962). A critical study of elite theory focusing particularly on the ruling class concept.

44. Shannon, Jasper B., "The Study of Political Leadership," in Jasper B. Shannon *et al.*, *The Study of Comparative Government* (New York: Appleton-Century-Crofts, 1949), pp. 314–30. A summary of the history of leadership studies, including several major propositions illustrated with historical materials.

45. Shils, Edward, "The Intellectuals and the Powers: Some Perspectives for Comparative Analysis," *Comparative Studies in Society and History*, **1**, 1 (October, 1958), pp. 5–22. The structure of intellectual elite groups and their traditions and functions are explored in terms potentially applicable to all societies.

46. Simon, Herbert, "Notes on the Observation and Measurement of Political Power," *Journal of Politics*, **15**, 4 (November, 1953), pp. 500–516. A conceptual discussion of the power concept which defines power as "an asymmetrical relation between the behavior of two persons" and includes discussions of feedback, anticipated reactions, and legitimacy in this context.

47. Spitz, David, *Patterns of Anti-Democratic Thought* (rev. ed.; New York: Free Press, 1965). A critical examination of antidemocratic thought that discusses elite theory in its intellectual context and focuses on questions of leadership sometimes overlooked by other authors.

48. Vidich, Arthur J., *et al.* (eds.), *Reflections on Community Studies* (New York: John Wiley and Sons, 1964). Eleven essays treating methodological problems in community research.

49. Weber, Max, *Essays in Sociology* (ed. H. H. Gerth and C. Wright Mills; New York: Oxford University Press, 1946). A selection from the works of a highly influential student of bureaucracy and leadership behavior.

50. Wolfinger, Raymond E., "Reputation and Reality in the Study of Community Power," *American Sociological Review*, **25**, 5 (October, 1960), pp. 636–44. A critique of the reputational approach in community leadership studies on the basis of the assumptions of the issue oriented approach.

Elites at the National Level

1. Aaronovitch, Sam, *The Ruling Class: A Study of British Finance Capital* (London: Lawrence and Wishart, 1961). Within the context of social stratification and bureaucratic theory, the author identifies and describes a key sector of British economic elites and its relationship as a ruling class to political leadership.

2. Armstrong, John A., *The Soviet Bureaucratic Elite* (New York: Praeger, 1959). This case study of bureaucratic elites in the Ukrainian S.S.R. analyzes their political behavior and the structural interrelation of their positions.

3. Barber, James D. (ed.), *Political Leadership in American Government* (Boston: Little, Brown, 1964). A collection of readings designed to illustrate "the inner

workings of executive, legislative, judicial, and city government institutions," by focusing on official leaders as individuals, as contrasting types, and as interdependent participants in the policy-maker process in the United States.

4. Bell, Wendell, *Jamaican Leaders; Political Attitudes in a New Nation* (Berkeley, Cal.: University of California Press, 1964). This study examines changing elite orientations in the context of a transition from colonial rule to independent national status, and uses social background information in combination with attitudinal data.

5. Bendix, Reinhard, *Higher Civil Servants in American Society* (Boulder, Colo.: University of Colorado Press, 1949). In exploring the role of administrators in the exercise of political power, the author treats the social backgrounds of higher federal administrators in the United States, the values in their "bureaucratic ethos," and problems in their professionalization.

6. Brzezinski, Zbigniew and Samuel P. Huntington, *Political Power USA/USSR* (New York: Viking Press, 1964). One of the major differences between American and Soviet systems is found to prevail at the elite level on the basis of a comparative analysis of elite socialization, recruitment, and value patterns, with reference to elite-elite and elite-mass relationships.

7. Buck, Philip W., *Amateurs and Professionals in British Politics 1918–1959* (Chicago, Ill.: University of Chicago Press, 1963). A study of social background and recruitment patterns in the House of Commons.

8. Deutsch, Karl W. and Lewis J. Edinger, *Germany Rejoins the Powers* (Stanford, Cal.: Stanford University Press, 1959). An analysis of contextual factors in German foreign policy making which includes data on the social background, political behavior, and recruitment patterns of relevant elites.

9. Edinger, Lewis J., "Continuity and Change in the Background of German Decision-Makers," *Western Political Quarterly*, 14, 1 (March, 1961), pp. 17–36. A social background study of decision-makers in the German Federal Republic which seeks to trace changes in recruitment patterns during the present century.

10. Edinger, Lewis J., "Post-Totalitarian Leadership: Elites in the German Federal Republic," *American Political Science Review*, 54, 1 (March, 1960), pp. 58–82. This essay examines "the theoretical assumptions concerning post-totalitarian leadership implied in the denazification directives by analyzing the occupational and political background and recruitment patterns of elites in the German Federal Republic a decade later."

11. Eisenstadt, S. N., *The Political Systems of Empires* (New York: Free Press, 1963). See the chapters on comparative leadership policy and style and their institutional context in historic bureaucratic empires.

12. Elliott, Osborn, *Men at the Top* (New York: Harper and Row, 1959). A narrative account of the American business elite commenting on its social background, career patterns, and current behavior.

13. Free, Lloyd A., *Six Allies and a Neutral* (New York: Free Press, 1959). A comparative study of legislative elites in the United States, Britain, France, West Germany, Italy, Japan, and India, based on interview data.

14. Frey, Frederick W., *The Turkish Political Elite* (Cambridge, Mass.: M.I.T. Press, 1965). A study of the recruitment and composition of deputies to the Grand National Assembly between 1920 and 1957 which presents extensive social background data and attempts to link these to elite behavior patterns.

15. Friedrich, Carl J., *Man and His Government: An Empirical Theory of Politics* (New York: McGraw-Hill, 1963). Included in this work are several impor-

tant chapters treating approaches to (and theory about) elites, individual leadership, power and authority.

16. Friedrich, Carl J. and Zbigniew K. Brzezinski, *Totalitarian Dictatorship and Autocracy* (Cambridge, Mass.: Harvard University Press, 1956). This analysis of the Soviet and Nazi regimes stresses aspects of political leadership sometimes not considered in studies focusing on Western democratic systems.

17. Gilbert, G. M., *The Psychology of Dictatorship* (New York: Ronald Press, 1950). A social-psychological study of leadership behavior and motivation in Hitler Germany based on postwar interviews with captured Nazi leaders.

18. Granick, David, *The European Executive* (New York: Anchor Books, 1964). A description of recruitment patterns, roles, and organizational contexts of economic elites in France, Germany, Belgium, and Great Britain.

19. Granick, David, *The Red Executive* (New York: Doubleday, 1960). A study of economic elites in the Soviet political system which treats their socioeconomic backgrounds, current leadership roles, and relations to the political system.

20. Guttsman, W. L., *The British Political Elite* (New York: Basic Books, 1963). This study of recruitment and circulation patterns in the British political elite presents a carefully documented social background analysis of changes in elite composition and their relationship to social stratification and political power.

21. Hunter, Floyd, *Top Leadership, U.S.A.* (Chapel Hill, N.C.: University of North Carolina Press, 1959). In this "exploration of the hypothesis that a power structure exists in concretely definable terms at the national level," the author employs a reputational method for elite identification, questionnaires, and interviews to posit inter-elite linkages.

22. Janowitz, Morris, *The Professional Soldier* (New York: Free Press, 1960). Authorthority structures, social background, career patterns, role conceptions, and behavior patterns are considered in this study of the military profession in the United States.

23. Jennings, Eugene E., *The Executive; Autocrat, Bureaucrat, Democrat* (New York: Harper and Row, 1962). A narrative study of executive images and roles in the United States.

24. Keller, Suzanne Infeld, *Beyond the Ruling Class; Strategic Elites in Modern Society* (New York: Random House, 1963). Industrialized societies are said to be characterized by multiple "strategic elites" which are functionally specific, compartmentalized, and achievement oriented, in contrast to traditional ascriptive ruling classes.

25. Kelly, David, *The Ruling Few* (London: Hollis and Carter, 1952). A descriptive treatment, by a former British diplomat, of elites in eleven political systems.

26. Kornhauser, William, *The Politics of Mass Society* (New York: Free Press, 1959). An attempt to delineate trends toward a homogeneous manipulating elite in the "post industrial" society of mass atomization.

27. Leites, Nathan, *The Operational Code of the Politbureau* (New York: McGraw-Hill, 1951). A study of the norms believed to have motivated Soviet elite behavior in the days of Stalin.

28. Leites, Nathan, *A Study of Bolshevism* (New York: Free Press, 1953). An expansion of *The Operational Code of the Politbureau* in which the norms are treated as the expression of rules to be found in the writings of Lenin and Stalin.

29. Lipset, Seymour Martin and Reinhard Bendix, *Social Mobility in Industrial Soci-*

ety (Berkeley, Cal.: University of California Press, 1959). A study which includes consideration of elite recruitment patterns in Western Europe and the United States and finds considerable social mobility in these societies.

30. Lewis, Roy and Rosemary Stewart, *The Managers* (New York: Mentor Books, 1961). A comparative study of career patterns and role behavior of English, German, and American economic elites which present social background data and examines relationships to elite groups and to non-elites in these political systems.

31. McKenzie, Robert T., *British Political Parties* (second ed.; New York: Praeger, 1963). The relationships between power and organizational structure in the Labour and Conservative parties are described as promoting similar leadership patterns in both parties.

32. Matthews, Donald R., *U.S. Senators and Their World* (Chapel Hill, N.C.: University of North Carolina Press, 1960). The author's careful examination of senatorial role perceptions and behavior patterns makes extensive use of social background and attitudinal data.

33. Mills, C. Wright, *The New Men of Power* (New York: Harcourt, Brace and World, 1948). A study of American labor union leaders and their organizational and societal environment.

34. Mills, C. Wright, *The Power Elite* (New York: Oxford University Press, 1956). Mills' thesis is that functionally interrelated corporation executives, military leaders, and political elites control the "big decisions" at the national level in the United States.

35. Newcomer, Mabel, *The Big Business Executive* (New York: Columbia University Press, 1955). A socioeconomic background study of American business elites over a fifty years period, treating trends in recruitment patterns across political generations.

36. North, Robert C., *Kuomintang and Chinese Communist Elites* (Stanford, Cal.: Stanford University Press, 1952). A study of recruitment and social background patterns among Kuomintang and Chinese Communist elites.

37. Ostrogorski, M., *Democracy and the Organization of Political Parties, Volume I, England; Volume II, The United States* (edited and abridged by Seymour Martin Lipset; New York: Anchor Books, 1964). An analytic study of organizational structure in Anglo-American political parties which remains one of the classic works in comparative politics.

38. "The Parliamentary Profession," *International Social Science Journal*, Part 1, 13, 4 (1961). Studies of legislative elites in France, Italy, Israel, Great Britain, the United States, and the Soviet Union.

39. Price, Don K., *The Scientific Estate* (Cambridge, Mass.: Belknap Press, 1965). The author analyzes the increasing interdependence of economic and political elites in the American polity, and finds them to be "converging" rather than "countervailing" power groupings.

40. Ranney, Austin, *Pathways to Parliament* (Madison, Wis.: University of Wisconsin Press, 1965). A study of recruitment patterns and processes in Great Britain based in part upon interviews and statistical analysis of background and attitudinal data.

41. Rosenau, James N., *National Leadership and Foreign Policy* (Princeton, N.J.: Princeton University Press, 1963). An analysis of questionnaire responses from a sample of United States opinion makers and organizational leaders in the foreign affairs policy area.

42. Rustow, Dankwart A., "The Study of Elites: Who's Who, When and How," *World Politics,* **18,** 4 (July, 1966), pp. 690–717. Several recent social background studies in elite analysis are reviewed along with some other recent theoretical works in the field.

43. Schlesinger, Joseph A., *Ambition and Politics* (Chicago, Ill.: Rand McNally, 1966). Analyzes the relationship between party structures and political ambitions in the United States.

44. Seligman, Lester G., *Leadership in a New Nation* (New York: Atherton Press, 1964). A study of Israeli legislative elites in the context of political development, which utilizes interview data.

45. Singer, Marshall R., *The Emerging Elite: A Study of Political Leadership in Ceylon* (Cambridge, Mass.: M.I.T. Press, 1964). Using an anthropological technique of special relevance for elite studies in small, modernizing political systems, Singer presents extensive social background data to delineate elite recruitment patterns in a new nation.

46. Syme, Ronald, *Colonial Elites: Rome, Spain and the Americas* (New York: Oxford University Press, 1958). A brief study of the political behavior of elites in three historic empires that relates elite characteristics to modes of political organization and change.

47. Thomas, Hugh (ed.), *The Establishment* (New York: Clarkson N. Potter, 1959). A collection of essays by a group of young English intellectuals that examines critically the role of the so-called "Establishment" in British politics and in the process presents a good deal of information about social stratification and political culture.

48. Tucker, Robert C. and S. F. Cohen (eds.), *The Great Purge Trial* (New York: Grosett and Dunlap, 1965). A revised edition of the verbatim report of the Moscow Trial of 1938 with a commentary that attempts to assess the significance of the trials in the context of a leadership purge in the totalitarian mass party.

49. Warner, W. Lloyd, *The American Federal Executive* (New Haven, Conn.: Yale University Press, 1963). A study of American civilian and military elites designed to be comparable to Warner and Abegglen's study of big business leaders (see also Warner and Abegglen, *Big Business Leaders in America*). Social background data are employed to trace recruitment patterns; socialization experiences and role orientations are also considered.

50. Warner, W. Lloyd and James C. Abegglen, *Big Business Leaders in America* (New York: Harper and Row, 1955). A study of recruitment patterns and socioeconomic backgrounds among economic elites in the United States which includes attitudinal and behavior materials obtained through interviews and psychological studies of representative elites.

51. Wilkinson, Rupert, *Gentlemanly Power: British Leadership and the Public School Tradition* (London: Oxford University Press, 1964). Elite socialization and recruitment through pre-adult educational institutions are studied in the context of systematic functions.

Elites at the Sub-National Level

1. Agger, Robert E., *et al., The Rulers and the Ruled* (New York: John Wiley and Sons, 1964). A study of evolving decision-making processes in four American communities over a period of sixteen years.

2. Banfield, Edward C., *Political Influence* (New York: Free Press, 1961). A theoretically oriented study of leadership patterns in Chicago, Illinois.

3. Barber, James David, *The Lawmakers: Recruitment and Adaptation to Legislative Life* (New Haven, Conn.: Yale University Press, 1965). An empirical analysis of Connecticut legislators based on interview and questionnaire data emphasizing the relationship between personality and recruitment in legislative roles.

4. Dahl, Robert H., *Who Governs? Democracy and Power in an American City* (New Haven, Conn.: Yale University Press, 1961). An investigation illustrating the issue oriented approach to the study of community power which focuses on participation in particular decisions, rather than reputation, for the identification of community leaders.

5. Epstein, Leon D., *Politics in Wisconsin* (Madison, Wis.: University of Wisconsin Press, 1958). A case study of the change from a one party to a two party system which includes analysis of the background and recruitment patterns of state legislators.

6. Eulau, Heinz and John D. Sprague, *Lawyers and Politics* (Indianapolis, Ind.: Bobbs-Merrill, 1964). A secondary analysis of data on four United States state legislatures which compares the recruitment patterns, role perceptions, and political behavior of lawyers with those of nonlawyers.

7. Flynn, Edward J., *You're The Boss* (New York: Viking Press, 1947). The autobiography of a former leader of the Democratic machine in Bronx County, New York.

8. Form, William H. and Warren L. Sauer, *Community Influentials in a Middle-Sized City* (East Lansing, Mich.: Michigan State University, Institute for Community Development, 1960). A study of Lansing, Michigan, this monograph identifies community elites by a reputational procedure and presents data on their social backgrounds, career patterns, and role perceptions.

9. Hollingshead, August B., *Elmtown's Youth* (New York: John Wiley and Sons, 1949). The impact of a highly stratified social structure upon adolescent socialization patterns is analyzed in a Middle Western community.

10. Hunter, Floyd, *Community Power Structure* (Chapel Hill, N.C.: University of North Carolina Press, 1953). A pioneering study of community power structure, using reputational and sociometric methods to identify a small group of leaders who make the major decisions in Atlanta, Georgia.

11. Janowitz, Morris (ed.), *Community Political Systems* (International Yearbook of Political Behavior; New York: Free Press, 1961). A collection of original essays presenting both empirical data and theoretical analysis—including an overview of the field by Janowitz.

12. Jennings, M. Kent, *Community Influentials* (New York: Free Press, 1964). A study of three major elite groups (economic dominants; prescribed influentials; attributed influentials) in Atlanta, Georgia identified by positional and reputational criteria, which considers their social backgrounds and roles in the decision-making process.

13. Lowi, Theodore J., *At the Pleasure of the Mayor* (New York: Free Press, 1964). A longitudinal analysis of political power in New York City which includes consideration of the social background recruitment, and circulation patterns of local elites.

14. Press, Charles, *Main Street Politics: Policy Making at the Local Level—A Survey of the Periodical Literature since 1950* (East Lansing, Mich.: Michigan State University, Institute for Community Development, 1962). A review of

the community power literature presented through summaries of the most important studies in the field, in which Press considers several central questions raised by the studies under consideration.

15. Prethus, Robert, *Men at the Top: A Study in Community Power* (New York: Oxford University Press, 1964). By using both reputation and issue approaches to study elites in two local communities, Prethus bridges the gap between stratification and pluralist studies, suggesting that different communities are likely to have different stratification patterns and that size may be a crucial variable here.

16. Schlesinger, Joseph A., *How They Became Governor* (East Lansing, Mich.: Governmental Bureau, Michigan State University, 1957). A study of the career patterns of governors in the American states.

17. Skinner, G. W., *Leadership and Power in the Chinese Community in Thailand* (Ithaca, N.Y. Cornell University Press, 1958). A study of the relationship of elite backgrounds and behavior patterns in relation to their subsystem and total system contexts.

18. Vidich, Arthur J. and Joseph Bensman, *Small Town in Mass Society* (Princeton, N.J.: Princeton University Press, 1958). Employing several tried methods, Vidich and Bensman find in Springdale a power structure similar to that of Hunter's Atlanta, though less conspicuous and without the same "aristocratic" base.

19. Wahlke, John C., *et al.*, *The Legislative System* (New York: John Wiley and Sons, 1962). A theoretically oriented study of state legislator's role orientations in four American states.

20. Warner, W. Lloyd, *Democracy in Jonesville* (New York: Harper and Row, 1949). In this early community power study the author's concerns are broader than the standard status and power focus of more contemporary studies; nevertheless, his findings on social stratification and elite circulation patterns are relevant to community leadership theorizing.

21. Wildavsky, Aaron, *Leadership in a Small Town* (Totowa, N.J.: Bedminster Press, 1964). A community power study of Oberlin, Ohio, which was designed as a replication and extension of the New Haven project by Dahl *et al.* Using the decisional approach the author finds that, as in New Haven, "Power is . . . fragmented among many different individuals and groups and rather widely dispersed . . . in the community."

22. Zink, Harold, *City Bosses in the United States* (Durham, N.C.: Duke University Press, 1930). A collection of case studies of twenty municipal bosses which serves as a basis for generalizations about patterns of personality, recruitment, and leadership style.

Small Groups and Organizational Behavior

1. Argyris, Cris, *Executive Leadership* (New York: Harper and Row, 1953). Drawing upon interviews and observations of leadership in an industrial plant, Argyris presents a collective portrait of the executive leader's traits and impact upon his followers in the context of industrial bureaucracy.

2. Barnard, Chester L., *The Functions of the Executive* (Cambridge, Mass.: Harvard University Press, 1938). An important early work on organizational leadership and its context in formal organizations.

3. Bass, Bernard M., *Leadership, Psychology, and Organizational Behavior* (New York: Harper and Row, 1960). A study of leadership behavior from a social

psychological viewpoint in which Bass attempts to synthesize much of the existing empirical work and to construct a systematic leadership theory of his own.

4. Cartwright, Dorwin, "Influence, Leadership, Control," in James G. March (ed.), *Handbook of Organizations* (Chicago, Ill.: Rand McNally, 1965), pp. 1–48. A survey of the literature on leadership in the organizational context.

5. Guetzkow, Harold S. (ed.), *Groups, Leadership and Men* (Pittsburgh, Pa.: Carnegie Press, 1951). A collection of essays on leadership in small groups and individual leadership behavior.

6. Hollander, Edwin P., *Leaders, Groups, and Influence* (New York: Oxford University Press, 1964). A series of essays by Hollander and others on leadership in formal structures. Among the more important points is the finding of a curvilinear relationship between group conformity and leadership.

7. Lipset, Seymour M., *et al.*, *Union Democracy* (New York: Free Press, 1956). A sociological case study of leader-follower relations in the International Typographical Union, based on interviews and including valuable methodological materials.

8. Michels, Robert, *Political Parties* (New York: Free Press, 1949; first printing, 1915). A classic statement of elitist theory and its relationship to organizational structures, in which Michels formulates his famous "iron law of oligarchy."

9. Presthus, Robert, *The Organizational Society* (New York: Vintage Books, 1965). An exploration of the interaction between organizational structure and executive personality type in the context of bureaucratic recruitment processes.

10. Selznick, Philip, *Leadership in Administration: A Sociological Interpretation* (Evanston, Ill.: Row, Peterson, 1957). A monograph which presents a theoretical perspective for the study of leadership in the organizational setting by analyzing the interaction between organizational structures and decision-making procedures.

11. Simon, Herbert A., *Administrative Behavior* (second ed.; New York: Macmillan, 1957). Institutional and large-scale organizational leadership is considered in this analysis of decision making.

12. Stinchcombe, Arthur L., "Social Structure and Organizations," in James G. March (ed.), *Handbook of Organizations* (Chicago, Ill.: Rand McNally, 1965), pp. 142–193. A study of the impact of the social system upon organizations and the effects of organizations upon the social systems in which they exist.

13. Verba, Sidney, *Small Groups and Political Behavior: A Study of Leadership* (Princeton, N.J.: Princeton University Press, 1961). Beginning with the premise that many political decisions are made in small groups, Verba demonstrates that much sociological small group research is directly relevant to the study of political decision making.

14. Whitehead, T. N., *Leadership in a Free Society* (Cambridge, Mass.: Harvard University Press, 1944). An empirical and philosophical study of leadership in the complex organizations of modern industrial society, contextually set within the problem of the role of economic institutions in societies at this level of socioeconomic development.

15. Young, Michael, *The Rise of the Meritocracy* (New York: Random House, 1959). A projection of assumed trends in bureaucratic evaluative procedures under which achievement becomes an organizationally prescribed criterion narrowly defined to exclude courage, imagination, and compassion in every aspect of modern social life.

Leaders Studied as Individuals

Some General Approaches

1. Bogardus, Emory S., *Leaders and Leadership* (New York: Appleton-Century-Crofts, 1934). A sociological study focusing upon recruitment criteria and leader-follower relations.
2. Bonham-Carter, Violet A., *The Impact of Personality in Politics* (Oxford: Clarendon Press, 1963). This book examines the independently "Great Man" versus deterministic "Social Forces" theme in modern British politics.
3. Borgatta, E. F., *et al.*, "Some Findings Relevant to the Great Man Theory of Leadership," *American Sociological Review*, 19, 6 (December, 1954), pp. 755–59. A report of an experiment in which "Great Men" were identified and their relationships to the groups they lead were explored.
4. Browne, C. G. and Thomas S. Cohn (eds.), *The Study of Leadership* (Danville, Ill.: Interstate Printers and Publishers, 1958). A comprehensive collection of essays by psychologists and sociologists focusing on problems in the scope and method of individual leadership studies.
5. Carlyle, Thomas, *On Heroes, Hero Worship, and the Heroic in History* (London: Oxford University Press, 1963). A classic study of the independently "Great Man in History."
6. Cohen, Morris R., "Great Men in History," Chapter in his *The Meaning of Human History* (LaSalle, Ill.: Open Court, 1947), pp. 214–24. A discussion of the "Great Man" versus "Social Forces" controversy which argues that the dichotomy is a false one to the extent that social forces "flow through the lives of outstanding individuals . . . ."
7. Danelski, David J., *A Supreme Court Justice is Appointed* (New York: Random House, 1964). An account of Chief Justice Taft's influence upon President Harding's decision to nominate Pierce Butler as Associate Justice of the Supreme Court, including a careful "transactional explanation" of Harding's choice.
8. Davies, James C., "Political Leaders and Followers," Chapter in his *Human Nature in Politics* (New York: John Wiley and Sons, 1963). Explores the leader-follower relationship in terms of a theory of motivation and proposes a leadership typology.
9. Devereux, G., "Charismatic Leadership and Crisis," in Muensterberger and Axelrad (eds.), *Psychoanalysis and the Social Sciences*, Vol. 4 (New York: International University Press, 1955), pp. 147–57. A discussion of the recruitment of charismatic leaders and their functions in crisis situations.
10. Edinger, Lewis J., "Political Science and Political Biography I and II," *Journal of Politics*, 26, 1 and 2 (May and August, 1964), pp. 423–29, 648–77. A review of interdisciplinary efforts in the study of individual leaders and presentation of a model which Edinger used in his study of Kurt Schumacher.
11. Friedland, William H., "For a Sociological Concept of Charisma," *Social Forces*, 43, 1 (October, 1964), pp. 18–26. An attempt to operationalize Weber's charisma concept by shifting from a psychological to a sociological perspective and concentrating on the social context rather than on "charismatics."
12. Friedrich, Carl J., "Political Leadership and the Problem of Charismatic Power," *Journal of Politics*, 23, 1 (February, 1961), pp. 3–24. The author considers

the concepts of power, rule, and Weber's typology of authority, presenting some thought-provoking alternatives of his own.

13. Garraty, John A., "The Interrelations of Psychology and Biography," *Psychological Bulletin*, 31, 6 (1954), pp. 569–82. A summary and bibliography of work relevant to the integration of psychoanalytic and biographical materials.

14. Gerth, Hans and C. Wright Mills, "Sociology of Leadership," in *Character and Social Institutions* (New York: Harcourt, Brace and World, 1953). Presents an analytic framework encompassing the interaction between the leader's traits and motive, his role choices and performances, and the environmental context for his activities.

15. Hitschmann, Edward, *Great Men: Psychoanalytic Studies* (New York: International Universities Press, 1956). Brief case studies illustrating the orthodox Freudian approach to biography.

16. Hook, Sidney, *The Hero in History: A Study in Limitation and Possibility* (New York: John Day, 1943). A student of philosophy examines and attempts to reconcile the "history makes leaders" and "leaders make history" theses by distinguishing between "eventful" and "event making" men.

17. Jennings, Eugene E., *An Anatomy of Leadership: Princes, Heroes and Supermen* (New York: Harper and Row, 1960). A typology of leadership and a call for more "great men" in American political and economic life.

18. Klapp, Orrin E., *Symbolic Leaders: Public Dramas and Public Men* (Chicago, Ill.: Aldine Publishing Company, 1965). A broadly conceived social-psychological approach to leadership in all kinds of situations.

19. Korten, David C., "Situational Determinants of Leadership," *Journal of Conflict Resolution*, 6, 3 (September, 1962), pp. 222–35. An examination of the situational factors which determine "centralized authoritarian" and "participative democratic" group leadership.

20. Lasswell, Harold D., "Political Constitution and Character," *Psychoanalysis and the Psychoanalytic Review*, 46, 4 (Winter, 1959), pp. 3–18. An analysis of the relationship between political structure and character structure with relevance to political stability.

21. Lasswell, Harold D., *Psychopathology and Politics* (Chicago, Ill.: University of Chicago Press, 1930); and *Power and Personality* (New York: W. W. Norton, 1948). Two seminal works employing a psychoanalytic approach to explain the behavior of political leaders on the basis of a number of case studies.

22. Machiavelli, Niccolo, *The Prince and The Discourses* (New York: Modern Library, 1950). A classic work which is particularly relevant for the study of political leadership in "nation-building" situations.

23. Neustadt, Richard E., *Presidential Power* (New York: John Wiley and Sons, 1962). A study of the politics of personal power in the office of the American Presidency: "what it is, how to get it, how to keep it, and how to use it."

24. Ogburn, William F., "The Great Man Versus Social Forces," *Social Forces*, 5, 2 (December, 1926), pp. 225–31. The author explores the influence of the individual in social change, concluding that he functions as a "medium through which the social forces play."

25. Pigors, Paul, *Leadership or Domination* (Boston, Mass.: Houghton Mifflin, 1935). A study that distinguishes between leadership based on "legitimacy" and leadership based on "power" and holds that legitimacy-based leaders are bound by the wishes of their followers more than power-based leaders are.

26. Ratman, K. J., "Charisma and Political Leadership," *Political Studies*, 12, 3

(October, 1964), pp. 341–54. A critique of the usage of the charisma concept in leadership studies which finds its vague usage detrimental to the study of authority—particularly in new nations.

27. Roche, John P. and Stephen Sachs, "The Bureaucrat and the Enthusiast: An Exploration of the Leadership of Social Movements," *Western Political Quarterly*, 8, 2 (June, 1955), pp. 248–61. A suggestive discussion of two types of leaders frequently found in social movements and of their relationships to these movements.

28. Rossiter, Clinton, *The American Presidency* (second ed.; New York: Harcourt, Brace and World, 1960). An institutional approach to the office of the American Presidency which includes analysis of role expectations, behavior of past incumbents, and the functions of the office in the American political system.

29. Rush, Myron, *Political Succession in the USSR* (New York: Columbia University Press, 1965). A study of the classical problem of leadership succession in tyrannical political systems and its ramifications for related patterns of political behavior.

30. Schlesinger, Arthur, Jr., "On Heroic Leadership," *Encounter* (December, 1960), pp. 3–11. An essay on the "Great Man in History" that relates him to crisis situations and explores the implications of this leadership type for democratic theory.

31. Schubert, Glendon, *The Judicial Mind* (Evanston, Ill.: Northwestern University Press, 1965). An analysis of Supreme Court justices' ideologies and attitudes from 1946 to 1963 which presents and examines a theoretical model of judicial decision-making.

32. Schubert, Glendon, *The Political Role of the Courts: Judicial Policy-Making* (Chicago, Ill.: Scott, Foresman, 1965). Employing a structural-functional approach, Schubert analyzes sociopolitical variables in judicial political behavior.

33. Selvin, Hanan C., *The Effects of Leadership* (New York: Free Press, 1960). A sociopsychological study of American army officers and their subordinates which examines the impact of different leadership styles upon the behavior of followers.

34. Strauss, Leo, *On Tyranny* (New York: Free Press, 1963). Including a new translation and interpretation of Xenophon's classic *Hiero* or *Tyrannicus,* this study considers totalitarian political leadership in the context of the social structure and control mechanisms of elite-mass relationships relevant to "movement-regimes."

35. Tucker, Robert C., "The Dictator and Totalitarianism," *World Politics*, 17, 4 (July, 1965), pp. 555–83. The author attempts a re-evaluation of the totalitarianism concept by means of developing a psychoanalytic approach to "the dictator as a personality type."

36. White, Robert W., *Lives in Progress* (New York: Holt, Rinehart and Winston, 1952). White combines psychological, biological, and sociological perspectives to present an approach to the study of personality genesis and its assessment which has considerable relevance for the analysis of political leadership.

37. White, Robert W. (ed.), *The Study of Lives* (New York: Atherton Press, 1963). A collection of essays on the analysis of leadership, personalities and processes, based on the work of psychologist Henry A. Murray.

38. Willner, Ann Ruth and Dorothy Willner, "The Rise and Role of Charismatic Leaders," *Annals of the American Academy of Political and Social Science,*

358 (March, 1965), pp. 77–88. A proposal for operationalizing Weber's concept of charisma by focusing on the perceptions of the followers rather than on the personality of the leader.

Standard Biographical Studies

1. Aron, Robert, *An Explanation of De Gaulle* (New York: Harper and Row, 1966). A study of leadership style and objectives that trace a life history back to the French President's childhood.
2. Bailey, Thomas A., *Presidential Greatness* (New York: Appleton-Century-Crofts, 1966). Personality and leadership characteristics of American presidents are analyzed and incumbents are "ranked" according to "Great Man in History" criteria.
3. Brecher, Michael, *Nehru: A Political Biography* (New York: Oxford University Press, 1959). A chronological treatment of the Indian leader's career which includes material on his political style and personality.
4. Bullock, Alan, *Hitler: A Study in Tyranny* (rev. ed.; New York: Harper and Row, 1962). Although this study avoids an explicit conceptual framework, it traces many of the political events of the Nazi era to Hitler's specific personality traits and political behavior rather than to historical determinants in German society and culture.
5. Bullock, Alan, *The Life and Times of Ernest Bevin* (London: Heinemann, 1960). A political biography of the British trade union leader and Labour Party minister which traces his political career in its organizational context.
6. Churchill, Winston S., *My Early Life* (New York: Charles Scribner's Sons, 1958). An autobiographical account of Churchill's life previous to his recruitment to politics which includes important materials on his childhood, adolescence, and value structure relevant to an assessment of his personality and leadership behavior.
7. Cole, Hubert, *Laval* (New York: G. P. Putnam's Sons, 1963). Biography of the French leader who served as Prime Minister of the democratic Third Republic as well as of the autocratic Vichy Regime that followed it in 1940.
8. Cowles, Virginia, *Winston Churchill, The Era and the Man* (New York: Harper and Row, 1953). A journalistic account containing material useful for a study of the British leader's personality and political behavior.
9. De Mendelssohn, Peter, *The Age of Churchill: Heritage and Adventure* (New York: Alfred A. Knopf, 1961). Focuses on Churchill's childhood and adolescent years.
10. Deutscher, Isaac, *The Prophet Armed; The Prophet Unarmed; The Prophet Outcast* (New York: Vintage Books, 1963). A three-part political biography of Leon Trotsky which analyzes his behavior both as a successful political leader and as a defeated one.
11. Deutscher, Isaac, *Stalin; A Political Biography* (New York: Oxford University Press, 1949). This book describes Stalin's career and leadership style in terms of the political context of his country and party.
12. Dickie, John, *The Uncommon Commoner: A Study of Sir Alec Douglas-Home* (New York: Praeger, 1964). A description of the British leader's recruitment into the office of Prime Minister.
13. Eyck, Erich, *Bismark and the German Empire* (London: George Allen and Unwin, 1958). An English summary of a three volume German study which includes extensive data for assessing Bismark's leadership style.
14. Fischer, Louis, *The Life of Lenin* (New York: Harper and Row, 1964). A stand-

ard political biography dealing primarily with Lenin's policies and leadership style after he achieved power.

15. Gandhi, M. K., *An Autobiography: The Story of My Experiments with Truth* (Boston, Mass.: Beacon Press Paperback, 1957). A life history, rich in material for the analysis of the Indian leader's political style.

16. Goldberg, Harvey, *The Life of Jean Jaurès* (Madison, Wis.: University of Wisconsin Press, 1962). The French Socialist leader's political style and values are analyzed in this account of his political career.

17. Heidenheimer, Arnold J., *Adenauer and the CDU* (The Hague: Nijhoff, 1960). A study of the German leader's accession to the leadership of his country and party.

18. Jackson, J. Hampden, *Clemenceau and the Third Republic* (New York: Collier Books, 1962). A descriptive biography of the French "crisis" leader of World War I that traces his career and political style in terms of the socio-political milieu of the Third Republic.

19. Jones, Thomas, *Lloyd George* (Cambridge, Mass.: Harvard University Press, 1951). A political biography of the British "crisis" leader in World War I.

20. Kennedy, John F., *Profiles in Courage* (New York: Harper and Row, 1955). A series of essays examining the leadership style of eight American political leaders, plus introductory and concluding chapters in which the late President advances some generalizations on the subject of leadership.

21. Kirkpatrick, Ivone, *Mussolini: A Study in Power* (New York: Hawthorne Books, 1964). This comprehensive political biography of the Fascist leader is primarily descriptive, but also ventures some analysis of Mussolini's motives and behavioral style.

22. Koenig, Louis W., *The Invisible Presidency* (New York: Holt, Rinehart and Winston, 1960). The role of "man behind the throne" in the American presidency is considered in a study of presidential advisors and assistants which examines their personalities, styles, and relations to the leader.

23. McKean, Dayton David, *The Boss: The Hague Machine in Action* (Boston, Mass.: Houghton Mifflin, 1940). A standard political biography of "Boss" Hague and the political machine of Hudson County, New Jersey.

24. Martin, Kingsley, *The Magic of the British Monarchy* (Boston, Mass.: Little, Brown, 1962). A study of the changing role of British monarchs since the middle of the nineteenth century with emphasis on the interaction between particular incumbents and institutional norms.

25. Moran, Lord Charles M. W., *Churchill* (Boston, Mass.: Houghton Mifflin, 1966). Based on a diary kept by Churchill's personal physician, this biography contains considerable material on the personality, political roles, and political style of the British leader.

26. Newman, Peter C., *Renegade in Power* (Indianapolis, Ind.: Bobbs-Merrill, 1964). A biography of John Diefenbaker, the Canadian Conservative party leader and Prime Minister, focusing on his years as Prime Minister, including some psychoanalytic variables explaining his leadership behavior.

27. Pringle, Henry F., *Theodore Roosevelt* (New York: Harcourt, Brace and World, 1956). A standard account of T.R.'s life and his political behavior in the presidential office.

28. Sherwood, Robert E., *Roosevelt and Hopkins* (New York: Harper and Row, 1948). A study of F.D.R.'s policies, personality, and political style, built around the relationship with an intimate aide.

29. Schlesinger, Arthur M., Jr., *A Thousand Days*. (Boston, Mass.: Houghton Mifflin, 1965). An account of the political style of John F. Kennedy by one of his close advisors.
30. Schoenbrun, David, *The Three Lives of Charles DeGaulle* (New York: Atheneum, 1966). An account of DeGaulle's successive roles as a soldier, resistance leader, and statesman.
31. Shub, David, *Lenin* (Garden City, N.Y.: Doubleday, 1948). Still one of the important political biographies of the Soviet leader because of the author's personal knowledge of the events and people he writes about.
32. Smith, Leslie, *Harold Wilson; The Authentic Portrait* (New York: Charles Scribners' Sons, 1964). This semi-official biography of the British Labour leader sympathetically traces his career before he became Prime Minister and goes back to his childhood in constructing an impressionistic sketch of his personality and political style.
33. Thomson, Dale C., *Alexander Mackenzie, Clear Grit.* (New York: Macmillan, 1960). A study of the Canadian Liberal leader's recruitment to the office of Prime Minister in the late nineteenth century, emphasizing his political style and policy as incumbent.
34. Tournoux, J-R., *Pétain and DeGaulle* (trans. Oliver Coburn; London: Heinemann, 1966). A comparative biography of the two French "crisis" leaders which includes information about DeGaulle's childhood and observations on his personality characteristics.
35. Tugwell, Rexford G., *How They Became President* (New York: Simon and Schuster, 1964). A study of the recruitment patterns of the thirty-five American chief executives forms the basis for a number of generalizations about the most successful career strategies for achieving the presidential office.
36. Ulam, Adam B., *The Bolsheviks* (New York: Macmillan, 1965). A political leadership study emphasizing Lenin's leadership style and accession to power.
37. Werth, Alexander, *Lost Statesman* (New York: Abelard-Schuman, 1958). Biography of the French "crisis" leader Pierre Mendès-France, whose interaction with the milieu of the Fourth Republic is related to both his successes and failures.
38. Wolfe, Bertram D., *Three Who Made a Revolution* (Boston, Mass.: Beacon Press Paperback, 1955). This study of Lenin, Trotsky, and Stalin offers insights into recruitment patterns and varying leadership styles in a successful revolutionary movement in terms of the interplay between contrasting backgrounds, personalities, goals, and political behavior of the leading actors.

Psychologically-Oriented Personality Studies

1. Burns, James MacGregor, *Roosevelt: The Lion and the Fox* (New York: Harcourt, Brace and World, 1956). An analysis of Roosevelt's "broker leadership" style and its relation to his political context, including an interesting appendix on the study of political leadership in general.
2. Clark, Leon P., *Lincoln: A Psycho-Biography* (New York: Charles Scribners' Sons, 1933). An orthodox Freudian psychoanalytic study examining the sources of Lincoln's attitudinal and behavior patterns.
3. Edinger, Lewis, J., *Kurt Schumacher: A Study in Personality and Political Behavior* (Stanford, Cal.: Stanford University Press, 1965). Based upon a model employing the role concept to link personality and environmental variables, this monograph about a German socialist underscores the need to study un-

successful as well as successful leaders in developing a theory of political leadership.

4. Erikson, Erik H., *Young Man Luther: A Study in Psychoanalysis and History* (New York: W. W. Norton, 1958). A psychoanalytic developmental analysis which traces Luther's leadership to a congruence between his personality needs and the exigencies of the dynamic social environment of his age.

5. Freud, Sigmund and William C. Bullitt, *Thomas Woodrow Wilson: Twenty-Eighth President of the United States; A Psychological Study* (Boston, Mass.: Houghton Mifflin, 1967). A psychoanalytic explanation of some of Wilson's political decisions, emphasizing early familial experiences in his character development.

6. George, Alexander L. and Juliette L. George, *Woodrow Wilson and Colonel House* (New York: W. W. Norton, 1956). Using Lasswell's framework for the study of political leadership, the authors examine Wilson's political behavior in terms of its psycho-generic origins.

7. Gottfried, Alex, *Boss Cermak of Chicago; a Study of Political Leadership* (Seattle, Wash.: University of Washington Press, 1962). Another attempt to employ Lasswell's psychoanalytic model to relate political behavior to personality needs stemming from childhood experiences.

8. Hargrove, Erwin C., *Presidential Leadership: Personality and Political Style* (New York: Macmillan, 1966). Six studies of American Presidents relating personality characteristics to leadership style through an "ego integration model" of role interpretation.

9. McRandle, James H., *The Track of the Wolf: Essays on National Socialism and its Leader, Adolph Hitler* (Evanston, Ill.: Northwestern University Press, 1965). An historian seeks to link the personality characteristics of the leader to the cultural characteristics of his political environment.

10. Merriam, Charles E., *Four American Party Leaders* (New York: Macmillan, 1926). A comparative psychopolitical analysis of the leadership traits and styles of Abraham Lincoln, Theodore Roosevelt, Woodrow Wilson, and William Jennings Bryan.

11. Possony, Stefan T., *Lenin: The Compulsive Revolutionary* (Chicago, Ill.: Regnery, 1964). A study of Lenin's career, including an attempt to explain his political attitudes and behavior in terms of psychological and somatic factors.

12. Robertson, Pearl L., "Grover Cleveland as a Political Leader," *Psychoanalytic Review*, **51**, 2 (Summer, 1964), pp. 130–54. Cleveland's leadership style is explored on the basis of a psychoanalytic model.

13. Rogow, Arnold A., *James Forrestal: A Study of Personality, Politics, and Policy* (New York: Macmillan, 1963). Also employing Lasswell's leadership model, Rogow relates incongruities between a rigid personality and the political context to a leader's guilt feelings, sense of frustration, paranoia, and ultimate suicide.

14. Wolfenstein, E. Victor, *The Revolutionary Personality* (Princeton, N.J.: Princeton University Press, 1967). A psychoanalytic study of Lenin, Trotsky, and Ghandi.

15. Zink, Harold, "A Case Study of a Political Boss," *Psychiatry*, **1**, 4 (November, 1938), pp. 527–34. A psychoanalytic study of David C. Stephenson, political boss of Indiana.

Index

NEW YORK INSTITUTE
OF TECHNOLOGY LIBRARY
NEW YORK
OF TECHNOLOGY LIBRARY

OLD WESTBURY LIBRARY